D1243428

*The Different Faces
of Motherhood*

Perspectives in
Developmental Psychology

Series Editor: Michael Lewis
Rutgers Medical School
University of Medicine and Dentistry of New Jersey
New Brunswick, New Jersey

The Different Faces of Motherhood

Edited by

BEVERLY BIRNS
State University of New York
Stony Brook, New York

and

DALE F. HAY
Institute of Psychiatry
London, England

PLENUM PRESS • NEW YORK AND LONDON

Library of Congress Cataloging in Publication Data

The Different faces of motherhood / edited by Beverly Birns and Dale F. Hay.
    p.   cm.—(Perspectives in developmental psychology)
  Includes bibliographies and index.
  ISBN 0-306-42887-3
  1. Motherhood. 2. Mother and child. 3. Motherhood—Cross-cultural studies. I.
Birns, Beverly. II. Hay, Dale F. III. Series.
HQ759.D54 1988   88-16878
306.8'743—dc19   CIP

© 1988 Plenum Press, New York
A Division of Plenum Publishing Corporation
233 Spring Street, New York, N.Y. 10013

All rights reserved

No part of this book may be reproduced, stored in a retrieval system, or transmitted
in any form or by any means, electronic, mechanical, photocopying, microfilming,
recording, or otherwise, without written permission from the Publisher

Printed in the United States of America

MQ
759
D54
1988

To Sylvia

Contributors

BARBARA HOLLAND BASKIN, Interdisciplinary Program in Social Sciences, State University of New York, Stony Brook, New York

NIZA BEN-NER, Departments of Sociology and Social Anthropology, Hebrew University, Jerusalem, Israel

BEVERLY BIRNS, Child and Family Studies Program, State University of New York, Stony Brook, New York

RUTH DE KANTER, Department of Development, State University of Utrecht, Utrecht, The Netherlands

MICHELE HARWAY, California Family Study Center, 5433 Laurel Canyon Boulevard, North Hollywood, California

DALE F. HAY, Institute of Psychiatry, De Crespigny Park, Denmark Hill, London, England

SHI MING HU, Asian Studies Program, State University of New York, Stony Brook, New York

JOAN F. KUCHNER, Social Science Interdisciplinary Program, State University of New York, Stony Brook, New York

MARSHA B. LISS, Department of Psychology, California State University, San Bernardino, California

KATHLEEN MCCARTNEY, Department of Psychology, University of New Hampshire, Durham, New Hampshire

ALISON NASH, Department of Psychology, University of Utah, Salt Lake City, Utah

DEBORAH PHILLIPS, Department of Psychology, University of Virginia, Charlottesville, Virginia

JANE PORCINO, Continuing Education Department, State University of New York, Stony Brook, New York

ELIZABETH P. RIGGS, (retired) Department of French, State University of New York, Stony Brook, New York.

SARAH HALL STERNGLANZ, Department of Psychology and Women's Studies Program, State University of New York, Stony Brook, New York

MARTHA B. STRAUS, University Associates in Psychology, 222 West Street, Keene, New Hampshire

JO ELLEN VESPO, Department of Psychology, Utica College, Utica, New York

VALORA WASHINGTON, Dean of Faculty, Antioch College, Yellow Springs, Ohio

Preface

The Different Faces of Motherhood began during a conversation between the two editors, developmental psychologists who have spent our professional careers working with infants and very young children. We are well aware of the importance of infants to their mothers and of mothers to their infants. However, we were particularly aware of the fact that, whereas our knowledge about infants increases exponentially each decade, our assumptions about mothers change relatively little. We were concerned about the theories that underlie the advice given to mothers and also about the assumption that mothers appear to be generic. More and more we have learned about individual differences in babies, but not more and more about individual differences in mothers. Our second concern has been to expand our knowledge about mothers. Our assumptions were few and our questions were many.

We believed that the experience of women would vary greatly, both in outlook and in behavior, depending on each woman's age, marital status, financial status, ethnicity, health, education and work experience, as well as a woman's own experience in her family origin and her relationship to her husband. If we are to understand child development and believe that the early years are important in a child's life, then it seems critical to examine our beliefs about mothers. If we are to understand human development, then being a mother is surely an important area of inquiry.

In conceptualizing this book, we had two major goals: to examine the diversity of maternal experience and to examine the underlying assumptions of the advice givers. We believe that to understand the present it is necessary to have some perspective on history and the cultural context in which mothers dwell.

After some discussion and many letters, we decided to invite some colleagues to join us in a session to brainstorm about the book. Our commitment to diversity as a theme included diversity in disciplines. Our authors included several psychologists (some who work primarily with children and families, one with aging), ethologists, a Chinese scholar in the field of education, and an educator concerned with the handicapped. All agreed to write original chapters for this book. We all concurred that the chapters would reflect current scholarship in our areas but also include some interview data—not to test hypotheses, but rather to generate them.

This volume is the collective effort of many colleagues, all women. For most of us, most of our professional lives are in the world of men. It is also true that most, although not all, of the "advice to mothers" books have been written by men. We were curious about a collaborative effort that would involve all women. We have not been disappointed.

Although there is frequently a time lag between the date that a manuscript is expected and the date that the actual book appears, this lag often means that by the time the book appears, the data are no longer relevant. We feel that this book is even more timely now than it would have been a few years ago.

Social change has never been more rapid than in the past few years, and nowhere is this more evident than in the area of family relations. The major changes are in the divorce rate and the number of women with young children who are now in the workforce. Although when we began the book we believed that we were writing about women whose images were poorly reflected in the literature, by now we feel that most women's experiences are represented in the book. The traditional nuclear family is not the modal family today. Most women in families are working and therefore concerned about child care. Almost half of married women divorce, often when children are present and young. Although much has been written previously about black mothers, there has been little consensus in this area, and much of what has been written has been false. Women who postpone childbearing are newly discovered as subjects of inquiry, and handicapped mothers may be the least visible of our many faces.

This volume is directed to students—both graduate and undergraduate— and persons working in or training to work in the helping or teaching professions. We believe that our efforts should be of interest to those working with children, youth, and families. Although this is not a book of advice, our hope is that it will be useful to professionals and also to mothers who may find information that is not available in most books written for and about mothers.

Beverly Birns
Dale F. Hay

Stony Brook and London

Acknowledgments

Acknowledgments also tell a story. Mine begins where we all begin, with my own mother, Sylvia Malkind. It was she who taught me that mothers could be kind, loving, sensitive, committed to making the world a better place, and be in the paid labor force. To the other important women who made it clear that children could love and be loved by more than one mothering person; Belle Krupnick, Lena Pressman, and Henri Schulman.

Among my friends and colleagues who contributed directly to this work: Jean Baker-Miller, long-time friend who as Director of Research at the Stone Center, Wellesley College, encouraged me to present an earlier version of my chapter on psychoanalysis at the Stone Center. To my colleagues at SUNY Stony Brook: Naomi Rosenthal and June Starr for their thoughtful questions and criticism. To my sister, Bernice Rosen, who read, commented and edited again and again and said that she never got bored. To my friends and colleagues whose devotion and collaboration to this volume far exceeded writing their own chapters. To Dale Hay, whose collaboration made me both proud and happy to be a developmental psychologist. Our hours of most intense work on both sides of the Atlantic were made even more pleasurable by the appearance and presence of Alex.

To my children, Susan, Peter, Matthew and Michael, who provided the joys and anxieties of motherhood, and as young adult friends make it clear that motherhood and work are not antithetical.

Yes, my world includes men as well as women. To my father, David Malkind, who at 90 is still smart and funny and cares and is proud of his daughters. To my former colleagues at Albert Einstein College of Medicine: Wagner Bridger for teaching me to think like a scientist; and to Mark Golden for sharing ideas, laughs and writing papers at the 11th hour. At Stony Brook, to Eli Seifman for providing protection and care in a not always friendly environment. To Eli Newberger, who at Children's Hospital, Harvard Medical School, provided a fellowship in family violence, where I learned about all the things that can go wrong with mothers and children, about the sadness and the rage.

To those who have been my closest partners in life: To Monroe Birns, who both predicted and insisted that I become "all that I am capable of being," but who did not live to see it happen. To Harold Atkins, for only rarely complaining about his wife's commitment to work and for sharing the sometimes difficult job of raising our children. Finally, to Dyllis Harvey, who for many years was another mother to my children, for her care and wisdom.

It is difficult to thank an institution. Nonetheless, SUNY Stony Brook has provided almost 2 decades of students from whom to learn as well as teach, and a profession that more than any other fosters and provides time to study, write and think.

Finally, I am especially grateful to the series editor, Michael Lewis, for his support and encouragement, to Robert Jystad, production editor at Plenum, for his cheerful and sensitive assistance, and last but certainly not least, Linda Joseph, for her unflagging persistence at the keyboard.

B.B.

Contents

PART II. CROSS-CULTURAL PERSPECTIVES

PART III. CONTEMPORARY AMERICAN MOTHERHOOD

Chapter 7. Motherhood and Child Care 157

Kathleen McCartney and Deborah Phillips

Chapter 8. The Black Mother in the United States: History, Theory,
Research, and Issues 185

Valora Washington

Introduction

BEVERLY BIRNS AND DALE F. HAY

Motherhood wears different faces. The experience of being a mother is affected by a woman's personal history, by the position she holds in her society, and by the social and economic forces operating in her culture. The experience of motherhood is also affected by the mother's health and present circumstances, by the quality of her relationships with family and friends, and, not least important, by the unique characteristics of her children.

The purpose of this volume is to highlight the diversity of maternal experience in the late twentieth century, which stands in contrast to cultural myths of the "good" mother, the "natural" mother. The chapters in this book examine how different groups of mothers lead their lives. The authors have explored what these groups of mothers have in common and what unique problems they face. In working on the book, we have found that, as social scientists, we have been ever ready to give advice to mothers but we actually know very little about their lives. We know far more about children than we do about mothers.

SPECIFIC AIMS OF THE BOOK

The volume as a whole is a collaborative endeavor. We met together with most of the authors at the outset, sharing ideas about the goals and research methods to be used in preparing each chapter. We all agreed that the chapters should reflect the current state of knowledge in the field, but that they should also point up new directions for research. As a group, we decided that each author should pursue the following objectives:

1. First, and most important, *motherhood should be studied with a focus on mothers in their own right and not simply as a reflection on the surface of child develop-*

BEVERLY BIRNS • Child and Family Studies Program, State University of New York, Stony Brook, New York 11794.   DALE F. HAY • Institute of Psychiatry, De Crespigny Park, Denmark Hill, London SE5 8AF, England.

ment. As it turned out, this was not an easy task. Most authors found a great deal of information about children, or about women in different groups and circumstances, but not about mothers in particular. For example, it is relatively easy to locate statistics about divorced women or studies about the effects of divorce on children, but it is much less easy to find out about the circumstances of divorced mothers. As we proceeded with our chapters, it became increasingly clear that, by focusing on motherhood in its own right, the contributors to this volume were defining a new, interdisciplinary field of inquiry.

2. Second, we asked each author to *look at mothers in the context of their more general life experiences.* The authors have cast their nets widely and have discussed the historical, social, and economic forces that impinge on the biological act of reproduction and the psychological experience of motherhood. They have asked, what kind of societies do mothers live in? Historically, has there been support for motherhood in a particular society? What factors make the task of mothering more difficult or less difficult? They have examined the experience of motherhood against the background of other dimensions of a woman's life, including her own childhood experiences, her education, her current relationships, and her opportunities for paid employment. We believe that the study of the mother–child relationship in isolation from the rest of the world has led to quite misleading conclusions, and the approach taken in this book is an attempt to address that problem.

A focus on the social context of motherhood is particularly important at this point in time because the twentieth century has witnessed nine decades of tremendous technological and social change. In hardly any area are these changes more dramatic than the domain of childbearing and family life. Technological advances in birth control mean that some women are able to have those children they choose to have when they choose to have them. The technology of abortion and its legalization mean that unwanted pregnancies can be terminated with little risk to the woman. New technologies concerned with genetics and fetal development permit the prediction of birth defects and the termination of pregnancies that would result in infants born with congenital anomalies. Advances in the treatment of infertility challenge our very definition of what it means to be a mother; a woman who is infertile can now mother a baby who is biologically her husband's child but who has been "grown" in the womb of another woman. Thus, in general because of the technological and social changes, women have more options than ever before, but options, no matter how desirable, also create confusion and ambivalence. An aim of the book was to highlight the many dilemmas, choices, and questions contemporary mothers face.

3. Finally, we asked the authors *to explore not just the objective status of mothers and their children, but the phenomenology of motherhood.* In other words, we asked the authors to listen to what mothers themselves had to say. Because of the many rapid changes in society as a whole, women are asking many questions. For example, they ask: Do I even want to become a mother? If I do become a mother, do I necessarily want to live with the father of the child? If I can't have a child, should I adopt a baby, and, if so, should it be of my ethnic and national

background? If I marry, and then have a child, can I still work for pay and be a "good mother" while doing my paid job well? If I raise my child as a single parent, can I support my family on one income? If I am well-educated, how shall I advance professionally while still being a good mother? Or if, like most women, I work in the low-paid service sector, how can I afford the best child care possible? Minority women ask: How can I overcome entrenched racism and provide my child with self-esteem and a good education? Disabled women must also ask: Am I strong enough to overcome all the myriad barriers to becoming a good mother?

To find out exactly what mothers are asking themselves and thinking about, the authors of the chapters in this book decided to talk directly to mothers. That is, in addition to combing through the available published literature on their topics, many of the authors conducted supplementary interviews with mothers. We believe that the results of these interviews bring each topic to life. Furthermore, even the very informal interviews that various authors conducted have generated many ideas for future research.

GENERAL THEMES

The authors have each pursued these objectives in unique ways, but three general themes recur throughout the book. One concerns the tension between theory and practice, myth and reality, what mothers are told they should do as opposed to what they do do. A second theme is the need to examine both myths about mothers and the realities of mothers' lives in their appropriate social and historical context. The third theme is the awareness many of the authors have articulated that, because of the rapid social and technological change in recent decades and because of some current resistance to and backlash against the changes, contemporary mothers in many different groups and societies have many questions and confront many dilemmas. The face motherhood wears in the late twentieth century is a puzzled one.

Myth, Theory, and Reality

Whether we call it mythology, ideology, or folk wisdom, there exist in all societies ideas about good mothers, women who are nurturant, kind, and selfless. These ideas about good mothers coexist with powerful myths about bad mothers, who are typified by the image of the wicked stepmother, who is vain, selfish, and at times sadistic, neglectful, and abusive. These myths become formalized in academic theories about motherhood, which in turn stimulate the empirical research that becomes translated into the advice experts give to women about how to mother. The result is a peculiar cycle of events; the myths and theories themselves do not accurately reflect the realities of motherhood, but they have the power to affect women's lives. Mothers may try to conform to the myths, to follow the advice given to them. When the myths bear no resemblance to reality, when the advice fails, mothers feel anxiety, guilt, and sometimes despair, which in turn powerfully affects their experience of motherhood.

The tension between myth and reality, theory and practice, is acute for contemporary mothers, but it is by no means a new problem. In many different societies, in many different historical eras, motherhood has been guided and constrained by the theories and world views espoused by the greater culture. Different societies subscribe to different myths, and different myths and theories lead to different childrearing practices. For example, most of us in Western society in the twentieth century think children have a right to a mother's love. We consider neglect and abuse of children abhorrent, regrettable, unnatural, and punishable by law. Yet belief in "mother love" may be a fairly recent development in thinking about mothers and children.

Elizabeth Badinter (1980), a French philosopher, has argued that just as the concept of "a child" is a new cultural invention, so "mother love" was conspicuously absent prior to the eighteenth century. Badinter argues that in early centuries infant mortality was not just a product of poverty. Even rich women sent their children out to wet nurses for their early years, the mothers being aware that few of their babies would survive. According to Badinter, it was only during the period of the Enlightenment that the survival of children came to be seen as important and mothers were urged to take care of their own children. Mother love as we think of it—a woman's investment of time, care, and affection in children—was, in Badinter's view, a concept invented to foster nurturance in women.

Of course, even within a given historical era, myths about mothers and children differ from culture to culture. For example, if Badinter is correct, children were devalued in seventeenth-century France, but their status in seventeenth-century colonial America was quite different. The low status of children in France may have been partly due to the fact that much of Western Europe was overpopulated. In contrast, children were needed to populate the new continent. The Puritans who came to America to avoid religious persecution had as one of their articulated goals a better life for their children.

What we know about childrearing in the Puritan colonies illustrates how theory and ideology influence motherhood. The Puritans' religious beliefs, as well as the harsh conditions of their lives, shaped their behavior toward their children. Biblical prescriptions and proscriptions, as well as the belief that "to spare the rod is to spoil the child," were important components of their implicit childrearing theories. Nonetheless, the need for farm labor and the development of new communities codetermined both harshness and kindness in the treatment of children.

Questions about the relationship between myth and reality, theory and practice, persist in contemporary Western society. With social changes come new myths and theories about mothers and children, and the new theories themselves are questioned and challenged. For example, many individuals fault the women's movement for a wide range of undesirable conditions, such as adolescent suicide, latchkey children, and child abuse. This view implies that feminist theory somehow arose on its own and created havoc. In fact, the movement appeared in response to the social, psychological, and economic realities of women's lives. Margolis (1984) argues that the women's movement did not arise because women read de Beauvior or Friedan, but because of post-World War II consumerism, families' need for two incomes, and discrimination against women in education and employment. Ideology in this case grew out of social and economic constraints on women.

The Historical and Social Context of Motherhood

The greater social order not only affects theories and ideologies about motherhood, it affects how women experience their lives as mothers. In order to understand the experience of an individual mother or group of mothers, we need information about the economic, social, and psychological environment of mother and child. For example, the experiences, thoughts, feelings, and behavior of a 25-year-old, single, impoverished Appalachian mother of three will be very different from those of a 35-year-old college-educated, urban, married mother of a 4-year-old only child. Differences in prenatal and postnatal medical care, maternal education, housing, and marital status will all affect how mothers relate to their children. In addition, the historical forces operating in a society influence the contemporary social context, which in turn shapes mothers' lives.

This can be clearly seen in contemporary American society. The American experience of motherhood is a paradoxical one that reflects a basic contradiction in American society as a whole. On the one hand, American culture claims to be a child-centered culture, one that highly values motherhood. At the same time, American culture is fiercely individualistic and places a high value on independence, privacy, and personal initiative. This tradition had made family life a very private concern.

Both strands in American views of mothers, children, and family life have been intertwined over the last two centuries. A major influence on American culture and therefore on American childrearing is the fact that the United States is a nation of immigrants. Whether it was the Puritans who came to escape religious persecution, the Irish who came to escape starvation, or the Jews who came in the 1930s to escape murder at the hands of the Nazis, most adults who emigrated to the United States believed that the New World would guarantee a better life for their children. The major exception of this, of course, was the Africans brought to America not to better their own and their children's lives, but to provide free labor for a developing nation. Nonetheless, as Valora Washington describes in her chapter in this book, a great concern for children is also a mainspring of Black American culture. In general, the child-centered quality of American life has been expressed in such ways as the commitment to public education and the growth of the child development movement in the universities.

At the same time that there is this general concern for the welfare of children, American society isolates mothers and children from the greater community. This isolation is made more acute by the fact that Americans are so mobile. Even before the invention of the automobile, the unusual mobility of the American people was predicated on the opportunities afforded by the vast land and its rich natural resources. In the early days, immigrants who were dissatisfied with their surroundings could move West. Today, Americans remain very mobile. Although the possibility of moving may be a source of optimism for American families, it may also profoundly affect the sources of support for mothers, who may raise their children thousands of miles away from their families and close friends. Alongside the myths of the hardy pioneers traveling great distances to establish their homesteads in the West is the image of the pioneer mother weeping at the small grave beside the wagon trail. Movement, opportunity, and loss have always been intertwined in the American experience.

Another factor related to both immigration and mobility is the fact that many immigrants came to America believing that "the streets are paved with gold," metaphorically if not in fact. The reality was that, as each wave of immigrants arrived, they were mostly impoverished and most remained so, for at least one generation and possibly for several generations. The non-English-speaking immigrants who arrived in the nineteenth and twentieth centuries were usually exploited and frequently despised by the first comers. They were given the hardest work, lowest pay, poorest housing and endured the most onerous health conditions. Their children's lives were not what they hoped for. In the early days of the factories, women and children worked 12 and 14 hours a day for starvation wages. Federal legislation banning child labor was not definitely accomplished until after World War II. Thus, the widely heralded child centeredness of American life must be seen against the background of the exploitation and abuse of children.

Alongside this basic contradiction between a child-centered society and one that considers childrearing private enterprise, there has long been a basic ambivalence within American culture about maternal employment. This is seen clearly in the recent history of the nation, since the Depression and World War II. American society has shunted women from home to workplace and back again several times over the last few decades and has blamed both working mothers and "overprotective," "domineering," stay-at-home mothers for their children's ills.

Because during World War II women were needed in the factories, Congress passed the Lanham Act in 1943, which provided federal funds to day-care centers for the specific purpose of freeing women with young children. As Kathleen McCartney and Deborah Phillips describe in their chapter in this book, the working mother became the "patriotic mother." Even in this period, however, when "Rosie the Riveter" was the focus of adulation and some children of working mothers were attending the well-staffed, attractive Lanham Day Care Centers, women were receiving mixed messages about combining gainful employment and motherhood.

One source of the mixed messages was the academic community. Although women were being encouraged to work and use child-care facilities, at this time psychoanalytic theories about the nature of women and motherhood were being elaborated, published, and disseminated. As Beverly Birns and Niza ben-Ner describe in Chapter 2, the psychoanalytic work elaborated on Freud's views of women as being passive, narcissistic, dependent, nurturant, and happy only when they were protected, loved, and provided for by men and engaged in childrearing. Thus, the generation of women who were raising their children during and following World War II were being told that their place was in the home.

Cultural ambivalence about women who did stay home was reflected in the publication of the book that many agree is the epitome of misogyny, Philip Wylie's *Generation of Vipers*. According to Wylie, men failed the military tests of physical and intellectual ability because they had been profoundly damaged by their mothers. With Wylie's book the notion that mother love may be uncontrolled and excessive is introduced into the contradictory American myths about motherhood.

Even in the 1950s, not all mothers were housewives; about one-fifth of married couples had two breadwinners (Margolis, 1984). Nonetheless, most mothers stayed home with their children, and the nature of the American home itself changed. The major social change of the postwar era was the massive migration of Americans to the suburbs. One sociological study (Rothman, 1978) indicated that the vaunted suburban privacy often deteriorated into isolation, and signs of familial distress were prevalent. Needless to say, American mothers who believed that they were living the American dream and subsequently found it a nightmare were confused by the paradox and blamed themselves for failing as wives and mothers.

The social changes in the 1950s and 1960s have set the stage for many of the current dilemmas facing American mothers. Among the most important are the civil rights and feminist movements that began in the 1960s. If the postwar era did not prove idyllic for whites, blacks who had served in the military and then returned to life in urban ghettos were even more disenchanted. Blacks faced segregation and extreme discrimination in housing, employment, education, and transportation. From both sources—the failure of the suburban dream for women and the continued oppression of blacks—came the movements for equality.

Among other changes taking place in the 1960s was the fact that the ideal of a society committed to the welfare of its children came much closer to being realized than ever before. As part of the War on Poverty, Head Start was enacted in an attempt to see that poor children would no longer begin school at an educational disadvantage. Federal money was allocated to the individual states to pay for health care for poor families. In 1971, Congress passed the ERA and the Child Development Bill. These two bills would have ended job discrimination against women and provided child care and health care for all children. This legislation would have radically altered the lives of American families. Furthermore, in 1973, the Supreme Court judged that terminating an unwanted pregnancy was a woman's decision. For the first time in American history, motherhood became a free choice.

In the 1970s and 1980s, however, the other strand in American views of family life, the emphasis on individualism and privacy, has once again become prominent. For example, the Child Development Bill was vetoed by Nixon, and the ERA was not ratified by a sufficient number of states to become law. The fight by the extreme right against both bills used "pro-family" rhetoric, including statements that the laws would destroy the family, that children would be "Sovietized," and that mothers would have to serve in the army. As we write, the 1980s are drawing to a close, and society as a whole is again ceding responsibility for the care of its children. Women are once again being exhorted to stay at home with their infants. The right to choose motherhood freely is being challenged by the right-to-life lobby. These historical trends create the array of dilemmas for contemporary mothers, in the United States and elsewhere, which is the third general theme taken up in the volume.

The Contemporary Mother

Who are today's mothers? What dilemmas do they face? In many societies across the globe, mothers in the 1980s differ from their predecessors a generation ago in a number of ways. For example, in the United States, if we picked an American mother to talk to at random, she might be an older woman, who has delayed childbearing and limited the size of her family to accommodate her professional development. Alternatively, she might be very young and rearing a child out of wedlock. In any case, the average mother is no longer likely to be a housewife, living with her employed husband and their three or four biological children in the suburbs. The so-called traditional family represents fewer than 10% of contemporary American families.

Today the typical mother is likely to be in the paid workforce; 60% of American mothers work for pay, including over 50% of mothers of children under 3 years of age (U.S. Department of Labor, Women's Bureau, 1986). She is fairly likely to be divorced, separated, or never-married; about half of American marriages end in divorce. If so, she is likely to be poor. More than half the women awarded child support do not receive it (Weitzman, 1985). The poverty rate for female-headed households is five times that for married couples. It is therefore not surprising that half of the poor in the United States live in families maintained by women.

In this time of rapid social change, many questions are being asked about motherhood and by mothers themselves. Can a woman be equally committed to work and family? Does, as Selma Fraiberg advocated (Fraiberg, 1977), every child have a right to full-time mothering for at least 3 years? If so, who pays? If maternity leaves become enacted into law, will such leaves be granted willingly, or will employers reconsider the hiring of women of childbearing age? What will this in turn do to the impoverished lives of many American mothers? What about the recent changes in the law and in social mores—for example, have the changing divorce laws helped mothers or made their lives more difficult? The questions are many, the answers are few. We hope that the information collected in this volume, especially the reports of mothers themselves, will increase our knowledge base, separate some myths from reality, and illustrate how children can be successfully reared in a myriad of ways. By portraying the different faces of motherhood, the chapters that follow show quite clearly that there is no single route to being a "good mother."

ORGANIZATION OF THE BOOK

The book is organized in terms of three main parts that correspond to the three general themes in the book as a whole: the tension between the theory and practice of motherhood, the need to examine motherhood in a broader social and historical context, and an appreciation of the dilemmas facing contemporary mothers. Part I is devoted to a review of some influential theories of the mother–child relationship. The theories we consider include evolutionary biology, psychoanalysis, and social learning theory. Each of these, but particularly psychoanalysis, affects the advice that is offered to mothers by authorities. Part II examines the social and historical context of motherhood in three different societies undergoing different sorts of major social changes: China, Morocco, and the Netherlands. Finally, Part III focuses on several different groups of contemporary American mothers in the 1980s who face common dilemmas as well as unique problems. The groups discussed include mothers who need child care, black mothers, divorced mothers, disabled mothers, and mothers who have delayed childbearing.

REFERENCES

Badinter, E. (1980). *Mother love: Myth and reality*. New York: Macmillan.

Fraiberg, S. (1977). *Every child's birthright: In defense of mothering*. New York: Basic.

Margolis, M. L. (1984). *Mothers and such: Views of American women and why they changed*. Berkeley: University of California Press.

Rothman, S. M. (1978). *Woman's proper place: A history of changing ideals and practice, 1870 to the present*. New York: Basic.

United States Department of Labor, Women's Bureau. (1986). *20 facts on working women*.

Weitzman, L. J. (1985). *The divorce revolution*. New York: Free Press.

Major Theories

Part I examines some influential theories about the mother–child relationship. Mothers, of course, have been theorized about in varying ways by obstetricians, fertility specialists, demographers, anthropologists, and family sociologists, among others. The focus in this section is more limited. Here we focus on three general perspectives: Sarah Sternglanz and Alison Nash examine the perspective of evolutionary biology; Beverly Birns and Niza ben-Ner discuss the psychoanalytic tradition; and Dale Hay and Jo Ellen Vespo review social learning accounts of the development of the mother–child relationship. These three theoretical perspectives have inspired much of the empirical research in developmental psychology that in turn provides a collection of "facts" about mothers and children that often end up in the advice books.

All three theories have influenced developmental psychology throughout the twentieth century, though the influence of each has waxed and waned from decade to decade. Theories do not remain static; each has undergone considerable internal development since the nineteenth and early-twentieth centuries, when Darwin and Wallace, Freud, Thorndike, and Watson were formulating their ideas. Some of these developments are described in detail in each of the chapters that follow. Before presenting each theory separately, however, it is useful to compare them in terms of a common set of dimensions. There are both commonalities and differences among the theories in terms of what they hypothesize as the causes and outcomes of motherhood, their relative preoccupation with the period of infancy as opposed to other parts of the life span, the levels of analysis that are used, and the nature of the evidence provided.

A COMPARISON OF THE THEORIES

Causes and Outcomes

The three theories attribute the development of the mother–child relationship to different causes but focus on similar outcomes. Biologists, psychoanalysts, and social learning theorists all link the mother–child relationship with the child's subsequent mature social behavior. None of the perspectives raises the possibility that mothers might have nothing to do with their children's social success.

The Preoccupation with Infancy

Developmental psychologists have always been preoccupied with the study of infants (cf. Hay, 1986) and, in particular, with the notion that experiences during infancy are critical. This belief is expressed in common proverbs, such as "As the twig is bent, so grows the tree," and translated into developmental theory with Freud's claim that the mother–infant relationship is the prototype for all future relationships. The three theories differ in the emphasis they place on infancy, with social learning theorists stressing the importance of cumulative experiences throughout life; in practice, however, social learning researchers have also placed disproportionate emphasis on studies of infants.

Levels of Analysis

Influences on the mother–child relationship have been discussed at three levels of analysis: what is happening in the immediate situation, as a mother and child relate to each other; what has happened over the lifetime of each; and what has happened over generations, as genes are transmitted and the species has evolved. Evolutionary biologists are primarily concerned with the third level, whereas psychoanalysts and social learning theorists are primarily concerned with the second. However, most of the empirical data used to test the theories is collected at the first level, the immediate situation. Grand conclusions about the nature of motherhood have been drawn from observations or reports of mothers and children in very particular circumstances.

The Nature of the Evidence

The three perspectives are associated with divergent methodological traditions and thus with divergent sources of evidence. The observational method has been used in all three perspectives, but to a differing extent. Experimentation is used by biologists and social learning theorists, though the scope of the experiments differ; biologists completely alter animals' experiences while growing up, while learning researchers attempt to simulate natural learning opportunities in the laboratory. Both psychoanalysts and social learning theorists have relied on parents' and children's retrospective reports about the mother–child relationship. Evolutionary biologists often are forced to argue on the basis of logic, rather than empirical evidence, insofar as social relationships do not leave a fossil record. At times their logical arguments about what mothers and infants are trying to do, in evolutionary terms, resemble the clinical interpretations made by psychoanalysts about their analysands' unconscious motivations.

Across all three perspectives (though perhaps less so for social learning theory) there has been considerable interest in using evidence about pathology to infer how the mother–child relationship normally develops. Thus, for example, biologists have examined the effects of rearing young animals in isolation from their mothers or with odd companions. Psychoanalysts have similarly paid a great deal of attention to the phenomenon of "maternal deprivation" and have studied children reared in institutions or under conditions of great privation. In general, the extensive, direct observations of mothers and their offspring in ordinary circumstances is a relatively recent development in all three perspectives.

THEMES IN THE CHAPTERS

In addition to noting the commonalities among these three theories, it is also important to note their unique features and the unique ways in which each has developed over time. The chapters in Part I provide an intensive look at the current versions of biological, psychoanalytic, and learning perspectives on the mother–child relationship.

Ethology

In their discussion of biological theories of motherhood, Sternglanz and Nash (Chapter 1) focus on the question of maternal instinct. They note that many people use biological theory to make claims about what is or is not "natural" for human mothers, and therefore that it is important to examine carefully what biological research actually tells us about motherhood. They explain in detail the nature of the evolutionary arguments about maternal instinct and then review the relevant empirical research on motherhood in other species. Sternglanz and Nash note that, if maternal behavior is completely instinctual, it should not be affected by the conditions under which the mothers themselves grow up; it should be similar in closely related species; and it should not differ from culture to culture in the human species. None of these premises is supported by the empirical literature. Rather they cite evidence to prove that maternal behavior varies in closely related species and also from culture to culture among humans. Further, they conclude that human mothers may or may not wish to stay at home full-time with their children but that it cannot be argued that it is "biologically natural" to do so.

Psychoanalysis

The notion that mothering is instinctual is also a theme in psychoanalytic formulations about motherhood. However, as Birns and ben-Ner note in Chapter 2, psychoanalytic theories of motherhood have themselves undergone evolution over the decades of the twentieth century. Instinct theory is one component of psychoanalytic theory, but Freud's greatest legacy is the notion that the mother–child relationship is not only the most important, because it is the basis of all future love relationships, but also that this early relationship is the basis for the mental health or emotional problems that appear later in life. It was because of Freud's credentials as a physician and scientist, as well as his brilliant style, that he made psychoanalysis a major thread in twentieth century literature as well as psychology.

However, today it is not so much Freud's original ideas that influence contemporary psychology and child development, but rather those of his followers—among them Bowlby, Fraiberg, Mahler, and Ainsworth—who have studied mother–child interactions and specifically attachment behavior. It is these authors, who insist on the importance of the first 2 years of life, who form the basis of much of the current debate about the needs of infants and the effects of maternal employment and nonmaternal care on very young infants. If today's working mothers feel a deep sense of guilt and uncertainty as they work and take major responsibility for child care, it is because of the profound effect of psychoanalytic theory on the experts. If women are afraid that by working they may be creating problems for their children, it is because many of the authorities take as gospel this theory. Birns and ben-Ner trace the evolution of the theory and the ramifications for mothers who in the late twentieth century continue to raise their children and join the paid labor force.

Social Learning Perspectives

Finally, in Chapter 3, Hay and Vespo examine the social learning perspective on the development of the mother–child relationship. Their chapter is also directed to the general question of whether motherhood is natural and instinctual or whether, in contrast, mothers and infants both have to learn to relate to each other. Hay and Vespo review three examples of explicit social learning theories of the formation of mother–infant attachment and note some strengths and limitations of each perspective. They then highlight what they refer to as a "disguised" social learning perspective in the more influential ethological theory set forth by John Bowlby and Mary Ainsworth. They note that although attachment theory is described as "ethological," most of the current research on mother–child attachment tests ideas about the effects of certain experiences on mothers and children. In other words, ethological attachment researchers are actually testing social learning hypotheses. Given this paradox in the empirical literature, Hay and Vespo conclude that prospects for a synthesis across theoretical perspectives on motherhood are in fact quite bright. However, such a synthesis will require going beyond the very mechanistic, paradigm-bound views of social learning that have been advanced in the past.

CHAPTER 1

Ethological Contributions to the Study of Human Motherhood

SARAH HALL STERNGLANZ AND ALISON NASH

Over the past few years, with the rise of sociobiology, it has become common for the popular press to give the impression that scientists have agreed that human motherhood has an innate biologically controlled basis. This conclusion is ostensibly based on work by ethologists and sociobiologists and supposedly generally accepted by psychologists. There is a further impression given that mothering as it was carried out in the mythical traditional 1950s home is known to be the best kind of mothering, best because it is most natural, most akin to mothering styles seen in other animals. There is a strong implication that variation from this natural biologically determined model will lead to disaster and damaged children—a feeling that people who fight Mother Nature on motherhood are asking for trouble. In fact, however, examination of the now extensive literature on the theory and practice of animal motherhood does not lead one to any of these conclusions. Further, using the criteria that ethologists and sociobiologists most commonly require, these "generally accepted" conclusions are easily shown to be false. Since public policy decisions (e.g., lack of governmental support of nonmaternal child care) have been based on those misconceptions, this issue is of more than academic interest.

We begin by considering the question of why animal research might be relevant to human motherhood and then move to a discussion of the theoretical and factual basis of sociobiologically based prescriptions for maternal care. This is followed by a survey of what a traditional ethological approach has to contrib-

SARAH HALL STERNGLANZ • Department of Psychology and Women's Studies Program, State University of New York, Stony Brook, New York 11794.   ALISON NASH • Department of Psychology, University of Utah, Salt Lake City, Utah 84112.

ute to our knowledge, and the chapter closes with a discussion of the implications of our conclusions.

WHY STUDY ANIMAL MOTHERS?

Before we begin this examination it is important to raise the question of why anyone would feel that findings from research done on animals would have any relevance to the central question of this book: What is human motherhood? The book explores the many different ways women mother. Why confuse the issue further by looking at animals?

The question of the relationship of animal research to human behavior is not unique to this issue. It is implicit whenever a rat or pigeon is placed in a Skinner box, and it is made explicit at the beginning of every comparative psychology class and raised as a larger issue by every animal rights activist boycotting drug companies that test their products on animals. It is important to review the question here again, however, because the qualifiers and subtleties of any answer display a not too surprising tendency to be dropped when the issue is something as controversial as "instinctual motherhood" or mothering.

Without a doubt there are many comparative psychologists who are interested in animal research for its own sake, who are interested in comparing the behavior of several nonhuman species or in thoroughly understanding the behavior of one. It is probably also true, however, that many people who work with animals do so because they are interested in a particular human behavior that can only be, or more easily be, studied in animals. In some cases (e.g., neurotransmitters or chemistry of the brain) only animals can be used because the research obviously will be physically or psychologically destructive to the subject, and such research on humans would be unethical. In other cases animals are the preferred subjects because they are not "cluttered up" with complicating "higher" systems (i.e., ability to transmit a culture through writing), so the reflex or other phenomenon can be studied in a purer state. In yet other cases animals are preferred because their genetic or environmental backgrounds may be controlled to an extent that is not possible or ethical with humans, so again the phenomenon may be studied in a purer state.

In all these instances the goal is to learn enough about a particular behavior to be able to identify it and measure its importance for humans. There is an implicit assumption that humans possess the same behaviors as "lower" animals (to be anthropocentric), but that in humans these behaviors are buried beneath accretions of culture and "higher" cognitive skills. There is also an implication for many that basic skills, those we share with animals, are more fundamental, essential, and important than purely human "frill" skills. Just as the foundation of a building is more fundamental and important to the survival of a building than is the top floor, so it is believed that behavior controlled at the "lowest," most phylogenetically primitive centers of the brain (e.g., breathing) is more important to the survival of the animal than some higher skills (e.g., solving mathematical problems, maze learning). By this reasoning, then, any fundamental animal instincts humans may have about mothering are more important, more dangerous to disturb, than any modern ideas about feeding schedules or optimal spacing of pregnancies that we have developed on the topic. Interfere with these fundamental urges, the analogy goes, and one may bring down the entire structure of successful mothering (defined as a happy mother and a healthy child). By studying animal mothers one may hope to identify the "basic" mother model, which can then be identified in all successful patterns of mothering, however different they may seem superficially.

The danger in drawing conclusions about human behavior from animal behavior is, of course, that it is just those cognitive "frills" and higher order abilities that make us human. Our advanced skills may indeed sometimes run counter to basic biological urges, but overall they have made us a more successful species than are the other primates (successful here meaning there are more of us, to use the definition of success of the evolutionary theorist). To pick a very basic example, although other mammals, including the other primates, use four limbs to locomote, most of the time, once past the age of 1 year, we use only two. Going on all fours is clearly the fundamental way to move—we even begin that way. Yet, except for the occasional specialist in back disorders, no one suggests that humans give up the advantages of bipedalism because of the minor side effects consequent to abandoning the more fundamental form of locomotion.

Hence, while it is often useful to understand our basic "animal" nature, this usefulness is likely to come from increased knowledge enabling us to counter it (e.g., the development of certain back exercises or hip belts for back packs) than in convincing us to abandon the human for the animal state. Unfortunately, it is just this point that is often forgotten. It is always advantageous to know more about ourselves, and the study of animals is often very helpful in this. It is not, however, always clear what recommendations should be made on the basis of this knowledge. Knowledge of our biologically based drives does not necessarily lead to a prescription to follow them.

In particular, this caveat tends to be forgotten when results are summarized by the popular press, by popularizers, and even by some professional sociobiologists. As we shall see, it is not necessarily clear what the basic pattern of motherhood is. Authors tend to seize upon that pattern that most fits their preconceptions and political beliefs and then announce that variations from this pattern are so dangerous as to destroy children and mothers. Rather than look for benefits from these variations and ways to counter any negative effects, they concentrate on maintaining (or rather restoring) what they believe to have been the *status quo* in some more natural time. Just as the social Darwinists used "survival of the fittest" to justify the existing social order (the "cream will rise" approach; if one is born poor and doesn't rise one obviously is not cream and does not deserve to live at the top of society's milkpail or pecking order), today conservatives are using sociobiology to legitimize calls for a "return" to particular patterns of motherhood. This is not a matter of mere exhortation; well-meaning legislation may indeed go far to forcing this one pattern on all by making any other pattern economically impossible.

It thus seems reasonable that research on animal motherhood will indeed be informative for humans. Other animals whose young need prolonged care face the same problems as humans, that is, who shall provide the care? The answers to questions such as whether animals show flexibility in their caregiving arrangements or whether care giving appears in a programmed fashion may help us trace the evolution of human child care. At best, these answers give us a feel for the breadth of choices that Mother Nature has found acceptable in mothering.

SOCIOBIOLOGICAL THEORIES: CARETAKING AS THE RESULT OF SELFISH GENES AND POTENTIAL INVESTMENT

Sociobiologists do not, of course, theorize at the level of "Mother Nature's wants and needs." In recent years, a complex theory has developed that attempts to explain existing animal and human sex differences in terms of differential investment of energy in offspring. This line of reasoning has been used to argue that women, for genetic reasons, have a greater and more inherent interest in childrearing than men, and that mothers are more biologically equipped to take care of babies than are fathers, or anyone else for that matter. This theory assumes at the outset that females give more care to offspring than males. The theory then attempts to explain this sex difference. We discuss later some of the difficulties with this assumption, but for the moment let us focus on the theoretical argument. The basis of the theory is the assumption that an animal that has already invested much in a particular offspring (e.g., a pregnant mammal) continues to invest energy in care so as not to lose the initial investment. An animal with little invested (e.g., a promiscuous male) has little incentive to invest more. To see why this follows, it is helpful to examine the concept of the "selfish gene."

Although the sociobiological explanation of traditional sex roles is stated most explicitly (and received most publicity) in Wilson's (1975) *Sociobiology*, the theoretical basis is more clearly spelled out by Trivers (1972) and Dawkins (1976). In their view, the force of natural selection would impel mammals such as humans into a situation in which females are, for biological reasons, primarily responsible for child care. To understand this view, it is important to note the recent focus of evolutionary theorists on a new unit of natural selection. Although at different times the unit upon which evolution acts has been seen as the individual or as a whole population, recently the emphasis has been on the gene. This variation on the chicken and the egg problem can be expressed in a simplified way as "A man is just the sperm's way of making more sperm." The more reproductions of a gene there are in the general population, the more successful that gene is.

What does this mean for the individual? Contrary to the views of social Darwinists, success in evolutionary terms is measured in quantity, not quality, of life. A slave with twelve surviving children is more of an evolutionary success than a king with two. The slave ceases to contribute to her success when she becomes too old or otherwise unable to reproduce, *unless* her activities lead to the increased likelihood that her offspring and their offspring will reproduce—that is, that more copies of her genes will appear in the population. So far the individual's interest in promoting the success of her descendants and the gene's "interest" in multiplying copies of itself are identical. However, from a genetic point of view, both children and full siblings (of the parent) are equally closely related to the parent. A sister carrying gene A who supports her brother who carries gene A is doing as much for the propagation of gene A as a mother (carrying gene A) who supports a child carrying gene A. By focusing on the gene, one can explain, in very "selfish" terms, apparent altruism toward one's relations (and by extension one's community, which presumably shares one's genes). A biological predisposition toward as least certain kinds of altruism, far from being suicidal, is evidence of evolutionary fitness and, by this quantitative definition of fittest, promotes survival of the fittest (Trivers, 1971).

This genetic view of fitness leads to some interesting options for childrearing. Given the limitations of the energies of the parent, one may either have many offspring and provide little care or one may have fewer offspring and provide more care. Either of these approaches should lead to a reasonable number of surviving descendants, but a species cannot both have many offspring and provide a high level of care for each. Offspring must be cared for from the parents' surplus energy, and there is only a limited amount available.

If this view of fitness is unfamiliar, the reader by now may be objecting that this approach requires a degree of conscious control of reproduction and knowledge of economics unlikely to be found in most people, much less animals. In the view of the sociobiologists, of course, all this is taking place at an unconscious genetic level. Those animals that have made incorrect choices (e.g., tried to raise large families while giving each offspring a great deal of care) have perished, or, more importantly, the genes that impelled them to such cost-ineffective behavior have been eliminated from the gene pool. The overworked, intensive care-giving mother of 12 has died young, leaving her offspring defenseless and helpless, resulting in their demise. Only mothers whose genes led them to the correct choices will have offspring who survive to pass these genes on. Note that because this genetically controlled behavior is seen as unconscious and because the unconscious is seen as more basic (the conscious is just the tip of the iceberg), psychologists as well as biologists will see this behavior as difficult and risky to change.

Generally speaking, fish, amphibians, and reptiles opt for the many offspring–little care approach and birds and mammals for the opposite. Both the females and males in most cold-blooded species make relatively small biological mass and behavioral energy contributions to their individual offspring (although there are exceptions). Please note that the mass of the female–egg contribution is apparently always a larger contribution than that of the male–sperm. In mammals, due to pregnancy and nursing, females make a very large biological mass contribution and males a very small one. This sex difference is extreme in humans, so extreme that the human female's investment at birth in a particular baby is so high it is clear her only "sensible" course is further investment in caretaking to ensure her genetic survival. This point is underlined by the fact that although infant mammals and birds in general require caretaking to survive (unlike many cold-blooded animals), the human infant requires an exceptionally long period of caretaking and is exceptionally unable to contribute to its care, even by clinging to a parent's fur.

The male, on the other hand, may be perceived as having a choice. If the female is able to take care of the child alone with a reasonable chance of success, his best genetic option may be to leave them and father as many more babies as he can. However, if it will substantially increase the infant's chances of surviving to reproduce for him to stay around, *and* if he is sure he is the father (questions of this sort illustrate the disadvantages of in-body fertilization), it will be to his genetic advantage to contribute his efforts to the child's survival. It is a question of which strategy is likely to result in the greatest number of offspring surviving to reproduce themselves. Note that from the gene's point of view, if not the father's, it is immaterial whether the child is living on welfare or in Scarsdale as long as its health is not so affected by deprivation that it will be unable to reproduce. From the gene's point of view, being carried by a line that produces a generation every 12 or 15 years is usually a much better sign of fitness than being carried by "yuppies" who postpone childrearing into their 30s or decide never to have children at all.

Following logically from this reasoning, one might expect monogamy (and potential shared child care) in human societies in situations in which it is clearly advantageous to the survival of the children to have two contributing parents and in which female "faithfulness" can be guaranteed (e.g., perhaps societies that place a premium on female virginity, even to the point of sewing the labia together, and that severely punish adulterous or even raped women, even by death). In the best of all worlds for the male's genes, the society would involve both polygyny and faithfulness of women. For the female's genes, monogamy (or polyandry) is clearly the most desirable choice, with polygyny only being allowed in situations involving males with superabundant resources. This reasoning can be used to explain the traditional American view that it is the woman who wants to be married and the man who prefers promiscuity—and also the myth that a man who "loves 'em and leaves 'em" can be changed by the love of a good (read "faithful") woman.

CRITICISM OF SOCIOBIOLOGICAL THEORIES OF CARETAKING

It has recently become apparent that there are some problems with the use of the selfish gene theory in explaining male–female patterns of relationships. Objections have been raised by less deterministic theorists and by ecological sociobiologists who take species' environments and individual life histories into account. The objections have been made to two crucial assumptions in the theory: (a) the relative "expensiveness" of eggs and (b) the belief that the promiscuous male fathers more offspring than the male who is in contact with his family and available for caretaking.

Central to the sociobiological model of maternal care, based on Trivers'

(1972) analysis of parental investment, is the difference in size between the sperm and the egg:

> The fundamental difference between male and female is the size of the gametes. Male produce tiny gametes and can be viewed as successful parasites of large female gametes. Because sperm is cheap and plentiful, males can increase their reproductive success by mating with many females. (Krebs & Davies, 1981, p. 134)

This view purports that this fundamental difference is what causes the general tendency for males to philander and females, who cannot increase the number of offspring that they produce by further matings, to remain faithful and to protect their initial large investment (eggs are not so "cheap and plentiful") by caring for the offspring. The end result of this tendency of the male to leave to philander and the female to remain with the offspring is that by necessity it is the female who is most available to parent and who therefore should be biologically programmed to parent.

The assumption of a large differential investment in eggs and sperm, with its corollary that males increase reproductive success via multiple matings whereas females do not, has been challenged. Gladstone (1979) asserts that there is no evidence for this initial differential investment in eggs and sperm. Although one egg may require more of the organism's energy to produce than a single sperm, Gladstone points out that many millions of sperm are released at each mating. The meiotic divisions alone necessary to produce these sperm consume energy. In fact, a century ago, Victorians used the expensiveness of sperm to rationalize male sexual behavior (Jacoby, 1977). Just as the cheap sperm of the 1970s and 1980s is used to explain male philandering in the 1970s and 1980s (Trivers, 1972; Dawkins, 1976; Daly & Wilson, 1978; Krebs & Davies, 1981), the expensive sperm of the Victorian era was used to promote sexual continence. Sexual continence was equated with thrift and ejaculation termed an expenditure (Jacoby, 1977). In other words, the economics of sperm, whether one is inclined to assign a "cheap" or costly value to it, has been used repeatedly to rationalize the mores of male sexual behavior, be it philandering or continence.

Just as there is a lack of concrete evidence that eggs are costlier to produce than sperm, likewise it is not evident that multiple mating is the optimal strategy for males and faithfulness for females. It was pointed out before that theoretically the ideal situation for a male mammal is one that involves female chastity and a large harem, a situation that inevitably leads to primarily female child care, and a situation not too dissimilar (it was thought) to the life of an alpha (most dominant) male in many baboon or macaque troops. Most observed copulations among the baboons and macaques involve this male and it was presumed, logically enough, that most offspring were also his. Recent paternity tests in macaque troops, however, have indicated that other males are fathering a far higher percentage of the young than had seemed possible (Curie-Cohen *et al.*, 1983; Smith, 1981). How this can be (sperm exhaustion in the alpha male? surreptitious couplings out of sight of both the alpha male and the anthropologists?) is not yet clear, but it does cast into doubt the explanation of the genetic advantages of this form of social structure.

One means by which males other than a dominant one can mate with estrous females has been documented in another monkey species, the olive baboon (*Papio anubis*). Pairs of males were observed to form alliances in which both members together harassed a dominant male while he was consorting with an estrous female. While one member of the team fought with the dominant male, the other mated with the female (Packer, 1977).

Dominant male deer mice have the same problem. It was thought that a dominant male did most, if not all, the breeding in a group. Birdsall and Nash (1973), however, provided genetic evidence of *frequent* multiple male parentage within single litters in a natural population. In addition, Bray, Kennelly, and Guarino (1975) vasectomized polygynous male red-winged blackbirds and found that the females in these males' harems still laid fertile eggs. In other words, while these harem leaders were supposedly increasing their reproductive success by mating with one of their females, other of their females were also busy mating elsewhere.

In all of these examples, the supposed advantage of polygyny—spreading a male's genes around—becomes a disadvantage, in that strategies developed by other males in the population may diminish the first male's chances of fathering offspring. While dominant males are away mating elsewhere, their females can mate with other males, whose sperm may then fertilize the females' eggs in place of the dominant male's. These observations also call into question the assumption that males benefit from multiple matings whereas females do not. According to sociobiological theory, it is advantageous for females to be faithful. It is advantageous for females to keep their mates and it is assumed they must be faithful to do so. Why then, in the examples cited above, are they not faithful? Sociobiologists regard multiple matings—males mating with females who have already mated—as an example of a conflict of interest between the two sexes resolved in favor of males. A female is not assumed to gain fitness as a result of additional copulations whereas a male does gain from mating with a previously inseminated female through sperm competition. Females may put up with these extra copulations because the cost of avoiding them is prohibitive (Alcock, Eickwort, & Eickwort, 1977). However, Gibson and Jewell (1982), by tethering male sheep, found that two-thirds of the ewes, *on their own initiative*, mated with more than one ram. Such multiple matings have been documented in many mammals, but had been assumed to be a result of male harassment of estrous females. Extra-pair copulations have been documented in many species birds as well (Gladstone, 1979).

Repeated matings (with different males) may benefit females by increasing the conception rate. There is evidence that male sperm counts decrease with progressive ejaculations in deer mice; in fact, this depression was found to last for two days (Dewsbury & Sawrey, 1984). To be sure of conception and of propagating *her* genes a female should seek a variety of "fresh" males, to increase the chances of a high sperm count.

Taken together, these studies show that the optimal strategy for males, in the judgment of sociobiologists, is not necessarily the one that always evolves, or the one that leads to increased reproductive success. The spreading of genes by mating with as many females as possible may be more costly to a male than originally assumed. First, the cost of sperm production as compared with egg production may be greater than presumed. Second, the cost to a male of leaving a female unattended while he mates elsewhere may be much higher than originally assumed, as it gives the female the opportunity to mate with other males whose sperm might then fertilize the female's eggs. In other words, male philandering is not necessarily more advantageous than male faithfulness. It may be at least as beneficial to male reproductive success to remain with the female.

Furthermore, in species in which both parents are needed to raise the offspring successfully, a male's abandoning his family to mate with others may seriously decrease his reproductive success. Nisbet, Wilson, and Broad (1978) have described the difficulties involved in caring for offspring alone in species in which two parents typically care for the offspring. The probability of the survival of these offspring is greatly reduced. A recent experimental study of parental care in marmosets (the young of which are typically cared for by fathers, mothers, and siblings) indicated that when some of the usual caregivers are drugged and unable to caretake, the others do not compensate—i.e., the young simply received less care (Locke-Haydon, 1984), which could decrease their chances for survival. Rasmussen (1981) presents a cooperative model of parental care (in contrast to the conflictual model presented by Trivers, 1972; Daly & Wilson, 1978; and Krebs & Davies, 1981) in which both parents benefit from remaining together and mutually rearing the young. Such benefits are apparent in Coulson's (1972) study of kittiwakes. She found that pairs remaining together for a long time raised more offspring than individuals who changed mates. This suggests another disadvantage to males of even temporarily leaving their mates and young to mate elsewhere. Weak ties to the family may erode the pairbond, and these females may then be more likely to form bonds with other males. A male who remains with his mate and family may be more reproductively successful in the long run (which is what counts in terms of evolution) than one who philanders.

Thus neither the difference between the sperm and egg nor the presumed advantages of promiscuity for the male appear to be useful in providing an explanation for the evolution of male promiscuity or female parental care. One could easily argue that it is to the male's reproductive advantage to be monogamous and, since he is present, to share care of the offspring.

Theoretically, then, there is no biological reason to assume that in general, mothers should be predisposed to caregive more than fathers. A multitude of factors determine caregiving arrangements, and indeed, species make these arrangements in a variety of ways. Unfortunately, as so often happens in the field of sex roles, the original assumptions and theory have been picked up by popularizers whereas the refutations have not.

Once they have decided mothers are biologically best fitted for caring for children, the next assumption made by some theorists and most popularizers, and certainly a debatable extension (one not necessarily supported even by Dawkins, 1976), is that if this interest or lack of it is biologically based it is unchangeable or at least it is undesirable to change it. Before we even begin to deal with this concept, however, let us return to the original assumption that women are inherently more interested and involved in child care than men and examine the evidence on this question using the traditional criteria of ethologists.

It should be noted that whereas sociobiologists in general reach the conclusion that women should do child care, they do not all follow the same path to this point. Wilson, for example, whose text *Sociobiology* (1975) caused a far larger public furor than Triver's work or even Dawkin's *The Selfish Gene* (1976), came to the same conclusion without this theoretical background. Although Wilson is the initial codifier of sociobiology, his arguments about human maternal instincts are supported by some of the traditional ethological lines of reasoning. He primarily argues from analogy to other primates and to today's nontechnological societies.

ETHOLOGICAL EVIDENCE FOR A MATERNAL INSTINCT

Three criteria are generally used by ethologists and scientists in related fields in deciding whether a behavior or a complex of behaviors, such as mothering, is innately based. These are: (a) *does the behavior appear in an animal raised in isolation from other members of its species,* either at birth or at some later time, through the process of maturation? To use the mechanistic analogy commonly employed, either the animal is wired for the behavior at birth or it is programmed so that at some later time (e.g., in adolescence) the wires are plugged into the appropriate slots; (b) *does the behavior appear in the same fashion in all (or at least all non-zoo and laboratory) groups of this species?* Even in groups so far separated as to have no cultural connections? The behavior need not appear in all members of the group, but it should appear in all animals of a similar age and reproductive status. In humans this is known as cross-cultural similarity; (c) *does the behavior appear in a similar fashion in related species? Is there phylogenetic continuity?* Let us examine each of these criteria in detail. First, however, a word of explanation for psychologists about the kind of data to be discussed.

The Nature of Ethological Data

Ideally, the data on which we will base our judgments about the naturalness of a particular type of parenting would be data of the highest order by psychological standards, as the implications and recommendations that would grow from these conclusions will be particularly far ranging, potentially making drastic changes in people's lives. Unfortunately, as so often happens in cross-disciplinary research, we discover that different disciplines have different standards for and approaches to data collection. Most psychological journals today, for example, use blind review (the name of the author is kept secret from the reviewer) when evaluating papers to prevent the reviewer's being biased by fame of the author or author's institution—or by personal animus; this practice is literally unheard of in most other social (or natural) science disciplines. Similarly, most psychological journals today would be reluctant to publish human behavioral data based on observations made by a single person. It is agreed in the field that observer bias, particularly in an area such as sex roles in which people hold strong opinions, is just too strong to make the data believable without the safeguards of multiple observers and reliability measures, and even then one may argue that observers share common cultural preconceptions that will bias their data in a common direction.

For various coincidental historical reasons, most primate field researchers are not psychologists; they come from an anthropological or biological background where because of expense and/or logistics and/or naivete such concepts are not yet accepted. Similarly, blind observations (observations in which the observers are unaware of the main hypotheses of the study or unaware of the "group" to which the observed subject belongs) seem to be nearly unheard of except in the inadvertent case of the first observer of a given species. It is perhaps not surprising then that the first studies of a given species produce uniform findings for a species and that it is only when the second generation of field workers appears, eager to find something new to publish, that variation begins to appear. From a psychologist's perspective much of the data on animal motherhood should be taken with a grain, or perhaps a teaspoon, of salt. Logically, then, one should be especially cautious about the conclusions that are drawn from this data.

Isolation Studies: Do Animals Reared Alone Show Maternal Behavior?

The Logic of the Isolation Experiments

Isolation studies are by far the most rigorous of the criteria used to indicate that a behavior is "instinctive." In the classical textbook example this technique was used experimentally to study the origin of bird song in different species (Hinde, 1966). Most species have a certain song that is produced by all members (or at least all members of the same sex) at a predictable point in the bird's growth cycle. For this research, eggs are hatched and the chicks hand reared in isolation from other members of their species so that they hear the song of their species only if the experimenter purposefully exposes them to it. When a variety of species are studied, a variety of findings appear indicating the range of possibilities, from biological control to primarily environmental control. If the song appears in its full form at the proper time without exposure, song production is said to be biologically based. In some species the full song appears whereas in others a rudimentary song or no song appears. In some species very brief exposure to the species' song suffices for the bird to learn the song; in some cases exposure before the bird is old enough to sing itself is sufficient; in others the bird must be exposed to the song repeatedly when she or he is old enough to sing. Cases midway on the continuum are interpreted as indicating a biological predisposition. In some cases, this predisposition is considered to be very strong, as when a bird receives its only exposure when too young to sing and as an adult can produce the song. To be so receptive to such a complex stimulus at such a young age and to remember it so well implies a biological predisposition for learning the song.

More recent research on nonsocial behaviors indicates that the situation may be a little more complex than this. It is possible for an animal to be born with a skill or ability and to lose it through lack of practice ("use it or lose it"). The now classical work of Wiesel and Hubel (1963), for instance, demonstrated that kittens are born with an ability to perceive pattern, but without stimulation of the pattern-sensing neurons (the kittens' eyes were covered with halved ping pong balls), the relevant parts of the brain pathways literally degenerated. Similarly, without proper visual–motor feedback experience, depth perception was lost (Held & Hein, 1963). Consequently, when a specific social behavior, such as mothering, does not appear when the animal has been raised in isolation, it might still be true that the animal was "wired" for this behavior but lost the skill through lack of stimulation.

Effects of Isolation Rearing on Mothering

What do we know about the effect of mothering behavior in animals raised in isolation? "Parental care" in many species consists of depositing the fertilized eggs in a more or less favorable situation (sometimes quite complexly favorable, as when they are sealed in a nest with food for the future) and abandoning them. Because the offspring never see their parents, parental behavior in these, usually "lower," species obviously always appears in isolation. Although other "lower" species as far apart as spiders and (male) fish demonstrate more interactive parenting, such as carrying their offspring about with them for some time, unfortunately, studies of isolate rearing on these parental behaviors have not been carried out.

Parental care in warm-blooded species is usually much more complex, although a few species, such as the cuckoo who leaves her eggs in another species' nest or the megapodes who lay their eggs in natural sources of warmth such as volcanic ash or rotting vegetation, manage to avoid it. These species obviously do not learn "maternal" behavior from their mothers.

There have been relatively few nonprimate isolation studies of parental behavior among those warm-blooded species that do display parental behavior involving contact with the young, and the results are mixed (e.g., see Buhler, Keith-Spiegel, & Thomas, 1973). One difficulty is that handrearing of many bird species is known to lead to later sexual confusion during mating (e.g., Hinde, 1966). We do not know of any research in which isolate-reared birds were artificially inseminated and then studied for their maternal behavior.

There have, however, been a number of isolation experiments on primates, which are of particular interest. In the rhesus macaque, mothers have primary responsibility for the care of young infants. Harlow and his co-workers (e.g., Harlow & Suomi, 1970) raised rhesus macaques in total isolation and found effects on many forms of social behavior. As well as being generally socially unskilled, these animals were sexually unsuccessful. Harlow made it possible for normal males to impregnate isolate reared females using a rack to maintain proper position. He found that isolate-reared rhesus were terrible mothers by the most fundamental criteria, such as damage to and survival rates of their offspring (Seay, Alexander, & Harlow, 1964). At least in rhesus monkeys, mothering is not "instinctive." Similarly, zoo-reared apes, often brought up in unintentional isolation from members of their own species, seem to have difficulty in mothering, particularly with their first offspring (e.g., Maple & Hoff, 1982).

On the other hand, rhesus monkeys raised with their mothers were fairly good mothers themselves and even isolate-reared monkeys were much better mothers the second time around than the first. Even the female offspring of the motherless mothers (those that survived) were not bad mothers (perhaps because motherless mothers are far more likely to abuse their sons than their daughters and to give adequate care to their daughters [Sackett, 1974]). Should one then conclude that female monkeys are biologically programmed to learn mothering from their own mothers? Is this what isolation rearing disrupts? No, because motherless monkeys raised with other motherless monkey peers were better mothers than those reared without peers (Harlow, 1969). Furthermore, male rhesus monkeys, as well as females, learn how to care for infants. Gomber and Mitchell (1974) found that although isolate-reared males showed less positive behavior toward infants than wild-born males, in time the isolate-reared males were able to form effective social relationships with infants. Thus it appears that in the rhesus macaque, genes and/or hormones alone are not responsible for caregiving behavior in females or males, and with some social experience both develop the capacity to interact with infants.

We could conclude from these studies that the biological basis of mothering can be activated by general social experience, or that mothering is a form of social expression and that experience with any other monkeys improves one's interaction with babies. Given the actual behavior of the peerless motherless monkeys with their infants—behavior that included biting and bashing the persistent infants (the infants seemed to have a clear biologically based image of the kind of mothering they needed), rather than just clumsiness with babies, the second explanation is the more likely. What appears, then, when animals are raised in isolation, is not normal parental nurturing, nor even an inadequate version, but rather its opposite, a finding that supports the conclusion that mothering behavior is not innate.

In summary, then, isolation studies of animals indicate that mothering behavior may be learned or innate, depending on the species. Studies of animals most closely related to humans indicate a substantial learning factor for both males and females.

Humans Reared with Minimal Mothering

The experimentally pure isolation experiment cannot be carried out with human beings for ethical reasons. Adult sex role behavior such as parenting cannot take place without a vast infrastructure of social behavior. Humans require social stimulation to develop and/or maintain innate abilities. Given the fact that we have not purposefully raised children in isolation since the time of

Dennis (1941), and we would not condone the use of a Harlow style "rape rack" with any children "accidentally" raised in this fashion when they reached maturity, we will never have data from isolate-reared humans except that from so called feral children. Such children, locked in attics or discovered in wolf dens, usually have great difficulty in learning to communicate and indeed seem to die young. Very few are old enough to have reached sexual maturity when they were discovered and no mixed sex pairs have been found. Consequently, there are no examples of "natural" human childrearing techniques, untouched by the effects of human culture. Many of these children never acquire speech, and most reports are concerned with speech acquisition and general socialization (e.g., toilet training). Sex roles are rarely mentioned. So far none of the children are reported to have borne a child, although according to a report by Skuse (1984) of a personal communication, the two boys described in Koluchova in the 1970s, who have adjusted well to ordinary society, were beginning to date. Only those children who do adjust to society are likely to have babies, and these isolate-reared adults have then been "contaminated" by their societies, rendering any conclusions about "natural parenting" based on their behavior invalid. In other words, although the cases are much studied they have little to contribute to this discussion. Pragmatically then, isolation, the most convincing of the three criteria, cannot be used to study humans.

There does exist one further "natural" study of humans somewhat comparable to Harlow's (1969) peer-raised motherless monkeys (these monkeys were raised without contact with adult models for mothering behavior and yet were reasonably good mothers themselves). At the end of World War II, a group of children rescued from a concentration camp were brought to England and while readjusting to a normal society were studied by Freud and Dann (1951). The children had had successive multiple adult caretakers who were repeatedly taken away from them; the only constant figures in their lives were each other, and all their emotional attachments, which were intense, were with each other. They "mothered" each other. Reentering a more stable environment the children again were able to form attachments to adult caretakers and seemed to be reasonably normal emotionally. Unfortunately, we do not know what kind of parents they became as adults (or much about what parenting experience they had had as small children before the camp), but so far as they can be followed their behavior seems similar to that of Harlow's peer-raised monkeys.

Studies of Cross-Cultural Similarity

The Logic of "Cross-Cultural" Comparisons

The second important criterion for the determination of biological input in the development of a social behavior is the level of cross-cultural similarity. If all langurs show the same style of mothering, or at least all wild-reared langurs do, no matter how far apart the langurs live, this adds support to the idea that mothering style in langurs is biologically determined. It would be expected that separated groups and troops of primates would show "cultural drift" in mothering style long before genetic drift would have any effect. If, on the other hand, some groups of langurs showed mother-only care, some allowed "aunts" to participate, and some entrusted much of the care to adolescents and others to adult males, one would conclude that while there might be generalized "caretaking genes" in the langurs, they are certainly not confined to or only biologically activated in mothers. It is important to note that *only* universal similarities in mothering styles in the langur provide convincing evidence of biological control of mothering behavior; every example of diversity strengthens the case for environmental control through learning.

Let us now apply this criterion to the research that has been done on wild-living nonhuman species. Since perhaps the strongest indication of the evolution of flexibility in caregiving arrangements comes from studies that document the variability *within* a species, let us first look at some species generally considered to be relatively inflexible.

Flexibility in "Lower" Species

Avian behavior is thought to be controlled more by innate predispositions than is mammalian, and particularly human, behavior. Yet, even in bird species there can be a good deal of flexibility in how individual mothers and fathers care for their young. In species in which the caregiving roles of the mother and father have been documented by long hours of observations of birds at the nest, much variability from couple to couple in how caregiving responsibilities are shared has been found. In ring doves (Silver, 1978), common terns (Storey, 1978), zebra finches, and spotted sandpipers (Nash, unpublished data), some mothers do almost all of the caregiving, whereas others may do almost none. Plasticity in the social system of acorn woodpeckers has been documented by Stacey and Bock (1978), who found that, in southeastern Arizona, the woodpeckers exhibited two different types of social organization: one of highly cooperative groups in which the young were cared for communally and the other in which only the two parents cared for the young.

Who cares for the young may depend on the mating system of a species, but, even within a given mating practice, diversity exists. For example, among spotted sandpipers in North Dakota (Oring & Knudson, 1972) and New York (Hays, 1972), females may be polyandrous or monogamous. The degree to which both monogamous and polyandrous females incubate and care for the young is quite variable. Some polyandrous females performed no parental care at all, whereas others helped as many as three males take care of their eggs and/or young (Nash, unpublished data). Flexibility in parenting has been documented in another polyandrous species as well, the American Jacana. In this species, females were found to perform no parental care at all for several breeding seasons and then to help the males brood the young for one season (Jenni & Betts, 1978).

Diversity within Mammalian Species

Such variability has been documented in primates as well. Among tamarins, some mothers do a lot of caregiving, and others very little (Cebul & Epple, 1984). Among Japanese macaques, in some troops males do much caregiving, whereas in other troops they do little (Itani, 1959). This intertroop variability is also seen in black howler monkeys (Bolin, 1981).

This flexibility is highlighted by situations that are unusual for a given species. In rhesus macaques, mothers may actively keep males away from their infants. Redican (1978) placed adult male rhesus monkeys, who when observed in the wild, have been described as "indifferent" to infants, in a situation in which they were allowed unrestricted access to infants, in order to explore their dormant or unexpressed caretaking potential. Longitudinal data were collected on four pairs of wild-born adult males and infants housed in the absence of mothers and peers. In the absence of "restrictive mothers" these males formed close relationships with the infants. Separation tests indicated infants developed as strong attachments with these males as they usually do with their mothers. Redican concluded that adult males were as suitable objects of attachment as adult females (i.e., mothers). Even in the rat, in which maternal care has been found to be strongly influenced by biological factors (hormones), parental care has been induced in virgin female and male rats simply by exposing them to newborn pups for 5 to 10 days (Rosenblatt, 1967).

This kind of variability based on external environmental changes also occurs in natural settings. Environmental effects can be strong: in high-density areas snub-nosed langurs are polygamous and "adults" interact with the young, whereas in low-density situations the langurs live in monogamous groups and no nonparental "adults" are available (Watanabe, 1981).

Diversity among Human Cultures

As these studies indicate, caregiving in bird and mammal species can in fact be quite flexible. It appears as though mating and parenting arrangements are not determined by inflexible genetic programs. Through evolution, species in which extensive care of the young is necessary seem to have developed many strategies to ensure that the young receive this care. In fact, unlike species in which extended care is not needed (many insects, fish, and reptiles), species that require extended care seem to be quite social in general. Extended care and general sociability seem to go together, thus providing the opportunity for a variety of individuals to be able to form relationships and help take care of the young.

One might well expect the same flexibility in humans as well. Evolution may not have uniquely prepared mothers for taking care of babies, but rather come up with a variety of caregiving arrangements. The young themselves are quite adaptable and can adjust themselves to a variety of caregivers, including, as mentioned earlier, their peers (Suomi & Harlow, 1978; Freud & Dann, 1951).

When we come to apply the criterion of cross-cultural uniformity to human parenting behavior it is particularly useful to remind ourselves of our goals by referring to other species. It is easier for humans to recognize the value of cross-cultural comparisons when talking about another species than when talking about their own. There seems to be a strong tendency to see one's own culture as normal and others as "exceptions to the rule." It is difficult to look at other cultures and realize that any functioning culture provides an equally strong "rule." There is no satisfactory way to decide which culture is the Platonic essence of the rule on any given issue. Each must be weighed equally. This is not to say that the solution lies in "culture counting" (46 cultures use babysitters of either sex, 101 use "aunts," 63 use mother-only care. . . .) or weighting by population (2% of the world's population use father-only care, 10% use siblings. . . .). What we are searching for is not the most common method of caretaking but for any evidence that there is one worldwide style for our species. If there is no such single style then we must abandon a hypothesis of a general biological basis for mothering before we go on to investigate which environmental variables interact with what biological substrate to produce the many variations we see.

As long ago as 1965 in Eleanor Maccoby's first book on sex differences, there appeared a compilation of tasks assigned to males and females by different cultures (D'Andrade, 1966, based on a 1937 table by Murdock). These tasks included such behaviors as weaving, potting, cooking, trapping, fishing, gathering food items, sowing, and clearing fields, and the author concluded that, except for the hunting of very large animals (a task not found in many cultures), there was no task assigned exclusively to males or to females. This is certainly true for child care, as we may see by just a few examples from the ethnographic literature. Note that, even in societies in which only adult women care for children, the woman who cares for a child need not be its mother.

The child-care arrangements of today's surviving hunter-gatherer societies are of particular interest because many sociobiologists (e.g., Wilson, 1975; Konner, 1976) believe them to be representative of our ancestral societies. It is thought that these societies live in an environment similar to the environment in which humans evolved and to which human instinctive behavior is adapted.

The !Kung women of Africa are the gatherers of their hunter-gatherer tribe, providing two-thirds of the tribe's food and walking an estimated 1,500 miles per year. They carry their children constantly for four years, and even when not moving the children are rarely more than a few paces from their mothers. Children are widely spaced (probably because of the high level of breast feeding until the child is 4 or 5), and among those !Kung who have not moved to settlements a new child is not born until an older child is fully able to walk long distances. The father rarely carries the child except on very long trips, when the mother is also carrying all the household goods. Because women have so few children and the children are so constantly carried, care of "preschool"-aged children belongs to the mother (Lee, 1979).

In contrast, the Australian aborigine women in Arnhem Land, who are also gatherers, leave their children with co-wives or other babysitters when they go out to gather (Lee, 1979). In yet another variation, the seminomadic hunters and gatherers of the Ituri Forest may leave or take their babies. Infants experience multiple caretaking including nursing by women other than their mothers. Women often go out in groups together and child care is shared at the work site, or mothers may leave infants behind with others while they are working. This shared care is the typical caregiving arrangement for the Éfé (Tronick, Winn, & Morelli, 1985).

There is also great variety in child-care arrangements among more settled groups. The Tikopia of Polynesia at first allow only the mother, her experienced adult female relations, and her husband's experienced adult female relatives to handle the infant. Older children are warned away and the father is considered so inept that at first he is not allowed to even hold the infant. As the baby grows, he is allowed to hold it briefly with much instruction from the experienced women on how to hold the head, and so on. However, as soon as the infant can crawl or walk, the father begins child care as a matter of course. After 1 year, the baby is "taken to work," with the father taking boy children and the mother taking the girls. In addition, the baby is likely to be carried about by other adult women and by older brothers and sisters (from age 4 years and including teen-agers). If the mother is overworked, her sister may move in to help with the children and may eventually become a co-wife (Firth, 1957).

Among the Swazi in Africa the husband again may not hold the infant when it is small (under 3 months), but in this society he never has much contact with the children. The mother–child relationship is the closest bond in this society (closer than husband–wife), and the mother with a young child is intensely involved with the child although she may borrow her sister's childern as nurse-maids and help. If she becomes ill her co-wives are not allowed to suckle her child and the child will be sent to the mother's mother or the mother's full sister (if she is not a co-wife) for care. Once the children are weaned they move in with the father's mother and live and sleep with her until puberty (Kuper, 1956).

As a final example, among the Trobriand Islanders, although the mother and child are very close, the father washes, plays with, and looks after the infant around the house (women are also helped in child care by their sisters). In this society, however, there is much less sibling interaction, as there is an extremely strong brother–sister incest taboo resulting in separation of male and female siblings (Fathauer, 1962).

Even within a culture, there may be a variety of caregiving arrangements. In fact, in the monogamous, nuclear-family-oriented society of the United States, is found such alternatives as the Apostolic United Brethren in Utah, a polygamist church. The wives of one husband may live together, raising their children communally (1985). Israel includes both nuclear families with primary maternal responsibility and the communally reared children of the kibbutz (Spiro, 1958).

In short, there is no single style of mothering worldwide, or anything close to it. In most societies (although not ours today), babies must interact with lactating women several times a day, but even this restriction does not neces-sarily mean the mother must be the constant caretaker. In all of these societies, with all of these methods of raising children, children grow up to be normal productive members of their societies. It may be that a particular mothering pattern produces an adult particularly well fitted for a specific type of society, but it is certainly not true that all humans must use one pattern to produce normal adults.

Studies of Phylogenetic Continuity

The Logic of Cross-Species Comparisons

The third approach that ethologists use to judge whether a behavior is "instinctive" is phylogenetic continuity. Do closely related species show similar forms of the same behavior? From the days of Tinbergen's gulls this has been a useful approach for establishing the plausibility of inheritance of a behavior.

Tinbergen (1960) compared communicative displays across different species of gulls and showed that one could trace the evolution of behavior just as one can trace the evolution of morphological traits. On the one hand, he found that the displays of closely related species of gulls were quite similar. On the other hand, there were some differences in these displays, which reflected the different habitats in which different species live. For example, unlike most gulls, which set up their nesting colonies on dunes or large flat grassy areas, kittiwake gulls nest on steep cliffs. Many of the signals in this species are adapted to their cliff-dwelling lifestyle. The face-away appeasement display in kittiwake chicks appears much earlier than in other gulls. Other gull chicks can simply move away when mobbed by their nest mates in an attempt to share food. If kittiwake chicks defended themselves in this way, they would fall off the cliffs. They therefore at an early age must signal appeasement to their attackers. An appeasement display similar in form appears at a later age in other gulls.

By showing that closely related species had similar displays, modified to suit each species' habitat, Tinbergen demonstrated that the principles of evolution could be applied to behavior. Ethologists, and later sociobiologists, then used these principles to explain a variety of behaviors in animals and also in humans. This approach proved fruitful. A problem, however, with some sociobiological analyses is that they do not adequately trace the phylogeny of the particular behaviors in question. That is, they do not show that the behavior is actually similar in form among closely related species. One of the difficulties in doing this with humans, of course, is that there are no living closely related species. Another problem is that it is very difficult to show that a whole complex of behaviors is similar across several species. Parental care is such a group of behaviors. Tracing the phylogeny of a particular communicative display is a very different task from tracing the phylogeny of the host of behaviors that go into caring for offspring.

This problem is illustrated by examining another group of shorebirds, which, like Tinbergen's gulls, belong to the same subfamily as one another. Among the 18 species of arctic/subarctic sandpipers belonging to the same genus, *Calidris*, can be found a wide variety of parenting arrangements. Some species are monogamous, and among these, in some species the female does no parental care (the male alone incubates the eggs), whereas in other species the male and female share parental duties. In other species, females lay two successive clutches of eggs, one which the female cares for, the other which the male cares for. A third arrangement is one in which a female lays two clutches of eggs, the first which her first mate cares for, the second which she and her second mate care for. Finally, some species are polygynous or promiscuous, with the female providing all the parental care.

This variability in parenting strategies in the species of this one genus living in a similar environment indicate the difficulty in tracing the phylogeny of a behavior as complex as parental care. Furthermore, the variability in parenting arrangements within these closely related species of birds indicates the difficulties in using phylogenetic continuity arguments in attempting to trace the evolution of human parenting strategies. If such different arrangements can be found within one genus, which species would we use to trace the evolution of human parenting arrangements? There are no other extant species in the human genus *Homo*, and even if there were, we would expect at least as much variability in their mating and parenting arrangements as is found within one genus of birds.

Still, it may be useful to look at the parenting arrangements if not in other-human species, then in species that are closely related to humans. In Tinbergen's day similar behavior was one technique used to establish phylogenetic closeness. Today, with numerous biochemical measures of genetic similarity, the "causation" arrow tends to go in the opposite direction: with genetic similarity established we can look for behavioral similarity. In particular, we look at species related to humans to discover the "natural" behavior of humans.

The most obvious answer to what are comparable species for humans is that we should look to those species that are genetically most closely related to us, that is, the other primates. An argument can also be made, however, for looking at nonprimate species whose social environment is similar to that hypothesized for ancestral humans. Similar environmental pressures are thought to frequently produce similar adaptations even in species that are genetically quite distinct. This process, called convergent evolution, is well documented in terms of physical adaptations, the most dramatic example perhaps being the "fishlike" shapes of dolphins and whales, whose ancestors were terrestrial mammals. The need to move through water shapes all aquatic animals into similar form whatever their ancestry.

By analogy it is argued that certain evolutionary behavioral "choices" may have inevitable "spinoffs." The most commonly discussed of these categories in reference to humans is that of the social carnivore (e.g., Lopez, 1978). It can be argued that the evolutionary "decision" to become a group-living hunter has certain inevitable consequences, particularly in terms of male–female relationships and child care, and that our best guide as to what these consequences are is to examine the lives of the other social carnivores. Similarly, one may argue that a species' "decision" for monogamy vs. polygamy has certain inevitable consequences for childcare and that comparison with other species that have made the same decision will be enlightening, even if these species are not primates.

Comparisons on the Basis of Genetic Similarity

From the point of view of a sociobiologist hoping to draw conclusions about human behavior on the basis of the other primates, the ideal case would be one in which all primates display the same style of mothering behavior. Unfortunately for the sociobiologist, no such similarity exists. As mentioned in the previous section, there is considerable variety in "mothering" behavior even within a species. Among primate species the range covers the entire spectrum, from species that would delight the most radical feminists to those that would warm the hearts of the Moral Majority.

Although most primate species have primarily female caretakers, these caretakers need not be the mothers and are not infrequently male. In some instances the primary caretaker from infancy is the father.

For example, among the prosimians (the most "primitive" of today's primates), we see a wide range of behavior. All troop members of the sifaka are interested in the infant and groom the mother and infant. (Grooming is a friendly social behavior in which the groomer picks through the fur of the groomee ostensibly removing insects, dirt, scabs, etc. It is a peaceful, relaxing activity usually performed by family members, friends, courting couples, and by subordinates to dominants. A human analogy might be a back rub.) *Lemur catta* infants are often carried by their juvenile siblings and groomed by their fathers, sisters, and other group members. Among the *Varicia variegata*, siblings and the father, but not strangers, are allowed to groom the infant (Klopfer & Boskoff, 1979). Among many lemur species, the mother may be removed from the weaned baby for a week without upset to the infant, as long as at least one other familiar adult is around. If no adult is present the infant appears depressed. This is true even for *Lemur fulvus*, which has the most exclusive lemur mother–infant pattern, in which only the father is allowed to groom the infant and he only a week after birth (Klopfer & Boskoff, 1979).

As an extreme example of the extent to which primates may dispense with child care we should mention the parental behavior of the tree shrew (which are either the most "primitive" of all primates or not primates at all, depending on where one stands in a continuing controversy). The male tree shrew builds a nest but never sees the offspring until they are weaned. The female sees the infants only every 48 hours when nursing and leaves them completely alone in the nest in between (Mitchell & Brandt, 1972). It should be noted that the tree shrew is atypical of primates in other behaviors as well; in contrast to the usual "laid-back" primate lifestyle, the tree shrew is constantly on the move while hunting food or eating.

The New World monkeys of South and Central America are the monkeys most people visualize at the word "monkey," that is, generally small monkeys that have prehensile tails. They are more distantly related to humans than are Old World monkeys (see p. 36). The New World monkeys include the marmosets, tamarins, howler monkeys, night monkeys, spider monkeys, squirrel monkeys, vervets, and titis, among others. As within the prosimians there is a wide variety of parental behavior.

There are several varieties of marmosets, all of whom live in nuclear family groups, have sexes of about the same size, parents that defend their territory jointly, and generally have twins. The twins are tolerated by both adults and can successfully beg food from either parent. The twins are carried by and almost totally cared for by the father and siblings, except for nursing, when they are returned to the mother (Hrdy, 1981; Passingham, 1982).

Male titis and night monkeys also hold and transport infants. The male titi holds the infant except when it is being fed. Among night monkeys both parents care for the infant, but after it is nine days old, it is always carried by the father except when nursing. Similarly, the male plays the most important role in the care of the twins usually born to tamarins (Epple, 1975; Lee, 1984).

Newborn primates are almost always attractive to other females, at least, and sometimes to males as well, and squirrel monkeys, howler monkeys, and vervets readily give up their newborns to others for holding and playing. One adult female spider monkey adopted and produced milk for first a spider monkey infant, and, 2 years later, a howler monkey infant (Estrada, 1982), so this attraction may even cross species lines.

The Old World monkeys live in Africa and Asia. Humans are generally considered to be Old World primates, as are the apes. The Old World monkeys include langurs, colobus, baboons, and macaques. Because of the convenience of their savannah dwelling habits baboons and macaques were among the first species to be extensively studied by primatologists in natural settings. As a consequence of this early exposure these species formed the basis of many sociobiologists' idea of a "typical" primate.

The langur lives in troops and is famous among primatologists for its extensively developed "auntie" system (or alloparenting, to use a less sexist term). Langur mothers allow other females to handle their young as soon as the infants are dry. A newborn langur may spend half the first day of its life with non-mother females. The infant seems to exert fascination for other females and spends much of its time being passed from hand to hand. It has been repeatedly noted that nulliparous females are more clumsy at handling the infants than are experienced mothers. Maternal skills seem to be learned through shared child care in the langur (Dolhinow, 1972).

Among the macaques and baboons, child care is primarily the mother's responsibility (infants do not visit others until some weeks after birth), but macaque males will look out for particular infants, even when they are not orphans. Usually, these are the infants of their consorts, females with whom they spend a lot of time during the female's estrous period; macaques are not monogamous. Male Japanese macaques will carry yearling infants whose mothers are having new babies (Wolfe, 1981). Further, adult males are far more likely to "adopt" orphans than are adult females (Hasegawn & Hiraiwa, 1980). Male Barbary "apes" (nearly tail-less macaques that live on the rock of Gibraltar) will often carry, cuddle, and wean infants (Passingham, 1982). In general, males are tolerant of infants, allowing them to play on their bodies and tug on their fur in a manner they would never tolerate from an adult, and they protect mothers and infants from predators.

Among the macaques and baboons, the most extreme example of male involvement in "child care" is probably found among the hamadryas baboons. Subadult males may briefly kidnap and even adopt infants and may protect juveniles from other members of their play groups. Eventually, a male becomes attracted to one preadolescent female and they form a pair. When she matures she becomes the first member of his "harem."

Among Barbary macaques, male care of the young is prevalent. Males may form close relationships with particular infants, and triadic interactions frequently occur involving two males and an infant (Taub, 1984). Originally, such triadic interactions were interpreted as "agonistic buffering"—i.e., a male was thought to "use" an infant to protect himself or advance his own status. By holding an infant, a male could inhibit another male's threats or attacks (Deag & Crook, 1971). Taub (1980) has shown, however, that this hypothesis does not explain triadic interactions very well. His study indicated that triads of two males and an infant were formed when two males took an interest in the same infant; the males were not "using" the infant to protect themselves but in fact were both taking care of the same infant. Thus in this species several individuals other than mothers may take care of infants. Such triadic interactions in which two males take care of the same infant have been found in chacma baboons as well (Busse, 1984).

Baboons and macaques are all attracted to infants and in some species low-ranking mothers (e.g., bonnet macaques [Estrada & Estrada, 1984]) may be forced to give up their infants. Unlike most other species a "borrowed" macaque infant is not always returned and an abandoned newborn may be adopted by a nursing female and raised as a twin (Fucillo, Scucchi, Troisi, & D'Amato, 1983). Interestingly, with regard to the effect of experience, in some species the animals most likely to be attracted to infants are very experienced mothers, whereas in others it may be the least experienced, and in still others the moderately experienced (Hirawa, 1981). There is limited support for the idea that parturition is a generally necessary and/or sufficient biological initiator of caretaking behavior.

The apes of Africa and Asia are our closest living relatives genetically and can most simplistically be distinguished from monkeys by lack of a tail. The apes include gibbons, siamangs, orangutans, chimpanzees, and gorillas, the last three of which are known as the great apes, being considerably bigger than the others. The great apes approximate human size.

Gibbons live in nuclear family units. The biggon male is tolerant of infant gibbons but not so of juveniles. Although he does not play with the youngest infants, he does once they are 6 weeks old (Mitchell & Brandt, 1972). Among siamangs, infants are dependent on the mother the first year, but on the father the second year, being carried by the father. Fathers groom and sleep with their juvenile offspring while mothers do so for infants (Taub & Redican, 1984).

The three great apes, the gorilla, chimpanzee, and orangutan, have quite different patterns of interactions with infants. The orangutan male generally lives alone when adult (except during courtship) and so has little contact with the mother and child grouping. The mother orangutan lives alone with her children (Schurmann, 1981). In captivity, however, when contact is forced, male orangutans are reported to show tolerance for and interest in infants and in one case, to even assist at a birth (Taub & Redican, 1984).

Gorillas and chimpanzees live in mixed age and sex bands containing several adults of each sex. Infant gorillas live in the same band as adult males but rarely have much contact with them. Females, usually the mother, do most child care, although juveniles may carry the infant for short stretches. The infant gorilla is probably the most helpless of the nonhuman primates, needing help even to cling to its mother at first. Infants are attracted to the dominant silver-backed males and play on and around them while the males tolerate them (Mitchell & Brandt, 1972). Males have also been observed to groom infants (Schaller, 1972).

The infant chimpanzee is carried and cared for almost completely by the mother for the first 6 months but then begins to interact intensively with and be carred and groomed by older infants, juveniles and adolescents, especially kin (Nishida, 1983). Although adolescent females are very eager babysitters, once a female has had infants of her own she loses interest in others (Nishida, 1983). To a lesser extent adult males will also initiate play with young chimpanzees (i.e., juveniles and infants [van Lawick-Goodall, 1971]) and will protect and tolerate infants (e.g., when the infant tries to push away a male copulating with its mother). Among the gorillas and chimpanzees it is clear that even in the wild experienced chimpanzee and gorilla mothers provide more adequate care than inexperienced mothers and that the individual mother improves with experience (Maple & Hoff, 1982). On the other hand, extensive experience is not necessary for an adequate level of mothering provided the animal has been raised by a mother herself (e.g., Beck's 1984 report of a zoo-born gorilla; Davis et al.'s 1981 report on a home-reared chimpanzee).

Recently, researchers have begun to study the pygmy chimpanzee as well. The results from this species may be the most interesting yet, as pygmy chimpanzees differ from other chimpanzees in a number of ways. For example, they lack strong antagonistic behavior between adult males (Mori, 1983), tend to travel in male–female groups, seem to be monogamous (Patterson, 1979), have ventral–ventral intercourse frequently, and have intercourse throughout the female's cycle, rather than just when she is in estrus as do most primates (Wallen & Winston, 1984). The female seems so far to have primary child-care responsibility, but not much as been reported, relatively, on child care as yet (Badrian & Badrian, 1984).

Thus among different species of our closest relatives, the contribution to caregiving of mothers as compared with others varies greatly. Such variability indicates that no one strategy (e.g., mothers are the best caregivers) is necessarily most adaptive.

Comparisons with Other Social Carnivores

As mentioned before, another alternative for the sociobiologist is to consider humans as a member of the class of social carnivores and to look for examples of convergent evolution. Similar environmental and social circumstances are thought to lead to convergent evolution in other social behaviors; like situations should produce like behavior. As all the social carnivores hunt in groups (and share their kills), and as our ancestors and current hunting and gathering societies are thought to (have) behave(d) similarly, it is thought that these characteristics lead inevitably to certain other social characteristics.

It should be noted, however, that arguments still rage in the anthropological world as to the importance of hunting in human evolution. Blurton-Jones (1972) has also made an interesting argument, indicating that human infants are physically better adapted for constant carrying as other primate infants are, rather than for cacheing as many carnivores do with their infants. That is, that our "primateness" outweighs our "carnivoressness" when it comes to infants. Nonhuman primates do not generally hunt, although van Lawick-Goodall's chimpanzees seem to be developing this skill (1971), and there have been isolated instances of hunting reported in other species. The social carnivores most studied and most often compared to man are the lion and the wolf. Unfortunately for the sociobiologist, no consistent social carnivore pattern appears.

The life of the lioness reminds one of the woman in the Enjoli perfume advertisement, and the old Billie Holiday song (she brings home the gnu, serves it up to her lions. . . .). Most lion groups consist of two adult males, several adult females, and their young. Lionesses do the hunting and killing of game cooperatively while the males wait with the cubs. The females then "allow" the males to drive them from the kill and to feed first. Males often allow cubs to feed with them. Females do not permit cubs to eat with them. Any cub who has not eaten with the males must wait for what is left, if anything, when the females finish. When cubs are young enough to nurse they are nursed not only by their mothers but by other lactating females as well. When, as happens every 2 to 4 years, a new pair of males drives out the old pair, the new males kill or expel all cubs and females spontaneously abort any pregnancies (Schaller, 1972; Gould, 1982).

In terms of the central question we are asking, the existence of a "maternal instinct," there seems to be relatively little "personal" interest by mothers in their cubs; indeed males show more interest in cubs (those that are their own offspring at least) than females. Dawkins (1976) explains this in terms of the selfish gene by pointing out that the males who live in a pride are usually brothers and the females are also usually closely related (to the other females). The males "know" they have only a short time to father and raise any offspring, who must be strong enough to survive expulsion from the pride by the time their fathers and uncles leave. The longer lived and more reproductively active females "know" that if this cub doesn't work out they have another chance with the new males next year. Brothers care for each other's offspring as do the sisters and female cousins. The closest analogy in humans would be a commune of house husband brothers living under threat of divorce. Few sociobiologists have found the lion a useful model for explaining human parenting roles.

The canine species, particularly wolves, have more supporters as possible models for human social arrangements. Hall (1978) points out that since species evolve to fill niches, and since that niche filled by our ancestral primates was unfilled in North America until relatively recently, a good argument can be made that the wolf has been shaped by ecological pressures similar to those that affected our ancestors. As similar pressures may lead to similar behavioral solutions, wolves might indeed provide us with hints as to our "basic" social pattern.

Wolves do indeed present a somewhat different picture of parenting than the lion, although there seems to be a considerable variation between packs. Adult wolves may live alone or in packs; the number of males and females need not be equal. There is a general tendency for only one female to give birth each year (Sullivan, 1978; Lopez, 1978) (although sometimes more do) and for non-mothers of both sexes to hunt and regurgitate food for the pups. When the pups are very young the mother stays in the den with them or nearby while the other adults hunt and bring back food for her, which is cached near enough that she may eat while still guarding the pups. By the time the pups are 3 weeks old, she begins to join the hunt again at times while another adult female stays with the pups. Murie described these "mother's nights out" in 1944 (reprinted in 1985) as follows:

> Each time she went off with the band she ran as though she was in high spirits, seeming happy to be off on an expedition with the others. (p. 29)

When the pups are old enough to come out of the den, the putative father (wolves are generally monogamous) (Mech, 1970; Sullivan, 1978; Brown, 1983) (although a nonalpha male is sometimes allowed to copulate with the alpha female [Lopez, 1978]) and all females seem very attracted to them, and other males are at least very tolerant (Murie, 1985). Wolves are not aggressive to pups and the general level of aggression is very low when they are around (Sullivan, 1978). If more than one female has had pups they may den near each other and rendezvous at times with all the pups (Murie, 1985). If the wolf pack consists only of the parents (as it does in the southwest United States, where wolves are under considerable pressure from man), if one parent dies the other takes over all parental duties, including feeding the pups and moving them to a new den if necessary (Brown, 1983).

Other canine species display similar patterns with small variations. Coyotes are also preferentially monogamous but live in pairs with nonadult offspring rather than packs. The father drags food to the mother when the pups are small and later both may regurgitate food for the pups. Both are very protective of the pups, and if one dies the other will continue to raise the offspring (McMahan, 1978). Similarly, in foxes (Murie, 1985) and African wild dogs (Schaller, 1972) both sexes feed the pups by regurgitation. Among wild dogs once pups are old enough to follow the hunt, regurgitation ceases, but pups receive total precedence at the kill (Schaller, 1972). The canine pattern then seems to be one of communal living (although in some species' sociological situations the commune equals the parents) and communally shared childcare once the early nursing period is past. Given Hall's (1978) remarks on the relevance of the canine model to human life this is certainly an interesting pattern.

Comparisons of Monogamous versus Polygamous Species

Rather then comparing species on the basis of genetic similarity or their general social arrangements, one might compare them on the basis of their relationships between the sexes—an area of social behavior that might relate more directly to child care than hunting. In particular, one might compare humans with species that are polygamous (usually polygynous) and with those that are monogamous. In terms of child care, monogamous relationships offer greater probability of (and according to a "selfish gene" theory, greater incentive for) shared child care.

Hrdy (1981) points out that there is tremendous variety between animal classes on this issue—90% of bird species are monogamous, for instance, while only 4% of mammalian species are—a difference that might give pause to those who suggest the life-mated swan as a human role model. On the other hand, about 37 of about 200 primate species are monogamous or about 19%, which makes primates somewhat more likely to be monogamous than other mammals. The "abouts" in the preceding sentences relate both to arguments about species definition and, more interestingly, to those species that may be either monogamous or polygamous depending on their circumstances.

Monogamous species tend to be those in which males and females are nearly of equal size (in some cases the female is slightly larger). Polygamous species tend to be those in which the males are considerably larger than the females (i.e., may weigh twice as much); this association is "explained" on the grounds that males have to compete with males for females—that is, polygyny "causes" size differential. That this need not follow logically may be seen in the bird species in which monogamous males "compete" to attract a female via song, coloration, dance and/or attractive territory (e.g., Gould, 1982).

Where do humans fall in this size categorization? Most people's spontaneous response is that we are dimorphic by size, and some sociobiologists also say so (e.g., Hinde, 1983). However, by the standards of the proverbial visitor from Mars, humans are nearly equal in size (that is, if the average female weighs 120 pounds, the average male does not weigh 240 pounds; in American society the average female is 5'4" and the average male 5'8", a difference of about 6% in height). From this one might conclude that humans are monogamous, which illustrates the dangers of such reasoning. According to Hrdy (1981) about 20% of human societies are monogamous (this includes those such as our own, which might better be called serially polygamous since, as mentioned above, surety of paternity is the issue); since our species has a variety of marital relationships we cannot use this issue to "predict" a child-care mode for all humans.

Summary of the Evidence for a "Maternal Instinct"

In sum, the three criteria by which sociobiologists would judge whether or not a behavior is biologically based do not lead one to conclude that mothers, in particular, are biologically more predisposed to child care than others. Indeed, if we have inherited any pattern from a primeval primate ancestor it is probably one of flexibility; thus, depending on the situation, a postweaning child (and even a preweaning child for much of the time) may be cared for by siblings, aunts, uncles, fathers, grandparents, mothers, or friends with no damage to the child. Based on the data, the use of sociobiology to "justify" a role for mothers as exclusive child caretakers is unjustified.

CONCLUSIONS

Arguments for the primary or exclusive role of human mothers in parenting have fallen into two general categories: those based on the greater investment of the female in offspring and those based on the ethnological criteria for biological inheritance—isolate rearing, cross-cultural similarity, and phylogenetic similarity. Apparent earlier support for these arguments has arisen from selective choice of species to cite and/or from inaccurate assumptions based on limited data. Arguments for exclusively maternal care are based on the belief that such care is an inviolable rule in the animal world, a belief that is easily shown to be false. By careful selection of examples it would be equally easy to build a case (easily toppled) for nonmaternal care, e.g., by citing the marmosets and their paternal care. The truth lies somewhere in between, and ethology's contributions to its identification apparently can be no more than to hint at the likelihood of a flexible plan.

Why have we invested so much time in showing that ethology has little to tell us about human caretaking, other than to demonstrate a range of possibilities? Does it matter if people mistakenly believe that human caretaking is biologically linked to one subgroup or another? The answer to this is, unfortunately, yes, that people act on such beliefs and/or use them to justify positions and behaviors they want to take or perform for other reasons. These false arguments have real-world consequences because people tend to believe that what is normative is prescriptive—that what is, should be—and act to make it so. For a behavior to have a biological basis provides the ultimate normative justification for the biologically and psychologically unsophisticated citizen. In contrast, developmental psychologists marvel at the flexibility of humans, at the ease with which even such a basic response as the newborn sucking reflex may be conditioned, changed, and controlled (e.g., Sameroff, 1968). Ethologists, too, state that we do not "have to follow every 'inner' value judgment" (Eibl-Eibesfeldt, 1970, p. 441). Unfortunately, these caveats do not reach most nonacademics.

Even if there were a consistent picture to be drawn from other animals as to what good parenting is, it is by no means obvious that this picture should be applied to modern humans as an ideal. Unfortunately, that is just how this misinformed picture has been applied. It is particularly striking that so few sociobiologists see the likelihood that it is just this way that it will be applied. Dawkins (1976), for instance, discusses at length his amazement at the emotional intensity with which a woman questioned a copanelist of his about the biological determination of sex roles. His conclusion was that she (and others) were misinformed about the resistance of biological programming to change, a conclusion that seems to indicate that he is out of touch with the use that nonscientists make of his work. For most people, the conclusion that sex roles are biologically determined would mean that they are very difficult to change, that we are stuck with that with which we are born. One can only (charitably) assume that Dawkins and other sociobiologists such as Wilson are politically very naive.

There is a strong tendency today for voices from many different backgrounds to cry out that mothers belong at home, that children cannot flourish without their mother's care. Fathers, friends, grandparents, sisters, and day-care centers are all inadequate substitutes. Some of these voices belong to psychologists (Fraiberg, 1959; or more moderately, White, 1985), some to fundamentalist ministers, and some to sociobiologists. The common theme is that children cannot become good adults without constant maternal care, and most of these prophets also feel that mothers cannot be happy and complete women unless they devote themselves full time to their children.

We will leave it to others to argue the psychological and religious issues. It is clear, however, that on both theoretical and evidential grounds there is no basis in sociobiology for recommending mother-intensive child care in our society. Other than for lactation, mothers seem no more predisposed to or innately skilled at child care than fathers, siblings, or nonparents. Day care in the home or out of the home does not violate our biological foundations. Father care will not produce biologically based maternal frustration. Our genes will not cause society to crumble if older siblings care for younger. If there are compelling arguments for a nostalgic return to a hypothetical 1950s world (which may never have existed outside of *Ozzie and Harriet, Father Knows Best* TV land—and certainly didn't outside middle-class America), these arguments are not to be found in sociobiology.

REFERENCES

Alcock, J., Eickwort, J. C., & Eickwort, J. R. (1977). The reproductive behavior of *Anthidium maculosum* and the evolutionary significance of multiple correlations by females. *Behavioral Ecology and Sociobiology, 2,* 385–396.

Badrian, A., & Badrian, N. S. (1984). Social organization of *Pan paniscus* in the Lonako Forest, Zaire. In R. L. Susman (Ed.), *The pygmy chimpanzee.* New York: Academic.

Beck, B. B. (1984). The birth of a lowland gorilla in captivity. *Primates, 25*(3), 378–383.

Birdsall, D. A., & Nash, D. (1973). Occurrence of successful multiple insemination of females in natural populations of deer mice (*Peromyscus maniculatus*). *Evolution, 27,* 106–110.

Blurton-Jones, N. (1972). Comparative aspects of mother–child contact. In N. Blurton-Jones (Ed.), *Ethological studies of child behavior,* Cambridge: Cambridge University Press.

Bolin, I. (1981). Male parental behavior in black howler monkeys (*Alouatta palliata pigra*) in Belize & Guatamala. *Primates, 22*(3), 349–360.

Bray, O. E., Kennelly, J. J., & Guarino, J. L. (1975). Fertility of eggs produced on territories of vasectomized red-winged blackbirds. *Willson Bulletin, 87,* 187–195.

Brown, D. E. (1983). *The wolf in the southwest—The making of an endangered species.* Tucson: University of Arizona Press.

Buhler, C., Keith-Spiegel, P., & Thomas, K. (1973). Developmental psychology. In B. B. Wolman (Ed.), *Handbook of general psychology.* Englewood Cliffs, NJ: Prentice-Hall.

Busse, C. (1984). Triadic interactions among male and infant chacma baboons. In D. M. Taub (Ed.), *Primate paternalism,* New York: Van Nostrand Reinhold.

Cebul, M. S., & Epple, G. (1984). Father–offspring relationships in laboratory families of saddle-back tamarins (*Saguinus fuscicollis*). In D. M. Taub (Ed.), *Primate paternalism,* New York: Van Nostrand Reinhold.

Coulson, J. S. (1972). The significance of the pair-bond in the Kittiwake. In K. H. Voous (Ed.), *Proceedings of the XVth International Ornithological Congress* (pp. 424–433). Leiden, Netherlands: E. J. Brill.

Curie-Cohen, M., Yoshihara, D., Luttrell, L., Benforado, K., MacCluer, J. W., & Stone, W. H. (1983). The effects of dominance on mating behavior and paternity in a captive troop of rhesus monkeys. *American Journal of Primatology,* 5(2), 127–138.

Daly, M., & Wilson, M. (1978). *Sex. evolution & behavior.* North Scituate, MA: Duxbury Press.

D'Andrade, R. (1966). Sex differences and cultural institutions. In E. E. Maccoby (Ed.), *The development of sex differences,* Stanford: Stanford University Press.

Davis, D., Fouts, R. S., & Hannum, M. E. (1981). The maternal behavior of a home-reared, language using chimpanzee. *Primates,* 22(4), 570–573.

Dawkins, R. (1976). *The selfish gene.* London: Oxford University Press.

Deag, J., & Crook, J. H. (1971). Social behavior and "agonistic buffering" in the wild Barbary macaque, *Macaca sylvana. Folia Primatologica,* 15, 183–280.

Dennis, W. (1941). Infant development under conditions of restricted practice and of minimal social stimulation. *Genetic Psychology Monographs,* 23, 143–189.

Dewsbury, D. A., & Sawrey, D. K. (1984). Male capacity as related to sperm production, pregnancy initiation, and sperm competition in deer mice (*Peromyscus maniculatus*). *Behavioral Ecology and Sociobiology,* 16, 37–47.

Dolhinow, P. (1972). The North Indian langur. In P. Dolhinow (Ed.), *Primate patterns.* New York: Holt, Rinehart & Winston.

Eibl-Eibesfeldt, J. (1970). *Ethology—The biology of behavior.* New York: Holt, Rinehart & Winston.

Epple, G. (1975). Parental behavior in *Saguinus fusciocollis* ssp. (Callithricidae). *Folia Primatologica,* 24, 221–238.

Estrada, A. (1982). A case of adoption of a Hower monkey infant (*alouatta villosa*) by a female spider monkey (*Ateles geoffroy*). *Primates* 23(1), 135–137.

Estrada, A., & Estrada, R. (1984). Female-infant interactions among free-ranging stumptail macaques (*Macaca arctoides*). *Primates,* 25(1), 48–61.

Fathauer, G. H. (1962). Trobriand. In D. M. Schneider & K. Gough (Ed.), *Matrilineal kinship.* Berkeley: University of California Press.

Firth, R. (1957). *We, the Tikopia—A sociological study of kinship in primitive Polynesia.* Boston: Beacon Press.

Frailberg, S. (1959). *The magic years.* New York: Scribners.

Freud, A., & Dann, S. (1951). An experiment in group upbringing. *Psychoanalytic Study of the Child,* 6. 127–168.

Fuccillo, R., Scucchi, S., Troisi, A.,& D'Amato, F. R. (1983). New adoption in a confined group of Japanese macaques. *American Journal of Primatology,* 5(3), 257–260.

Gibson, R. M., & Jewell, P. S. (1982). Semen quality, female choice and multiple mating in domestic sheep: A test of Trivers' sexual competence hypothesis. *Behavior,* 80, 9–31.

Gladstone, D. E. (1979). Promiscuity in monogamous colonial birds. *The American Naturalist,* 114, 545–557.

Gomber, J., & Mitchell, G. (1974). Preliminary report on the adult male isolation-reared rhesus monkeys caged with infants. *Developmental Psychology,* 10, 298.

Gould, S. (1982). *Ethology—The mechanisms & evolution of behavior.* New York: Norton.

Hall, R. L. (1978). Introduction. The anthropology of the wolf. In R. L. Hall & H. S. Sharp (Eds.), *Wolf & man—evolution in parallel.* New York: Academic.

Harlow, H. (1969). Age-mate or peer affectional system. In D. S. Lehrman, R. A. Hinde, & F. Shaco (Eds.), *Advances in the study of behavior* (Vol. 2). New York: Academic Press.

Harlow, H., & Suomi, S. J. (1970). Nature of love—simplified. *American Psychologist,* 25, 161–168.

Hasegawa, T., & Hiraiwa, M. (1980). Social interactions of orphans observed in a free-ranging troup of Japanese monkeys. *Folia Primatologica, 33*(1–2), 129–158.

Hays, H. (1972). Polyandry in the spotted sandpiper. *Living Bird, 11,* 43–57.

Held, P., & Hein, A. (1963). Movement-produced stimulation in the development of visually guided behavior. *Journal of Comparative and Physiological Psychology, 56,* 872–876.

Hinde, R. A. (1966). *Animal behavior: A synthesis of ethology and comparative psychology,* New York: McGraw-Hill.

Hinde, R. A. (1983). Cambridge University lecture on ethology and sex roles, Cambridge, England.

Hiraiwa, M. (1981). Maternal and alloparental care in a troop of free-ranging Japanese monkeys. *Primates, 22*(3), 309–329.

Hrdy, S. B. (1981). *The woman that never evolved.* Cambridge: Harvard University Press.

Itani, J. (1959). Parental care in the wild Japanese monkey (*Macaca fuscata*). *Primates, 2,* 61–93.

Jacoby, R. M. (1977). Science and sex roles in the Victorian era. In the Ann Arbor Science for the People Editorial Collective, *Biology as a social weapon* (pp. 58–68). Minneapolis, MN: Burgess.

Jenni, D. A., & Betts, B. J. (1978). Sex differences in nest construction, incubation, and parental behavior in the polyandrous American Jacana (*Jacana spinosa*). *Animal Behavior, 26,* 207–218.

Klopfer, P. H., & Boskoff, K. J. (1979). Maternal behavior in prosimians. In G. A. Doyle & R. D. Martin (Eds.), *The study of prosimian behavior.* New York: Academic.

Konner, M. J. (1976). Aspects of the developmental ethology of a foraging people. In N. Blurton-Jones (Ed.), *Ethological studies of child behavior,* Cambridge: Cambridge University Press.

Krebs, J. R., & Davies, N. B. (1981). *An introduction to behavioral ecology.* Sunderland, MA: Sinauer.

Kuper, H. (1956). Kinship among the Swazi. In A. R. Radcliffe-Brown & D. Forde (Eds.), *African systems of kinships & marriage,* Oxford: Oxford University Press.

Lee, P. C. (1984). Early infant development and maternal care in free-ranging vervet monkeys. *Primates, 25*(1), 36–47.

Lee, R. B. (1979). *The !Kung San—Men, women & work in a foraging society.* Cambridge: Cambridge University Press.

Locke-Haydon, J. (1984). The caregiving/care-seeking balance in captive common marmosets. *Animal Behavior, 32,* 806–815.

Lopez, B. H. (1978). *Of wolves & man.* New York: Scribner's.

Maple, T. L., & Hoff, M. P. (1982). *Gorilla behavior.* New York: Van Nostrand Reinhold.

McMahan, P. (1978). Natural history of the coyote. In R. L. Hall & H. S. Sharp (Eds.), *Wolf & man—Evolution parallel,* New York: Academic.

Mech, L. D. (1970). *The wolf: The ecology & behavior of an endangered species.* Garden City, NY: Natural History Press.

Mitchell, G., & Brandt, E. M. (1972). Paternal behavior in primates. In F. E. Poitter (Ed.), *Primate socialization.* New York: Random House.

Mori, A. (1983). Comparison of the communicative vocalizations and behaviors of group ranging in Eastern gorillas, chimpanzees and pygmy chimpanzees. *Primates, 24*(4), 486–500.

Murie, A. (1985). *The wolves of Mount McKinley.* Seattle: University of Washington Press. (Originally published in 1944 as No. 5 in the series "Faura of the National Parks" by the U.S. Government Printing Office)

Nash, A. Unpublished data.

Nisbet, I. C., Wilson, K. J., & Broad, K. (1978). Common terns raise young after death of their mates, *Condor, 80,* 106–109.

Nishida, T. (1983). Alloparental behavior in wild chimpanzees of the Mahale mountains, Tanzania. *Folia Primatologica, 41*(1–2), 1–33.

Oring, L. W., & Knudson, M. L. (1972). Monogamy and polyandry in the spotted sandpiper. *Living Bird, 11,* 59–73.

Packer, C. (1977). Reciprocal altruism in *Papio anubis. Nature, London, 265,* 441–443.

Passingham, R. E. (1982). *The human primate.* Oxford: Freeman.

Patterson, T. (1979). The behavior of a group of captive pygmy chimpanzees (*Pan paniscus*). *Primates, 20*(3), 341–354.

Rasmussen, D. R. (1981). Pair-bond strength and stability and reproductive success. *Psychological Review, 88,* 274–290.

Redican, W. K. (1978). Adult male-infant relations in captive rhesus monkeys. In D. J. Chivers & J. Herbert (Eds.), *Recent advances in primatology: Vol. 1. Behavior.* New York: Academic.

Rosenblatt, J. S. (1967). Nonhormonal basis of maternal responsiveness in the rat. *Science, 156,* 1512–1515.

Sackett, G. P. (1974). Sex differences in Rhesus monkeys following varied rearing experiences. In R. C. Friedman, R. M. Richart, R. L. VandeWiele, & L. O. Stern (Eds.), *Sex differences in behavior.* New York: Wiley.

Salt Lake Tribune (1985, December 15).

Sameroff, A. J. (1968). The components of sucking in the human newborn. *Journal of Experimental Psychology, 6,* 607–623.

Schaller, G. B. (1972). *The Serengeti lion. A study of predator–prey relations.* Chicago: University of Chicago Press.

Schurmann, C. L. (1981). Courtship and mating behavior of wild orangutans. In A. B. Chiarelli & R. S. Corruccini (Eds.), *Primate behavior & sociobiology,* Berlin: Springer-Verlag.

Seay, B., Alexander, B. K., & Harlow, H. F. (1964). Maternal behavior of socially deprived Rhesus monkeys. *Journal of Abnormal Social Psychology, 69,* 345–354.

Silver, R. (1978). The parental behavior of Ring doves. *American Scientist, 66,* 209–215.

Skuse, D. (1984). Extreme deprivation in early childhood II. Theoretical issues and a comparative review. *Journal of Child Psychology and Psychiatry, 2514,* 543–572.

Smith, D. G. (1981). The association between rank and reproductive success of male rhesus monkeys. *American Journal of Primatology, 1,* 83–90.

Spiro, M. E. (1958). *Children of the kibbutz.* Cambridge: Harvard University Press.

Stacey, P. B., & Bock, C. E. (1978). Social plasticity in the acorn woodpecker. *Science, 202,* 1298–1300.

Storey, A. (1978, October 20–23). *Coordination of incubation activities in common terns.* Paper presented at the Northeast Regional Meeting of the Animal Behavior Society, Monmouth College, West Long Branch, NJ.

Sullivan, J. S. (1978). Variability in the wolf, a group hunter. In R. L. Hall & H. S. Sharp (Eds.), *Wolf and man—Evolution in parallel,* New York: Academic.

Suomi, S. J., & Harlow, H. F. (1978). Early experience and social development in Rhesus monkeys. In M. E. Lamb (Ed.), *Social and personality development.* New York: Holt, Rinehart & Winston.

Taub, D. M. (1980). Testing the "agonistic buffering" hypothesis. *Behavioral Ecology and Sociobiology, 6,* 187–197. Taub, D. M. (1984). Male caretaking behavior among wild Barbary macaques (*Macaca sylvanus*). In D. M. Taub (Ed.), *Primate paternalism.* New York: Van Nostrand Reinhold.

Taub, D. M., & Redican, W. K. (1984). Adult Male-infant interactions in old world monkeys and apes. In D. M. Taub (Ed.), *Primate paternalism.* New York: Van Nostrand Reinhold.

Tinbergen, N. (1960). The evolution of behavior in gulls. *Scientific American, 203*(6), 118–130.

Trivers, R. L. (1971). The evolution of reciprocal altruism. *Quarterly Review of Biology, 46,* 35–57.

Trivers, R. L. (1972). Parental investment and sexual selection. In B. Campbell (Ed.), *Sexual selection and the descent of man.* Chicago: Aldine.

Tronick, E. Z., Winn, S., & Morelli, G. A. (1985). Multiple caretaking in the context of human evolution: Why don't the Efe know the western prescription for child care? In M. Reite & T. Field (Eds.), *The psychobiology of attachment and separation.* Orlando, FL: Academic.

van Lawick-Goodall, J. (1971). *In the shadow of man,* New York: Dell.

Wallen, K., & Winsten, L. A. (1984). Social complexity and hormonal influences on sexual behavior in rhesus monkeys (*Macacca mulatta*). *Physiology and Behavior, 32*(4), 629–637.

Watanabe, K. (1981). Variations in group composition and population density in two sympatric Mentawaian leaf monkeys. *Primates, 22*(2), 145–160.

White, B. L. (1985). *The first three years of life* (rev. ed.). Englewood Cliffs, NJ: Prentice-Hall.

Wiesel, T., & Hubel, D. (1963). Single cell response in striate cortex of kittens deprived of vision in one eye. *Journal of Neurophysiology, 26,* 1003–1017.

Wilson, E. O. (1975). *Sociobiology.* Cambridge, MA: Belknap Press of Harvard University Press.

Wolfe, L. D. (1981). A case of male adoption in a troop of Japanese monkeys (*Macaca fuscata fuscata*). In A. B. Chiarelli & R. S. Corruccini (Eds.), *Primate behavior & sociobiology.* Berlin: Springer-Verlag.

CHAPTER 2

Psychoanalysis Constructs Motherhood

BEVERLY BIRNS AND NIZA BEN-NER

INTRODUCTION

The image of mother and child pervades Western culture—from Michelangelo to Kollwitz, from Sophocles to Virginia Woolf, and from Locke to Freud. For centuries, mothers have been portrayed in extremes: the "good" mother, like a Madonna, is pale, serious, but gentle; the "bad" mother is big, ugly, and wicked. These images of motherhood can influence how women provide for their children and how they feel about themselves.

In addition to images, other cultural factors influence how women care for their children. Throughout history, the goal of adequate mothering is to raise a child who conforms to the existing culture. In nonliterate societies, adults teach children to hunt and gather, to eat with their fingers, and to grow the foods they will consume. In colonial America, where the realities of life were harsh, mothers used cold water to toughen their babies for long, cold winters. During slavery, Black women taught their children obedience to protect them from the extreme cruelty of the slaveholders. In our postindustrial society, we teach our children to read and write, to eat with forks and knives, to use machines, and to learn about the world from television, books, and computers, as well as from direct exposure.

In modern society, childrearing in the home is a relatively private experience, occurring most often in the nuclear family. Despite the changing definition of what a family is, mothers remain the primary caretakers of their children. A culture's view about mothers often depends on its beliefs about the nature and needs of children.

BEVERLY BIRNS • Child and Family Studies Program, State University of New York, Stony Brook, New York 11794. NIZA BEN-NER • Departments of Sociology and Social Anthropology, Hebrew University, Jerusalem 91905, Israel.

During the twentieth century, the century of the child (Ehrenreich & English, 1979, p. 189), our understanding of childhood has greatly increased; so have our beliefs and theories. As our knowledge of child development has increased, the role of the mother in the development of the child has come under close scrutiny.

Among the theories that attempt to explain human behavior, the one that has had the most influence on twentieth-century thought is psychoanalysis. Perhaps its power lies in the fact that, as our lives become increasingly influenced by science, technology, knowledge, and mobility, psychoanalysis maintains, although not uncritically, the importance of the family and the evolution of emotions as the source of human behavior. Psychoanalytic theory, as originated by Freud in the early-twentieth century and since then elaborated and altered by his followers, has had a profound influence on late twentieth-century thinking about all human relationships, particularly that between mother and child. Freud's theories about mothers were very preliminary, but provided a framework for many contemporary views. Developments and elaboration of his ideas remain very important today.

In this chapter, the evolution of psychoanalytic theory shall be discussed as it informs theories and beliefs about motherhood. The current prevalent view about mothers is that maternal behavior, attitudes, and personality shape and determine the behavior and the mental health of children. First, the evolution of the theory is described. Following this, ways in which the tendency to blame mothers for children's problems found in psychoanalytic theory has influenced research and public policy are discussed. Evidence is then cited that questions some of the basic premises of psychoanalytic theory concerning the primacy of infancy and the mother–infant bond. We then identify some of the factors other than the mother that we believe are ignored when mothers are considered the primary determinants of child development. Finally, a perspective on motherhood is offered that includes but delimits the power of mothers. Our basic premise is that mothers play a crucial role in the development of their children and that infancy is an important time of life. However, we believe that mothers do not *construct* their children, and that development during infancy is only one among a myriad of factors that determine personality and behavior.

PSYCHOANALYTIC VIEWS OF MOTHERS AND CHILDREN

Freud and the Evolution of Psychoanalytic Theory

Insofar as Freud was a physician and scientist, his theories were far more influential than those of the philosophers and theologians before him. Freud based his theories on his clinical experience with patients who had emotional disorders. In a most compelling manner, he explained neurosis on the basis of early childhood experiences. Although Freud's ideas remain controversial today, particularly as they pertain to women, some of his ideas are basic to most personality theories. Orthodox Freudians consider Freud's emphasis on the resolution of the Oedipal conflict to be the cornerstone of his theory. Others, who we discuss here, have expanded and revised his views about the nature of the early mother–infant tie.

Freud (1949) wrote that the infant's relation to the mother is "unique, without parallel, established unalterably for a whole lifetime as the first and strongest love-object and as the prototype of all later love-relations—for both sexes" (p. 45). Freud did not elaborate on the nature of this early relationship because he believed that at birth the infant's behavior is solely determined by powerful instincts. The mother's importance is initially as the person who gratifies these powerful impulses. Freud believed that gradually the infant develops love for the mother because she becomes identified with need gratification. By satisfying the infant's hunger and alleviating distress, the mother reduces pain and increases pleasure, a fundamental principle of psychic life. Although Freud believed that the mother is important for the development of the infant, he did not consider the mother's personality or behavior to be the crucial factor in normal or pathological development. Moreover, during the early years, the mother and, increasingly, the father also set limits to the child's need gratification. Early development is therefore conflictual, because parents both give and withhold, gratify and constrain.

For Freud, the critical conflict occurs at 3 or 4 years, and the resolution of this conflict determines future development. The early childhood conflict concerns the child, mother, and father. For boys, it is the Oedipal conflict. The conflict concerns the boy's love for his mother, which Freud considered to be sexual, and his love for and fear of his father. Father represents society and its constraints, and also is perceived as a competitor for the child's love. The boy fears father's retaliation, and in normal development renounces his Oedipal love for his mother, accepts his father, and resolves the conflict by becoming "like" father. The path for girls is different. According to this theory, because girls identify with their mothers, they remain immature and imperfect.

Freud's legacy includes an emphasis on personality development deriving from early relationships between children and parents, the importance of emotions in development, and the belief in unconscious factors as determinants of attitudes and behavior. It is the period of early childhood rather than infancy that Freud believed was critical. Although Freud did say that the infant's love for the mother would be prototypical of later love relationships, it was the Oedipal crisis rather than infancy that he believed to be the crux of psychological development. Theorists and practitioners in the second half of the twentieth century extended the study of the roots of behavior to the period of earliest infancy. Freud speculated about the early development of infancy based on the retrospective accounts of his patients. However, it was his adherents and students who actually observed and studied infants and young children who were developing normally, as well as those who exhibited problems.

After World War II and the rise and fall of fascism, psychiatry increasingly sought an explanation for man's inhumanity to man in the early experiences of the growing child. It was both the cruelty displayed in the war, as well as the large number of homeless children whose parents were killed in the war, that intensified the search for explanations of antisocial behavior. The effect of loss of parents early in life on later behavior became of particular interest. The most prominent theoretician to emerge from the wartime period was John Bowlby.

"Ethological" Attachment Theory: Bowlby and Ainsworth

John Bowlby was being trained as an analyst at the time of World War II. After the war, at the request of the World Health Organization, he produced a monograph entitled "Maternal Care and Mental Health" (1951). This monograph reviewed many studies of the 1930s and 1940s that demonstrated the negative impact on children of early separation from the mother. Bowlby claimed that sustained separation of the infant from the mother leads to mental retardation and/or the development of affectless psychopaths.

Although some of Bowlby's conclusions were widely criticized (Casler, 1961; Yarrow, 1961), Bowlby's work led to reforms in many countries concerning the care of children orphaned by the war. Early adoption or foster home placement replaced the ware-housing of children in large institutions, prevalent at that time. However, another outcome of this work was the development of a new field of inquiry—attachment theory.

In his 1951 monograph, Bowlby stated that the basis for mental health is established in infancy, when mothers provide a warm, continuous, and loving relationship with their infants. He drew on studies by Spitz, Ribble, Goldfarb, and others to demonstrate the devastating effect of separation of the infant from the mother in the early years of life. He indicated that children who were either totally deprived of maternal care and love or those who had early contact with their mothers but were then separated would suffer severe psychological sequelae. The disorders due to "maternal deprivation" involved cognitive as well as emotional deficits. For example, Bowlby claimed that babies separated early suffer from depression and delayed speech onset. Most important was his contention that early deprivation leads not only to delayed development, but to irreversible damage. Bowlby concluded that there is a causal relationship between prolonged separation in the early years and later affective and cognitive deficits.

If separation from or loss of the mother is so devastating, then understanding the mother–infant bond, which Bowlby termed "attachment," is important (Ainsworth, 1964, 1969). What then is the nature of the "bond" and how did it develop?

Bowlby disagreed with Freud's view that the baby's primary bond to the mother derives from the feeding experience. He later cited Harlow's studies of monkeys, which found that monkeys who were maternally deprived preferred a soft, terry cloth artificial "mother" that did not provide milk to a hard, wire "mother" that did (Harlow & Zimmerman, 1959). Bowlby concluded that the mother–infant tie was not based primarily on the feeding experience, but could be attributed to other factors, such as warmth, smiles, softness, and so on. For Bowlby, the mother is not just the breast or the provider of food, but rather the person who provides the infant with emotional sustenance so important for the maintenance of life.

Contrary to Freud's theory, which emphasized the Oedipal period at 3 or 4 years, and contrary to the ideas of some of the other psychoanalytic theorists, who stressed the first months of life, Bowlby believed that the crucial period in the life of the infant is the end of the first year as well as the second year of life. Bowlby believed that babies are innately programmed to behave in ways that elicit caregiving responses from their mothers and that maternal behavior is also biologically programmed. For Bowlby, it is not physical care but the specific relationship between an infant and *its* mother that is crucial for development. His work, emphasizing the uniqueness and specificity of mother–infant attachment, supported the view that maternal dedication, warmth, love, support, and attention, as manifested in feeding, holding, smiling, touching, and playing, would lead to the normal development of infants, who would grow up to be healthy, well-adjusted adults.

In 1969, based on her own observations of infants in Uganda and on Bowlby's early work, Mary Ainsworth refined the concept of attachment and designed a procedure to measure it (Ainsworth & Wittig, 1969). According to Ainsworth, the toddler's response to separation from and reunion with the mother could be used to measure the quality of attachment between mother and child. The measure, which was called the "Strange Situation," consists of a 20-minute laboratory procedure during which the mother and a stranger enter and leave the laboratory in a predetermined sequence (see also Hay and Vespo, Chapter 3; McCartney and Phillips, Chapter 7). Based on the infant's response to the mother's leaving and return, babies are classified as securely or insecurely attached. A baby who accepts the mother's leaving and is happy at her return is considered to be securely attached. In contrast, a baby who either cries profusely when the mother leaves and then is angry at her when she returns or is totally unresponsive to her is considered insecurely attached.

Proponents of this theory (e.g., Sroufe & Waters, 1977) claim that this short experimental procedure provides an indicator of the quality of the relationship between infant and mother. They also claim that the relationship as measured at this particular moment in time reflects the mother's previous caretaking skill and feelings for the baby. They argue that the mother of the securely attached infant is the mother who has previously been attentive, responsive, and loving to her child (cf. Hay and Vespo, Chapter 3, for an analysis of this assumption). Because the security classification derived from the Strange Situation is considered to be a reliable and valid measure, that is, stable over time and actually measuring the qualities of the relationship it purports to measure, the procedure has been used in dozens of studies.

It is our contention that the attachment classifications in the 1980s may be similar to the concept of IQ that was prevalent in the 1950s. IQ was then believed to be a stable, reliable measure of children's intellectual functioning. Some felt that an infant who was developmentally advanced would surely be a gifted child and that a baby with a below-average score on tests would be a retarded child. IQ scores were used when considering adoption and for placement in special classes for the retarded or gifted. Decades of research have shown that IQ is best seen as a measure of a child's functioning on a series of tasks at one moment in time. It is reliable over short time intervals, but it is also subject to change over time. Even normal children in unchanging environments change in IQ (Kagan & Moss, 1962), and for special groups of children, such as those born prematurely or fetally malnourished children who may be developmentally delayed, the test measures may have little predictive value (Birns & Noyes, 1984).

It seems to us that measuring how a child responds to its mother's departure and return at the age of 1 year is a behavioral measure, and one may choose to call it attachment behavior. However, it seems much less likely that this 20-minute procedure is an index of good or bad mothering, or that it will be very useful in predicting how children develop in years to come. Belief in attachment security as a quality measure in infancy that reflects mothering skill may lead to the assumption that we have uncovered secrets that are as yet not fully explored. It also leads to the belief that behavior in infancy is completely predictive of later behavior, an idea that is challenged by many psychologists (Kagan, 1984; Clarke & Clarke, 1979).

Object Relations

Whereas attachment theory and research stressed the second year of the infant's life and the mother's role in attachment behavior, another revision of Freud's theory was object relations theory. Object relations theorists (Mahler, Pine, & Bergman, 1975; Winnicott, 1968) consider themselves to be Freudians, but have revised orthodox theory in several ways.

One revision was the decline in importance of the Oedipal conflict and therefore the Oedipal period. The major shift, however, was the replacement of Freud's drive model by an "object-seeking" model. For Freud, satisfying drives (the pleasure principle) was the primary force in human behavior. Therefore it was the strength of the original instincts and the conflicts they engendered that was primary. For the object relations theorists, it was the "object" (person) of the drives that was critical. By perceiving the formation of the self in infancy through the specific relations with the mother (the object of the drives), these theorists stated that the mother–infant tie is the core of emotional and psychological development. Consequently, they believe that fusion with and then separation from the mother represents the beginning of self-identity.

Mahler's Theory

One theorist who had a major impact on contemporary thought about child development, specifically on the mother's role, was Margaret Mahler. Her earliest work in the United States focused on psychotic children who either failed to relate to the mother (as in autism) or failed to emerge from the "symbiotic fusion" with the mother to attain autonomy. In 1952, Mahler stated that a universal separation–individuation phase marks the "psychological birth" of the infant, who emerges from a symbiotic unity with the mother with a new awareness of self. In 1967, Mahler wrote:

> I believe that the symbiotic phase of the mother–infant unity . . . together with inborn constitutional factors, determines every human individual's unique somatic and psychological make-up. (p. 749)

Mahler observed mother–infant interaction of both normal and problem children during the early months and years, studying the separation–individuation phase and its significance for normal identity formation. According to Mahler (Mahler *et al.*, 1975), every child confronts a crisis in separating from the mother. In the first few months of life, the infant behaves and functions psychologically as a fused system with the mother, a "dual unity within one common boundary." Mahler emphasized the concept of dual unity with the mother, as mother–infant relationships, according to her, are based on a reciprocal need-satisfying system. The mother attends to the child's many cues while the child in response adapts to the mother's needs, emotions, and demands. Engaged in a need-satisfying relationship, the mother is the infant's psychic regulator and an undifferentiated person in both reality and fantasy for the infant. However, as the child matures, the process of separating from the mother becomes more and more important to the child. Separation is not only marked by measuring physical distance from the mother, but also represents an intrapsychic differentiation of the "I" from the "not I," and the external from the internal. Cognitive and mental recognition of the separated self marks the end of the separation–individuation phase.

In contrast to Bowlby, Mahler was originally impressed by her own clinical experience and descriptions of psychotic children who she believed suffered from early distortions in the mothering experience. However, Mahler then studied the development of the mother–infant relationship in normal children. Her observations and theoretical formulations have profoundly affected the terminology as well as thinking about the importance of this early relationship. It is to her credit that she also wrote about the importance of the child's temperament and the many chance occurrences that codetermine a child's development in the early years. Mahler was clear in speaking about the importance of the birth of a sibling, changes in employment in one of the parents, or changes in the parents' or the child's health that would influence the relationship and also the child's life directly. It is interesting, however, that, as her theories filter down to the general public her contribution to the understanding of the broader issues that affect how mothers mother is frequently lost.

Winnicott's Theory

Although Mahler's ideas may be the best known to psychologists and other professionals and parents in the United States, several other object relations theorists have influenced thinking about mothering. One influential figure in the British psychoanalytic movement who emphasized the mother–infant tie was D. W. Winnicott, a pediatrician and child analyst.

Winnicott may have been the most influential of the psychoanalysts writing in the 1950s and 1960s because he wrote not only professional papers and books but also gave lectures to and produced books for parents (Winnicott, 1968). In fact, he may have been the British equivalent of Dr. Spock.

More than any of the analysts, Winnicott stressed the role of the mother as the primary determinant of the infant's well-being and later mental health. Although he claimed to be a follower of Freud, he did not believe, as Freud did, that the infant's instincts are the most powerful force shaping development (Greenberg & Mitchell, 1983). Nor did he accept Mahler's formulation of the infant as psychologically fused with the mother during the first weeks of life, only later to separate. Rather, Winnicott believed that, from the first day of her child's life, it was the mother's behavior and her competence in providing the child with the ideal environment that is the critical factor in determining the infant's normal or pathological development.

At an International Psychoanalytic Congress in 1961, Winnicott, in stating his position, said: "There is no such thing as an infant . . . whenever one finds an infant one finds maternal care, and without maternal care there would be no infant" (p. 586). Although few would argue with that statement, what Winnicott meant was that qualitative aspects of the mother's care were critical from the first day of life. In his lectures to parents, Winnicott (1964) disclaimed really under-standing the experience of mothering, as he was a man. He lectured and wrote to parents, giving advice, although he ended every talk advising mothers to do what comes naturally, rather than following books. Many of Winnicott's ideas and concepts have become part of the everyday language of parenting books, as well as being used by professionals concerned with children.

Among his better-known ideas are those concerning the "good enough mother." Winnicott differed from other analysts (Sullivan, 1953) who spoke of the "good mother" and the "bad mother," and concerned himself rather with the "good enough mother." The "good enough mother" does what comes naturally, which means that in the earliest days she provides the perfect en-vironment and gradually both gratifies and inhibits her children. Other concepts attributable to Winnicott are the concepts of "mirroring," whereby the mother reflects the child's state, which helps develop the infant's sense of self. Win-nicott (1953) also wrote extensively about "transitional objects," which help the infant "represent" the mother in her absence.

Winnicott stressed the importance of the infant's earliest experience in nurs-ing, not because the infant is dependent on food, nor because pleasure in nurs-ing would lead to love of the infant for the mother, but rather because successful nursing conveys the mother's love for the baby. Feeding without love, Winnicott believed, would be destructive.

Although Winnicott wrote that there are factors other than a mother's care that influence child development, by stressing the naturalness of "good enough mothering" and telling mothers to listen to their own feelings and not the experts, he implied that it is maternal behavior that is also fortunately in-stinctive. It is interesting that someone who devoted himself to educating moth-ers about child care did so because he proclaimed that experts, whether midwives or physicians, were not to be taken as seriously as the mother's own feelings. Winnicott thus represented the British point of view that infant development depends most on the love of the mother for her infant.

Klaus and Kennell: Bonding

The concerns raised by the object relations theorists about the first few months and even weeks of an infant's life are taken to an extreme in another application of psychoanalytic theory as seen in the work of Klaus and Kennell (1976). Klaus and Kennell introduced the term "bonding" as a reference to a unique relationship between mother and child that is both specific and enduring, and claimed that, in the very first hour after birth, both mother and infant are unusually receptive to forming this critical bond.

In their study, they divided a sample of mothers into experimental and control groups matched according to certain criteria such as neonatal birth weight. The control group of infants was provided with traditional hospital care, which consisted of separating the infant from the mother at birth. Contact between the infant and mother was primarily at regular feeding times. In contrast, the experimental group of mothers were permitted 16 additional hours of contact with their infants during the infants' first 3 days of life. Some of this contact occurred during the first hours immediately after birth.

Klaus and Kennell (1982) reported that mothers in the experimental group were more attentive to their babies during infancy, spoke to them more than did control mothers when the children were 2½ years old, and had children who were more intelligent at 5 years. The investigators assumed that differences at 5 years were due to the early experience with the mother during the first few days of life, which set the subsequent mother–child relationship.

Fraiberg's Plea for Full-Time Mothering

Yet another variant of the psychoanalytic perspective on the mother–infant relationship suggests not only that sensitive maternal care is important from the earliest days and even hours of life, but that being cared for by persons other than the mother can actually be harmful. Among the psychoanalysts who studied the normal and pathological development of children, few were as popular as Selma Fraiberg. Her book, *The Magic Years* (1959), was a readable and informative work describing the first 3 years of life. Fraiberg had the unique ability to translate complex Freudian ideas into a comprehensible popular test. She also considered herself to be an advocate for children.

Therefore, her 1977 book, *Every Child's Birthright*, was perceived as an authoritative text. The stated goal of her book was to present a case for welfare reform that would provide adequate financial support to impoverished mothers so that they would not have to work and deprive their infants of maternal care.

Fraiberg stated that the right of every infant to good early care could only be met by a 24-hour-a-day mother.

Fraiberg's argument is based on several faulty beliefs: (a) that a baby's love for its mother is necessarily exclusionary; (b) that only mothers can and do love their own babies; and (c) that economically disadvantaged babies are in double jeopardy if they are in day-care, because poor mothers will only be able to afford and therefore can only have poor day-care.

Fraiberg built her argument on traditional psychoanalytic doctrine and the work of Bowlby on institutionalized infants. She supported Freud's belief that love and aggression were basic drives and that the infant's love for the mother ultimately tames aggression. She then drew on Bowlby's work to argue that infants deprived of mother's love during the first 2 years of life will grow up unable to form human relationships.

Fraiberg expanded on Freud's belief that the infant's love for the mother becomes prototypic of all future love relationships and attributed to the mother and infant the development of the "language of love." She eloquently described the evolution of this language. The infant's love for the mother is seen as exclusionary and she compared the feeling of desperation at separation to the feelings of adults who first fall in love. She stated that infants cannot tolerate separation from the mother, and even the 2-year-old grieves at the mother's temporary absence. Of prime importance, it is only because the mother is so highly valued and loved that the infant modifies his or her aggressive impulses, and it is only 24-hours-a-day mothers who can provide this love. She claimed that survival of the human race is as dependent on the mother's ability to provide adequate love as it is on international peace.

Feminist Neo-Freudians

Although some feminist psychologists are very critical of Freud's views (Chesler, 1972; Weisstein, 1971), other feminist scholars embraced certain psychoanalytic concepts. Some feminist theorists have adopted certain of Freud's and the object relations theorists' ideas, but have drawn rather different conclusions. They draw on psychoanalytic theory but then consider the possible drawbacks of a view of mothers as sole caregivers.

Dorothy Dinnerstein's (1977) book, *The Mermaid and the Minotaur*, claimed that rage against women was rooted in early infantile experience. Because the infant is a primitive being, and originally the mother gratifies but also thwarts the infant's gratification, the child associates power and denial of gratification with the mother. Therein lies the source of hostility toward women. Because the father is not involved in child rearing until the baby is older and more rational, he is perceived as more rational than the mother. Therefore, she claims adults believe that men are more rational than women. After a complicated analysis, Dinnerstein concludes that, in order to correct distorted views of men and women, men should become involved in child care early in their children's lives, so that infantile rage can be shared. The early participation of men in child care, according to Dinnerstein, will also contribute to increased nurturant behavior in men.

The recommendation that men become more nurturant is very appealing and none would argue against greater paternal involvement in child care. However, to believe that women will gain economic equality and become more highly valued if men do more child care ignores the social, political, and economic bases of inequality between men and women. Dinnerstein's book is an example of the extreme form of "infant determinism" that derives from psychoanalytic thinking.

Whereas Dinnerstein is an experimental psychologist, who invoked psychoanalytic theory to explain sexism, Nancy Chodorow is a sociologist who seeks the explanation for social roles and personality development in mother–child interaction. Chodorow analyzed the crucial role of the mother in both female and male identity formation (Chodorow, 1978). She claimed that girls learn nurturance by virtue of their identification with their mothers. Boys, however, must turn away from their mothers to establish male identification. She argued:

> Women's mothering produces asymmetries in the relational experiences of girls and boys as they grow up, which account for crucial differences in feminine and masculine personality, and the relational capacities and modes which these entail. (p. 169)

Although both Dinnerstein and Chodorow consider greater participation of fathers imperative, their views on how mothers influence children are quite different. Dinnerstein borrows most from orthodox psychoanalytic theory, in that she invokes infantile impulses (rage) as the fundamental psychic force. Chodorow does not invoke earliest infancy and instincts as explanations for adult behavior, but rather considers identification as the critical process. In this way she is closer to Freud's own emphasis on early childhood rather than infancy.

Summary of Psychoanalytic Viewpoints

The preceding section has traced the development of the psychoanalytic perspective on mothers and children from Freud's explanations of adult neurosis as an outgrowth of infantile instincts and their gratifications to some contemporary feminist analyses of socialization that borrow certain key psychoanalytic assumptions. In the process, we noted how the object relations theorists transformed Freud's original ideas by emphasizing the role of the mother as object and the critical nature of the earliest months of the infant's life. Their emphasis on very early mother–infant relations in turn influenced the major empirical concerns stimulated by psychoanalytic theory: the impact of the security of the original attachment relationship with the mother on the child's later development, the impact of successful or unsuccessful bonding with the mother during the earliest hours of life, and the effects of various kinds of separation experiences, including being cared for part of the time by persons other than the mother. We shall critically evaluate each of these issues emanating from the psychoanalytic perspective. First, however, we examine how the various psychoanalytic theories about mothers and children fit into a general tradition of blaming mothers for what happens to their children.

MOTHER BLAMING

Mother Blaming in the Common Culture

Once the child's needs have been stated, and the essential characteristics of the good mother described, then blaming mothers for their children's problems becomes not only possible but likely. If good mothers produce good children, then bad children are produced by bad mothers.

Psychoanalytic theorists did not invent the destructive mother or the ideology of mother blaming. Centuries before, there were books telling mothers how to rear their children and paintings depicting drunk mothers neglecting their children as they tumbled downstairs or into rivers. As long as mothers have been responsible for their children, they have been blamed for inadequately fulfilling their responsibilities. However, images of the child and images of the mother do change. In fairy tales, forlorn, victimized children had mothers who had been beautiful and kind but were either dead or sleeping. Mother substitutes, most often stepmothers, were cruel and scheming. However, in contemporary Western culture, one need not be a stepmother to be portrayed as cruel and destructive.

Although mother blaming is very ancient, and continues to be prevalent today, the 1950s may well have been its peak period. At the end of the war, the family was much romanticized. Soldiers who had been away from home for years returned and mother was encouraged to leave the factory and return to full-time homemaking. The American dream reappeared. Father, living at home, would be employed, and mother no longer needed at the factory, would stay at home in the suburbs, having and mothering three or four children.

Of course, not all Americans shared this experience. For those who did, "mother love" was the prescription of the time. In the conservative 1950s, as mothers were told of the joys of housewifery, they were also vilified for providing either too little or too much love. The most vituperative image of the mother was drawn by Phillip Wylie in *Generations of Vipers* (1942). He claimed that a whole generation of American men were infantilized and grew up to be army rejects because of their self-indulgent and nagging mothers. His writing heralded the mother blaming of the 1950s.

Mother Blaming by Psychiatrists

Psychoanalysis, predicated on the belief that the child comes into the world preformed with instincts and drives that are both loving and aggressive, demands of the mother that she be the ideal "object of the child's love," satisfy the child's wishes and desires, and provide the controls for his or her aggressive drives until the child develops internal controls. Currently, specific acts, attitudes, and even unconscious wishes of mothers are held responsible for "problem" children or children's problems. Winnicott's assertion that "there is no infant without a mother" has become "There is no problem child without a problem mother" (Chess, 1964, 1982). The mother is no longer seen only as a person, who molds a child the way a sculptor does clay, but rather the provider of nourishment, love, and control, and, above all else, the mediator between the child's instincts and the demands of reality, as well as the provider of mental health.

In describing psychosexual development and the importance of the unconscious, the mother as well as the child is considered to be ruled by needs, drives, and conflicts, most of them unconscious. Moreover, as the mother is the child's primary love object, she is also the purveyor of mental health and mental illness. In many cases of child pathology, it is the mother's "dark continent," her needs and wishes, that are highlighted. In psychoanalytic theory, at the root of all neurosis, psychosis, and character disorders is the mother who is either rejecting, punitive, immature, seductive, narcissistic, neglectful, or overprotective, and sometimes all of the above.

In the 1950s, at the height of the mother-blaming tradition, research in the field of mental health began to receive attention from the federal government. Large grants were awarded to scientists seeking the cause of mental retardation and mental illness. Careful research involving technology that allowed for precise psychophysiological and psychological measures of mother and child coexisted with clinical descriptions of negative mother–child interaction.

Clinical descriptions of psychotic children supported the analysts' claim that mothers caused their children's psychopathology. For instance, Boyer (1956) wrote:

> The amnestic material from Maria, her mother and her aunt reveal that mother was hostile to this girl and minimized Maria's needs. The girl's wants were ignored and mother's were heeded. Mother could not let the child be separate and bound her through feeding experiences. (p. 248)

It is still true, as Caplan and McCorquodale (1985) have demonstrated, that "mother blaming is a significant and serious problem that continues in the current clinical literature" (p. 352). Too many clinicians, they stated, still indict mothers for "making or breaking their children."

Today, in the scientific literature on child development, mother blaming appears in different forms. In particular, the issues raised by psychoanalytically oriented researchers like Klaus and Kennell (1976) and Fraiberg (1977) about early bonding and the effects of day-care fall into this tradition. For example, with respect to the concerns about bonding, Chess (1982) suggested that "whereas the schizophrenogenic mother is no longer an acceptable concept, bonding and failure of bonding may be its current counterpart" (p. 96).

Similarly, the positions of some experts on child development concerning the effects of maternal employment and nonmaternal day care illustrate contemporary mother blaming, and seem likely to contribute to maternal guilt. For example, Berry Brazelton (1986), a popular pediatrician who writes compassionately about mothers and children, stated that women who return to work too soon after their infants' births are fulfilling their own needs and sacrificing the needs of their infants. Furthermore, he states that pregnant women who plan to return to work soon after their babies' births feel differently about the birth and the forthcoming baby than do women not planning to return to work. His conclusions, he says, are based on clinical impressions but not research, but, because he is considered an authority, his opinions are taken very seriously.

Another researcher (Belsky, 1986), who formerly supported day care as nonharmful to children or parents, has recently revised his views. Belsky now claims that employed mothers are either selfishly depriving their infants or selfishly "overwhelming their babies with excess attention in order to alleviate their guilt." Belsky writes:

> By trying to make up for lost time, mother may inadvertently exceed the information processing capacities of their infants causing them to avoid interaction and contact. In essence, these mothers may be meeting their own needs at the expense of their babies, whom they have missed so dearly during the day. (unpublished manuscript)

Belsky cites studies that indicate that working mothers spend as much time with their infants as nonemployed mothers, but that fathers with working wives spend less time with their infants than fathers with nonemployed wives. He uses these data to claim that the employed women are therefore overstimulating their infants and preventing the fathers from having their share of play time. Thus, in Belsky's statements, mother blaming takes a slightly different form: Mothers, in this case, are indicted for providing too much rather than too little love.

CRITIQUE OF PSYCHOANALYTIC THEORY: THE MYTH OF MATERNAL POWER AND INFANT AS FATHER OF MAN

Criticisms of Existing Theory

In tracing the history of psychoanalytic perspectives on mothers and children, we began with Freud in the first half of the twentieth century and concluded with the feminist embrace of analytic theory in the second half of the century. We then examined how these views fit into the more general tendency to blame mothers for their children's problems. Because we believe that ideas emanating from Freud's work have profoundly influenced ideology, social policy, and mothers' feelings about themselves, we would now like to offer several criticisms of the theory and its derivatives. Our criticisms fall into two categories, conclusions that we consider to be false and errors of omission.

Because of the breadth of Freud's theories, their derivation from a clinical sample, and their dependence on constructs that are difficult to operationalize, it is unlikely that most of his ideas will ever be "proven" correct or false. However, certain errors have been found. Freud was wrong about female sexuality and wrong about women's fantasies about childhood molestation. Attempts to explain culture and personality in terms of early weaning or toilet training have likewise failed. However, Freud's belief that mothers are critical players in the drama of life is unlikely to be false. The recurrent clinical observation that seriously abused children want to remain with their mothers is just one compelling example of evidence for the strength of the bond.

However, because at this time it is not possible to prove or disprove clinical descriptions and intuition, we will turn to the writings of scientists who did research addressing issues drawn from psychoanalytic theory. In particular, we shall look at the evidence bearing on the following issues raised, as we have already seen, by researchers in the psychoanalytic perspective: the impact of mother–neonate "bonding," as discussed by Kennell and Klaus, and the possible "toxicity" of day care, as discussed by Fraiberg, Brazelton, and Belsky. After considering each of these issues in turn, we shall consider the evidence bearing on the more general assumption at work in all these manifestations of psychoanalytic theory, namely, that early experiences critically influence the child's later development.

Bonding

As we have seen, Klaus and Kennell claimed that experience during the first few days of life determined later behavior. They made no attempt to consider other factors in the lives of the children they studied, such as the birth of siblings, changes in parents' economic situation, or other stresses. They also neglected to consider the possibility that the health care providers in the study were aware of the two different treatments and might have conveyed to the mothers in the experimental group that their babies were special, thus enhancing maternal care.

The initial study done by Klaus and Kennell has been discredited by Svejda, Campos, and Emde (1980), who, using meticulous procedures, failed to replicate the original finding, and by Egeland and Vaughn (1981), who compared babies who were being adequately taken care of with a group of those who were not. These authors found that, in looking at the birth and postpartum histories of the babies and mothers, the well-cared-for babies were not distinguishable from those who were not. Babies who had been separated from their mothers at birth because of postnatal problems were no less "bonded," nor at any higher risk for neglect or abuse than those who were placed in immediate and extended contact with their mothers.

The "Toxicity" of Nonmaternal Care

Developmental psychologists have shown that infants can and frequently do form attachments to more than one person (Schaffer & Emerson, 1964; Lamb,

1976). Additional objects of attachment include fathers, siblings, grandparents, paid child-care providers, and other loving adults. Furthermore, it is not always true that biological mothers provide the best care for children, as those working in the field of child abuse and neglect have demonstrated. Furthermore, the claim that poor mothers can only pay for poor day care implies that the only way to fund day care is through parents' fees and removes the responsibility for the care of children from the larger society. Well-funded programs for disadvantaged infants have been shown to be not only adequate, but to vastly improve the quality of life for these infants (Ramey, Yeates, & Short, 1984).

In an attempt to advocate for infants, children, and their mothers, Fraiberg used questionable research and strong personal biases in writing a book that could only create guilt in all working mothers and misinform public policy. The inadequate schools provided for impoverished children or inadequate care of impoverished patients has not led anyone to call for an end to public education or public hospitals. Rather, most advocates for children and the poor recommend excellent schools, excellent health care, and excellent day care to provide adequately for all children and families. Although we acknowledge Fraiberg's good intentions and appealing writing style, we are concerned about the influence of this kind of application of psychoanalytic theory to analyses of vital social issues.

We observe that the increasing participation of women in the work force influences family structure and interpersonal relations. Therefore, the concern about the influence of nonmaternal care on children, and particularly the very young, becomes a major issue, for mothers, employers, and policy makers. Selma Fraiberg was an advocate for federal and state financial assistance to permit poor mothers to stay at home and not abandon their children to inadequate day care, but she did not call for good day care. Today's experts are concerned with the psychological effect of maternal employment on mothers, fathers, and their babies, even when families can afford good day care.

As we noted earlier, Belsky (1986) has recently added his voice to those who claim that being cared for by someone other than the mother is not in the best interest of the child. He claims that mothers damage their children, not because of inadequate attention but rather, since they miss their babies and guilty about leaving them, they overstimulate the babies when they return from work. How strong is the evidence for his contention that working mothers overstimulate their babies and deprive them of opportunities for father–child interaction?

It seems very likely that some working mothers do miss their infants when they are at work. However, in blaming mothers for overstimulating their babies, Belsky overlooks another possible explanation for the fathers' behavior. It may be that those mothers who have been at home all day with their small babies may be so tired of child care that, when the father walks in at the end of the day, they may immediately hand the baby over to him. It may also be that, when both parents are away all day, mothers may make more of an attempt to nurture their infants. There is, however, no evidence that we know of that this attention is harmful. There have been singularly few studies of new parents and their feelings about being parents. However, one study (Mahoney, 1985) suggests that mothers of 4-month-old infants, whether the mothers are employed or not, feel somewhat depressed and overwhelmed. Independent of employment status, these women indicate that they have very little time for themselves, their husbands, or their friends. Maternal employment and day care have not been shown to negatively affecf mothers or children.

The Effects of Early Experience: Early Deprivation Revisited

The important general question posed in this chapter is whether knowledge about early maternal and infant behavior provides clues to the infant's later development. For example, Bowlby and the attachment researchers suggest that a warm, sensitive, responsive mother paired with a securely attached happy infant predicts that the infant will become a psychologically healthy adult. The concerns about early "bonding" and the impact of nonmaternal care similarly are questions about the effects of early experience. It is thus important to examine the evidence that exists concerning the effects of very drastic forms of early deprivation, that is, the situation where one would most expect to see long-lasting damage to the child.

Studies of the devastating effects of early institutionalization and early deprivation have captured the national imagination. However, there have also been studies demonstrating the remarkable ability of children with serious early damage to recover when moved to favorable environments (Skeels, 1966; Kulchova, 1972, 1976). These latter studies have been largely ignored or disparaged by those who claim that early damage due to early institutionalization or other forms of "maternal deprivation" is irreversible. Rather than relying on early studies that can be dismissed because of flawed designs or inadequate measures, we examine the findings of an ongoing study by Barbara Tizard, which was begun in Britain in the mid-1970s.

In that study, babies separated from their mothers were provided with good physical care but denied the opportunity to "attach" or "bond" to one parenting person. A group of 60 infants was placed in residential care before they were 4 months old and remained until they were at least 2 and in some cases 4, 5, or 6 years old (Tizard, 1977). The nurseries were spacious private homes that each housed about 15 babies who were provided with beautiful facilities, toys, and abundant but impersonal care. Child-care providers were women training to be baby nurses. They therefore rotated shifts, were not always caring for the same group of children within a facility, and rotated through different centers. The division of tasks and arrangements of shifts discouraged the formation of close relationships between the nurses and individual children. One analysis of the personnel in the nurseries indicated that the average child had 24 caretakers by the time she or he was 2; those who stayed in care for 4 years had an average of 48 caretakers. After 2 to 6 years in the nursery, the children were then adopted or in some cases returned to their biological mothers.

According to attachment theory, object relations theories, or even conventional wisdom, this kind of care should be totally disastrous. How then have the children fared?

When the children were tested at 2, their speech was somewhat delayed

and their average Development Quotient was 22 months (Tizard, 1979). However, by age 8, after they had been adopted, they were of average intelligence.
Many of the children were considered by their teachers to be excessively demanding, but they did not differ markedly from the children in a control group.

Perhaps what is most interesting is that the children's behavior correlated
most highly with their current life situation rather than with their experience or
level of functioning in the nursery. The children who had the longest stays in the
nurseries, the lowest IQs, or the highest number of problem behaviors were *not*
the most likely to have problems at age 8. Children placed in economically
comfortable homes with older, eager to adopt parents had the fewest problems.
Those children who were returned to their biological mothers did not fare so
well. Most of these mothers married men not biologically (or psychologically)
related to the child, and had other children by their current husbands. The
children who were restored to their biological mothers had many more behavior
problems, as reported by both parents and teachers.

Tizard does not claim, nor do we, that early experience is unimportant. The
study does demonstrate, however, that even if the first 2 or even 4 years of an
infant's life are spent without one primary mothering person, postinfancy experience alters the results of early deprivation.

A quotation from Jerome Kagan's most recent (1984) book, *The Nature of the
Child*, addressed this issue. Kagan wrote: "Every society needs some transcen-
dental theme to which citizens can be loyal." He said that because contemporary
society made it difficult to have absolute faith in knowledge, God or romantic
love, "the sacredness of the parent–infant bond may be one of the last unsullied
beliefs." He suggests that the excessive concern with earliest infancy may be a
reaction to the fact that infants do need care and attention, but the evidence
suggests that individuals other than the mother may also provide it, and that
this idea may provoke too much anxiety.

FACTORS OTHER THAN MOTHER

In evaluating the influence of psychoanalysis on our knowledge and theories about mothering, it is important to understand that there may be errors of
omission as well as errors of commission in the theory. In their emphasis on the
role of mothers in the psychological development of their children, most analytic
theorists ignore or minimize other important factors. In this section, we discuss
some factors other than mother that have been shown to be important determinants of behavior. Among these factors are fathers, temperamental characteristics of the infant, and social class.

The Father's Influence

If the 1950s was the decade of the mother, the 1970s ushered in the decade
of the father (Lamb, 1976; Kotelchuck, 1976). Earlier research had emphasized

"father absence," whereas current research concerns the positive role of fathers. Beginning in the 1970s, in response to women's increasing participation in the work force, the women's movement, and to fathers both as subjects and objects of research, fathers began to be considered active parenting figures. Although work in the 1960s (Schaffer & Emerson, 1964) had indicated that babies often become as attached to their fathers as to their mothers, and occasionally more so, the message wasn't heard until recently. It has now been established (Lamb, 1976; Yogman, 1983) that fathers can be as nurturant as mothers, that fathers are important in the socialization of their children, that they play more vigorously and in more diversified ways than mothers, and that they are more involved in fostering sex-role stereotypic behaviors.

Given the fact that fathers may have important effects on children, does interaction with children have critical effects on fathers and on society as a whole? We have already noted that one variant of the psychoanalytic perspective on motherhood, the feminist theories of Dinnerstein and Chodorow, has called for increased father involvement in child care. Of course, we believe that loving care by fathers will enhance family life, make motherhood less stressful, and perhaps foster nurturance in men. However, we find the belief that closer proximity of men and babies will decrease male violence or even alter existing stereotypes to be simplistic. There is some evidence that, during the past decade, contact between men and children has increased. Undoubtedly, many fathers provide loving care for their children, and some single fathers are more than adequate parents. However, there is no evidence of broad social change attributable to greater involvement of fathers in child care. Thus, fathers' behavior should continue to be studied to determine its influence.

We now know that good maternal care, good day care, and nurturing paternal care are positive influences on a child. Likewise inadequate care, whether administered at home, by mother or father or in a poorly staffed center, is harmful. However, the notion that "more" paternal involvement will automatically enhance family relationships has not been proven.

The Child's Temperament

In examining factors that influence children's lives, we cannot ignore the children themselves. One issue that continues to plague psychology and medicine concerns the relative importance of nurture and nature. Today most scientists agree that it is a false dichotomy and adopt an interactional or transactional stance. Classic articles by Bell (1968) and Sameroff (1975) state that infants are subjects as well as objects and that they influence the behavior of caretakers. Nonetheless, behaviorists and social learning theorists stress maternal behavior, whereas others stress the tempermental characteristics of infants and their biological determinants.

Just as babies are born with blue eyes or brown eyes, they are also born with nervous systems that may be differentially responsive to stress. We think that this is important because, in studies of attachment and bonding, there is an implicit assumption that the infant's attachment to the mother, whether secure or insecure, is primarily based on maternal behavior, when in fact it may be that avoidant or insecurely attached infants may be temperamentally inhibited and vulnerable to fear. In general, it is useful to examine continuities in temperament across the life span to measure the importance of this factor.

One of the best-known studies of temperament is the New York Longitudinal Study conducted by Stella Chess and Alex Thomas, which was begun in the early 1950s (Thomas, Chess, Birch, Hertzig, & Korn, 1963). These psychiatrists were particularly interested in the role of temperament in development. They examined the nature of development as a function of the child's characteristics and the relation between parental practices and child characteristics. They followed a homogeneous sample of 133 children of New York middle-class professionals from infancy to adulthood. Their major source of information was maternal reports. Mothers were interviewed every 3 months during the children's first year of life and then less frequently as the children grew up. The children were observed and tested and interviewed as young adults.

Chess and Thomas derived a series of behavioral characteristics such as activity level and adaptability that were then used to classify the children as "easy," "slow to warm up," and "difficult." They examined styles of parenting, life events, and temperament, and found that, whereas some of the "difficult" children did become "difficult" adults, the relationship was not linear. Parents who could accommodate to their difficult children were more likely to have well-functioning adolescents than parents who did not make this adaptation. Similarly, some children labeled "easy" in early life did not grow up without problems. Nonetheless, temperament early in life was a better predictor of later behavior than factors relating to childrearing patterns.

Chess and Thomas's research is based on maternal reports and began when infants were 3 months old. To understand the role of temperament in development more fully, it is desirable to study younger infants and observe them directly. The senior author did such work at the Albert Einstein College of Medicine, focusing on individual differences in the first few days of life when mothers had little contact with their infants. We were able to demonstrate that differences in response to a wide variety of stimuli were present during the first 48 hours of life and that these differences remained stable during the first few days of life. We measured differences in response to sounds, visual stimuli, and mildly noxious stimulus, and a pacifier. We demonstrated stable individual differences in the intensity of response to stimuli and also found that babies who responded vigorously to one stimulus tended to respond vigorously to other stimuli (Birns, 1965). Moreover, we found that we could demonstrate differences in how easily babies could be soothed (Birns, Blank, & Bridger, 1965). In addition to what we considered to be temperamental factors present at birth, some measures of temperament observable during the first few days of life correlated with behavior at 4 months (Birns, Barton, & Bridger, 1969).

Kagan and Moss (1962) found only one characteristic among the many that were studied to be stable from infancy to adulthood. Boys who were fearful and shy as adults had chosen careers that were consistent with this early-appearing trait. Although initially the researchers attributed fearfulness to maternal behaviors, Kagan now believes that fearfulness is attributable to biological predisposition. Kagan's ongoing research indicates that babies who are at the extremes of the continuum on vulnerability to fear at 21 months demonstrate the same behavior at 4 years. Furthermore, psychophysiological measures taken of children at both time periods indicated that stability of behavior is matched by stability of heart rate. This finding supports the importance of biological predispositions (Kagan, 1984).

In raising the issue of temperament and the possible biological aspect of temperamental qualities, we do not imply biological determinism. We do not believe that what is observed at birth is in any way fixed for all time. Rather, individual differences present at birth may or may not be predictive of later behavior, but certainly influence early and later infant–caretaker interaction. For example, an infant who is considered to be easy will evoke different feelings than a baby who cries readily and often is hard to soothe. This position is consistent with current transactional theory.

Socioeconomic Influences

The factor that may be most important in determining the developmental outcome for any one infant or group of infants, and which can be determined even before birth of the baby, is social class. Numerous studies indicate that being born rich or poor is the single most important factor in child development (Birns & Bridger, 1977; Keniston, 1977).

In evaluating the psychoanalytic views of motherhood, it is important to note that most psychoanalytic patients and most of the children studied intensively by analytically oriented students of child development have been from the middle class. Based on observations of children whose mothers are married, receive good prenatal care, and parent one, two, or at most three children, have not worked, and whose basic needs have been adequately met, generalizations have been made and advice offered that may have very little to do with the experience of a large number of minority and/or poor children. The life experiences of poor children are markedly different from those of their more affluent peers. Patients who come from psychoanalysis or those studied intensively as children may report dreams of deprivation, too little or too much love, or feelings of abandonment when younger siblings were born; the problems of the poor include a host of additional factors.

A poor child is more likely to be unplanned, to have only one parent in the house, to be born too early or too small, and to have serious illnesses that may not be treated. The very poor child is also likely to be inadequately nourished, poorly housed, and subjected to many childhood illnesses and accidents that may have permanent effects. Rather than fearing castration, the poor child may be more afraid of cockroaches and rat bites.

Inadequate school performance of poor children has led to programs like

Head Start (Zigler, 1985) and other programs that address the nutritional, health, and education needs of poor children (Birns & Noyes, 1984). Nonetheless, 20 years after the War on Poverty, being born poor in the United States may be the greatest hardship, both physical and psychological, that a child can endure. We will cite just one series of studies that addresses this issue. The studies were conducted by the senior author and colleagues at the Albert Einstein College of Medicine in the 1960s, when national attention and research money were focused on poor children as part of the War on Poverty.

We wanted to find out how early in life children who were economically impoverished, but not deprived of health care, would reflect the influence of extreme poverty (Golden & Birns, 1971). Our measures were measures of cognitive development. We wanted to see whether babies, being raised without toys and books, by mothers who were undoubtedly stressed by their poor housing and minimal income, would be less well functioning than babies reared with all the comforts most of us consider to be necessary.

The sample included babies between the ages of 1 and 2 years. One group was defined as "welfare babies," some of whom lived in apartments with one light bulb, no linen on the beds, no cribs, and barely enough food. A second group of infants was poor or near poor, but their basic physical needs were adequately met. The third group consisted of privileged babies, whose parents earned a sufficient income to provide for the children's physical needs, as well as toys, books, and many outings.

We found, much to our surprise, that, between the ages of 1 and 2 years, the extremely impoverished babies were developing as well as the middle-class infants. They could walk, stack blocks, imitate sounds and gestures, and find hidden objects as well as the other groups could. Our hypothesis that extremely poor infants would be developmentally delayed even in infancy was not confirmed.

However, when we retested these babies at the age of 3, they were developmentally delayed (Birns & Golden, 1972). This finding suggests one of the many ways that poverty influences development. Poor mothers provide the love, affection, and stimulation necessary for early development. However, babies raised in homes with few toys, books, or games, by mothers whose verbal skills are limited by their insufficient education, are by the age of 3 less verbally mature than their more affluent agemates. Many studies, such as the Carnegie Commission Report (Keniston, 1977), have concluded that poverty is the single most serious deterrent to children's normal physical and emotional development.

SUMMARY AND CONCLUSIONS

This chapter briefly described and criticized some psychoanalytic theory because much of the current advice being given to mothers is predicated on this theory (Brazelton, 1986; Fraiberg, 1977). During a period when parents have less and less influence on the lives of their children (Keniston, 1977), our belief in infancy as the critical period may be reassuring because it is the period when parents are most in control. For parents to believe that behavior with their infant is the single most important determinant of what their children will be like as adults may be comforting, but it may not be true.

Psychoanalytic theory has greatly enriched our understanding of human behavior. Freud and his followers expanded our knowledge and interest in early childhood and fostered the search for the origins of personality development. Among the analytic researchers, some like Mahler *et al.* (1975) provided rich observational data on normal as well as pathological development. Their studies provide careful descriptive narratives of mothers interacting with their babies and stress the importance of the interaction of maternal behavior with infant temperament.

It is wonderful to observe loving and sensitive mothers interacting comfortably and affectionately with their infants. It is likewise very difficult to watch mothers who appear insensitive to their children's needs, mothers who do not respond to their infants' cries, or mothers who do not engage in gazing, smiling, and responsive vocalization. However, to date there is no evidence that this very early period in the relationship between mother and child is the sole determinant or even the major determinant of the developmental outcome of the early years.

We have argued in this chapter that, when a securely attached infant becomes a cheery 4-year-old, it is most likely that the infant had an easy temperament at birth, that the mother may have been very loving and sensitive, that no untoward events occurred, and that the mother who was positive in her approach to her baby during infancy remained so. However, it seems equally plausible to us that this same secure infant of a caring mother, if raised in a family that is stressed by unemployment, illness, severe conflict, and/or an alcoholic father, will most likely exhibit behaviors consistent with these events in her or his environment. At the same time, infants hospitalized for an extended period at birth, or those who spend their early life in a group home (Tizard, 1977), or those who are severely abused and neglected during early childhood (Kulchova, 1976) may, when placed in an optimal environment, become well-functioning adolescents and adults.

We have argued that psychoanalytic theory, by placing so much emphasis on early infancy and intrapsychic development, ignores many of the most potent factors that influence children. We are further concerned about the implications of this theory for mothers and for those concerned with social policy. We can understand that, in a world that is increasingly technological, in which TV is our children's most constant companion, computers are replacing teachers as educators, and the threat of nuclear war is forever with us, it is very reassuring to believe that, by providing A+ mothering, we guarantee our children happiness and mental health.

Nevertheless, if we believe that parents, and mothers in particular, construct their children like Detroit builds cars, we diminish our efforts to insist on guaranteed child health care, excellent day care for the children of working mothers, good schools and after-school programs, and the provision of services to all children and families who require social solutions to social needs. It is our hope that studies of the developing child will expand horizons to include all the "other than mother" factors, as we continue to search for the key to optimal childrearing in a rapidly changing society.

Kurt Weill wrote in *A Threepenny Opera* that a man can be civil only after he has had his proper dinner. Mothers, too, may be most loving and kind when they are well cared for, provided with food, clothing, shelter, health care, and knowledge about children. Mothers are usually their infants' first and primary caretakers. They most often remain very important in their children's lives. However, by focusing only on the mother–child relationships, psychoanalysts and all of us, as authors, teachers, physicians, and policy makers, overburden mothers, and are not acting in the best interest of the child.

Additional research on mothers' experience, as well as supportive services should enhance maternal experience, child development, and family well-being.

References

Ainsworth, M. D. (1964). Patterns of attachment behavior shown by the infant in interaction with his mother. *Merrill Palmer Quarterly, 10,* 51–58.

Ainsworth, M. D. (1969). Object relations, dependency and attachment: A theoretical review of the infant–mother relationship. *Child Development, 40,* 969–1025.

Ainsworth, M.D. , & Wittig, B.A. (1969). Attachment and exploratory behavior of one year olds in a strange situation. In B.M. Foss (Ed.), *Determinants of Infant Behavior* (Vol. 4). London: Methuen.

Bell, R. Q. (1968). A reinterpretation of the direction of effects in studies in socialization. *Psychology Review, 75,* 8–95.

Belsky, J. (1985). Day care reconsidered. Unpublished manuscript.

Birns, B. (1965). Individual differences in human neonates' responses to stimulation. *Child Development, 30,* 249–256.

Birns, B., Barton, S., & Bridger, W. H. (1969). Individual differences in temperamental characteristics of infants. *Transactions of New York Academy of Sciences, 31,* 1071–1082.

Birns, B., Blank, M., & Bridger, W. H. (1965). The effectiveness of various soothing techniques on human neonates. *Psychosomatic Medicine, 23,* 316–322.

Birns, B., & Golden, M. (1972). Prediction of intellectual performance at 3 years on the basis of infant tests and personality measures. *Merrill Palmer Quarterly, 18,* 53–58.

Birns, B., & Noyes, D. (1984). Child nutrition: The role of theory in the world of politics. *International Journal of Mental Health, 12(4)* 22–42.

Bowlby, J. (1951). *Maternal care and mental health.* Geneva: World Health Organization.

Bowlby, J. (1969). *Attachment and Loss; Vol. 1, Attachment.* London: Hogarth.

Boyer, B. (1956). On maternal overstimulation and ego defects. *Psychoanalytic Study of the Child, 11,* 236–256.

Brazelton, T. B. (196). Issues for working parents. *American Journal of Orthopsychiatry, 56,* 14–25.

Caplan, P. J., & McCoquodale, I.H. (1985). The scapegoating of mothers: A call for changes. *American Journal of Orthopsychiatry, 55,* 610–613.

Casler, L. (1961). A critical review of the literature. *Monograph of Society for Research in Child Development, 26,* 2.

Chesler, P. (1972). *Women and madness,* Garden City, NY: Doubleday.

Chess, S. (1982). "Blame the mother" ideology. *International Journal of Mental Health, 11,* 95–107.

Chess, S. (1964). Mal de Mere. *American Journal of Orthopsychiatry, 34,* 613.

Chodorow, N. (1978). *The reproduction of mothering.* Berkeley: University of California Press.

Clarke, A. M., & Clarke, A. D. B. (Eds.). (1976). *Early experience: Myth and evidence.* New York: Free Press.

Clarke, A. M., & Clarke, A. D. B. (1979). Early experience: Its limited effect upon later development.

In D. Shaffer & J. Dunn (Eds.), *The first year of life: Psychological and medical implications of early experience*. New York: Wiley.

Dinnerstein, D. (1977). *The mermaid and the minotaur*. New York: Harper & Row.

Egeland, B., & Vaughn, B. (1981). Failure of "bond formation" as a cause of abuse, neglect and maltreatment. *American Journal of Orthopsychiatry, 51*, 78–84.

Fraiberg, S. (1959). *The magic years and Carnegie Council on Children*. New York: Scribner's.

Fraiberg, S. (1977). *Everx child's birthright: In defense of mothering*. New York: Bantam.

Freud, S. (1949). *An outline of psychoanalysis*. New York: Norton.

Golden, M., & Birns, B. (1971). Social class and cognitive style in infancy. *Child Development, 42*, 269–277.

Greenberg, J. R., & Mitchell, S. A. (1983). *Object relations in psychoanalytic theory*. Cambridge: Harvard University Press.

Harlow, H.F. , & Zimmerman, R.R. (1959). Affectional responses in the infant monkey. *Science, 130*, 421.

Kagan, J. (1984). *The nature of the child*. New York: Basic.

Kagan, J., & Moss, H. A. (1962). *Brith to maturity: A studx in psychological development*. New York: Wiley.

Keniston, K. (1977). *All our children: The American family under pressure*. New York: Harvest.

Klaus, M. H., & Kennel, J. H. (1976). *Maternal–infant bonding: The impact of early separation or loss on family development*. St. Louis: Mosby.

Klaus, M. H., & Kennell, J. H. (1982). *Parent–infant bonding*. St. Louis: Mosby.

Kotelchuck, M. (1976). The infant relationship to the father: Experimental evidence. In M. Lamb (Ed.), *The role of the father in child development*. New York: Wiley.

Kulchova, J. (1972). Severe deprivation in twins: A case study. *Journal of child psychology and psychiatry, 13*, 107–114.

Kulchova, J. (1976). A report on the further development of twins after severe and prolonged deprivation. In A. M. Clarke & A. D. B. Clarke (Eds.), *Early experience: Myth and evidence*. London: Open Books.

Lamb, M. E. (Ed.), (1976). *The role of the father in child development*. New York: Wiley.

Mahler, M. (1952). On child psychosis and schizophrenia: Autistic and symbiotic infantile psychosis. *Psychoanalytic study of the child, 7*, 286–305.

Mahler, M. (1967). On human symbiosis and the vicissitudes of individuation. *Journal of the American Psychoanalytic Association, 15*, 740–763.

Mahler, M., Pine, F., & Bergman, A. (1975). *The psychological birth of the human infant: Symbiosis and individuation*. New York: Basic.

Mahoney, M. A. (1985). *Social support: The meaning of relationship for employed and nonemployed mothers*. Unpublished Stone Center working paper.

Ramey, C. T., Yeates, K. O., & Short, E. J. (1984). The plasticity of intellectual development: Insights from preventive intervention. *Child Development, 55*, 1913–1925.

Rode, S. S., Chang, P. N., Fisch, R. D., & Stroufe, L. A. (1981). Attachment patterns of infants separated at birth. *Developmental Psychology, 17*, 188–191.

Sameroff, A. J. (1975). Early influences on development: Fact or fancy? *Merrill Palmer Quarterly, 21*, 267–294.

Schaffer, H. R., & Emerson, P. E. (1964). The development of social attachments in infancy. *Monograph of the Society for Research in Child Development, 29*.

Skeels, H.M. (1966). Adult status of children with contrasting early life experiences. *Monographs of the Society for Research in Child Development, 31*. Sroufe, L.A. and Waters, E. (1977). Attachment as an organizational construct. *Child Development, 48*, 1184–1199.

Sroufe, L. A., & Waters, E. (1977). Attachment as an organizational construct. *Child Development, 48*, 1184–1199.

Sullivan, H. S. (1953). *The interpersonal theory of psychiatry*. New York: Norton.

Svejda, M. M., Campos, J. J., & Emde, R. (1980). Mother–infant "bonding": Failure to generalize. *Child Development, 51*, 775–779.

Thomas, A., Chess, S., Birch, H. G., Hertzig, M. E., & Korn, S. (1963). *Behavioral individuality in early childhood*. New York: New York University Press.

Thomas, A., & Chess, S. (1977). *Temperament and development*. New York: Brunner/Mazel.

Tizard, B. (1979). Early experience and later social behavior. In D. Shaffer & J. Dunn (Eds.), *The first year of life: Psychological and medical implications of early experience*. New York: Wiley.

Vaughn, B., Egeland, B., & Sroufe, L. A. (1979). Individual differences in infant–mother attachment at twelve and fifteen months: Stability and change in families under stress. *Child Development, 50*, 971–975.

Weisstein, N. (1971). Psychology constructs the female. In V. Gornuk & B. Moran (Eds.), *Women in sexist society: Studies in power and powerlessness*. New York: Basic.

Winnicott, D. W. (1953). Transitional objects and transitional phenomena: A study in the first not-me possession. *International Journal of Psychoanalysis, 34*, 89–97.

Winnicott, D. W. (1964). *The child, the family and the outside world*. New York: Penguin.

Winnicott, D. W. (1968). The relationship of a mother to her baby at the beginning. *The family and individual development*. London: Social Science Paperbacks.

Wylie, P. (1942). *A generation of vipers*. New York: Farrar and Rinehart.

Yarrow, L. J. (1961). Maternal deprivation: Toward an empirical and conceptual re-evaluation. *Psychology Bulletin, 58*, 459–490.

Yogman, M. W. (1983). Competence and performance of fathers and infants. In A. MacFarlane (Ed.), *Progress in child health*. London: Churchill Livingstone.

CHAPTER 3

Social Learning Perspectives on the Development of the Mother–Child Relationship

DALE F. HAY AND JO ELLEN VESPO

INTRODUCTION

The authors of the two previous chapters have examined the contributions of evolutionary biology and psychoanalysis to the study of motherhood. A third, centrally important perspective on the mother–child relationship is that of social learning theory. The purpose of our chapter is to examine the current status of that third perspective. In particular, we focus on social learning accounts of attachment formation, or, in other words, how the relationship between mother and child is initially established. Social learning perspectives generally hold that mothers and children must learn to relate to each other, and thus that neither maternal caregiving nor infants' attachment behavior is completely instinctual.

Learning on the part of both mother and child is assumed to continue as the infant grows older, and so the period of infancy is not seen as critical in quite the same way as it is in the psychoanalytic perspective. Still, learning theorists, like psychoanalysts, have been somewhat preoccupied with the earliest beginnings of the mother–child relationship, and our focus on the topic of attachment formation reflects that preoccupation.

There is of course not one but a family of social learning theories (for a history of the social learning perspective, see Cairns, 1979). Nonetheless, some commonalities obtain across family members. In this chapter, we define social learning generally as *psychological change of a relatively permanent nature that occurs as a function of multifaceted experience in the social world.* To the extent that formation of the relationship between mother and child conforms to this definition, it

DALE F. HAY • Institute of Psychiatry, De Crespigny Park, Denmark Hill, London SE5 8AF, England. JO ELLEN VESPO • Department of Psychology, Utica College, Utica, New York 13501.

qualifies as social learning. We explore some different ways in which attachment has been examined as a social learning process. First, we consider three statements about attachment that explicitly fall within the social learning perspective. We shall discuss both commonalities and divergences among these statements and assess their mutual strengths and limitations. Next, we review work conducted in a rather different tradition, Bowlby's (1958, 1969) "ethological" attachment theory (for a summary, see Birns and ben-Ner, Chapter 2); we examine some studies in the ethological tradition in which social learning hypotheses have been set forth, but not in so many words. By doing so, we hope to find some prospects for a synthesis across theoretical perspectives. Finally, we discuss some ways in which the social learning perspective can be revised and broadened, in order to account more fully for the dynamic, developmental qualities of human relationships, including the one between mother and child.

EXPLICIT SOCIAL LEARNING ACCOUNTS OF THE ATTACHMENT PROCESS

Commonalities among Social Learning Approaches

The three illustrative statements about the attachment process that we review in this section by no means represent a unified theory; however, they share some common features. In the social learning tradition and outside it, the term *attachment* is variously defined, but three general sources of evidence are usually consulted to determine that an attachment between infant and caregiver exists. These are the behaviors shown by the mother and infant in each other's presence, the behaviors shown by each when separated, and the responses of the infant to persons other than the mother. In contrast to Bowlby and his colleague Mary Ainsworth, who have been preoccupied with the topics of separation and reunion, researchers in the social learning tradition have focused more upon what mothers and infants do when they are interacting together. In general, the notion of *behavioral interdependence* between mother and infant is at the heart of these descriptions of the attachment process.

In addition, these writers see attachment between mother and child as one example of a more general social and developmental process. They do not see it as Freud (1938) did, as "unique and without parallel." Rather, they seek general principles that may be applied to other sorts of learning tasks, or to the formation of attachments in other species, or to diverse sorts of social relationships beyond mother–infant attachment. This is a somewhat dangerous enterprise, in that one may discern common principles at one level of analysis but divergent facts at another. Nonetheless, in the view of social learning theorists, the existence of the latter need not preclude search for the former. This characteristic quest for generality is possibly the greatest strength and the greatest limitation of the social learning perspective.

In comparing three examples of social learning perspectives on attachment, we shall examine how, with respect to each, the attachment process is being described and conceptualized and then what explanatory processes are being invoked. In other words, exactly what is developing between mother and child? And what forces are responsible for its development? The three statements are now presented in the order in which they have appeared in the literature on attachment.

An Operant Approach: Attachment as Mutual Conditioning

Operant approaches to the study of the mother–infant relationship were offered in the 1960s (Bijou & Baer, 1961, 1965; Gewirtz, 1961, 1969), at a time when principles of operant conditioning were being applied, willy-nilly, to all sorts and conditions of human behavior. The operant approach to attachment thus derives from the tradition of American experimental psychology and stands in contrast to the British and European roots of the psychoanalytic and ethological traditions synthesized by John Bowlby.

The major operant theorist who has tackled the topic of attachment is Jacob Gewirtz. Gewirtz initially presented his learning analysis of attachment at the first conference on infant development organized in London by Brian Foss, at which Bowlby and an influential group of other psychiatrists and psychologists virtually defined the field of inquiry. Since that time, Gewirtz has continued to present his formulations as an explicit theoretical alternative to Bowlby's theory.

What Develops between Mother and Child

Gewirtz viewed the formation of an attachment relationship as a process whereby the mother's behavior comes to be rewarding for the child and vice versa. In those cases where the mother is primary caregiver, she consistently provides the infant with experiences that are inherently rewarding. Not only does she take care of the infant's basic survival needs, feeding it, keeping it warm, and so on, but she also provides physical comfort and perceptual and intellectual stimulation. Gewirtz assumes that infants gradually make the connection between these rewarding experiences and the mother's presence and behavior, and so she eventually becomes rewarding in her own right, apart from the primary reinforcement that she provides. This means that she has acquired the power to shape the child's subsequent behavior. The child develops those skills and tendencies that lead to rewarding interaction with the mother. Hence the child's attachment behavior is conditioned by the mother's contingent reactions.

At the same time that the mother's behavior is rewarding for the child, the child's behavior is rewarding for the mother. Thus, infants can condition mothers as well as be conditioned by them. Infants' smiles, coos and babbles, and differential responding to particular people seem to be potent reinforcers in most cultures (Gewirtz, 1969). Laboratory experiments have further demonstrated the

reinforcing value of infants' behavior (Gewirtz & Boyd, 1977b). Gewirtz speculated about why infants' behavior would be reinforcing for adults. Is it because
they are species-characteristic behaviors, thus signifying the child's membership
in the human community? Or because they provide information about the infant's state and well-being, which is an important matter to a concerned adult?
Or because they may be interpreted by the adult as a sign that the infant is
becoming attached?

Whatever the reason, in Gewirtz's view, the infant's behavior leads to
changes in the caregiver's and vice versa, with complex stimulus–response
chains becoming established and maintained. The development of attachment
thus consists of the progressive changes that take place as infant and mother
condition each other, and so become mutually interdependent.

Contributing Processes

Gewirtz has resolutely attempted to explain the emergence of attachment in
terms of a single learning process, operant conditioning. The perspective he
offers is not necessarily incompatible with Bowlby's (1969) emphasis on biological constraints on the learning that takes place between mother and child, but
such constraints are not explored. At the same time, there is no attempt to
invoke higher order learning processes or cognition. In addition, the central
question of how emotions as well as behaviors are conditioned, how feelings
change over time, is raised but not dealt with adequately.

In presenting a learning analysis of attachment, Gewirtz was striving for
scientific rigor. Philosophers of science note that a scientific theory should be
falsifiable, that is, its hypotheses should be stated in such a way that they can be
proven wrong. Gewirtz has hypothesized that attachment is the product of
conditioning; how could he be proven wrong?

Simply attempting to identify functional relationships in naturally occurring
interaction would not suffice; proper control procedures are required. On the
other hand, laboratory demonstrations that infants and mothers can condition
each other's behavior (e.g., see discussion in Gewirtz, 1977; Gewirtz & Boyd,
1977b) show what might be going on in natural settings, but do not prove that
that is what is, in fact, going on. Thus Gewirtz's account of attachment formation proves less easy to test than might first be thought.

The fact that is seen by many observers (e.g., Rajecki, Lamb, & Obmascher,
1978) as the most telling point against an operant account of attachment formation is the observation that parental abuse does not seem to punish infants'
attachment behavior. Quite what the implication of this fact might be for
Gewirtz's theory is not completely clear. Abuse is associated with qualitative
differences in attachment relationships, a point to be explored later in this chapter, and so it may be incorrect to say that attachments are invulnerable to
punishment. At the same time, it is not clear that abuse necessarily represents
contingent punishment; an analysis of links between the child's displays of
attachment behavior and the parent's abuse would have to be demonstrated.
Furthermore, even if under some circumstances abuse does technically qualify

as punishment, it is not clear whether the failure to disrupt attachments that are already formed tells us much about the processes whereby they were formed originally. Thus, it would seem that the role of operant conditioning as a process contributing to attachment formation has not been successfully established nor discredited.

In contrast to Gewirtz's emphasis on operant conditioning, the next accounts to be discussed invoke additional learning principles and also discuss both biological constraints and higher order processes.

A Psychobiological and Learning Synthesis: Attachment as Behavioral Adaptation

What Develops between Mother and Child

The next statement we examine is an attempt to synthesize biological and social learning perspectives. Robert Cairns's (1966a, 1972) account of attachment formation owes much to the tradition of social learning theory, particularly as it was developed in the 1950s by Sears and colleagues (e.g., Sears, 1951). At the same time, his theory is explicitly biological. He sees attachment as one form of social adaptation, which he defines as "adjustment to environmental conditions; specifically modification of an animal or plant (or its parts or organs) fitting it more perfectly for existence under the conditions of its environment" (Cairns, 1977, p. 1). Cairns notes that adaptation is not "synonymous with health, normality, happiness, or contentment" and that "Social adaptation to some environments requires the development of activities that may depart markedly from the norm of the species" (p. 1). For a newly born organism, one of the most central features of its environment to which it must adapt is its mother. To the new parent, one of the most salient features of its changed environment to which it must adapt is the newborn.

In describing the infant organism's emerging relationship with its mother, Cairns (1972) drew attention to the fact that the mother constitutes both a *focal stimulus* and a *contextual stimulus*, that is, in the infant's view, is both figure and ground. He contended that both these roles are important for understanding the infant's subsequent adaptation. That is, the infant would interact directly with the mother as a focal stimulus, and thereby possibly condition and become conditioned by her, in much the way that Gewirtz has described. At the same time, for most young mammals, the mother serves as the background against which most important things in life take place; she provides a context in which the infant pursues its own existence. Thus the infant's own, independent activities become associated with the mother's overarching presence, and they become disrupted in her absence. Such associations between the mother as context and the infant's behavior would take place, even in the absence of overt rewards.

Cairns (1977) notes that, in most mammalian species, adaptation between mother and infant takes place on a physiological level as well as a behavioral one. However, the physiological adjustments that are made may be neither necessary nor sufficient for social attachments to emerge. For example, for many mammals, the mother's eating the placenta is an important facilitatory event in establishing mutual regulation between herself and her offspring. Nonetheless, both camels and humans manage without this meal. Furthermore, the mother's role as a contextual stimulus may derive primarily from the fact that, under ordinary circumstances, she happens to be the most salient figure in the infant's environment, and not from her biological identity as such. This possibility was suggested by observations of lambs reared without their mothers but with another perceptually complex, salient object in their environments, namely, a television set. The lambs displayed species-characteristic attachment behavior to the television sets and became notably distressed when their video companions were taken away (Cairns, 1966b).

Cairns sees infants' reactions to separation from and reunion with their caregivers in terms of an ongoing process of adaptation to the vicissitudes of the environment. He notes that studies of mother–infant separation typically stop observing during the period of initial disruption, when both mother and infant have each lost the central portion of their home environments. Continued observations, when done, reveal a gradual recovery and return to self-sustaining behaviors, with additional social relationships gradually becoming established or adaptation to life alone taking place. The picture that is drawn here is of the young mammal as a flexible, coping organism who adapts to changing circumstances, whatever they may be, and not one of a fixated organism whose life course is completely determined by events that took place during an early critical period.

Contributing Processes

In describing attachment and reactions to separation as part of an ongoing process of social adaptation, Cairns is clearly invoking learning principles. His argument is not, however, tied to the demonstration of an operant conditioning process. Indeed, he contends that ". . . it is necessary to develop concepts that are closer to the actual phenomena of social interchanges than the traditional ideas of social learning theory permit (e.g., social reinforcement, modeling)" (Cairns, 1977, p. 18).

The processes Cairns invokes include biological and psychological synchrony, social facilitation, and contiguity learning, rather than operant conditioning. He argues that one can understand social development (including the formation of attachments) only in terms of the properties of dyadic interactions. Such properties include *mutual synchrony, escalation, recurrence,* and *consolidation.* By this he means that social partners have a tendency toward synchrony, that is, to produce similar or complementary, but not necessarily identical, behaviors when interacting with each other. This property of synchrony thus extends beyond mere imitation. The person's interactions tend to increase in intensity over time, be repeated, and consolidate across partners and settings. All this may happen in the absence of contingent reinforcement or punishment.

Cairns's version of social learning theory is more flexible than that of the operant theorists' in that it is not so closely tied to stimulus–response learning. Is it as rigorous? Can it be proven wrong? Descriptive studies of social interaction may reveal synchrony and escalation, for example, but they do not prove that such processes underlie the development and maintenance of attachments. In addition, by striving for a very general theory that accounts for attachment formation across mammalian species, Cairns's account seems to downplay the role of higher order cognitive processes and the distinctive features of human attachments, in particular, their self-conscious qualities. The next statement that we review is an attempt to deal with that issue.

A Social-Psychological Perspective: Attachment as Relationship Formation

What Develops between Mother and Child

As we noted earlier, the social learning perspective is characterized by its quest for general principles that may apply across tasks, settings, and species. Another version of this characteristic quest for generality is a recent attempt by one of us to identify commonalities in the way infant–mother attachments and other sorts of human relationships are formed (Hay, 1985). It was argued that six general steps are taken when any two persons form a mutual relationship. First, each person must identify the other as a suitable person with whom it is possible to relate. At the simplest level, this entails noticing that the other is an animate object and a member of one's species. Second, each person begins to communicate with the other, sending signals and decoding the other person's signals in turn. Third, the two partners begin to engage in patterned, contingent interaction. Interaction requires one to pace and regulate his or her own behavior, in coordination with the partner's, whether the interaction be one of harmonious cooperation or antagonistic conflict. The interaction that emerges as two persons become acquainted may be described in terms of stimulus–response chaining (e.g., Gewirtz, 1969) or processes of synchrony and consolidation (e.g., Cairns, 1977); thus, with respect to this attainment, this perspective is compatible with the ones discussed earlier.

It is with the next steps to be discussed that a relationship takes on a more abstract life of its own, beyond the overt behavior of the two partners. Fourth, as two persons become acquainted and maintain their relationship, each person, as Cairns (1972) has also noted, becomes a context for each other's independent activities. This process subsumes the phenomenon of stimulus control discussed by the operant theorists, but is more general, including other forms of social facilitation, such as the "secure base" phenomenon described by the ethological attachment theorists (e.g., Ainsworth & Bell, 1970). Fifth, as two persons continue to relate, their interactions and impact on each other become more and more unique, so that they become more and more distinguishable from other pairs of persons. Thus meaningful individual differences begin to emerge at the level of relationships as well as persons. Finally, each participant in a particular relationship gradually develops a generalized concept of the partner and of their mutual relationship. Such a concept has both cognitive and affective dimensions. Thus both mother and child come to have hopes and fears, expectations and beliefs about each other and about the relationship that exists between them.

These six steps in the formation of relationships are not to be thought of as discrete stages. The timing and sequencing of the attainments is a matter for empirical investigation. Moreover, persons who have acquired a generalized concept of their relationship continue to communicate and interact, and there are feedback properties in the system. Their shared or diverging theories of the relationship may be expected to constrain the types of communication and interaction in which they engage. When an adult couple decides, for example, that they are or are not in love, their interactions will change accordingly, and those changes will in turn feed back into strengthening or weakening their conviction of their mutual affection.

It is proposed that these six steps are taken by a mother and infant in developing a mutual attachment. It is true, however, that with respect to that particular type of relationship, there is an imbalance between the two partners. The mother, as a mature, sophisticated adult, has the capacity to take all six steps in forming a relationship with her infant within days, if not within hours of its birth. In her decision to reproduce, she may already have identified a human infant as a potential partner with whom it is both possible and desirable to relate. Indeed, as a result of both her membership in the human community and her particular sex-role socialization (see Berman, 1980), she is likely to identify infants as particularly compelling stimulus objects.

The mother may also be expected to try to communicate and interact with her infant immediately, adjusting her own behavior and expectations in terms of the infant's limited capacities, and her relationship with the infant, even before its birth, becomes an important context within her life. It seems likely that a particular mother's interactions with her infant take on an idiosyncratic character from the very outset, distinguishing them from other mother–infant pairs and even from that same mother's relations with other offspring. Finally, to the extent that humans are compulsively cognitive organisms, a mother is likely to have constructed a general theory about her child and their relationship even before that child is born. Indeed, such a theory of the "child ideal" may have been constructed long before and may have been instrumental in her decision to conceive or bear or rear the child. This all is not to imply that the mother does not change as a function of experience relating to her actual child. Rather, the picture that emerges when looking at attachment development from the mother's point of view is one of an integrated system continuing to develop and regulate itself over time, rather than a sequence of discrete attainments.

The picture is somewhat different when we examine it from the child's point of view, because capacities for communication, interaction, certain kinds of emotional expression, and thought emerge only gradually over the first 2 or 3 years of life. Thus, as an infant's particular relationship with the mother is developing, so is his or her capacity for relationships in general.

It is obvious that, for family-reared children, these important capacities for forming relationships may be clearly seen within the relationship that is developing between mother and infant. As an infant forms a relationship with its mother, that infant is acquiring skills and exercising capacities that will enable him or her to form relationships with other people in general. Does that imply, however, that the formation of the mother–infant relationship is a critical prerequisite for relating to others, that development must take place in this domain first before the lessons learned can be applied to other relationships? In Freud's (1938) terms, does the mother–child relationship truly serve as a "prototype" for future relationships?

The available empirical evidence would suggest that this is not the case. It has long been noted that infants form multiple attachments (Schaffer & Emerson, 1964). No evidence has been provided for the claim that later relationships derive from an initial bond between mother and child. Rather, the six steps of relationship formation taken by infants with their mothers are almost simultaneously taken in other contexts, including, most unexpectedly, in their emerging relationships with same-age peers (see Hay, 1985). For example, a detailed comparison of infants' interactions with their mothers and with a peer revealed that newly acquired interactive skills were applied simultaneously to relations with the mother and with the peer (Nash, 1986).

These data suggest that both general and specific lessons are learned by both mother and infant in the course of forming their mutual attachment. The relationship that emerges between them has unique content, unique qualities, unique meaning; at the same time, at a more general level of analysis, it has a number of features in common with all other human relationships. It may seem more "unique, without parallel" from the mother's point of view than from the infant's. In any case, an adequate social learning perspective must eventually explain how both the general and the specific lessons come to be learned.

Contributing Processes

Like Bowlby, Hay (1985) suggested that human infants are biologically prepared to learn certain social lessons. It was argued, however, that what they are prepared to learn is to affiliate with members of their species in general; human infants come into the world biased in favor of interacting with other humans. They respond to the stimulus properties of the human face and voice (and, as the operant theorists noted, those properties are potentially reinforcing). Furthermore, infants are able to produce communicative signals such as the cry and the smile that have clear impact on their fellow humans, and they show rhythmic variations in their behavior that make patterned interaction with other humans probable. These biological endowments, however, do not account for attachment formation to the mother in particular; to explain the development of that particular relationship, the learning processes at work when infants interact with their mothers and others must be invoked.

Like Cairns (1972), Hay (1985) stressed the operation of processes other than operant conditioning in the formation of social relationships. Such processes include social facilitation, perceptual learning, emotional synchrony and conditioning, modeling and identification, and direct instruction. In particular, it was noted that attachment formation represents intentional as well as incidental learning. Developmental psychologists tend to think of attachment as something that just happens naturally, for better or worse, whereas they think of socialization as more deliberate tutelage and inculcation of values. In contrast to this view, it seems likely that parents do deliberately teach their children to love them and to understand human relationships and that this call for intentional learning may be one more reason why the parent–child relationship stands apart from other sorts of relationships, despite the obvious characteristics all human relationships have in common.

Questions about the possibilities for falsification of this version of the social learning perspective need to be raised as well. The central proposition that attachments are formed in the same way that other social relationships develop would be proven wrong if certain dimensions of the mother–child relationship were found to be unique and, in particular, if the development of attachment was found to be controlled by unique processes. Thus this theory would seem to be ultimately falsifiable, but the current absence of convincing evidence that attachment development is unique is somewhat difficult to interpret.

Strengths and Limitations of the Explicit Social-Learning Perspectives

All three of the preceding accounts of attachment formation as social learning are characterized by an attempt to describe precisely what happens as mothers and infants develop their relationships and by hypotheses about contributing processes. They also all portray attachment formation as a complex, flexible process that may take multiple pathways and that can occur between various people, not just the child and its biological mother. This perspective is quite different from the notion of a "normal" course of events, with deviations from that course being seen as pathological.

However, where all three perspectives fail is where the psychoanalytic–ethological perspective taken by Bowlby and Ainsworth is at its strongest. None of the social learning perspectives, as currently stated, deals adequately with the phenomenon of affect, particularly positive affect. That is, these perspectives do not explain the love that is manifested between mother and infant, as opposed to their mutual distress at separation, which both Gewirtz and Cairns see as behavioral disorganization and breakdown. Nor do any of these three perspectives identify clear, systematic patterns of individual variation in attachment relationships. Their hypotheses about contributing processes could powerfully explain individual differences, but they have not been applied to that task. To address these issues, it becomes necessary to review the evidence collected by researchers in the Bowlby-Ainsworth tradition (cf. Birns and ben-Ner, Chapter 2). Some of their accounts of the ontogeny (as opposed to the phylogeny) of attachment curiously resemble social learning hypotheses.

"DISGUISED" SOCIAL-LEARNING HYPOTHESES

Several researchers within the Bowlby-Ainsworth tradition (e.g., Main, Kaplan, & Cassidy, 1985; Stayton, Ainsworth, & Main, 1973) have studied attachment as a phenomenon that develops and is maintained as a function of particular social experiences. As such, these theorists may be said to be viewing attachment as a form of social learning, in accordance with the definition we are using throughout this chapter. The difference from the explicit social learning accounts lies in the emphasis on individual differences and, ultimately, pathology. Ainsworth and her colleagues are asking, what social influences knock a mother and child off their expected, biologically based trajectory? How do social experiences create deviations in attachment relationships?

To address these questions, the attachment researchers have spent a great deal of time figuring out how to measure such deviations, and they have raised hypotheses about the role of social influences on a somewhat *ad hoc* basis. The "disguised" social-learning hypotheses that they have generated thus do not follow directly from Bowlby's (1969) theory of the evolution of attachment relationships.

The Bowlby-Ainsworth Account of What Develops

Bowlby (1969) described the eventual outcome of the attachment process as a "goal-corrected" partnership between mother and child; he noted that this would not be fully established until the child was 2 or 3 years of age, a year or so after the infant first begins to seek proximity to or resist separation from the caregiver. Thus, unlike some other psychoanalytic theorists, Bowlby took notice of important attainments in attachment relationships made after infancy.

Bowlby's (1969) description of the goal-corrected partnership was subsumed under his general theory of the evolution and normative development of attachment relationships. However, his interests as a psychoanalyst and clinician seem to have focused attention on differences among children in their opportunities and abilities to engage in such partnership.

The task of describing and analyzing those individual differences has been pursued most systematically by Mary Ainsworth (e.g., Ainsworth & Wittig, 1969; Stayton, Ainsworth, & Main, 1973). Prior to working with Bowlby, Ainsworth had studied with the Canadian personality theorist William Blatz, who had stressed the importance of security in adult adjustment (Blatz, 1966). Not surprisingly, security became the abstract construct Ainsworth chose to describe the individual differences she observed in infants' reactions to separation from and reunion with their mothers. She argued that differing patterns of behavior on those occasions showed that different infants felt more secure or less secure in their relationships with their mothers.

To assess security, Ainsworth designed a brief laboratory procedure to observe infants' reactions to meeting a stranger and separation from and reunion with their mothers; she called this procedure, accurately, the "Strange Situation" (Ainsworth & Wittig, 1969). The method itself deserves careful scrutiny. Because the procedure entails a series of brief events (meeting the stranger, being left alone with her, reunion with the mother, etc.), and these brief episodes occur in a fixed order, the nature of the various experiences is confounded with the order in which they are presented. Furthermore, the brief time allotted to each type of experience permits little possibility for adaptation to one before being buffeted by the next. Thus, as an experiment, the "Strange Situation" is flawed and useless for assessing infants' normative reactions to strangers or to separation and reunion. It should not, therefore, be viewed as an adequately controlled experiment, but rather as a stress interview for babies. In that "interview," under conditions of mild stress, systematic and reliable individual differences appear to emerge.

Ainsworth's "Strange Situation" is discussed in detail elsewhere in this volume (Birns and ben-Ner, Chapter 2; McCartney and Phillips, Chapter 7). For present purposes, it suffices simply to emphasize that what Ainsworth sees developing is the infant's affective evaluation of the attachment relationship, his or her degree of felt security in that relationship. It is the development of that affective phenomenon that Ainsworth is attempting to describe and explain. She seems not particularly interested in describing or explaining chains of actions and reactions between mother and child, and so the task she set for herself is quite different from that pursued by the operant theorists (e.g., Gewirtz, 1969).

Ainsworth thus pointed to affect as a core phenomenon in the development of attachment relationships, and, in that way at least, her formulations succeed where those of the learning theorists fail. Interestingly, however, current extensions of Ainsworth's work emphasize the cognitive dimensions of attachment relationships; current researchers analyze the patterns of insecure and secure attachments described by Ainsworth in terms of the infant's "working model" of the mother and their mutual relationship (Bretherton, 1985; Main et al., 1985). Their notion of "working models" closely resembles the notion of a generalized concept of the partner and the mutual relationship discussed in the social psychological perspective presented earlier (Hay, 1985). Both of these notions, however, fail to come to terms adequately with the affective coloring of the attachment experience. It seems, therefore, that the welcome emphasis placed on affect in the Bowlby-Ainsworth perspective is being somewhat deemphasized in these more recent statements.

There is another important difference between what investigators in the Bowlby-Ainsworth tradition and the learning theorists are trying to explain. In contrast to the emphasis in the learning perspective on mutual development by mother and child, Ainsworth's characterization of attachment relationships as secure or insecure seems fundamentally one-sided. The relationship between mother and child is being described in terms of the child's point of view. What the abstract construct would be that defines differences among attachment relationships from the mother's point of view is not quite clear; surely it is not the mother's security in her infant's presence. Researchers in the Bowlby-Ainsworth tradition have argued strongly that the "Strange Situation" measures secure or insecure relationships, not secure or insecure children; that is, the classifications are interpreted to reflect qualities of relationships, not temperamental characteristics of individual children (cf. Main *et al.*, 1985; Sroufe, 1985). These claims rest on the fact that a child's security classification when tested with the mother does not predict that same child's classification when tested with the father (Main & Weston, 1981; Main *et al.*, 1985). Thus the two assessments are presumed to characterize the mother–child and father–child attachment relationships, respectively, not global temperamental characteristics of the child that would be shown with both parents.

This conclusion rests on the absence of a statistically significant correlation; it thus suffers from all the usual problems encountered when a scientist tries to accept the null hypothesis. Nonetheless, even assuming that the attachment theorists' interpretation is a correct one, they are still describing the attachment relationship from the child's, not the mother's or father's, point of view. As Bretherton (1985) remarked, ". . . it is unfortunate that studies of attachment relations as experienced and represented by the attachment figure are almost non-existent" (p. 33). Bretherton is of course excluding from consideration those studies undertaken within the learning perspective (e.g., Gewirtz & Boyd, 1977b).

In general, when trying to synthesize the "disguised" social learning hypotheses with the explicit ones, it is important to note that the investigators in the different perspectives are trying to explain different things. Those in the Bowlby-Ainsworth tradition are seeking explanations of systematic individual differences in a child's feelings of security in or "working model" of the attachment relationship. They see these individual differences as important predictors of a child's lot in life. They are relatively unconcerned with explaining how normative mother–child interaction develops and changes over time.

Social Influences Contributing to Attachment Security

At the present time, researchers in the Bowlby-Ainsworth tradition are developing methods that extend beyond Ainsworth's "Strange Situation" (e.g., Main *et al.*, 1985; Waters & Deane, 1985). Most of the extant research on social influences on attachment, however, has relied upon the use of Ainsworth's paradigm, and so we restrict our discussion here to studies that have used the "Strange Situation" to measure security.

As we have noted, Ainsworth and her colleagues claim that the procedure measures relationships, not individual children, but they have described the individual differences assessed by their measure in terms of the child's point of view. We believe that this decision to describe attachment relationships in terms of the child's feelings of security or insecurity has led these researchers to set forth unidirectional hypotheses about the effects of the mother's behavior on the child's security. This fits in, of course, with the common tendency to account for deficits in children by blaming mothers (cf. Birns and ben-Ner, Chapter 2), despite the lip service almost always given to the popular concept of bidirectional effects in development.

When attempting to look at the impact of maternal characteristics on the child's feelings of security, as measured by Ainsworth's procedures, the attachment researchers have examined at least five things about the mother: (a) her particular style of interacting with the child; (b) her maltreatment of the child; (c) her own developmental history, especially the quality of her own attachment relationships; (d) her cultural heritage; and (e) her current life circumstances. We now consider each of these social influences in turn.

The Mother's Interactive Style

In abbreviated form, one of the most central hypotheses in contemporary attachment research is that propounded by Ainsworth, namely, that *sensitive mothers create secure babies*. Ainsworth has claimed that patterns of mother–infant interaction in the early months of life predict the security classifications made around the time of the infant's first birthday (Stayton, Ainsworth, & Main, 1973). Of particular concern in her analyses were global ratings of the mother's sensitivity to the infant's signals, which predicted secure attachment and stood in contrast to the mother's avoidance of and remarked-upon dislike of physical contact with the baby, which predicted insecure attachment. Thus, Ainsworth and her colleagues have argued that infants of sensitive mothers learn that they can count upon the relationship and feel that they are secure within it. In contrast, infants of mothers who avoid them begin to avoid their mothers in turn.

These claims clearly represent hypotheses about forms of social learning, although Ainsworth and her colleagues protest against such statements being framed in operant terminology. In particular, Ainsworth has argued strongly that a mother's sensitive responsiveness to a young infant's distress does not reinforce crying, but rather predicts less crying (more secure behavior) at later ages (see Bell & Ainsworth, 1972; Gewirtz & Boyd, 1977a, for a debate on this point).

The correlation that Ainsworth noted between early patterns of mother–infant interaction and later security classifications has been reproduced in other samples, but it is not quite clear whether the available evidence convincingly supports the hypothesis that maternal sensitivity produces secure attachment (for an extended, critical review of these data, see Lamb, Thompson, Gardner, & Charnov, 1985, Chapter 5). In general, the confusion results from the fact that the attachment theorists have tried to force a causal link between prior maternal sensitivity and subsequent child behavior. What they have in fact documented is a correlation between a measure of mother–child interaction at an early age with another measure of mother–child relations, the "Strange Situation," at a later age. Because the former is labeled in terms of the mother's sensitivity and the latter as a measure of the child's feelings of security, a causal hypothesis emerges. This stands in contrast to the learning theorists' characterization of attachment as a process of mutual learning.

The Mother's Maltreatment of the Infant

Another dimension of mother–infant interaction that might be expected to affect the development of attachment is abusive maternal behavior, which might be said to be the opposite of maternal sensitivity. Maltreatment does not prevent attachments from developing, a fact that, as we have seen, has been widely regarded as a major challenge to operant analyses of attachment formation (cf. Rajecki *et al.*, 1978). At the same time, maltreated infants do not seem to experience the same degree of security in their relations with their mother as do infants whose mothers do not abuse them. Thus, the implicit social learning hypothesis being set forth in the Bowlby-Ainsworth tradition seems to be that *maltreated infants become attached, but their attachments are rather likely to be insecure.*

Support for this hypothesis was obtained in a comparison of maltreated and nonmaltreated infants from lower income families (Schneider-Rosen, Braunwald, Carlson, & Cicchetti, 1985). A majority of the maltreated infants were classified as insecurely attached at 12, 18, and 24 months of age; in contrast the majority of infants who were not maltreated were classified as securely attached at all three ages. Longitudinal analyses indicated that there was more change in classification over time for the maltreated infants, and most of the change took the form of moving from the secure to an insecure classification, or from one insecure group to the other. Thus maltreatment would seem to be a detrimental social influence on the quality of attachment, even though it does not prevent attachments from being formed.

The Mother's Own Attachment History

Those attachment researchers who have hypothesized that maternal sensitivity creates secure attachment have also speculated about what experiences in the mother's own development promote her sensitivity and hence the child's experience of security. Thus, yet another implicit social learning hypothesis is the notion that *a child develops "working models" of his or her own mother and father that persist into adulthood and influence that child's own behavior as a parent.* For example, Ricks (1985) argues that, in early attachment relationships, one forms a mental representation of the relationship and, simultaneously, one's own self-worth. Maladaptive representations formed in early life guide future relationships. Thus one would expect cycles of insecure attachments throughout generations, if subsequent experiences do not alter these representations.

This hypothesis has been addressed by means of retrospective interviews of the parents of infants tested in the Ainsworth "Strange Situation." For example, in one study, an "Adult Attachment Interview" was developed to classify adults' accounts of their own attachment histories as secure or insecure (see Main *et al.*, 1985). These classifications of the parents were reliably correlated with their children's security classifications. The predictive power of the retrospective reports was stronger for mothers than for fathers, but statistically significant for both. Interestingly, a predictor of secure attachment in the children seemed not simply the parent's own happy childhood, but, rather, the parent's sense of being at peace with childhood experiences, however distressing they might have been.

The Mother's Cultural Heritage

Other factors in a mother's own socialization hisotry, beyond her memories of her own early attachment relationships, are invoked to account for differences in her child's experience of security. One important determinant appears to be the general culture in which both mother and child reside. In addition to any personal "working models" that mother and child have constructed, cultural groups collectively seem to construct their own theories of motherhood and child development. Thus, another implicit social-learning hypothesis emerging in attachment research is that *cultural expectations of babies and childrearing customs shape the qualities of attachment relationships.*

This hypothesis does not follow directly from Bowlby's or Ainsworth's theoretical writings; rather, it was forcibly brought to the attention of attachment theorists by data indicating considerable cross-cultural variations in the distribution of security classifications (for a review, see Lamb *et al.*, 1985). Of particular interest were attempts to replicate Ainsworth's procedures for classifying security in Germany and Japan (Grossmann, Grossmann, Spangler, Suess, & Unzner, 1985; Miyake, Chen, & Campos, 1985). Samples of northern German and Japanese infants revealed a greater preponderance of responses to separation and reunion that, in American samples, would have been classified as "insecure." In Germany, a relatively high proportion of children show one type of "insecure" behavior; they avoid close contact with their mothers in the test situation. In Japan, no infant was observed to show such avoidance; rather, a fair proportion of Japanese babies showed the other subcategory of "insecurity," namely excessive separation distress.

These data are most easily interpreted in terms of the expectations society holds for a 12 month old in Germany, Japan, and the United States, respectively. In Germany, 12 month olds are already expected to be somewhat independent; in Japan, 12 month olds are not expected to ever have been separated from their mothers, even briefly. Thus, Ainsworth's procedures for measuring "security" take on very different meanings in different cultures. It thus becomes most important to recognize the cultural relativism of the concept of security and to avoid equating "normal, biologically adaptive" behavior with "the way American babies tend to act." Moreover, the cross-cultural variations underscore the importance of socialization influences, as opposed to species-characteristic maturational processes.

The Mother's Current Circumstances

It is also clear that social factors other than a mother's history with her own parents and her cultural background are likely to affect her relationship with her child. In particular, her own current life circumstances are important. Another *ad hoc* social learning hypothesis emerging in the field of attachment research is that *when mothers' lives change, the quality of their children's attachment to them is likely to change as well.*

Some longitudinal research has shown security classifications to be quite stable over the course of the infant's second year (Waters, 1978). However, other evidence indicates that changes in family circumstances, and particularly the mother's own independent life, are associated with changes in security classifications (Thompson, Lamb, & Estes, 1982). In that latter study, infants were observed at 12 and 19 months of age, and only 53% of the classifications remained stable.

Based on the parents' responses to questionnaires, it was learned that changes in the child's security classification were related to the mother's return to work or to changes in the identity of the primary caregiver and not to general changes in family circumstances, such as moving to a new house. Interestingly, however, this does not mean that secure babies inevitably became insecure when their mothers went back to work; the change could go in either direction. Rather, change occurred more often for the babies who were initially classified as insecure. They were more likely to become securely attached over time than to remain insecure. Why this might be is not quite clear; no doubt a host of influences might be responsible for the change. At least one other factor in the mother's social circumstances might contribute. In general, the mother's level of social support seems to be predictive of her child's security in the Ainsworth procedures (Crockenberg, 1981). At least in some circumstances, a woman's return to work might increase the overall level of social support she receives, which would then be a positive influence on her relationship with her child.

The Quest for Contributing Processes

Throughout this section, we have spoken of "disguised" social learning hypotheses. Perhaps a better term than "disguised" might be "latent." All of the topics just reviewed—the effects of the mother's interactive style, maltreatment of the infant, own attachment history, culture, and life circumstances—underscore the importance of social, as opposed to biological, influences on attachment formation. Thus these hypotheses are certainly social ones, but do they invoke learning?

The correlational data used to generate and test the hypotheses about social influences do not provide information about the actual processes responsible for the observed associations. In reviewing the correlational data, attachment researchers have invoked general representational processes, in terms of children's and mother's construction of "working models" (see Bretherton, 1985), but the processes that would actually contribute to the construction of such models are not precisely specified.

Strengths and Limitations of the "Disguised" Social-Learning Perspective

One of the greatest strengths of the work just reviewed is also a limitation, namely, the almost complete reliance on Ainsworth's laboratory procedure for classifying the security of attachment. Use of a standard procedure gives coherence to the literature and permits important comparisons across studies; at the same time, Ainsworth's procedures are limited in scope and application. They are most appropriately applied to infants in the second year of life; moreover, the focus on reactions to separation and reunion lead to an analysis of only one dimension of the emerging relationship between mother and child. A complete developmental theory of that relationship must deal with constructs other than security.

In general, these "disguised" social-learning hypotheses provide data in search of a proper developmental theory. They do not constitute an adequate theoretical alternative to the explicit social-learning perspectives; they do, however, highlight some important social influences that those perspectives must account for. In particular, the evidence concerning family and cultural influences and the mother's current life circumstances clearly shows the need for a social learning perspective that extends beyond molecular analyses of dyadic interaction. These findings argue for an analysis of the sociology as well as the psychology of attachment relationships.

PROSPECTS FOR A SYNTHESIS

At this point, it seems that neither the social learning perspective nor the more influential perspective of Bowlby and Ainsworth provides a sufficiently encompassing developmental theory of attachment. The explicit social learning perspectives reviewed here all tended to neglect the role of affect in personal relationships and failed to come to terms with systematic patterns of individual differences. Bowlby, Ainsworth, and their colleagues attempted to deal with those issues and provided longitudinal analyses of at least one dimension of mother–child relationships, their security from the child's point of view; however, they have almost completely neglected the question of underlying process. The learning perspective promotes very detailed, molecular analyses of interaction; in contrast, the Bowlby-Ainsworth tradition has focused almost entirely on a global classification system based on patterns of response to separation and reunion and virtually ignores what mothers and children do when they are together (for an exception to this tendency, see Waters and Deane, 1985). In sum, neither perspective alone seems satisfactory. But what are the prospects for a synthesis?

More than a decade ago, Cairns (1972) remarked that "To continue to be useful in developmental analyses, social-learning theory requires major revisions in both methodology and orientation" (p. 73). It seems to us that an updated version of social learning theory would in fact provide a useful framework in which to study the development of human relationships, including the one between mother and child. Such a revised social-learning theory would subsume many of the current concerns of attachment researchers, who, as we have seen, are essentially exploring social learning hypotheses in a "disguised" fashion. Before this synthesis of perspectives can be envisioned, however, increased attention must be paid to three major issues in the study of social learning: (a) the active role of the learner in his or her own development; (b) the ways in which social and developmental factors constrain or enhance the learning that occurs; and (c) the limitations of traditional paradigms for explaining development in natural settings and for testing important social learning hypotheses. We now offer some comments about each of these issues in turn.

The Active Learner

One of the least appealing characteristics of the traditional social-learning approach is its mechanistic portrayal of both mothers and children. The operant perspective, in particular, describes mothers and infants as response-emitting stimulus objects and not as living, thinking, feeling human beings. The picture is one of passive responding to arbitrary contingencies.

This portrait of mother and infant as passive entities, however, is not a necessary component of a social learning perspective on attachment. Some years ago, Harriet Rheingold (1969) characterized the human infant as active, responsive, modifiable, and capable of modifying the behavior of others. In retrospect, that statement seems almost radical, because Rheingold was both stressing the role of learning in the infant's development—its modifiability—and its status as an active organism who was simultaneously modifying the behavior of other people.

What are some implications of this view of the learner as an active organism for social learning theories? One important implication is the fact that organisms select certain things to learn and ignore others. For example, young infants do not reflexively imitate everything they see modeled (Hay & Murray, 1982). To understand what an infant is actually likely to learn about people and about relationships from interacting with its mother, one must take into account the infant's tendency to select from a menu of possible experiences.

Likewise, the mother is selective in what she learns. Recent work on learning has stressed the role of prior knowledge and expertise (e.g., Chi, 1978). Thus, when attempting to trace how the mother's behavior comes to be controlled by the infant's, it is necessary to recognize her status as a competent, knowledgeable, motivated human adult. What she can do, what she knows, and what she cares about are all going to affect what she takes out of the experience of relating to her infant.

Some of the selectivity shown by both infant and mother may derive from the biological constraints on social behavior described by Bowlby's (1969) theory of attachment. Attention to the learner's active role in what is learned thus provides one possibility for synthesis across perspectives. It is important to bear in mind, however, that biology is not the only determinant of the infant's and mother's selection of what to learn.

The Social and Developmental Character of Social Learning

Just as human learners are not passive organisms, so they are not isolated or static ones. Rather, they are social, and they develop over time. One of the more curious things about traditional social-learning theory is that it seems blithely to ignore the special qualities of social life. Furthermore, a developmental perspective is almost entirely absent. As Cairns (1972) has noted:

> Traditional analyses of social learning typically have held ontogenetic factors constant empirically, then ignored them theoretically. The fiction that maturation-paced changes in social interactions are uninteresting, irrelevant, or beyond our comprehension is no longer acceptable. (p. 73)

If the social learning perspective is to survive in any form, it must be forced to be more truly social and more developmental.

This implies that when we are trying to describe and explain what goes on as mother and child become attached, we must recognize the fact that they are engaged in a social enterprise. Each is learning from the other, and their learning is synchronized. We must explore ways in which to describe such mutual learning experiences, beyond a mechanistic analysis of stimulus–response chaining. We must chart what each is deliberately trying to teach the other, as well as what each is picking up incidentally, unconsciously. Affective and cognitive links between the two learners, as well as behavioral ones, must be examined.

Similarly, we must not forget that mother and child are each pursuing a developmental path through time and that learning capacities, as well as motivation to learn, change with age. This is as true for the mother as for the infant. Development does not cease in adulthood, and it is important to view mothers as well as infants as developing organisms.

The Limitations of Traditional Paradigms

One major revision in social learning theory that certainly seems called for, and that has not yet been undertaken, is a reevaluation of the usefulness of the traditional classical conditioning, operant conditioning, and modeling paradigms for explaining how social relationships develop in natural settings. A major assumption has always been that the same general learning principles can be applied to social and nonsocial behavior. For example, Bandura (1969) admonished us that, with respect to imitation, "Unless it can be shown that the vicarious learning of matching behavior is governed by separate independent variables, distinctions proposed in terms of the form of emulated responses are not only gratuitous but breed unnecessary confusion" (p. 219). In other words, if a model's nonsocial actions are likely to be copied, so should his or her social ones.

This assumption continues to hold sway in social learning accounts of the attachment process. The operant theorists, in particular, have asserted that the conditioning processes they believe to be at work in the development of mother–infant attachment are the same as those at work in other types of learning tasks. This is but one other example of the characteristic quest for generality in the social learning perspective.

There is undeniably a certain appeal to this faith in the existence of general learning principles. Unfortunately, a number of empirical studies of early social development have presented some challenges to that view. These studies raise the question of whether social behavior in infancy in fact develops in a way that conforms to traditional learning paradigms.

Consider, for example, an important tenet of the operant theorists' account of attachment formation, namely, the straightforward proposal that the infant's social behavior is reinforced by the mother's contingent reactions. This point is more controversial than it might seem. For example, a classic study providing evidence that young infants' vocalizations can be conditioned with social reinforcement (Rheingold, Gewirtz, & Ross, 1959) has been reinterpreted; when the study was replicated with proper controls for pseudoconditioning effects, it was found that the social stimulation being used to reinforce the infants' vocalizations was actually not serving as a reinforcer but as an unconditioned stimulus that evoked sounds from infants (Bloom & Esposito, 1975). Noncontingent social stimulation was just as effective in getting the infants to coo and babble.

This fact raises important concerns about Gewirtz's (1961, 1969) interpretations of naturally occurring patterns of mother–child interaction. Do such sequences in fact represent stimulus–response chaining? The fact that certain kinds of maternal and infant responses tend to occur around the same time would not prove that mutual conditioning had been established.

Similar evidence also indicates that other learning processes, such as punishment and modeling, do not always operate in natural settings as they do in the laboratory. For example, modeling is not always an effective influence on infants' social behavior. In one study, 12 month olds were less likely to perform a target social action when that act was modeled than when they were simply asked to do it (Hay & Murray, 1982). This finding, taken together with the evidence that adults' noncontingent social behavior gets infants to coo and babble (Bloom & Esposito, 1975), underscores the importance of general processes of *social facilitation* in development. That is, the diverse ways in which human infants and adults are stimulated and transformed by each other's presence, behavior, and expectations are critical events in social development, but these interpersonal influences do not easily reduce to familiar laboratory paradigms.

It thus becomes the task of the social learning theorist to move beyond tradition and attempt to describe the processes that are actually at work when people relate to each other in natural settings. The notion of one person serving as a context for another's activities is at the heart of the matter (Cairns, 1972; Hay, 1985). It remains to be understood, however, exactly how that attainment is made. Cairns's (1977) concepts of interactive processes such as synchrony, escalation, recurrence, and consolidation provide directions to explore. However, these concepts must be much more precisely specified, and they must be expanded to account for cognitive and affective change, as well as behavioral acquisition. It becomes increasingly clear that an adequate theory of social learning cannot be a purely behaviorist one.

CONCLUSIONS

In sum, prospects for a synthesis across theoretical perspectives on the mother–infant relationship now seem bright. Work within the Bowlby-Ainsworth tradition, despite its roots in the theories of psychoanalysis and evolutionary biology, has become increasingly focused on the importance of social influences on the development of attachment. These "disguised" social learning hypotheses require further explication and integration into a coherent account of attachment formation. At the same time, the social learning position itself has largely moved beyond mechanistic behaviorism. The work that we have reviewed in this chapter, undertaken within an explicit social learning perspective and outside it, has uncovered a number of facts about social influences on attachment that may be incorporated into the revised theory we envision. More generally, this review of attachment research underscores the fact that reproduction is a biological process, but motherhood a social one. We need not only to understand how social events influence how mothers and infants become attached initially, but how their continuing relationship is shaped, maintained, and sometimes challenged and destroyed by their social worlds.

REFERENCES

Ainsworth, M. D. S., & Bell, S. M. (1970). Attachment, exploration, and separation: Illustrated by the behavior of one-year-olds in a strange situation. *Child Development, 41,* 49–67.
Ainsworth, M. D. S., & Wittig, B. A. (1969). Attachment and exploratory behavior of one-year-olds in a strange situation. In B. M. Foss (Ed.), *Determinants of infant behaviour* (Vol. 4). London: Metheun.
Bandura, A. (1969). Social learning theory and identificatory processes. In D. A. Goslin (Ed.), *Handbook of socialization theory and research.* Chicago: Rand McNally.
Bell, S. M., & Ainsworth, M. D. S. (1972). Infant crying and maternal responsiveness. *Child Development, 43,* 1171–1190.
Berman, P. (1980). Are women more responsive than men to the young? A review of developmental and situational variables. *Psychological Bulletin, 88,* 668–695.
Bijou, S. W., & Baer, D. M. (1961). *Child development: Vol. 1. A systematic and empirical theory.* New York: Appleton-Century-Crofts.

Bijou, S. W., & Baer, D. M. (1965). *Child development: Vol. 2. Universal stage of infancy.* New York: Appleton-Century-Crofts.

Blatz, W. E. (1966). *Human security: Some reflections.* Toronto: University of Toronto Press.

Bloom, K., & Esposito, A. (1975). Social conditioning and its proper control procedures. *Journal of Experimental Child Psychology, 19,* 209–222.

Bowlby, J. (1958). The nature of the infant's tie to its mother. *International Journal of Psychoanalysis, 39,* 350–373.

Bowlby, J. (1969). *Attachment and loss: Vol. 1. Attachment.* London: Hogarth.

Bretherton, I. (1985). Attachment theory: Retrospect and prospect. In I. Bretherton & E. Waters (Eds.), *Growing points of attachment theory and research. Monographs of the Society for Research in Child Development, 50,* (Serial No. 209).

Cairns, R. B. (1966a). Attachment behavior of mammals. *Psychological Reviews, 73,* 409–426.

Cairns, R. B. (1966b). Development, maintenance, and extinction of social attachment behavior in sheep. *Journal of Comparative and Physiological Psychology, 62,* 298–306.

Cairns, R. B. (1972). Attachment and dependency: A psychobiological and learning synthesis. In J. L. Gewirtz (Ed.), *Attachment and dependency.* Washington, DC: Winston.

Cairns, R. B. (1977). Beyond social attachment: The dynamics of interactional development. In T. Alloway, P. Pliner, & L. Krames (Eds.), *Attachment behavior.* New York: Plenum Press.

Cairns, R. B. (1979). *Social development: The origins and plasticity of interchanges.* San Francisco: Freeman.

Chi, M. T. H. (1978). Knowledge structures and memory development. In R. S. Siegler (Ed.), *Children's thinking: What develops?* Hillsdale. NJ: Lawrence Erlbaum.

Crockenberg, S. B. (1981). Infant irritability, mother responsiveness, and social support influences on the security of mother–infant attachment. *Child Development, 52,* 857–865.

Freud, S. (1938). *An outline of psychoanalysis.* London: Hogarth.

Gewirtz, J. L. (1961). A learning analysis of the effects of normal stimulation, privation, and deprivation on the acquisition of social motivation and attachment. In B. M. Foss (Ed.), *Determinants of infant behaviour.* London: Metheun.

Gewirtz, J. L. (1969). Mechanisms of social learning theory: Some roles of stimulation and behavior in early human development. In D. A. Goslin (Ed.), *Handbook of socialization theory and research.* Chicago: Rand McNally.

Gewirtz, J. L. (1977). Maternal responding and the conditioning of infant crying: Direction of influence within attachment acquisition process. In B. C. Etzel, J. M. LeBlanc, & D. M. Baer (Eds.), *New developments in behavioral research: Theory, methods, and applications.* New York: Wiley.

Gewirtz, J. L., & Boyd, E. F. (1977a). Does maternal responding imply reduced crying? A critique of the 1972 Bell and Ainsworth report. *Child Development, 48,* 1200–1207.

Gewirtz, J. L., & Boyd, E. F. (1977b). Experiments on mother–infant interaction underlying attachment acquisition: The infant conditions the mother. In T. Alloway, P. Pliner, & L. Krames (Eds.), *Attachment behavior.* New York: Plenum Press.

Grossman, K., Grossman, K. E., Spangler, G., Suess, G., & Unzer, L. (1985). Maternal sensitivity and newborns' orientation responses as related to quality of attachment in Northern Germany. In I. Bretherton & E. Waters (Eds.), *Growing points in attachment theory and research. Monographs of the Society for Research in Child Development, 50* (Serial No. 209).

Hay, D. F. (1985). Learning to form relationships in infancy: Parallel attainments with parents and peers. *Developmental Review, 5,* 122–161.

Hay, D. F., & Murray, P. (1982). Giving and requesting: Social facilitation of infants' offers to adults. *Infant Behavior and Development, 5,* 301–310.

Lamb, M. E., Thompson, R. A., Gardner, W. P., & Charnov, E. L. (1985). *Infant–mother attachment: The origins and developmental significance of individual differences in Strange Situation behavior.* Hillsdale, NJ: Lawrence Erlbaum.

Main, M., Kaplan, N., & Cassidy, J. (1985). Security in infancy, childhood, and adulthood: A move to the level of representation. In I. Bretherton & E. Waters (Eds.), *Growing points in attachment theory and research. Monographs of the Society for Research in Child Development, 50* (Serial No. 209).

Main, M., & Weston, D. R. (1981). The quality of the toddler's relationship to mother and to father: Related to conflict and the readiness to establish new relationships. *Child Development, 52,* 932–940.

Miyake, K., Chen, S-J., & Campos, J. J. (1985). Infant temperament, mother's mode of interaction, and attachment in Japan: An interim report. In I. Bretherton & E. Waters (Eds.), *Growing points in attachment theory and research. Monographs of the Society for Research in Child Development, 50* (Serial No. 209).

Nash, A. (1986). *A comparison of infants' social competence with mother and peer.* Paper presented to the American Psychological Association, Washington, DC.

Rajecki, D. W., Lamb, M. E., & Obmascher, P. (1978). Toward a general theory of infantile attachment: A comparative review of aspects of the social bond. *The Behavioral and Brain Sciences, 1,* 417–464.

Rheingold, H. L. (1969). The social and socializing infant. In D. A. Goslin (Ed.), *Handbook of socialization theory and research.* Chicago: Rand McNally.

Rheingold, H. L., Gewirtz, J. L., & Ross, H. W. (1959). Social conditioning of vocalization in the infant. *Journal of Comparative and Physiological Psychology, 52,* 68–73.

Ricks, M. H. (1985). The social transmission of parental behavior: Attachment across generations. In I. Bretherton & E. Waters (Eds.), *Growing points in attachment theory and research. Monographs of the Society for Research in Child Development, 50* (Serial No. 209).

Schaffer, H. R., & Emerson, P. E. (1964). The development of social attachment in infancy. *Monographs of the Society for Research in Child Development, 29* (Serial No. 94).

Schneider-Rosen, K., Braunwald, K. G., Carlson, V., & Cicchetti, D. (1985). Current perspectives in attachment theory: Illustration from the study of maltreated infants. In I. Bretherton & E. Waters (Eds.), *Growing points in attachment theory and research. Monographs of the Society for Research in Child Development, 50* (Serial No. 209).

Sears, R. R. (1951). A theoretical framework for personality and social behavior. *American Psychologist, 6,* 476–483.

Sroufe, L. A. (1985). Attachment classification from the perspective of infant–caregiver relationships and infant temperament. *Child Development, 56,* 1–14.

Stayton, D. J., Ainsworth, M. D. S., & Main, M. (1973). Development of separation behavior in the first year of life: Protest, following, and greeting. *Developmental Psychology, 9,* 213–225.

Thompson, R. A., Lamb, M. E., & Estes, D. (1982). Stability of infant–mother attachment and its relationship to changing life circumstances in an unselected middle-class sample. *Child Development, 53,* 144–148.

Waters, E. (1978). The reliability and stability of individual differences in infant–mother attachment. *Child Development, 54,* 516–520.

Waters, E., & Deane, K. E. (1985). Defining and assessing individual differences in attachment relationships: Q-methodology and the organization of behavior in infancy and early childhood. In I. Bretherton & E. Waters (Eds.), *Growing points in attachment theory and research. Monographs of the Society for Research in Child Development, 50* (Serial No. 209).

Cross-Cultural Perspectives

Part II provides data on the relationship between social, religious, philosophical, and political theories and the realities of women's lives. Each chapter provides some historical background as well as information on contemporary women. Three chapters are too few to reflect the diversity of the faces of motherhood in different nations. Rather, these three chapters illustrate factors that determine social change in ideology and demonstrate how potent a force ideology is for both continuity and change.

We chose these three cultures to demonstrate different forms of social change driven by ideology as well as other factors. In Moslem Morocco, Islam as both religion and cultural mandate constrains change in an emerging nation. In the People's Republic of China, social change has been dramatic and revolutionary following political, ideological, and economic reforms. In the Netherlands, a stable Western industrialized nation, the social change involves a very small group of people who chose an alternative, collective form of childrearing in a society that is individualistic and based on the nuclear family.

MOROCCO

First, Harway and Liss (Chapter 4) show how ideology—in this case the Islamic religion—has been used to explain the slow pace of social change with respect to motherhood in Morocco. These authors illustrate how religion is only one of the many cultural factors in society that affect the lives of women and children and constrain social change.

The authors state that Islam is more than a religion; it is a philosophy that influences law, sexual behavior, and all aspects of family life. Differences in social class profoundly affect women's attitudes and behavior toward their children. Another factor that is of great importance to emerging nations is the conflict between tradition and westernization. Islamic women in Morocco are caught between the old and the new, and many mothers are still living in extreme squalor. Interviews with Moroccan mothers of different social classes portray the diversity of mothers' experiences, all influenced by Moslem religion and culture, but also by different social class experience and exposure to Western culture and technology.

CHINA

Perhaps the most dramatic example of the relation between social change and ideology is the situation in the People's Republic of China. "The Chinese Family: Continuity and Change" (Chapter 5) deals with the dramatic political and social changes that have taken place in China. Hu discusses the solutions that the Chinese have adopted to deal with the problems facing the most heavily populated nation in the world as it attempts to achieve its goal of socialist modernization before the end of this century. Political ideology as well as population considerations changed the position of women in Chinese society and also made small, rather than large, families the cultural norm. Contemporary mothers in China are most likely to have only one child, to work, and to have been taught contemporary doctrine.

Hu's interviews with young mothers indicate that they are indeed living different lives than their mothers did; however, attitudes and beliefs, such as the greater value placed on males, may be harder to change than the actual conditions of life. Even mothers who were most influenced by current realities still retained many beliefs from the previous generation. Thus, in China today, new theory has indeed influenced practice, but it has yet to be completely assimilated into each individual's personal system of beliefs.

THE NETHERLANDS

Whereas the lives of mothers in China and Morocco are vastly different from those of mothers in the United States, the lives of women in Holland and other Western European nations in many ways resemble those of contemporary American women. Like other Western industrialized nations, Holland provides most women with modern medicine, sanitation, education, and housing. Birth control is available and maternal and infant mortality rates are low. Chapter 6 (de Kanter), therefore, is not about the general state of motherhood in Holland.

Rather, de Kanter describes a very small group of feminist women (and some men) who established a unique living arrangment for themselves and their children. For these women, their own theoretical beliefs—rather than factors endemic to their culture—led to their creation of an alternative lifestyle that involved collective childrearing.

De Kanter describes an ideologically based attempt to create a new form of childrearing in the Netherlands. This approach involves a group of unrelated children who live together. However, unlike the children in the kibbutzim in Israel, these children are not cared for by professional child-care workers but by their parents, who take turns at 24-hour stints of child care. This collective approach to childrearing derived from both feminist and socialist beliefs about the family; the parents felt that children need not and, in fact ought not, be reared in the nuclear family setting. Chapter 6 details the theoretical basis and the practical functioning of two such children's collectives and indicates both the satisfaction and the problems resulting from this application of radical theory to parenting practice.

In order to protect their privacy and because of other political beliefs, the parents would not allow their collective to be studied or evaluated. Nonetheless, de Kanter's knowledge about and interviews with members provide an interesting analysis of group childrearing in an environment whose dominant ideology is individualistic and privacy oriented.

CHAPTER 4

Arab Mothers in Morocco
Responsibilities without Rights

MICHELE HARWAY AND MARSHA B. LISS

INTRODUCTION

Morocco has been described as a world of many faces. This comment usually refers to the wide diversity of ethnic groups, geographical terrain, and traditional and westernized customs of the country. However, the expression is even more appropriate as a description of the women of Morocco, who experience widely varying lifestyles as wives and mothers depending on their cultural and economic subgroups. Despite these differences there is an underlying consistency in childrearing practices, which are inextricably interwoven with pure economic factors affecting the family's daily life. Thus, we cannot consider how different groups of mothers in Morocco fulfill their parenting roles without considering how living conditions, health care, literacy, access to education, and sanitation enhance or interfere with their ability to focus on their children.

It will be clear from the descriptions of Moroccan women that follow that most are too busy scraping together a living and providing food and shelter for their children to focus on the finer points of childrearing as in the West. Philosophies of childrearing are not developed; they emerge out of necessity or have been transmitted from one generation to the next. This is reflected in the lack of reference materials on Moroccan mothers. The psychological, sociological, and anthropological literature focuses almost entirely on women and Islam, the role of cultural factors in subrogating women, and the overall economic conditions of the country (Mernissi, 1984; El Saadawi, 1980; Dwyer, 1978; Bowen, 1981; Youssef, 1978; Davis, 1983; Smith, 1980). In this chapter, we extrapolate from the existing literature on Moroccan women and combine those results with interview material to create a portrayal of Moroccan mothers and their situation.

MICHELE HARWAY • California Family Study Center, 5433 Laurel Canyon Boulevard, North Hollywood, California 91607.   MARSHA B. LISS • Department of Psychology, California State University, San Bernardino, California 94207.

ECONOMIC BACKGROUND

Overall Economic Conditions

Morocco is a primarily agricultural nation just a stone's throw from the European continent but in many ways a million kilometers from Europe. Morocco's major industry is that of exporting citrus fruits, olives, grain, and other agricultural products as well as canned sardines. The tourist industry is the other major means of support supplemented by the sale and export of leather goods and other craft articles. Morocco is the leading exporter of phosphate in the world, but this provides only a small fraction of the country's income. Morocco has little industry, with the exception of American or Western-owned plants that produce tires, soap, assemble European automobiles, and manufacture a small portion of industrial products necessary for daily life.

The Moroccan economy cannot provide even the basics for most of its citizens, in part as a result of a costly war (between Morocco and Mauritania over a part of the Sahara), which has diverted funds that might otherwise provide relief for Moroccan social programs. Mothers struggle to survive on a day-to-day basis within the context of the large national economic hardship. Because there are few organized efforts at economic development, the individual mother must herself provide the impetus for any change in status.

One of the ways diversity is seen is the contrast between rural and urban life. Economic factors play an important role in creating the differences in the standard of living of rural and urban women. This is further compounded by the growing westernization of the cities and the continuing adherence to traditional mores in the rural areas. Daily life in Morocco is much more rudimentary than a Westerner can imagine, especially in the countryside where many Moroccans live in haystacks or shacks constructed of corrugated metal and sometimes cardboard. Most homes, even fairly elaborate ones in some cities, have no running water and women or children must sometimes walk as much as 13 miles each day to fetch water, which they carry back in reusable 5-liter plastic bottles. Moroccan cities tend to be relatively modern. The roads are good, a legacy from the French protectorate, and allow good access to all parts of the country. One result of this has been large amounts of migration to the cities from the rural areas and the sprouting up in the cities of "Bidonvilles"—shanty towns—with a consequent increase in crime and increased poverty and malnutrition for the inhabitants.

Whereas country women are secluded at home, city women tend to be somewhat more emancipated than rural women regardless of economic level. It is rare for a city woman to be a prisoner at home. However, many city women still wear the djellaba—a shapeless neutral colored robe with a hood that covers the woman from head to toe—and usually the veil. Whereas the veil used to cover most of the woman's face, as of the late 1960s it has dropped from above the nose to just below the nose and in some cases is dispensed with altogether. The more westernized young women in Casablanca and Rabat may wear western dress.

Population Parameters

The literacy rate is low, especially for women (only 6% of females over 15 are literate), which is partially due to a shortage of schools and partially due to the belief that women should not be educated. Thus we find only 36% of school-aged girls in primary school, compared with 72% in Indonesia, 83% in Tunisia (International Labor Organization, 1973). Among the elite, many of the children are educated in France, especially at the postsecondary level. A number of Centres d'Education Feminine have sprouted up throughout Morocco, but their role has been restricted to teaching girls skills to be practiced within the home— embroidery, baking, and the like. The assumption, of course, is that young women will be getting married early and will need only these kinds of skills.

Morocco's population is spiraling. Women get married young to husbands selected by their parents and then they have many babies. Thus in 1969, 54% of girls 15 to 19 were already married (in contrast to 19% in Tunisia; 1969 U.N. Demographic Yearbook). The mean number of births per woman was 5.3 from 1980 to 1985 (U.N. Department of Economic and Social Affairs, 1986). Unless the young woman's work is required for the survival of the family, she will of course not participate in the labor force. Since only 15% of the economically active labor force was female in 1980 (the number has probably risen somewhat but not much since), working out of the home is not an option for very many women (U.N. African Statistics Yearbook, 1980). If a woman's income is necessary for survival, she may work as a domestic (if she is lucky), perhaps do craft work, or she may sell the crops she has grown at the market, gather twigs and branches for firewood, and carry huge loads on her back for several miles. She may also be responsible for watering the animals, another job that requires a hefty 4 to 5 mile hike. Poor women tend to work very hard, whereas it is not uncommon to find city men lolling about in the cafes in front of an interminable glass of mint tea.

As women's economic participation in the work force becomes more of a necessity, a large number of young women are finding themselves without the necessary skills to earn a living. Embroidery and other crafts may sell well to tourists, but the price they bring is very low and competition for this meager income is very great. A recent U.S. Agency for International Development (USAID) funded project had as its objective the training of young women in nontraditional fields: typewriter repair, canning of agricultural products, luxury leather work, and child care. However, it is unlikely that the projects will be maintained once U.S. funding is terminated.

SOCIAL CIRCUMSTANCES

As just indicated, the economic and cultural factors create diverse social groups. In the sections that follow, we describe the diverse social circumstances in which Moroccan women find themselves and illustrate how these different lifestyles affect motherhood. Adapting Maher's (1978) categorizations, we describe the elite, the urban bourgeoisie, the working class, the country women, and the factory workers. We will demonstrate that the woman's social circumstances dictate not only how she lives but also proscribe her cultural behaviors within the family circle.

The Elite

The elite in Morocco comprise a small portion of the population but control most of the wealth:

> Mrs. Hasnoui is a member of the elite. Her husband is a highly respected doctor. She is educated, fluent in French and has at times in her life been involved in charity benefits. She has five children, all but the youngest of whom are in universities and secondary schools in France. She has at times fallen into periods of deep depression accompanied by tears, in discussing the emptiness of her home without the children. She makes frequent, lengthy (and very expensive by American standards) telephone calls to France. At first meeting, since she is the more verbal of the couple, it appears that she is the dominant force in the home. However, it soon becomes clear that she addresses her husband with deepest respect referring to him as Sidi (Excellency) Hasnoui, both in talking to him as well as about him. It is he who has decreed that the children must be educated in France and that the boy must at least obtain a college degree. Mrs. Hasnoui has a staff of three maids who do most of the chores in the home including many of the less rewarding aspects of motherhood.

The elite mother as typified by Mrs. Hasnoui leads a life free from economic worries and daily chores or decision-making. Moreover, being a mother involves many of the privileges—such as belonging to the husband's family and attaining status by virtue of having produced children—but brings with it few of the obligations. Among the rewards that elite women have in raising children is the fact that much of their sense of self is developed in conjunction with the achievements of their children. When the children grow up, the mother's status amplifies as she becomes the matron of the family, and as the offspring, particularly the sons, marry and produce children of their own, her status peaks and she becomes the reigning monarch of her "queendom" (Mernissi, 1975a).

Because mothers in this group have no worries about day-to-day economic problems they can devote more time to their children. However, that they have the time to devote does not necessarily assure that they spend the time in direct contact with the child. More than likely, a maid is hired to take care of major childrearing chores and the mother may restrict her involvement with her child to fondling, kissing, and generally permissive acquiescence to his or her every wish. Mothers in this group, as in others, rarely discipline their children; in fact, interviewed men indicated that Moroccan women "love their children too much."

Discipline is usually the father's job, but the overloving mother intercedes to try to protect her offspring—oftentimes running the risk of personally incurring the father's wrath. Whereas the mother may decide what the child is to wear or eat, important decisions regarding the child's future are the father's prerogative. This decision may include what type of schooling to give the child, for how long, and who goes to school. Members of the elite are often educated, having usually completed a secondary education; many of them finished their schooling abroad, usually in France.

A foreign education, however, does not necessarily mean for girls, though it may. This education has brought with it a tendency to adopt western mores such as dress and international cosmopolitan values. Although many of the girls from westernized families obtain schooling, many young Moroccan women from well-to-do traditional families never leave their homes with the exception of their wedding day. This is further evidenced by Njoku's (1980) observation "where strict seclusion of women is practiced the Western type of education at times may be impossible" (p. 11).

Another example of the split within this social stratum involves childbirth. The westernized elite woman will retain a western-trained obstetrician to treat her during her pregnancy and confinement and is likely to give birth in a private clinic. If she nurses her baby, she will only do so within a private setting. In contrast, the traditional elite woman may call upon a traditional midwife (the Kablate) to birth her child at home; the father will be informed about the baby after the birth. Because the Koran advocates breast feeding for 2 years, the traditional woman still will nurse her baby for a long period of time (232rd verse of the Koran, as translated by Ali, 1964).

The Urban Bourgeoisie

The urban bourgeoisie represents a small but somewhat larger percentage of the Moroccan population. Like the elite, most of these families represent inherited established wealth and status and live primarily in the old towns such as Rabat, Fez, and Meknes:

> Hassan and his bride, Anissa, are an urban bourgeoisie couple. Hassan, age 28, is an educated young man from a good home. His parents made a good match for him from among the upper bourgeoisie in Meknes. Even though Anissa (18) frequently comes to visit his family in Tangier (where upon arrival she is secluded from the outside) the young couple is forced to wait to live as husband and wife until the religious ceremony can be performed. They have already been married in a legal civil ceremony. Only after Hassan pays his bride's parents the bridewealth will they be able to consummate the marriage. Of course, the fact that he is young and only recently employed has delayed his ability to amass enough funds for the bridewealth.

In fact, Anissa is not typical of the urban bourgeoisie, in that her marriage has been arranged with a young man. Other young girls are not so lucky and may be married off to a much older man (sometimes in their 60s). Once married, the young wife goes to live with her husband's family and she is often kept secluded until she has produced many children. Her children serve to cement her identification and allegiance to her husband's group. The children are in a sense payments conferring status upon a woman who otherwise would have none of her own.

Seclusion in this social stratum is facilitated by the wealth of the group. Money in part serves to employ servants who do the tasks in the outside world that the woman's seclusion prevents her from doing. When necessary, the outside world (e.g., seamstress, doctor) comes to her just like to an imprisoned princess. The babies are delivered at home by doctors or midwives and are usually nursed by the mother until the next child is born. Because nursing is valued so highly in this group, a nursing woman may have an abortion if she discovers she is pregnant (Mernissi, 1975b). Among the more westernized within this group, bottle feeding may have been adopted as evidence of modern ways. However, there has been much concern by health organizations (World Health Organization, 1977) about the misuse of prepared infant formulas, often thought to be a boon in the industrialized world. The lack of education of many Third-World mothers and sanitary conditions in their countries has led to abuses, such as overdilution and the use of unsterilized water, in the preparation of these formulas.

The men in this group, more than any other, exercise strict control over the women with the belief that this is necessary in order to ensure the survival of the family. In describing the urban bourgeoisie, Lahlou (1968) says, "Before being himself, the individual belongs to his family. This is even truer of women" (p. 422). This is accomplished by strict seclusion of women—to prevent them from finding their own husbands and from being corrupted by western customs unmarried girls are not allowed to leave the house. Shopping and all forms of interaction with the outside world are conducted by the men in the family or by servants. It is not surprising that all discipline and decision-making about the children's future and present activities are carried out by the father.

Seclusion starts at puberty. Young girls may attend school and go outside the house for play and chores along with a sibling or supervisor. Those young girls who are sent to school often go to Koranic schools lest the Western schools teach them disrespect for parents. The seclusion of women serves the practical purposes mentioned above but also is considered the high-status "thing to do," much as buying furs or jewels is in some western circles. If the woman must venture into the outside world, she wears the djellaba and veil. Some women will wear Western clothes underneath their djellabas. Because of this seclusion, a woman's time is spent primarily with her children and later her grandchildren.

The Working Class

The working class consists of the state-employed "fonctionnaires." The men may be policemen, customs inspectors, teachers, and comprise a substantial portion of the population. This group is not as wealthy as the ones we have already described; their financial situation is tight but they enjoy more than a subsistence standard of living. Essentially, they comprise a lower middle class that bears no resemblance in economic terms to definitions of middle class in most western cultures:

> Mr. Laayoune and his wife are members of the working class. Mr. Laayoune is educated, Westernized and seemingly very modern. In fact, he is employed as an accounting clerk in a leading Western Embassy and fits in very well with the other Western

employees. He is invited to and often attends Embassy functions. Mr. Laayoune also plays tennis and attends tournaments; Mrs. Laayoune does not accompany him. In spite of his extended professional and social contacts with Westerners Mr. Laayoune epitomizes the working class in his attitude toward his wife and family. While at work and in social situations he deals in an egalitarian way with both men and women, he makes a sharp dichotomy between his treatment of women out of the home and within the home. Mrs. Laayoune is strictly secluded. Mr. Laayoune speaks often and enthusiastically about his children but would never think of talking about his wife. One might think she does not exist. Mrs. Laayoune's life is centered totally on the home. Mrs. Laayoune does not have a maid. She has no input in decision making beyond the children's daily hygiene and caretaking needs.

The men in this group try to imitate the urban bourgeoisie in their customs and seem to adopt a upwardly mobile social status in the outside world. However, in their private lives they differ dramatically from the urban bourgeoisie. It is among this group that the fiercest expression of male supremacy is found. Women, like Mrs. Laayoune, are strictly secluded. Because families in this group are often unable to afford servants, a foster child or poor female relative may serve as an indentured servant to do the tasks that require contact with the outside world. Unlike the elite and the urban bourgeoisie, not only is the man's word final regarding the children's future lives, the woman has no input into decision-making whatsoever. She is informed when necessary.

The women tend not to be educated beyond a rudimentary level with the exception of the domestic skills that are taught at home. As they are secluded, they receive little prenatal care; their babies are delivered at large public maternity hospitals or by traditional midwives. The women nurse until the next child is born. All forms of discipline are the father's responsibility; the mothers are expected to teach the children to respect their father and to be obedient. The women know little of modern western customs since they receive all their education or experience from their mothers. This is a social group whose styles of childrearing and family interactions have been passed down from mother to daughter. The paucity of contact with the outside world makes it difficult to learn more about them; they are not seen, nor heard from in public.

The Country Women

Individuals in this category comprise the largest proportion of Moroccan citizens. Just under 60% of Moroccan women fit into this category (Population Reference Bureau, 1982). Country dwellers are primarily agricultural workers; sometimes they farm theor own land but most often they work the land of others and in many cases they struggle to maintain a subsistence standard of living:

> Fatna and her children till a small piece of land adjoining the straw hut they call home. Everyday they climb up to the top of the small mountain adjacent to their home and gather logs and twigs. Fatna then gathers them into a large bundle which she carries down the mountain on her back to sell in the village. Although she is only 38, she looks closer to 70 and is permanently bent into a stooped position from years of carrying the heavy loads.

Jamilia is also a country woman. She too has a small plot of land and also raises eight chickens. Twice a week, on market days, she walks 6 miles to the nearest town and displays her wares: usually 2 dozen eggs, 2 or 3 bunches of seasonal vegetables and a dozen potatoes. Sometimes she also has herbs for sale. Jamila is 20 years old, and has 3 children. She was abandoned by her husband 2 years ago and is raising the children alone. While Jamila would like to provide an education for her children, at this time she is totally dependent on the labor they provide; she also cannot afford to buy them clothing and school supplies so that they can attend the already overcrowded one-room schoolhouse.

Fatna and Jamila are representative of this group of women—struggling, married young, several children and often deserted by their husbands. In contrast, it is exceedingly rare in the urban bourgeoisie and elite for a husband and father to desert his family. Men in this group are not committed to their homes, yet when they are with their families they expect respect and service from their wives.

It is rare for country children to receive an education, although in recent years a number of programs have begun to draw from this population. Despite the adverse circumstances of their lives, the women remain faithful to their religion and when they do send their children to school it is likely to be to a Koranic school (where they are trained in the memorization of the Koran).

From a very young age (6 to 7 years), children are required to work and help the family financially. In contrast to poor city women, these country women are somewhat better able to meet the nutritional needs of their children since they can use the fresh farm products they produce; however, they have less access to health care and sanitation. The women are assisted in childbirth by a midwife or a female relative. Breast feeding their infants is a given in this group.

Some mothers think there is a way out of this subsistence standard for their children. The route is through migration to the cities. The young boy or girl (perhaps as young as eight) may be sent to live with relatives or former neighbors who had migrated earlier. Once there the young child is put to work as an indentured servant/apprentice to a craftsperson, as a servant in the home (maid or gardener depending on the child's sex), or in a factory. These factories usually produce crafts for sale to tourists. The children work sometimes as much as 10 to 12 hours for the equivalent of $2 a day.

Tourists are often amazed at the complex designs and high quality of the work but their western senses are offended by the poor conditions under which such children labor. Typical is the rug factory just outside Rabat. Sixteen youngsters work from 8 a.m. to 8 p.m. with few breaks. There is no time for free play or recess breaks, let alone for education. Although this may appear to be a bleak situation, their mothers still regard it as a step up from the total poverty of their homes. In some ways they are correct—the children do get meals and shelter. The children who work as servants may have a better or worse situation depending on the family for whom they work.

In spite of their moves to the city, these migrants retain their ties to their original villages and families. The children return for feasts, family milestone events (births, marriages), and to select a mate. They in turn might be next in line to bring a village child to the city to work as a servant for their own employers:

> Aisha was brought to Casablanca as a girl of 12 by a very distant relative who worked as a cook for a wealthy European family. She was employed as a maid for the same family. She retained her village ties, returning to see her family. When the family she worked for needed a washerwoman, it was Aisha's turn to find the new employee from her village. While feeling sad about the separation from her daughter, Aisha's mother felt satisfied that at least one of her children was living in the city, being fed, being clothed and housed. Aisha's mother regrets that she could not find more positions for her children. While she misses Aisha and the labor at home Aisha would have provided, she feels secure and satisfied about her daughter's future.

The move from the village to the city presents the child with a great deal of culture shock. The number of people, the modern surroundings, and the seemingly emancipated life-style combined with the child's loneliness increase the sense of vulnerability. As a result, these children are the easy prey of unscrupulous individuals who exploit their labors and their lives. As the young girl enters puberty this may mean early seduction by a man promising marriage but delivering nothing. The girl then has no options—she cannot go home to the village, she is no longer marriageable, and if she should become pregnant she loses her value as a worker. Her mother's dreams for her become shattered.

The Factory Workers

The majority of factory workers are women. Factory work is usually the last resort of these women who are also heads of households:

> Saadia works in one of the large sardine canning factories in Agadir. When the boats come in she and the other workers must be there and cannot leave until there are no more sardines to can. This may mean paid work from one hour to 100 hours at a stretch. She is 25 and has five children ranging from 2 to 8 years; her husband, Mohammed, abandoned them before the youngest was born. When she is at work, the children are left alone. There are no day care facilities and no family members to supervise. The older children usually spend their time playing in the streets, while the babies cry without getting any relief. When she returns from a long stretch, Saadia is too tired to care for the children; she leaves them some food and hopes that somehow they will get out of this cycle.

The pay in the factories is poor, the working and living conditions are terrible. Yet women like Saadia have no viable alternatives. Once they have been abandoned by their husbands, they are abandoned by the rest of their families for the shame they have brought; they have no system of support and no one will empathize. Thus, the abandoned woman cannot rely on the extended family available to other poor women. Had she been widowed, "the man's immediate relatives assume the guardianship," comfort her and take her back home (Njoku, 1980, p. 24). The problem of the children's situation has become so acute in Agadir that Moroccan governmental agencies in cooperation with USAID have set up child-care training programs to provide day-care workers for these children (Tyzka, personal communication). The results of these programs are still to be seen.

Other women also seek out factory work, but do so as a last resort. These women are the wives of sick, old, or unemployed husbands. For example, 50% of the women living in a bidonville (slum) of Casablanca fall in this category (Forget, 1964). Because all these women live in the city, their sanitary, health, and nutritional status resembles that of the other city women. Their lack of education does not allow them to seek more lucrative jobs or to pursue more satisfying life-styles. They can work as domestics if they have the right connection or they can become "free women" (prostitutes), which may not seem to many an acceptable choice. Whichever way they choose, they will have little or no time or energy to supervise or interact with their children or to think about how to plan for their children's lives or what style of childrearing they want to practice.

Some women, in spite of the odds against them, do manage to make a better future for their children. They are, however, exceptions and represent only a small fraction of the number of poor and oppressed women and mothers:

> Amina, 23, is typical of this exceptional group. She was abandoned by her husband shortly before her son was born. While completely illiterate and unsophisticated, she learned one lesson very early from seeing the families around her and hearing stories about the families for whom her sisters work: She who pushes and persists may pull herself and her family out of a bleak situation. Her most impressive success was her efforts to secure an education for her five-year-old son. She has managed to enroll him in an exclusive preschool attended predominantly by westernized wealthy children. Through sheer persistence, daily visits to the school and contact with a charitable organization which funds scholarships for needy children, she has managed to obtain one of the rare scholarships available. This is no ordinary accomplishment, especially since Moroccans, especially women, are more likely to give in to authority than to see their goals come to fruition. Her son is now on his way out of this cycle of poverty with a chance to a better job than those of the other neighborhood children. Amina's future, as a result, is also less bleak as her child will be in a better position to provide for her future in years to come.

It is unclear how women like Amina become motivated to change their lives in these directions and to put all their efforts into their children's lives. They stand in stark contrast to most Moroccan mothers who are either not allowed to make future planning decisions (the elite, the urban bourgeoisie, and the working class) or are to weary to push and plan (the country women and the factory workers).

THE ROLE OF RELIGION

The Roles of Women and Men

One of the factors that may explain why it is so difficult for Moroccan mothers to make decisions about the future or be assertive on the part of their children is the impact of the Muslim religion. The teachings of Islam are not only a religion, but they are embedded in the very laws of the society, affecting notions of family and of property and describing how to deal with people who deviate from the mainstream. The Koran, which legislates women's status, is seen as the literal word of God revealed by the prophet Mohammed and is incorporated into the laws of the land. Thus, it is because the Koran legitimizes multiple wives that it is legal to have up to three wives in Morocco—but only if the husband is able to support all three. Women's dress and all aspects of behavior are described by the Koran and thus pass into the laws of the society. At the time the Koran was written, the status of women it prescribed was a great improvement over theirs (Beck & Keddie, 1978). Thus, the Koran and the Moslem religion by themselves cannot be held responsible for the lowly status of women in Moslem countries. It is the case, though, that change has come about much more slowly in Moslem countries, in all areas, but especially with regard to the status of women, and this it seems can be related at least indirectly to the role of the religion in these countries.

The Moslem religion also contains a multitude of prescriptions (translated into civil law) regulating the interactions between the sexes, including but not limited to the rights and duties of marital partners, sexual interactions, and the legal status of the partners. More specifically, Islam prescribes the role of the mother vis-à-vis her children and her spouse.

In order to understand the role of the mother in Morocco, it is first necessary to understand how she has traditionally been viewed in her sexual role. Islam views women as intensely sexual beings whose very sexuality makes for the need to control their sexual behavior (in order to control procreation):

> Women have very great sexual desires and that is why a man is always necessary to keep them from leading men astray. Why else call women "hbel shitan" (the Rope of Satan)? That is why women must be cloaked when in public, live in houses with small windows placed so that others cannot see in, and be married off before they can give their fathers any trouble. The saying is appropriate: "A woman by herself is like a Turkish bath without water" implies that because she is always hot and without a man she has no way to slake the fire. (quoted in Rosen, 1978, p. 568)

Thus, virginity at marriage is one of the most important Moslem traditions that affect the young woman. Proof of virginity is required, with certain divorce or perhaps death as a consequence if a nonvirgin is discovered in the marriage bed:

> Latifa, a young Moroccan student of humble background (her father works a small plot of land in Southern Morocco near the desert) is typical of the young women who are educated, somewhat Westernized, and yet very much mindful of tradition. Latifa is very beautiful and behaves seductively to men and women alike. She has a boyfriend and she can be seen in town walking arm-in-arm with him and necking in the quadrangle of her university. She and another female student were once discovered in the beds of two male students in the men's dormitory. The men were expelled, the women's scholarships cut back. Latifa is obviously sexually active and does not hide the fact. However, she notes: "I intend to be a virgin when I get married. I have to be, otherwise my family will kill me (not a euphemism, but meant literally)." When asked how she can be a virgin when she has obviously already engaged in intercourse, her eyes twinkle and she says: "There are ways."

Virginity is so important that a new phenomenon has developed since the late 1960s. This phenomenon involves the creation of an artificial virginity, in which minute stitches are taken in the remains of the ruptured hymen for the purposes of making it whole again. Such a medical procedure is quite expensive, costing between 500 and 1000 dirhams (compared with the average yearly expenditure for an agricultural family of 565 dirhams, Mernissi, 1979), attesting to the importance to the young women of recreating virginity. Within marriage, women are required to be sexually available to their husbands on demand, to be faithful to the men even when the latter avail themselves of other sexual partners, and to be ever wary of repudiation (instant divorce, which can happen for cause or without by the husband repeating three times: "I repudiate thee").

The Importance of Motherhood

One ground for divorce or repudiation is the failure of the woman to "procreate [which is] the function of women" (Mikhail, 1979, p. 118):

> Soumaya, 26, is a sad example. She comes from an urban bourgeoisie home. She was university educated and met her husband, Brahim, while a student. They are both very westernized, are young and attractive, hold good jobs in the city, and travel to France frequently. They were married 4 years ago and Soumaya has had 6 miscarriages. Frequent visits to private doctors both in Morocco and France and even exploratory surgery have not helped the situation. Soumaya cries every night and has been threatened by Brahim on multiple occasions. Despite her western successes, she is treated with contempt and seen as a failure by both her husband and his family. Even though Brahim fully understands that her problems are medical and beyond her control, he has been under pressure from his family, and has threatened repudiation if an offspring is not forthcoming within the next year.

Soumaya's situation is reminiscent of the well-publicized repudiation of Soraya by the Shah of Iran over 25 years ago because of her inability to produce an heir. Similarly, the Moroccan folklore is full of tales of women "that indicate the repudiation of a sterile woman to be replaced by one hopefully fertile" (Mikhail, 1979, p. 119). So strong is the need for the Moroccan woman to become a mother!

Being barren has other consequences beyond possible repudiation. Not only do children serve as a protection against repudiation, they are, as we have seen earlier, a source of labor and income for the family. But further, children also confer special status on the Moroccan woman. For many Moroccan women, the first time they have control over any aspect of their lives is when their children are born. Thus, woe to the woman who remains barren!

The Role of the Mother

Bouhdiba (1975), in describing the mother's role in her family refers to "The 'Kingdom' [sic] of the Mother." Because of her lack of power and control in other areas of her life, when her children are born, the Moslem mother focuses all of her attention, emotions, and love on her children, becoming at times overly possessive and affectionate, other times virtually abusive. Having children represents a change in status for a woman, especially if she is lucky enough to produce a male child. Not only does the woman finally have an arena in which to exert control—in the raising of her children—but her children represent security for her old age, protection against repudiation in her marriage, useful allies against the father, and sometimes her only contact with the outside world.

Not only is the mother's life enhanced by her bearing offspring, but the relationship between mother and child is special in the Moslem family because of the masterful position of the father in the family. The father is both his wife's lord and master, and he is also seen as a colossus and a powerful being by the children. His word is law and he often behaves autocratically. Just as women are devalued, so are children. Offspring are not valued by the father for their being but only for what they will become. Children are virtually ignored by the father, except for discipline, and the upbringing of the very young is left entirely to the mother. The mother is often seen as a harbor from the father's rage. The result is that an alliance is formed between mother and children to secretly defy the father. In disputes between father and children, the mother often serves as mediator. Thus, the mother (but not the woman) is a venerated individual—venerated by men for having produced heirs and by their children for having loved them.

Abdellah, a student commenting on why it is so difficult to control the numbers of births in Morocco, indicated that as long as children are seen as Morocco's social security system, the birth rate will remain high. This attitude is also reported by Sukkary/Stolba and Mossavar-Rahmani (1982) who note that:

> Throughout the Near East children are valued for a host of reasons—infant morbidity, social security in old age as well as a genuine love for 'the little ones.' (p. 53)

Bouhdiba (1975) concurs that one of the benefits to a woman of having numerous children is that they provide a stabilizing factor in her current life and a protection for the future.

Beck and Keddie (1978) in the introduction to their book argue that it is not Islam *per se* that is responsible for the low status of women in most of the Moslem countries (since many of those repressive customs preceded the birth of Islam in those countries). They note, however, that Moslem countries have been slower than others to change. They ask: "Why has Islamic society been more conservative in its maintenance of the old laws and traditions?" To attempt an answer to Keddie's question, let us examine again what Bouhdiba (1975) had to say about the role of the mother in Islamic society and her ties to her children. In Moslem countries, although the woman is devalued in just about every way, she retains her power in one crucial area: she is seen as the liberator of life, as the key to procreation. And so a cult of the mother has arisen in Islamic society and Bouhdiba asserts that it is the key to understanding the personality of the Islamic society:

> It is normal that robbed of so many joys, suffering such a painful life condition,
> working under such miseries, the woman focusses on her children all of her affec-
> tion. . . . The relationship between mother and child is transformed into a long term
> psychological unity. . . . The umbilical cord is maintained for a long time. (p. 262,
> translated from the original French)

This unity and tie is illustrated in Boudejdra's (1970) novel *La Repudiation*, where
the author portrays "the suffocating motherly love."

As we have seen, the mother becomes a central figure of the family although she herself never makes any pivotal decisions—she takes on the form of
the benign and impotent figurehead.

THE CONFLICT WITH WESTERNIZATION

The role of the Moroccan mother is changing, as indeed much of Moroccan
society has been changing in the 1980s as a result of the conflict between the
increasing westernization of the country and the traditional values. These mothers are torn between what their history and tradition demand of them and the
modern mores and customs brought in by the western colonizers along with
technological advances and machinery. Most of Morocco was under French
protectorate status. The French brought with them modernization on a technological level, education, "advanced" notions of sanitation but also values,
lifestyles, and expectations that were uniquely Western. The conflict experienced by Moroccan mothers as a result is apparent on the surface in employment and aspects of daily life, but in addition causes a deep emotional
confusion that may be the most critical issue facing mothers and their futures.

Let us return to some of the women we have described earlier. Mrs.
Hasnoui is an example of a woman torn between traditional values of submission and a desire to contribute to her society and her children by working within
her chosen field of teaching. She has often been called upon to translate business
conversations and correspondence of her husband but still has no input in
decisions. Even though the children are being educated in France, it is her
responsibility to see that they are indoctrinated in the customs and do not
deviate from them. In spite of the desire to educate the children, she and her
husband may still select their children's mates.

Khadija is a college professor, educated in France and from an urban bourgeoisie family. Her cultural conflict is greater than most. She is in her 20s,
attractive, and very lonely. Unfortunately, even the educated professional men
want their wives to be traditional in values and submissive, which at this point is
no longer the way Khadija sees herself. Her last relationship with a colleague
ended when he chose to marry a young uneducated girl from his village. Khadija is worried that she will not be able to be a mother and be a part of her society
and culture. Most of the other women in her neighborhood and of her age
cohort are married with many children and do not understand her problems.
Khadija has considered moving to France to settle but does not want to be
permanently separated from her family and be an outcast. She has committed

herself to her students, her surrogate children, and helps them with their decisions about their own lives. Ideally, Khadija would herself like to explore options about family life—she would like to marry and have children but at this point that appears unlikely.

Zohra, a woman in her mid-30s with two teenage children, contrasted her own experiences with those of her mother. She first reported that she was one of 14 children. Her own mother had had 10 of those children, and died at a very young age (24) leaving Zohra an orphan at age 3. Shortly after his wife's death, her father remarried an even younger woman (13), who gave him four additional children before he passed away at 56. Thus most of Zohra's experience with a mother figure was with her stepmother who at age 13 not only had to assume responsibility for raising her own children but also the ten that had been brought into the world before her marriage to Zhora's father. As a stepmother, she was unusual; she was very loving, allowed her stepchildren to stay in contact with their mother's family, did not beat them more than her own children, and taught the girls all of the social graces expected of them. She supervised the girls; the boys were supervised in most of their education and upbringing by the father.

As an adult, Zohra now represents the westernized emancipated group of Morocco. When asked how her life as a mother was different from that of her own mother she said, "One very large difference, of course, is that I work outside the home." While working women still represent a fairly narrow slice of the Moroccan female population, this lifestyle is becoming more and more of a trend in the large cities such as Casablanca and Rabat. As more and more Moroccan women begin to work outside the home, more and more children are being brought up by maids. Indeed, the Moroccan working woman usually has a maid, either to do the more demanding of the household chores and/or to take care of the children. This is true whether the working woman comes from the elite or from the working class, working as a secretary or teacher or hairdresser. However, when asked about values and childrearing practices, Zohra could not distinguish between hers, her mother's or her maid's—they all blended.

A recent study by Filal and Benabdenbi (1983, 1984) consisted of interviews with 50 Moroccan working couples. The researchers examined the changes in the daily lives of these working mothers and found that while all had domestics, the mother's life and her use of leisure time had not changed dramatically. The mother most often finds all of her leisure nonworking time occupied in the preparation of meals, food shopping, and the completion of various household chores. Rarely does the woman use the time to take care of her own needs. The mother has to satisfy herself with the knowledge that by making concessions to others, she is maintaining the servile role of woman prescribed by the Koran— humility and submission. Using leisure time for family pursuits rather than to satisfy her own needs is a way for the woman to continue the tradition in nontraditional ways.

The amount of time left for the couple is never mentioned. When the children are very young, diapers and bottles are the woman's responsibility. When a child is older, it is the father who begins to take prime responsibility for a child's homework; however, westernized women are increasingly involved in supervision of their children's work to ensure that it is done properly and will bring the father satisfaction.

We must remember that these Westernized women represent only a small proportion of Moroccan mothers; they are found in the elite, the urban bourgeoisie, and sometimes in the working class. Change has not yet come for the country women and the factory workers. However, as their children emigrate to the city or receive public education, they begin to bring home the cultural conflict brought on by exposure to Western mores. This in turn leads generally to intense family conflict and specifically to questions about tradition, customs, and the fundamental beliefs of the social strata.

Conclusions

When one of the authors taught Developmental Psychology to university students in Morocco, she was often struck by the students' reactions. She was surprised to find that students had a great deal of difficulty accepting information about developmental sequences and changes or about parenting. The typical reaction was "That doesn't happen here." However, when challenged to describe what did apply, the Moroccan students were unable to describe or define childhood or parenthood. This all shows how little Moroccans, even educated Moroccans, think about these processes—it just happens as it has for generations. Likewise, in Crapanzano's (1980) book *Tuhami: Portrait of a Moroccan*, the interviewer repeatedly asked Tuhami for recollections about his childhood—Tuhami could not recall much about how his parents interacted with him, his circumcision, or the birth of his siblings.

As we indicated earlier, most of the literature (Bowen, 1981; Dwyer, 1978; El Saadawi, 1980; Beck & Keddie, 1978; Mikhail, 1979; Mernissi, 1984; Bouhdiba, 1975; Sukkary/Stolba & Mossavar-Rahmani, 1982; Davis, 1983, 1988; Smith, 1980; Youssef, 1978) on women in Morocco has focused on economic changes, legal status, or women vis-à-vis the religion itself. The lack of literature on mothers may be attributed to its status as a taboo subject to explore, one that is so very basic to the fiber of the society that it cannot yet be discussed or differentiated. As the changes the literature on women so widely addresses come about, they will inevitably infiltrate the family environment making motherhood and childrearing more than assumptions, givens of life, and taboo subjects and thereby more open to flexibility and growth.

References

Beck, L., & Keddie, N. (1978). *Women in the Muslim world.* Cambridge, England: Cambridge University Press.
Boudejdra, R. (1970). *La Repudiation.* Paris: DeNoel.
Bouhdiba, A. (1975). *La Sexualite en Islam.* Paris: Quadrige Presses Universitaires de France.

Bowen, D. L. (1981). *Contemporary Moslem religious attitudes towards family planning in Morocco.* Unpublished doctoral dissertation, University of Chicago.

Crapanzano, V. (1980). *Tuhami: Portrait of a Moroccan.* Chicago: University of Chicago Press.

Davis, S. S. (1983). *Patience and power: Women's lives in a Moroccan village.* Cambridge: Schenkman.

Davis, S. S. (1988). Factors influencing modern and traditional health care choices in rural Morocco: Convenience and courtesy. In C. Zeichner (Ed.), *Modern and traditional health care in developing societies: Conflict and cooperation.* Lanham, MD: University Press of America.

Dwyer, D. H. (1978). *Images and self-images: Male and female in Morocco.* New York: Columbia University Press.

El Saadawi, N. (1980). *The hidden face of Eve: Women in the Arab world.* Boston: Beacon Press.

Filal, S., & Benabdenbi, F. (1983, Dec.–Jan.). Les couples Marocains et le travail. *Lamalif, 142,* 50.

Filal, S., & Benabdenbi, F. (1984, October). *La dynamique du changement dans le role des sexes dans la famille et le travil.* Paper presented at meetings of the International Colloquium on Differential Psychology, Tunis, Tunisia.

Forget, N. (1964). Femmes et professions au Maroc. In P. Chombert de Lauwe (Ed.), *Images de la femme dans la societe.* Paris: Editions Ouvrieres.

International Labor Organization. (1973). *Statistical Yearbook.* Geneva.

Lahlou, A. (1968). Etude sur la famille traditionelle de Fez. *Revue de l'Institut de Sociologie, 3,* 407–441.

Maher, V. (1978). Women and social change in Morocco. In L. Beck & N. Keddie (Eds.), *Women in the Muslim world.* Cambridge, England: Cambridge University Press.

Mernissi, F. (1975a). *Beyond the veil: Male, female dynamics in a modern Muslim society.* Cambridge: Schenkmen.

Mernissi, F. (1975b). Obstacles to family planning practices in urban Morocco. *Studies in Family Planning, 6*(12), 418–425.

Mernissi, F. (1979, June/July). Virginite et patriarcat. *Lamalif, 107,* 25.

Mernissi, F. (1984). *Le Maroc raconte par ses femmes.* Rabbat, Moracco: SMER.

Mikhail, M. (1979). *Images of Arab Women.* Washington, DC: Three Continents Press.

Njoku, J. E. E. (1980). *The world of the African woman.* Metuchen, NJ: Scarecrow Press.

Population Reference Bureau. (1982). World Data Sheet.

Rosen, L. (1978). The negotiation of reality. In L. Beck & N. Keddie (Eds.), *Women in the Muslim world.* Cambridge, England: Cambridge University Press.

Smith, J. (1980). *Women in contemporary Muslim societies.* Cranbury, NJ: Associated University Press.

Sukkary/Stolba, S., & Mossavar-Rahmani, Y. (1982, September 30). *Fertility in cultural perspective: Egypt, Jordan, Morocco, Tunisia and Yemen.* No. NEB-0035-C-00-2024-00. Agency for International Development.

The Holy Q'ran. (Y. Ali, Trans., 1964). Mecca.

U.N. African Statistics Yearbook (1980). Economic Commission for Africa. New York: United Nations.

U.N. Department of Economic and Social Affairs (1970). *Demographic Yearbook, 1969.* New York: United Nations.

U.N. Department of Economic and Social Affairs (1986). *World Population Prospect: Estimates and Projections as Assessed in 1984.* Population Studies No. 98. New York: United Nations.

UNESCO. (1972). *Literacy 1969 to 1971.* Paris: Author.

World Health Organization. (1977). *Special Programme of Research, Development and Research Training in Human Reproduction.* Geneva: Author.

Youssef, N. (1978). The status and fertility patterns of Moslem women. In L. Beck & N. Keddie (Eds.), *Women in the Muslim world.* Cambridge, England: Cambridge University Press.

CHAPTER 5

The Chinese Family
Continuity and Change

SHI MING HU

THE TRADITIONAL CHINESE FAMILY: A HISTORICAL OVERVIEW

China has undergone a major revolutionary transformation since the establishment of the People's Republic of China in 1949 ("Liberation") and the "Cultural Revolution," the 10-year period of struggle and turmoil from 1966 to 1976. In the aftermath of the Cultural Revolution, China has embarked upon a new program of "socialist modernization" that promises to bring about additional changes in the society. The conventional wisdom holds that the traditional Chinese family has consequently experienced similar revolutionary changes and transformation. This is based on the assumption that the political ideology of the Chinese Communist Party contradicts the values of the traditional Chinese family. However, whether this assumption is correct, that is, whether the values of the traditional Chinese family have in fact changed, and if so, to what degree, are questions that call for more careful investigation.

In order to gain a better understanding of the Chinese family in contemporary society, it is necessary to have a brief historical overview of the major factors that have played such an important role in shaping the basic structure and fundamental values of the traditional Chinese family.

Prerevolutionary China

Most accounts indicate that the history of China before 1911 is, in reality, a story of changing dynasties. The idea of imperial dynasty continued for almost 3,000 years until the Qing Dynasty (1644–1911 A.D.), when China's contact with the western countries began to increase rapidly (Latourette, 1957, pp. 141–149).

SHI MING HU • Asian Studies Program, State University of New York, Stony Brook, New York 11794.

The essence of the imperial dynasty was a centralized bureaucratic state with the emperor as the absolute ruler who demanded "subordination" from all of his subjects. It is important to note that Chinese society, under such a centralized political institution, was held together by custom and ethics rather than by law and power. As a matter of fact, ethics and politics were viewed as a unity, and the family provided the mortar of the social and political structure. Because the family was the basic unit of Chinese society, the family was expected to bring up the kind of people desired by the society.

As for ethics, unquestionably the most long-lasting and influential figure in Chinese history is Confucius (551–479 B.C.), who long ago prescribed the ethics and social code for Chinese society. His basic doctrines have indeed dominated Chinese society until this very day. Confucianism actually provided a stable bureaucratic system and furnished the basis for an ethical rationalization for the emperor to exercise his authority. Confucius contended that the welfare of the state would be ensured by well-controlled families—the "subordination to authority" inculcated in the family was eventually extended to the emperor and to the ruling hierarchical class (Hu, 1960, pp. 157–170).

As we know, the traditional Chinese family usually included several generations living under one roof. Following the Confucian social codes, the authority of the eldest generation is supreme in the family hierarchy, which is similar to the relationship of the emperor to his subjects. Thus, the concept of "subordination to authority" was instilled in the family.

One of the Confucian social codes is the famous "five relationships" (*wu lun*), which advocate the proper behavior between soverign and subject, father and son, elder and younger brother, husband and wife, friend and friend (Latourette, 1957, p. 158). Based upon the "five relationships," Confucius further derived the "four virtues" (*si de*) and the "three obediences" (*san cong*) for the behavior of women. The low status of women in the Chinese family and society was thus institutionalized and perpetuated; this irreparable damage to the status of women in Chinese society persists to the present day.

The so-called "four virtues" are (a) "women's virtue" (*fu de*), which decrees how women should behave in agreement with the feudal ethics; (b) "women's speech" (*fu yan*), which requires women to talk less and speak properly at the right place and the right time; (c) "women's appearance" (*fu rong*), which instructs women to be graceful and pleasant; and (d) "women's task" (*fu gong*), which demands that women perform domestic chores dutifully and willingly. The so-called "three obediences" refer to the requirements of women at different stages of their lives. They are first, "to obey her father before her marriage"; second, "to obey her husband after she is married"; and third, "to obey her son when her husband dies" (Croll, 1978, pp. 12–44). These behavioral codes specifically demanded of women by Confucius not only made Chinese women "walk behind men," but also reinforced the very definite role of women in the strict patriarchal family structure of China.

According to the patriarchal structure of the traditional Chinese family, the inequality between sons and daughters begins at birth, as described in one of the early works of Chinese literature, *The Book of Poetry* (quoted in Croll, 1978, p. 23):

When a son is born
Let him sleep on the bed,
Clothe him with fine clothes,
And give him jade to play with.
How lordly his cry is!
May he grow up to wear crimson
And be the lord of the clan and the tribe.

When a daughter is born,
Let her sleep on the ground,
Wrap her in common wrappings,
And give her broken tiles for playthings.
May she have no faults, no merits of her own
May she well attend to food and wine,
And bring no discredit to her parents.

The favoritism of sons over daughters was largely due to the fact that the son was expected to carry on the family's name, to perform all kinds of ceremonial tasks such as ancestor worship and mourning, and to support the parents in their old age; in return, the son had the right to inherit his father's property and prestige. On the other hand, the daughter went to live with her husband and his family after her marriage, and she was not allowed to participate in any of the ceremonial rituals for her own parents, nor had she any rights to the inheritance of her parents.

Revolutionary China

The favoritism for sons, together with the Confucian "four virtues" and "three obediences," had defined the relationship between mother and child. For generation after generation, the Confucian ideal became the accepted "Chinese way of life," which remained virtually unchallenged until the establishment of the People's Republic of China in 1949.

The most serious condemnation of Confucianism, however, took place during the Cultural Revolution (1966–1976), when traditional Chinese ideas, including artifacts, whether or not they were related to Confucius, were severely criticized and indiscriminately attacked by the "Red Guards," who were charged by Mao Zedong with the mission of destroying the "four olds" (old ideas, culture, customs, and habits) and fostering the "four news" (new ideas, culture, customs, and habits) of the proletariat (Hu & Seifman, 1976, p. 191). As a result, Chinese society was in a state of chaos and disorder, and China's current leaders now refer to the Cultural Revolution as a "10-year calamity" for the nation and the people of China.

After the death of Mao Zedong in 1976 and the subsequent end of the Cultural Revolution, China's leaders launched a program called the "four modernizations"—the modernization of agriculture, industry, national defense, and science and technology. The goal of this program is to build a modern socialist society with Chinese characteristics, and it calls for a new reexamination of Chinese traditions, including Confucianism. Although the Confucian concepts of the "four virtues" and the "three obediences" for women have not and probably will never be revived, the idea of respect for age, knowledge, authority, and so on, are definitely being encouraged again, and students are now being taught to respect teachers, which in one sense represents a return to the traditional Confucian concept of "subordination to authority."

THE CHINESE FAMILY AS SEEN THROUGH THE EYES OF CHINESE MOTHERS AND DAUGHTERS

In order to achieve the goal of the "four modernizations," China must catch up with the advanced and developed countries of the world. Toward this end, the Chinese government has increasingly "opened up" China to the West and engaged in numerous programs to exchange ideas with the developed countries of the world.

In recent years, at the invitation of the Ministry of Education of the People's Republic of China to develop teacher training programs in different regions of China, the author has had the opportunity to travel extensively throughout the country, to work with and to meet a great number of people, and to observe firsthand some of the major changes that have taken place in Chinese society.

Fortunately, in the new climate of opinion following the Cultural Revolution, the Chinese have been more relaxed and open in speaking about their own experiences to "foreigners." This has made it possible to gather more reliable data concerning the perceptions of the Chinese themselves about the "Chinese family."

Interview Procedures

The author interviewed a number of "sets" of mothers and their daughters—the daughters were also married and had children of their own. The interviews were conducted in Chinese and were tape recorded with the permission of the interviewees. At least one member of each "set" of mother and daughter was someone with whom the author had had personal contact for a period of several months prior to the actual interview, thereby contributing to the willingness of participants to share their views with the author.

For the purpose of consistency and facilitating comparative analysis, a number of common questions were used in all the interviews. These questions are numbered in the text as a reference for the reader. Occasionally, a response to one of the common questions would prompt the interviewer to ask an ancillary question (which is indicated in parenthesis) before returning to the pre-established pattern of common questions.

Interview Questions

The interview questions focused on the following aspects of the Chinese family:

1. The number of children
2. Positive and negative experiences of rearing children
3. Possible different ways of rearing boys and girls
4. Possible different expectations for boys and girls
5. Solutions to children's behavioral problems
6. Concepts of "ideal parents"
7. Responsibility of society in rearing children
8. Possible changes in childrearing after "Liberation" (1949)
9. Miscellaneous questions

The young "daughter-mothers" were also asked some additional questions dealing with such topics as feelings toward their parents, expectations for their own children, and comparison of their own experiences of growing up with those of their children.

From the collection of sets of interviews of mothers and their daughters, the author has selected two illustrative interviews (which took place in July and August of 1983 in Yunnan Province) representing two very different social classes—intellectuals and workers—which have been transcribed, translated, and edited in a manner designed to preserve the authenticity of the original rhetoric. To preserve anonymity, the interviewees have not been identified by name.

MOTHER–DAUGHTER INTERVIEW SET NUMBER 1

Mother: Mrs. X.

Age 51, college professor and mother of three children (two daughters and one son).

Q: What I would like to ask you today is how you feel about raising children and other related questions as parents, to see if there have been any changes during the last three generations in China; all right Mrs. X?

A: Yes, very well; I hope I can make myself understood.

Q: First of all, how many children do you have?

A: I have three children, two girls and one boy; they are all grown up now. In fact, the elder daughter is married and has a baby girl; she is the one who will be joining us shortly.

Q: Fine. Perhaps you can tell me something about your own experience first. Later, I'll ask your daughter when she joins us. So, can you tell me your experience in rearing children?

A: As you know, in China offspring are very important to a family; so I feel very good to have three children, particularly to have both a boy and girls. However, my experience was a hard one.

Q: Why? What were the most stressful aspects about being a mother?

A: Well, because of the Cultural Revolution, I had to go to the Cadre School in Kaiyuang county. [Cadre Schools were generally located in the countryside, where individuals were sent for fixed periods of time—ranging from several months to several years—to take part in manual labor and ideological purification.] I left my home and my three children. (Q: Who took care of them? A: No one.) The oldest one was 11, her brother was 9, and her sister was 8. I was very worried about them. Every month, I gave them some money; the 11-year-old took care of her brother and her sister.

Q: Sorry to hear that. In spite of the difficulty, did you have any joyful experience as a mother?

A: Yes, my children are very nice; if I have work to do at home, they all help me. When they were growing up, they helped me to do a lot of chores such as washing clothes, shoveling coal and buying rice in the store. The happiest experience is to see them grow up without problems; my children are good in nature.

Q: Do you have different ways of rearing boys and girls?

A: No, about the same. As a matter of fact, because of the Cultural Revolution, I feel that I did not take care of them.

Q: Do you have different expectations for boys and girls?

A: Yes and no. As you know, the Chinese society has a long history of male domination; it is still true at the present time, although women's status has been raised after the Liberation of 1949. When people get old, sons are expected to take care of their parents. Therefore, most of the Chinese families expect their sons to do more for the family, and expect them to have better jobs so they can take care of their parents. We have the law stating that the children must take care of their parents when they are old. As for girls, we expect them to go to school and be able to work and eventually to get married to a good man. Since we have a son, the girls are not expected to take care of us when we are old; besides, we will have enough retirement to live on. Of course, it is their duty to show their gratitude to their parents.

Q: Where did you go for advice when your children had developmental problems?

A: Before the Cultural Revolution, my mother was still alive, so I brought my kids to my mother's home. Almost every Sunday, we went back to my mother's for dinner and lunch, etc. If there were problems, I asked my mother.

Q: Where did you go for advice when your children had behavioral problems?

A: My husband and I took care of them. I must say that we had very good kids. Only last year, when a friend of my son introduced a girlfriend to my son, I had some problems. You see, the girl was not very good. She doesn't work but likes to eat and dress up. I disliked her, so I advised my son not to be in touch with her. At first my son did not agree with me; but in a year or two, my son found her shortcomings and he himself decided not to be involved with her any more. Now this year, he got married to another girl; she is very nice. (Q: Did you know her before she was married to your son? A: Yes, I did.)

Q: What are your goals for your children?

A: In China, every family wishes their children to study in the university to get a good job, then to get married to a good man or a good woman. Since both my husband and I are professionals, we definitely want our children to get higher education. However it is not easy in our country because of the few universities. Particularly, my children went through the period of the Cultural Revolution when everything was upside down. In addition to education, we want our children to be an honest person and have good friends.

Q: How do you expect your children to behave toward you?

A: I would like them to respect us and to take care of us when we reach old age.

Q: What are the qualities you most want to develop in your children?

A: As I just mentioned, I want my children to be an honest person, not to do bad things such as drinking or smoking.

Q: What is your idea of an "ideal mother"?

A: I think that an "ideal mother" should be able to see her children eat well, have enough to wear, have good habits, to have her children follow good teaching.

Q: Do you think that you are an "ideal mother"?

A: No, I don't think so, because I did not take good care of my children—particularly during the Cultural Revolution when I had to leave them by themselves.

Q: What role do you think fathers play in childrearing?

A: I think that in China, most fathers are still the major figures to discipline children at home. As for actual physical care, I don't think that fathers do much; perhaps the younger generation nowadays is different. It is true that now more and more young men are helping out at home in taking care of children, especially when their wives are also working.

Q: What is your idea of an "ideal father"?

A: An "ideal father" is full of love but strict in discipline; he should be able to provide all the needs for his children and be considerate to his wife.

Q: Do you think that your husband is an "ideal father"?

A: Yes, because he loves our children; in particular, he likes the oldest girl. He never helped me, but this was because he was too busy with his own work.

Q: Do you think that men can/should be child caretakers?

A: I think so. For instance, my daughter's husband has been taking care of his daughter ever since she was three months old. He does a good job, too.

Q: In your opinion, what is the responsibility of society for childrearing?

A: I feel that education is the main responsibility of society for childrne. In our country there are very few universities, and the young people don't have the chance to go on for higher education. My children want so much to go to the university, but there are no chances; so they go to the evening school to learn something.

Q: Have there been any changes in childrearing in China after Liberation?

A: Not really, because the basic methods of child care are the same except for material goods; the majority of mothers continue to breast feed babies, and mothers of young mothers remain the main source of advice. It is true that nowadays there are more fathers helping out at home, but women are still the major persons in childrearing— even in the factory where there are child-care centers, the children are cared for by women.

Q: If you were rearing children now, would you do it differently? Why?

A: Probably not too much different. Childrearing is almost like a family practice which is passed on from generation to generation. New medical developments may change some of the care of illness, but not the major methods. Old customs are very hard to change.

Q: What else would you like to tell me?

A: You see, before the Cultural Revolution, our country learned from the Russians. Mothers were expected to have more children. When I had two children at that time, I did not want to have the third because of my busy work. However, the government would not allow me not to have any more children. So I was very upset because it was terribly hard to have a full-time job and to take care of three children at the same time. Now, the "one-child" policy seems to have another kind of problem; every family is spoiling the only child. I wonder how this "one-child" generation is going to be (Hu, 1983a).

Daughter: Mrs. W.

Age 26, medical technician and mother of one daughter.

Q: I was just talking to your mother about her experiences as a mother. I am glad to have this opportunity to talk with you about your experience. Do you mind?

A: No, not at all.

Q: How many children do you have?

A: Just a little girl, as you know, the "one-child" policy is a big campaign in our country—because of the large population in China.

Q: Yes, I understand and have read a lot about the efforts made by the government to enforce it. I have seen lots of posters and billboards about the "one-child" policy. How old is your child?

A: Only 2.

Q: Can you tell me about your experience as a mother?

A: Well, since this girl is the first one and the last one according to our government policy, I am extremely excited and also anxious to take good care of her. I just don't want anything to go wrong, which makes me nervous sometimes.

Q: In these 2 years, what were the most stressful aspects about being a mother?

A: In my situation, I hardly had any bad experience because my husband and I work in different units and do not live in the same place. I live in the quarter provided by my work unit and my husband lives in his. Since housing in the city is crowded, my place is relatively small; so I have my daughter live with my husband in his quarter which is in the countryside with large space. (Q: So you are not taking care of your daughter? A: No, I only see my daughter on weekends. Q: How do you manage that? A: Well, we alternate the visit, either I go to see them or they come to the city to visit me.)

Q: I see, so you are the new generation which has the husband taking care of the baby, right?

A: Yes. I am lucky in a sense because of the housing shortage and the working conditions which make it impossible for us to be together. (Q: How do you feel about this? A: Not too bad; I feel a sense of freedom and not being tied down by a baby. I am able to go to the evening school to learn.)

Q: I understand that the national population policy of one child per family will not allow you to have two or more children. However, suppose that you could, would you have different ways of rearing boys and girls?

A: No, I don't think so. My husband and I both have jobs, so we would have to rear our children according to our living conditions.

Q: Again, suppose that you had boys and girls, would you have different expectations for boys and girls?

A: No, but it is not completely fair for me to say "no," because of the Chinese tradition that families expect more from a boy than from a girl. It is likely that I'd expect a boy to get more education and have a better job.

Q: Getting back to your own situation, where do you go for advice when your child has problems—developmental and/or behavioral?

A: As you can see, I go to my parents for advice whenever my child has problems. Right now I have not had any serious problems, because my daughter is only 2 years old. Generally, we have much more material things for our child than our parents had for us.

Q: What are your goals for your child?

A: I would like to see her get a good education, grow up as an honest person, and eventually married to a nice man.

Q: How do you expect your child to behave toward you?

A: I expect my daughter to respect me and to take care of me when I need her.

Q: What are the qualities you want most to develop in your child?

A: Honesty is one of the qualities I want most to develop in my daughter, because during the Cultural Revolution we had many good qualities damaged in young people. I am so afraid that it might even affect the next generation. So, even at this early age of my daughter's life we emphasize "honesty" and good behavior. But I must admit that I am not really very strict, since I have only one child.

Q: What is your idea of an "ideal mother"?

A: My "ideal mother" is a mother who is intellectual and devoted; she is willing to spend a lot of time with her children and is very patient to teach them—of course, she takes good care of her children's daily routine.

Q: Do you think you are an "ideal mother"?

A: No, no, by no means—I am far from it. As you know, I don't even have time to take care of my daughter's basic needs because my job is far away from my husband's work unit. Besides, I am not all that patient.

Q: What role do you think a father plays in childrearing?

A: I think a father should assist in child rearing; my case is different as I pointed out previously.

Q: What is your idea of an "ideal father"?

A: My "ideal father" is the man who can discipline children and has a good job with enough income to provide a good living for his children.

Q: Do you think that your husband is an "ideal father"?

A: I think so. He has a good job and can discipline children; in fact, in my situation he does more than just assist.

Q: Do you think that men can/should be child caretakers?

A: Yes, I think they can, like my husband. He is doing a good job in taking care of my daughter; however, generally I think that they don't have to if there is no such need.

Q: In your opinion what is the responsibility of society in childrearing?

A: I think that education and health care are the responsibilities of society for children, because children have to go to school for education. When they are sick, they have clinics to go to; when they are in child-care centers, they should have regular check-ups to keep them healthy.

Q: Have there been any changes in childrearing in China after Liberation?

A: Not much—as far as I can remember. I am doing almost the same thing as my mother did when she reared us, except for the material things. I mean, we have a lot more for our child than my parents had for theirs.

Q: Getting back to your own childhood, what were the happiest experiences you had as a child?

A: It is hard to say, but I think that my school years were the happiest because I had lots of playmates.

Q: What were the most difficult experiences you had as a child?

A: That is not difficult to pinpoint. The most difficult experience was the time when I had to take care of my younger brother and younger sister when my parents were away for

3 years. I was only 11 then and did not know what to buy or when I would get money from my parents because I did not even know where they were. So we three children ran around wild. Still, even today, I do not know how we grew up.

Q: How do you feel about your parents?

A: I feel that they could have spent more time with us, but I guess it was difficult during the Cultural Revolution when people were sent by the government to various places to work. Under the circumstances they did their best to send us money for food and clothing so we could grow up.

Q: Would you like your child to grow up the same way you did?

A: No. because we did not have the opportunity to go to higher education. I want my daughter to be able to go to university for higher learning. As for materials needs, things are now much more plentiful. I also hope that I would be able to spend more time with her, when we would be able to work in the same place some day.

Q: Would you like your child to behave toward you the same way you do toward your parents?

A: Yes, I would like my daughter to respect me and help me when I need her, just as we are helping our parents now. (Q: However, isn't it true that your parents are helping you out financially? A: Yes, but that is because of our low salary right now.)

Q: What else would you like to tell me?

A: Well, I understand that our country really has a huge population and it is necessary to control the population increase, but it is also very difficult for young people—and as a matter of fact for old folks—to have only one child around. It makes us very nervous, particularly when the child is sick (Hu, 1983b).

MOTHER–DAUGHTER INTERVIEW SET NUMBER 2

Mother: Mrs. Z.

Age 55, part-time service worker (housekeeper) and mother of four children (three daughters and one son).

Q: Mrs. Z, when you finish your washing this morning do you mind if I ask you some questions about raising children and being a parent?

A: No, it is my honor; but to be very frank with you, a few years ago I would mind for fear of getting in trouble.

Q: Thank you. What I would like to ask you today is how you feel about raising children and other related questions about being a parent, to see if there have been any changes in China during the last three generations. So, first of all, how many children do you have?

A: I have four children, three girls and one boy. One daughter is married and has a child of her own. (Q: Is it a baby boy? A: Yes, she is very fortunate to have a boy. Q: Why? A: Because you know that our government is enforcing the "one-child" policy now. If she had a baby girl now, she would never have a chance to have a son.)

Q: Can you tell me your experience in rearing children?

A: Yes, it was very difficult because my husband was a worker with very low wages before the Liberation in 1949. After the Liberation, things have changed a lot and the worker's life has been improved. However, then the general income was low and with a family of six, plus my husband's mother, it was hard. For me it was even harder, since the spacing of my children was quite close. I had four kids ranging from 6 months to 6 years old. Although I did not work outside at that time, it was extremely difficult to care for four kids in one room. You know that the housing is limited in China; one family in a room is still common even today. I felt happy when my first child was born, because I didn't have too much work then. However, a year later I had the second one, and 3 years later I had the third one, a boy, who really gave joy to the family since he was the first boy. Finally, 5 years later, I had the last child, a girl again. With four little ones, you can imagine how it is!

Q: I understand; what were the most stressful aspects about being a mother?

A: As you know, everyday care of four children is hard enough, but the worst time is when kids are ill. If one came down with a cold, almost all the others got it too. My husband did not help then, because we were the "old fashion" type family where men don't do housework.

Q: In spite of headaches and hardship, did you have any joyful experience as a mother?

A: As I mentioned a while ago, I felt happy when my first child was born because I felt the joy of being a mother for the first time; later, the joy was overwhelmed by the care of more children.

Q: Do you have different ways of rearing boys and girls?

A: Generally no, but sometimes it is hard to get rid of "favoritism." You know, boys are still preferred to girls in this country. For instance, among the children, the boy always gets better food and clothing; particularly in my case, the girls could share clothing but the only boy could not. Therefore, in terms of care, I might have treated the boy slightly different.

Q: Do you have different expectations for boys and girls?

A: Yes, because boys are expected to take care of their parents. We expect our son to have more education and to find a better job so that he would be able to take care of his own family and us as well.

Q: Where did you go for advice when your children had developmental problems?

A: Since our parents died early, I had to go to relatives for advice. Of course, if there were serious problems, like illness, I would go to the doctor. Luckily, my children are quite healthy and have had few problems.

Q: Where did you go for advice when your children had behavioral problems?

A: As I just said, our parents died early, we had no place to go for advice. We disciplined our children, particularly when they were lying or doing things that they were not supposed to—we really punished them. My husband would never allow such behavior, so my son got spankings a couple of times.

Q: What are your goals for your children?

A: We hope that they will get more education and grow up to be a useful person; in the case of the girls, we hope that they would be married to good men.

Q: How do you expect your children to behave toward you?

A: I hope that they are obedient and dutiful, and that we will be cared for when we are old.

Q: What are the qualities you most want to develop in your children?

A: Being honest, diligent and dutiful.

Q: What is your idea of an "ideal mother"?

A: My "ideal mother" is a mother with consideration and patience, who also helps her children with their homework from school.

Q: Do you think that you are an "ideal mother"?

A: No, I don't think so, because I don't have patience and I can't help children with their homework.

Q: What role do you think fathers play in childrearing?

A: I feel the most important responsibility of a father is to be able to provide children with their needs and to discipline them. We Chinese say, "If you want to have children, you have to be able to bring them up." Before Liberation, we were poor and life was terrible. After Liberation, it has been better; still, it is hard to provide a family of six with enough food and clothing. My husband works and has little time to stay home to discipline children; he is also very temperamental.

Q: What is your idea of an "ideal father"?

A: I think an "ideal father" is strict in discipline and able to provide all the needs of his children.

Q: Do you think that your husband is an "ideal father"?

A: I don't think so, because he did not have enough education and was unable to help the children with their school work.

Q: Do you think that men can/should be child caretakers?

A: I don't think that men can take care of children; they may help, but that is about all. Even if they could, I don't think they would be willing. Men in our country would probably take a long time to learn how to take care of children.

Q: In your opinion, what is the responsibility of society in childrearing?

A: I think the responsibility of society to children is building schools for children to get education—perhaps also nurseries and day-care centers for younger children whose mothers are at work.

Q: Have there been any changes in childrearing in China after Liberation?

A: Not much, the rearing process is basically the same. Perhaps some working mothers, those who don't have older persons at home to help out, have to leave their children in day-care centers and feed them with some powdered milk.

Q: If you were rearing children now, would you do it differently? Why?

A: I don't think so; the only possible difference might be the spacing of the children. However, the younger generation doesn't have that problem now, since the government is enforcing the "one-child" policy—their problem is how to have a son!

Q: What else would you like to tell me?

A: I think that our government helps us to improve our living. My husband has a better job with better pay now, and I am able to have a part-time job to earn some money. However, after the Cultural Revolution, a lot of youngsters have picked up a lot of bad habits such as drinking and smoking; they also do not respect the elderly. So I hope that their bad behavior would be corrected and they would be useful persons (Hu, 1983c).

Daughter: Mrs. C.

Age 28, factory worker and mother of one son.

Q: Welcome, Mrs. C. I am so glad to have finally met you. I suppose your mother already told you about this meeting, right?

A: Yes. It is my honor to meet you today. My mother speaks of you a lot. She says, it makes such a difference to work for people you can understand. She was a housekeeper for foreign experts who couldn't speak Chinese.

Q: Yes, a couple of days ago I spoke with her about motherhood in China, and we had a good time. I hope that you won't mind answering some questions for me. First of all, how many children do you have?

A: I have one baby boy.

Q: Can you tell me something about your experiences in childrearing?

A: I feel extremely occupied, not free anymore, because the baby needs all my attention. My mother lives far away and I can't run to her all the time. The baby is just 1 year old and weaned; he can't walk too well as yet. Luckily, there is a day care in our factory so I can put him there till I get out of work. (Q: How about the time when he was still breast fed? A: No problem, because workers are allowed to take time off to feed the baby.)

Q: What are the most stressful aspects of being a mother?

A: No special stress as yet, because I have been a "mother" only 1 year. During this year, the only time I was terrified was when the baby caught a cold and refused to take milk.

Q: Do you have any joyful experience as a mother?

A: Not really, because as I just said, it is too short a time to have both bad and good experiences.

Q: Suppose that you had both boys and girls, would you have different ways to raise them?

A: I am not sure, since I have only a boy right now. However, I am quite sure that we spoil him.

Q: Do you think that you would have different expectations for boys and girls?

A: Although I expect both boys and girls to be good, I still think that boys are expected to do more. (Q: What do you mean by that? A: I mean that boys have to take care of their parents, in addition to their own family.)

Q: Where would you go for advice when your children have developmental problems?

A: I think that I would go to my parents first; if they couldn't help, I would go to the doctor.

Q: Where would you go for advice when your child had behavioral problems?

A: So far, I have not had any problems, and I hope there would not be problems in the future. We try to bring him up properly.

Q: What are your goals for your child?

A: I hope that he would get good education, be able to pass the entrance examination for college to have higher education. That way, he could have better jobs and take care of his family.

Q: How do you expect your child to behave toward you?

A: I would like him to obey and to respect us.

Q: What are the qualities you most want to develop in your chijd?

A: I want him to grow up to be a useful man, with good habits.

Q: What is your idea of an "ideal mother"?

A: My "ideal mother" is the mother with patience, who spends a lot of time with her children, and particularly spends time to coach them with their schoolwork.

Q: Do you think that you are an "ideal mother"?

A: No, because I have not had enough education. I am afraid that I would not be able to help my son with his homework when he goes to school.

Q: What role do you think a father plays in childrearing?

A: I think that a father should provide all the needs for his children, and be willing to help them when their mother is not available. (Q: What do you mean by "not available"? A: I mean when the mother is sick or something.)

Q: What is your idea of an "ideal father"?

A: An "ideal father" cares for his children and sets up good examples for his children, so when he disciplines them they know what is expected of them.

Q: Do you think that your husband is an "ideal father"?

A: No, he is not, because he has some bad habits, such as smoking—which he learned during the Cultural Revolution.

Q: Do you think that men can/should be child caretakers?

A: I think they can be trained, but they should not be child caretakers if there is no such need.

Q: In your opinion, what is the responsibility of society in childrearing?

A: To provide children with schools and clinics; this way the children would grow up healthy and educated.

Q: Do you think that there have been changes in child rearing in China after Liberation?

A: I don't think there have been too many changes; basically I do the same thing as my mother did to bring us up. Of course, we have more material goods for children nowadays.

Q: Getting back to your own experiences, what were the happiest ones you had as a child?

A: I think my early childhood experience was a happy one because I was able to go to school to play with other kids.

Q: What were the most difficult experiences you had as a child?

A: I don't think that I had a really difficult experience, except during the Cultural Revolution when most of the young people of my generation suffered. We left our home and went to the countryside to work; we had little food to eat and hardly any money to spend.

Q: How do you feel about your parents?

A: They are good parents. My mother is a hard-working woman, very clean. However, my father is a bit temperamental; we are afraid to talk to him.

Q: Would you like your child to grow up the same way you did?

A: No, I don't want him to go through the Cultural Revolution experience and pick up bad habits.

Q: Would you like your child to behave toward you the same way you do to your parents?

A: Yes, but I would like him to have a better job which would enable him to take care of me when I am old.

Q: What else would you like to tell me?

A: I am very glad to have a son, because we are not allowed to have more children. My mother-in-law is especially happy for us. The only worry I have is the fact that the boy is developing his temper as the result of all the attention he is getting. I hope you understand what I mean (Hu, 1983d).

CONCLUSION

The preceding illustrative interviews reveal that although Chinese society has experienced a revolutionary transformation since 1949, under the political ideology of the Chinese Communist Party, the "Chinese family" has retained many of the values associated with pre-revolutionary traditional China.

Notwithstanding the well-known Chinese saying that "women hold up half the sky," sons continue to be perceived as being more desirable than daughters. Sons are expected to take on more responsibilities in the family and for their parents and are therefore expected to go on for more education—which most Chinese view as "the way" to alter the course of one's life. Almost all the interviewees, irrespective of the generation to which they belonged, had similar responses to the questions dealing with "having sons and daughters" and "expectations for boys and girls."

Women themselves seem to perceive the role of the father in the childrearing process as different from that of the mother. The father is considered as the "provider" and the "disciplinarian," while the mother is considered as the "real" child caretaker, who has responsibility for the physical welfare of the children. As Elisabeth Croll states in her study of Chinese women since Mao Zedong, "It is the mother who is still conceived as the primary childminder in health and in sickness" (Croll, 1978, p. 71).

Young mothers seeking help to resolve their children's developmental and/or behavioral problems are apt to run back to their mother for advice and guidance. In the event that the new couple settle in the bridegroom's home, that is, live with the groom's parents—a traditional pattern of Chinese family residence that remains common even today—then the mother-in-law will likely be the main source of advice in matters dealing with childrearing.

Generally speaking, there has been very little change in the basic childrearing practices. Breast feeding remains the most common way of feeding babies, even among working women; most of the work units allow women time off to feed their babies. It is interesting to note that certain traditional "local" diets (reflecting taste preferences in different regions) are still followed in the belief that they will stimulate the nursing mother to produce more milk.

Personal observation and informal conversations with women in different regions of China indicate that other childrearing practices, such as weaning and toilet training, are also carried out pretty much in the same traditional way. In spite of the greater availability of nurseries and day-care centers for working mothers, one can only conclude that the Chinese family is still the main agent for the socialization and rearing of children.

In terms of education, most of the mothers interviewed felt that it is the responsibility of society to build more schools for children to provide educational opportunities. This response should not come as any surprise, since being an "intellectual" has long been associated with fame and fortune in Chinese history. Traditionally, only those select few who passed the civil examination—after long years of study and memorization of the Chinese classics—could become officials and obtain the power, wealth, and respect that came with these positions of authority. Although the civil examination was replaced by the modern school system at the turn of the century, the importance of schooling and of being well educated continues to be seen as the most effective vehicle for changing one's situation in life. This traditional respect for the power of education permeates virtually all levels of Chinese society.

During the Cultural Revolution, there was a dramatic reversal of this traditional attitude toward education. Egalitarianism carried the day, and highest priority was given to the "correctness" of one's political ideology. Intellectuals were considered as elitists, they were severely criticized, and many were sent to the countryside for "reeducation"—a term used by the Chinese government for having intellectuals engage in manual labor, supposedly to "learn from the workers and peasants." At the same time, numerous workers and peasants were put into positions formerly held by the intellectuals—in the hope of reversing the traditional attitude that glorified the intelligentsia.

However, as China is now denouncing the Cultural Revolution as a 10-year period of turmoil and disorder, the traditional respect for intellectuals has not only been revived, but it has been given "official" support in the government's pronouncements on the important role that intellectuals are to play in helping China achieve its goal of socialist modernization.

Highly competitive college entrance examinations have been restored, along with academic titles and formal degrees. A number of "key schools"— with preferential funding and specially selected faculty and students—have been established to serve as models of academic excellence (Seifman, 1981). Most of the interviewees expressed a strong desire to have their children go on for higher education in order to have better jobs. Eagerness for learning is very obvious in China these days; young people with books in hand are to be seen almost everywhere. While working in China, the author was often approached by service workers in hotels and even stopped in the streets by young students who requested "lessons."

The traditional virtues of integrity (which the interviewees implied when they used the word "honesty") and respect for the elderly are now also strongly encouraged among the young. Almost all of the interviewees stated that they wanted their children to grow up to be a person of integrity and with respect for the elderly. Interestingly, hardly anyone mentioned the idea of "serving the people," which during the Cultural Revolution was one of the most well-popularized desirable virtues.

Clearly, in the current drive toward the goal of socialist modernization, the Chinese people are thinking more about the quality of life, and the government has introduced a number of social and economic programs designed to improve the standard of living. One such program is the "one couple, one child" policy designed to curb the rapid population growth in what is already the world's most populous country. In 1982 the Chinese government issued a directive calling on every urban couple to limit themselves to the birth of only one child and widely advocating the same principle for couples living in the countryside. In "unusual cases," couples may receive permission to have a second child if their cases conform to the following exceptions: (a) those whose first child has a noncongenital defect, (b) remarried couples of whom at least one partner had no child in the first marriage, (c) those whose child is adopted, and (d) people living in remote areas or overseas Chinese settling in rural areas. The directive further stipulated that under no circumstances is the birth of a third child allowed (New China News Agency, 1982; Qian, 1983). This policy has, and will continue to have a major impact on women and the Chinese family. So strong is the desire for a male child that the Chinese press has reported tragic stories of female infanticide—especially in the rural areas—and has publicly condemned such practices (*Zhongguo Qingnian Bao*, 1982).

Mothers of both generations shared a common concern that with the new "one-child" policy, parents might have a tendency to spoil their "only child." In discussions with teachers and parents, both groups noted a greater frequency of "undesirable behavior" exhibited by some of the children attending kindergarten. This behavior was described as "selfishness" and "ill temper."

A Chinese journal for parents, *Essential for Parents* (*Fumu Bidu*), reported that Chinese parents suffer from "four overdones" (over-protection, over-indulgence, over-concern, and over-expectation), and "four fears": the fear that their children will (a) turn out badly, (b) not be talented, (c) refuse to support them when they are old, and (d) fall ill or even die. There is genuine concern that these factors, taken together, will result in immaturity, inability of children to get along with their peers, and lack of initiative (*Beijing Review*, 1985).

It will be very important to study the long-term impact that the "one-child" policy will have on childrearing practices and the value structure of the Chinese family.

REFERENCES

Beijing Review (1985, July, 8), p. 28.

Croll, E. (1978). *Feminism and socialism in China*. London: Routledge & Kegan Paul.

Hu, C. T. (1960). *China*. New Haven, CT: HRAF Press.

Hu, Shi Ming. (1983a, July). [Interview with Mrs. X: Yunnan Province, China]. Unpublished interview.

Hu, Shi Ming. (1983b, July). [Interview with Mrs. W: Yunnan Province, China]. Unpublished interview.

Hu, Shi Ming. (1983c, August). [Interview with Mrs. Z: Yunnan Province, China]. Unpublished interview.

Hu, Shi Ming. (1983d, August). [Interview with Mrs. C: Yunnan Province, China]. Unpublished interview.

Hu, Shi Ming, & Seifman, E. (1976). *Toward a new world outlook: A documentary history of education in the People's Republic of China, 1949–1976*. New York: AMS.

Latourette, K. S. (1957). *A short history of the Far East*. New York: Macmillan.

New China News Agency. (1982, November 6). Summary of world broadcasts, the Far East (1982, November 11), p. BII/24.

Qian, Xinzhong. (1983, February 14). China's population policy. *Beijing Review*, pp. 21–24.

Seifman, E. (1981, April). On the "key" colleges and universities in the People's Republic of China. *Asian Thought & Society*, pp. 25–35.

Zhongguo Qingnian Bao. (1982, November 9). Foreign broadcasts information service, China (1982, December 7), pp. K55–56.

CHAPTER 6

The Children's Home
An Alternative in Childrearing Practices in the Netherlands

RUTH DE KANTER

INTRODUCTION

With the development of the women's movement in the late 1960s and early 1970s, the nuclear family became a central focus of political and personal concern (Segal, 1983). Women questioned traditional ideas about the nuclear family, especially the central role of the mother as a primary caretaker for children (Comer, 1971). In response to these concerns, the Children's Collective was created as an alternative childrearing environment by feminist and socialist women and men at the beginning of the 1970s in Amsterdam, the Netherlands.

These feminist mothers and progressive fathers were looking for an alternative to the nuclear family. Single and married parents who participated in the Collective shared common views about the necessity of economic independence for women, greater participation of fathers in childrearing, and less rigid sex roles. All the parents participated in caring for the children and housekeeping. The parents together bought a home where their children could live together without each parent's continuous presence. The parents lived in several houses close by. At least one parent took care of all the children during one 24-hour period, once a week. On the weekends, the children left the Children's Collective and went to their parents' homes. The Children's Collective thus reflects one of the most radical ideas in the field of childrearing. Two similar Collectives were established 8 years later in Rotterdam, the Netherlands; they are still functioning.

In this chapter, I first discuss the historical and theoretical background for the Children's Collectives in the Netherlands. Second, I discuss the origins of

RUTH DE KANTER • Department of Development, State University of Utrecht, Utrecht, The Netherlands.

the collectives and their practical organizations as well as indicate similarities and differences between the Amsterdam and Rotterdam collectives. Finally, I evaluate the advantages and disadvantages of the Collective in Amsterdam. The descriptions of the Collectives draw upon some interviews with participating parents and articles they have written.

HISTORICAL AND PHILOSOPHICAL BACKGROUND

The Netherlands in the 1960s

The philosophy behind the Children's Collectives reflected the particular historical time and cultural background in the Netherlands in the late 1960s and early 1970s. This period was characterized by rebellion against authority. Spontaneous gatherings and organized demonstrations against the State were common. Many people wanted to be freed from institutional power.

Institutions of different kinds were challenged, including universities, other educational institutions, the law, religion, the family, and political institutions. The student movement challenged the power structure of the universities, claiming the one-person, one-vote system in the university boards. Teachers challenged the authoritarian relations in the school system. Progressive lawyers organized collectives and challenged the class-based law system. Student priests left the religious institutions. Feminists rebelled against marriage and the nuclear family. The continuity of the monarchy was questioned.

Within this changing political climate, the antiauthoritarian, antipatriarchal feminist movement formulated a critique of the ideological basis of the nuclear family. In women's consciousness-raising groups, women analyzed the effects of this ideology on their lives. They realized that traditional ideas about the family kept women as nonpaid housekeepers and mothers within the confines of the home. Being married was also seen by some as oppressive, as it created possessiveness, jealousy, and exclusiveness. More efficient contraception liberated women from certain sexual constraints, but not from sexual subordination to men. Thus women were trying to liberate themselves on different levels, asking for the right to free abortion and for more child-care facilities, adult education, and economic independence (Smit, 1967).

Women who were involved in the women's movement and had small children to look after felt the constrictions of their situation. They went to meetings, participated in political activities, wrote articles about the position of women, and tried to combine paid work with child care. They were inspired to try to change their own situations. Some women dissolved their marriages because they could not accept their dependent economic positions, and they could not persuade their husbands to share the responsibility for child care and household activities. Some mothers demanded paid work outside the home, while others completed their education.

Thus women who were trying to formulate a fundamental critique of the traditional ideology about the family were simultaneously making changes in their own lives. In particular, the women who founded the Children's Collective protested against the burden of having to be omnipotent, perfect mothers. They realized that they were not only mothers but also women with separate needs and desires for work and sexuality, which they wanted to achieve outside the home or marriage. All these women had paid work outside the home and participated in different activities in the women's movement.

These women also sought sexual freedom, as opposed to confining their sexuality to marriage. They contested the views of Rich (1976) and Rossi (1981), who identified motherhood with sexuality, and rejected the idea that the foundation of women's liberation and fulfillment is located in the "repossession of their maternal bodies" (Chodorow, 1980, p. 60).

One of the women said: "I could never combine my love relationship with my love for the children. For me these seem to be two separate worlds."

Another woman said:

> I have different lives. I am married. We spend the weekend as a small family together, my husband, daughter, and myself. During the week I work. I spend one day in the Children's Collective and one day with my lover. These worlds do not meet.

These women asserted their autonomy within these different spheres, although it was also sometimes very difficult to integrate them. Within a marriage, women have to unite them. However, these feminists accepted the fact that the structure of their lives was split. Reorganizing parenting presupposes reorganizing the structure of work and sexuality, as these are also important dimensions of life. But individuals cannot restructure the labor market without the intervention of the state. In the 1970s, neither the state nor the major industries were willing to restructure the labor market. This placed great limitations on alternative forms of childrearing like the Children's Collective.

Critique of the Ideology of the Family

The parents who began the Children's Collective tried to free themselves from the dominant childrearing perspective that stressed the natural bond between biological parents and their children. Instead, they argued that social ties between adults and children are as important as biological ones. They saw the traditional nuclear family as a system in which parents owned their children. They opposed the view that "a man owns a wife and a women owns her children." Instead, they wanted to reorganize the family in such a way that children's dependency and parents' control and repression would be minimized. As one of the mothers said in an interview:

> The family is repressive for both women and children. Mothers repress their children because they do not know what to do themselves. They have no place to express themselves other than in or through their children.

Another woman said: "Children need their own social system—a children's collective will help them to have an independent existence."

Hence these women and men developed a theory of emancipated motherhood in which women could combine sexual freedom and work with liberal childrearing. They no longer believed in the image of the biological nuclear family as a harmonious and homogeneous unit.

How does the philosophy behind the Children's Collective compare with other critiques of the traditional nuclear family? Most critics directed their criticism against mothers. For example, Robert Laing attempted to outline the "operations" whereby the family destroys and mystifies children. In his view, parents who are insecure and anxious must hold to the image of the family as a secure refuge. This contradiction causes madness. Laing believed that it was "the unhappy, insecure, cold, and possessive mother who prevents her daughter from having an autonomous life: She causes by her contradictory messages her daughter's madness" (Laing, 1976). Thus the mother became the target of Laing's critique of family life.

Feminists agreed only in part with Laing's analysis. They showed how the mother's position was defined by her economic dependency on her husband as breadwinner (Chodorow, 1978). As Ilene Philipson stated 10 years later:

> It is not the mother but the ideology and the policy that attempt to bolster the nuclear family by compelling mothers to remain at home with their children, which contains a fundamental contradiction. (Philipson, 1982)

Similarly, one of the mothers from the Children's Collective said: "I did not want to be in the same position as my mother. Because of her economically dependent position, she was blackmailed by my father."

For this woman, it was clear that the nuclear family was not the place in which women could find their ultimate fulfillment. The basis of the nuclear family is the heterosexual relationship between a man and a woman. Women are economically, sexually, and psychologically dependent on their male marriage partners. The power of the mother, as Laing analyzed the situation, is equal to the power of a bird in a cage.

Both the position and the behavior of the mother are affected by the division of labor between the sexes within and outside the family. As Ilene Philipson remarks:

> Unless mothers' working outside the home is accepted and supported ideologically and materially, so that they can approach their children with physical and emotional energy, and freedom from guilt, so that they accept themselves for being both mother and a person with interests, responsibilities and involvements that are separate from those of their children, faulty empathy possibly could arise not so much from mothers' isolation with their children but from the weariness and guilt they experience. (p. 39)

The Ideology of Motherhood

The traditional ideology of motherhood is transmitted through magazines, books, television, and advertisements. These external texts and images become internalized, so that most women have images of mothering and the ways in which they do or do not wish to mother. The external texts and internal images then produce guilt.

The ideology of motherhood tells women how they ought to mother and what a "real mother" ought to do. The following central points are made:

1. All women want to be mothers.
2. A biological mother always loves her biological children.
3. The biological mother is the best caretaker for her children.
4. Mothers know intuitively what their children need.
5. Infants need the constant presence of their mothers.
6. Love, marriage, and motherhood are naturally linked.
7. Motherhood within the heterosexual structure of marriage is the best way to raise children.

The mothers who formed the Children's Collective questioned these assumptions. For example, one woman said:

> When I see myself in a photograph with my two children, I have to realize that it is "me" with two children. It gives me the impression of the mother role which I do not want to play. This dependency of mothers on their children is what I dislike about it. . . . Mothers can only exist because of their children. I blame women for that.

When the mothers chose to oppose this view of motherhood, they met all kinds of resistance from other people and also from themselves. For example, one of the mothers said:

> My mother-in-law always sends letters and cards to my daughter to my home and never to the address of the Children's Collective. She simply does not want to acknowledge our way of life.

This woman also reported that it was very difficult for her to step back from her own daughter so others could have an intimate relationship with her. She said:

> My daughter always knew that I came back. When she cried as a small girl when I left, I knew she was really sad. She asked, "Mother, why are you leaving?" I felt guilty, but I knew that I had to go. It was not always easy to accept.

Freeing oneself from the ideology of motherhood means freeing oneself from the all-nurturant aspects and disciplinary power projected on mothers. It also means rejecting the dominating image of mother in the mirror, the symbolization of "The Mother," and accepting mothers' possible failure. At the same time it means accepting the subjectivity of the mother. Or, as Nancy Chodorow (1980) sees it:

> The idealization of mothers is an infantile fantasy. No human being can be perfect. . . . The fantasy of the perfect mother, however, has led to the cultural oppression of women in the interests of a child, whose needs are also fantasized. (p. 71)

Restructuring Sexuality, Child Care, and Domestic Labor

The Children's Collective attempted to retain the warm and caring aspects of the traditional family but to eliminate the repressive aspects, such as the division of labor between men and women and, especially, the confinement of women to the maternal role. In principle, this should decrease conflict between women and men. Essentially, then, the Children's Collective intended to alter power relationships, between women and men and between parents and children.

In practice, sharing of child care and domestic labor releases time for women to work for pay. The political appeal was the challenge to the nuclear family as the only life-style in which production, reproduction, sexuality, and socialization could take place. According to Wilson (1977), the way in which these four functions are interrelated and organized creates the repressive role of women in the family. The sexual division of labor is not so much based on biological arguments as on social coercion. From this point of view, there was a need, recognized by feminists, to reorganize these four functions into a new structure that would be less repressive than the nuclear family.

Simone de Beauvoir (1972) held that neither economic nor political independence were sufficient conditions for the liberation of women:

> The women who is economically independent of men is still in her moral, social, and psychological situation not equal to the men. . . . The woman is only a complete individual and equal to the men as she becomes also a sexual human subject.

Hence the reorganization of sexuality outside marriage would be necessary to liberate women.

Within marriage, women are primarily mothers and female sexuality has always been seen in terms of reproduction. Beginning in the 1960s, sexuality was no longer automatically linked to reproduction, and thus sexual liberation for women became possible.

The separation of sexuality and pregnancy also made it possible for women to rethink their position toward children. Never before have women had a choice about bearing children. Not wanting children within the nuclear family has been interpreted by some people as a rejection of children. Although this is not accurate, many feminist women were thought to be hostile toward children. Some feminists rejected the belief that serving as mothers and housekeepers within the nuclear family was their only possible role.

The Children's Collective provided an opportunity for women to care for their children but not to be confined to that role. It also provided an alternative for women to deal with the problems of their newly acquired sexual freedom. The children had a house of their own and thus did not need to be exposed to their mothers' changing moods related to sexual freedom.

Specific Assumptions and Aims of the Children's Collective

The Children's Collective parents had a number of goals. All the participants wanted to combine paid employment with child care. Because of inadequate provision of day care, these parents faced the dilemma of the choice between work and children. Because most elementary schools in the Netherlands do not provide lunch, children go home at lunch time. Someone, usually the mother, is at home between noon and 1:30 in the afternoon. These mothers did not want to choose between their work and adequate care for their children.

The parents had the following beliefs:

1. They rejected Bowlby's (1971) neopsychoanalytic contention that children need one mothering figure to achieve attachment. The mothers did not see themselves as the sole providers of warmth and care.

2. The struggle between men and women over the sharing of domestic labor could be resolved by the transformation of child care. Within the Collective, fathers as well as mothers would be responsible during one 24-hour period each week for housekeeping in the Collective.

3. Men would be required to look after their own and other people's children. Although most women occasionally care for other people's children, it was beleved that, by caring for children, men would acquire nurturant abilities.

4. Parents with only one child of their own would provide a living situation where other people's children would be accepted as brothers and sisters. Both biological and social ties would exist within the newly created family.

5. The creation of the Collective was expected to transform the traditional idea of a child as the private property of its biological parents. Parents would no longer talk about "my daughter" or "my son," but would consider other people's children "my children, our children." Shared responsibility would stimulate a collective identity.

6. Children would have a greater number of male and female identification figures. They would not just have one parent of either sex as the representations of "the mother" and "the father," but the mother would be represented by different women and the father by different men. This would diffuse the power attached to those figures and free them from a heavy psychological burden.

7. The parents would more easily share their childrearing problems with other parents. The collective would provide a setting in which such problems could be discussed.

8. The children would not be faced with, nor have their homes disrupted by, the potentially unstable love relationships of the parents.

THE PRACTICAL ORGANIZATION OF THE CHILDREN'S COLLECTIVE

The Collective in Amsterdam

A group of five parents, one couple and three divorced parents, two women and one man, bought an additional apartment where all of their six children, aged 1 to 9 years, lived together during the work week for a period of 17 years. The parents themselves lived apart near the Children's Collective. Unlike the Israeli kibbutzims' trained professional child-care workers, each parent alternately provided 24-hour child care in the Children's Collective. On the weekends, the children went to their parents' homes.

The women knew each other from the first women's consciousness-raising group in Amsterdam and shared common views. As one of the mothers stated:

> We wanted to raise the children collectively. Two separated parents wanted to share their child rearing. I have only one 2-year-old child, and I did not want to have another one. So for her it would better to have a home with more children to play with. I had the feeling that the Children's Collective freed me from daily mothering. I could see my child daily without the continuous responsibility of having to be home to look after her. I could combine child care for six children with four days of work outside the home, without guilt feelings. I felt rich having six children to look after, work, a husband, and a lover.

Another mother said:

> Being a single mother who was often ill, I needed other people to take over some of the daily care of my children. Apart from that, my children did not see their father, and I hoped the other men would be substitute fathers for my children. With our changing relationships and troubles with love and family life, we did not want to confront our children with these matters. . . . Within the women's consciousness-raising group, we always talked about the repressive sides of motherhood. None of us wanted to accept the image of the all powerful mother-figure. We knew we could not play this role.

Among the six children were three girls and three boys, including two sets of brothers and sisters. When the Collective started the boys were 1, 6, and 9 years old, the girls 1½, 7, and 8 years old. At that time, some of the children were in a stressful situation because of their parents' divorces. For instance, four children were bedwetting. However, despite their stressful lives, they liked each other very much and got along so well it seemed advantageous to set up a situation where they could live together. Initially they liked the home very much. The parents seemed to have more trouble adjusting to the cooperative situation than the children did.

Daily Schedule

The Collective was open from Monday morning until Friday evening. At least one parent each day took the entire responsibility for all six children, as well as the housekeeping, shopping, cooking, and so on. As it is usual in The Netherlands for parents to bring children to school, the caretaking parent brought all the children to school and fetched them back. The caretaker slept in the Collective that night and handed over the responsibility to another parent the next day. Once a week the house was cleaned by a domestic worker.

During the evenings, parents had their dinner either in the Collective or elsewhere. One of the women recalled:

> We usually had dinner with twelve people. It was always crowded and noisy. The adults talked a lot to each other and the children did not find it easy to talk. Teenagers want to tell their stories and my son sometimes had a hard time. After dinner the caretaking parent worked at full speed to do the dishes with the help of the oldest children, put the youngest to bed, read a little story to them. At half past eight, by the time those chores were finished, the oldest children were busy with their own activities. We needed the weekends to talk to our children or teach them special things. In the Children's Collective we did not always have the opportunity.

Authority within the Home

Parental authority was split across five adults and, in principle, there was no hierarchy among them. Nor was there consensus; rather, discipline was arbitrary. One of the girls, now in her twenties, recalled:

> The five adults did everything in their own way. Everybody had something they found important. I had to get used to it. Sometimes biological parents made distinctions between their own children and the others.

In some respects, the children saved some of their problems and experiences for their own biological parents. At other times, minor conflicts were resolved without any involvement of the biological parents.

Every fortnight there was a meeting of all parents and children in which children could discuss and propose changes they would like to make. For example, on one occasion they asked for a special telephone. The parents refused on the grounds that it was too expensive. The children came to the next meeting prepared with better arguments, and the parents accepted their suggestions. Within these meetings, the power relations between parents and children could be tested, and the different parties could listen to different kinds of arguments. So the struggle between parents and children about all sorts of things was spread among various people.

The parents considered the children's apartment to be the children's own home, where they could have their own rules. For example, the children could sleep wherever they wanted and could arrange it among themselves. The children's friends enjoyed visiting the Collective because they believed the children were free and had fun.

Material Arrangements

The parents did not invest a lot in the home, and so it did not always have to look attractive. The parents did not have the money or much time and energy to arrange the interior, which distressed some of the children. At one point, two teenagers invited their friends to their mother's home, because they liked it better.

There was a house budget to pay for food, electricity, gas, and pocket money for the children. The children did not know the financial arrangements.

Emotional Ties among the Children

Because the parents did not want their children to be the objects of psychological research, it is difficult to describe changes in the relationships among the children or between the various adults and the children. Particular bonds between the older and younger children existed. However, the goal of minimizing the biological ties of parents and children and establishing broader ties of attachment and emotional intimacy was not achieved.

The Children's Collective in Rotterdam

Another Children's Collective was started in Rotterdam 8 years later, in the summer of 1980. At the outset, the children ranged in age from 3 weeks to 4 years. All 10 parents lived next door, in different apartments. The parents had already known each other for 10 years from the student movement, the anti-authoritarian childrearing movement, and from a small communist group, the KEN (United Dutch Communist Movement). The collective is still in existence.

These parents perceived a contradiction between their social ideals and private lives, which motivated them to start living together. They aimed to break through the dependency relations between parents and children in the hope of creating free and nurturant children. They are trying to raise girls and boys to be caring and to occupy a successful position in society. These parents believed it necessary for additional people to participate in the education and care of their offspring. One of the criteria they set for successful education was a favorable emotional relationship between child and adult. Thus every adult in the group was committed to responding to the needs of all the children. All the adults take responsibility for the children, alternating caretaking duties, as in the Collective in Amsterdam. Not only parents but members of the Collective who are not parents participate in child care.

Emotional Aims and Methods

The adults perceive themselves as the most important identification figures for the children and so try to demonstrate free, androgynous ways of being. They discuss their private lives and their emotional resistance to changing male or female behavior. They regard it as important for men to learn to be nurturant and for women to have close contacts with other women. The emotional ties between all the parents are seen as very important.

Task Division among the Parents

Every day and night there are at least two parents in the Collective. They follow different work schedules, so one parent may be doing the shopping while another is responsible for contact with schoolteachers, another takes care of the financial administration, and a fourth is responsible for rebuilding the children's apartment.

Daily Schedule

During the night there are two parents in the Collective. In the morning, they have breakfast with the children, bring the children to school, and clean the house. In the afternoons there are always three or four adults present, parents and other adults who participate in the children's education and play with them. One of these adults is also responsible for household activities. In the evenings all the children eat together with the two caretaking parents and other caretakers of the day. Every month the adults make a schedule so children and adults know who will be home when.

Relations with Friends

The Collective frequently has contact with three other collectives. Some of the adults in the other collectives take on the role of social parent for the children.

The three collectives have a common place to eat where members can have dinner together and invite outsiders as well.

The children also have many school friends who come to the Collective to play. The Collective offers itself as an open house to friends and neighbors. There is room for discussion, parties, and musical sessions. They have already acquired a video station, which they use for role-playing sessions.

Material Arrangements

All the parents have a basic minimum income. They are either employed or have social security assistance. The children's apartment is totally adapted to the needs and wishes of the children. The interior is bright and cheerful.

Emotional Ties

All the children have attachment relations with at least three adults. In the beginning they were all very attached to their mothers, the primary caretakers. After several months, however, more people became emotional involved. Slowly the mothers were able to free themselves from the exclusive emotional claim. Eventually, mothers were able to have a more objective and realistic view of their children because others participated in the children's education and daily care and so could discuss what was going on between mother and child.

Fathers as well as mothers were more or less forced to rethink their own youths and socialization periods. They were confronted with their own patterns of sex-typed behavior, which they wanted to change with the help of other adults in the Collective.

Similarities and Differences between the Collectives

Both Collectives organized a 24-hour alternation in child care among adults as an expression of the wish to change the traditional view of the family and of motherhood. This implied a change in the division of labor between men and women inside the home as well as outside in the labor market. It also implied a change in monogamous marriage as the basis of the family. In both collectives, there was a desire to change the sexual arrangements between men and women, though this was less explicit in the Amsterdam Collective.

The Children's Collective in Amsterdam was begun by pioneer members of the women's movement. The women formulated their ideology and goals, and the men more or less adjusted to them. In contrast, the Rotterdam Collective was begun by parents and nonparents of both sexes who were involved in the student and communist movements. Its ideology was formulated more by men than by women and is more ideologically rigid.

One main difference between Collectives was the involvement of the Rotterdam Collective in a wider network of friends, especially the members of other collectives. These friends participate in child care as co-parents and in the discussions of family ideology and personal and political change. Furthermore, the Collective in Rotterdam is more open to friends and neighbors, and many people come in and go out. Many neighborhood children come to play. The Collective in Amsterdam was more of an isolated island. The adults in Rotterdam seem to have more political and intimate relations with each other than did the parents in Amsterdam. The Amsterdam parents were more individualistic in their way of living, beyond their duties in the Children's Collective. They were also more individualistic in the ways in which they educated their children.

Another difference seems to be the accent on sexual liberation, which is more important to the Rotterdam Collective. Some of the parents, influenced by Reichian psychology, stress the need for the sexual liberation of men, women, and children. As in the German collectives of the early 1960s, the Collective in Rotterdam explores the children's sexual wishes, and the parents respond to them as openly as possible. They challenge the sexual taboos in parent–child relationships.

The children in the Rotterdam Collective are young and demand more care from their parents than did the children in Amsterdam. For this reason, the biological and social parents are more involved, spending more time with the children than the parents did in Amsterdam. The Collective in Rotterdam seems to be more child-centered, from both an emotional and a material point of view. In contrast, the Collective in Amsterdam was more woman-centered. The women in the Collective in Amsterdam were very much involved in the women's movement.

Members of the Collective in Rotterdam have started to publish articles about their experiences and have made slides of their living arrangements. One of their aims is to get publicity and show that collective childrearing is possible as an alternative to the nuclear family. By publishing the ways they have organized parenting, and their liberal educational and sexual philosophy, they are vulnerable to criticism from the Dutch public and the State.

Evaluation of the Children's Collective in Amsterdam

Because the Collective in Rotterdam is still young, it is too early to evaluate its effects on the adults and children. However, the parents and children who lived collectively in Amsterdam have reflected on their experiences. Looking back, they make both positive and negative comments.

The members of the Collective stayed together for 7 years. This provided a solid basis for the children being together during their primary school years. During this time, the parents went out together a good deal, spent every year's 10 days' holiday together, and undertook small excursions in the afternoons when the children were not in school. It seems that, as in all families, the children had fun together and also had their struggles. As one of the girls, now in her twenties, said in an interview:

> I think it was nicer for us in the Collective than it would have been with my brother and mother alone. We were good friends, though we also had our fights.

Growing up in the Collective seems to have affected the living arrangements the children now adopt as young adults. One of the older girls lives alone but spends her holidays with friends. Her brother lives with other people, and the other brother and sister stayed in the apartment with the two other boys. Being raised together did not create needs for extreme privacy or individuality later on, nor did it create a longing for early romantic love or marriage. On the other hand, though they may live communally with other people, some of the children raised together do not often see or speak to each other. Thus the ideal of their becoming brothers and sisters was not realized.

Their current attachment to the adults of the Collective does not seem very strong. They do not often see or speak to the adults who cared for them, even though they may have positive memories of their experiences. As one girl said:

> It was a special period in my life. I had a lot of contact with other adults, more than children from ordinary families would have had.

The various women in the Collective provided different identification figures for the girls. The participating women were all very different, combining work with child care and love relationships in different ways. Thus the girls were provided with more than one image of womanhood. One another has speculated about what this meant for her daughters:

> This gave her strength. She seems to know what she is up to. She feels secure about herself. It did not seem to make her ambivalent about womanhood.

At the same time, the ideal of becoming mothers for each other's children was not realized. As one of the women said:

> There was not enough continuity. You had a very intimate relationship with all the children for one day, but then you went away and the children knew that. You felt it as a deficiency. This is the reason why we are not so close and intimate with the other children. If you were either irritated or had a nice time with the children one day, it would be gone the next. Sometimes you did not even bother to come back to the issue.

Although the women did not become mothers for each other's children, they felt that the collective childrearing bolstered their own strength as mothers. For example, one mother said that the Children's Collective actually saved her relationship with her children:

> I was always ill and knocked out. Children can get bored or fed up with a mother who always feels miserable. Children do not like that and could easily worry about their

mother. But in my case there were other women who gave my daughter other examples of womanhood. Even if they were not real mothers to her, they were good caretakers with whom she had a nice time.

The mother of the youngest girl felt that she had been in danger of overwhelming her daughter. She felt that she would completely take on the maternal role while taking on both the total responsibility and the guilt for not fulfilling the role perfectly. She believes that the Children's Collective saved her from doing so. Her daughter is still very much attached to her and, as one of the other mothers said, "likes to play the perfect daughter."

Six years after the experience, that mother has said:

> I do not have to feel guilty anymore. I think the Children's Collective was a good decision. But I still find it difficult to admit that I have a daughter whom I love very much but did not see for 48 hours each week. I left the Children's Collective in the morning after breakfast, went to work, had dinner with my lover, slept with him, and saw her only two days later. It was sometimes difficult, but I did not change this pattern because I thought it was good theoretically.

For the radical lesbian mother, the Children's Collective provided the opportunity for leaving the care of her children to the father and the group of parents. She took on the traditional wage earner's role and gave material support, seeing her children on weekends. One of the other participating parents remarked that:

> Her children probably need more emotional support; neither their father nor their mother could give them what they needed emotionally, I think. Their parents always said, "They will look after themselves, and they need their own social system."

This ideal of emotional independence of course reflects the ideology of the 1960s. As Lynne Segal (1983) wrote:

> Women in their roles as girl-friends, wives, and mothers have always been doing most of the emotional giving and nurturing which men have been receiving characteristically providing less adequate nurturing in return. (p. 56)

It is clear that this radical lesbian mother did not want to reproduce this kind of woman's role. Instead, she devoted herself to intellectual work and to activities in the women's movement.

In general, all these women had reflected on their roles as mothers, which enabled them to change what seemed natural within the two-parent nuclear family. For all of them, collective childrearing meant an emotional readjustment within a society that is very critical of the ways in which women mother. As pioneers within the women's movement, they had to resist the image of what Nancy Chodorow (1980) calls "an all-powerful mother with on the one side the blaming of the mother and on the other side the idealization of her and her possibilities" (p. 57).

The experience of collective childrearing also required an emotional readjustment on the part of the children, who were living in a society where the two-child nuclear family is normative. As I see it, the Children's Collective had more positive effects for the girls than for the boys. The girls had strong and courageous women with whom to identify; the boys had more difficulties.

The Collective was feminist, and from the beginning there was an ambivalent and sometimes negative attitude toward men. On the other hand, male intellectual values dominated, and emotional resistance toward sharing of the love relationship between mother and child had to be overcome. Members of the Collective, including the participating fathers, rejected male dominance. Aggression among the children was not accepted and in fact did not seem to exist. As one parent said:

> There did not seem to be any fighting over the attention of one's own parent. All the children had to share their parents with the other children. The special bond between biological parent and child could be expressed on the weekends or during the holidays.

It was not easy, however, to eliminate male dominant behavior from the Collective. One of the fathers was verbally authoritarian; as one of the mothers put it, "In a way he was able to let the children choose whatever he wanted them to do." Furthermore, when the two eldest boys became teenagers, they sometimes dominated the other children; one had a "big mouth." This kind of behavior was not accepted at all and caused problems for that boy. He became very insecure about himself and his male identity and he wanted to leave the Collective. He wanted to live in his mother's apartment, but that was not initially accepted. A meeting of parents and children was held to try to settle the problem. It turned out that he was in fact the first child to leave the Collective, thereafter staying in his mother's house next door. At the moment he is in his early twenties; he does not want to discuss his time in the Collective. His mother reports:

> He did not have a good time the last 2 years in the Collective. He became very vulnerable and felt threatened. The two fathers were not real fathers or identification figures for him, as I hoped they would have been. As I see it now, he started having relationships with girls very late, and did not have any sexual experiences with girls until his early twenties. He is shy about it.

She continued:

> I think we were not able to express heterosexual love in the collective. There was a taboo against showing love or intimacy between men and women; this happened outside the collective and was hidden from the children. So I think it was threatening for my son to start a heterosexual relationship.

She also admitted:

> I had to work very hard for years to gain his trust. For him, the Collective was probably too difficult. The two boys were confronted with too much aggression towards their gender. The male gender was attacked, and they felt it personally, at the very time that they had to take up their male identities.

Both boys, now in their twenties, are studying very hard and trying to establish their identities in intellectual work.

In general, the outcome of the Amsterdam Collective suggests that the discontinuity of care and the alternation of responsibility of the caretakers had positive, liberating effects on mothers and daughters and more negative effects on sons. The daughters had a greater number of women with whom to identify and hence gained different images of womanhood. However, the lack of intimacy and the taboo against showing heterosexual love, as well as the discrepancy between dominant male intellectual values and the dismissal of dominant male behavior, seemed to cause more problems for boys than for girls. Nevertheless, the boys did see men participating in household activities and child care. They are probably more inclined to do this kind of work later in life and may not regard it as discordant with the male identity. Still, in their adolescence and early twenties, they are confused about it.

These differences between the sons and daughters of the Collective suggest that, in a male-dominated society, where work and achievement are highly valued, women's work outside the home is more likely to be accepted than child care provided by men. Male identity seems more resistant to change than the identity of women.

REFERENCES

Bowlby, J. (1971). *Child care and the growth of love*. Harmondsworth: Penguin.

Chodorow, N. (1978). *The reproduction of mothering*. Berkeley: University of California Press.

Chodorow, N. (1980). The fantasy of the perfect mother. In B. Thorne & M. Yalon (Eds.), *Rethinking the family*.

Comer, L. (1971). *The myth of motherhood*. Nottingham: Partisan Press.

de Beauvoir, S. (1972). *The second sex*. Harmondsworth: Penguin.

Laing, R. (1976). *The politics of the family*. Harmondsworth: Penguin.

Philipson, I. (1982). Narcissism and mothering: 1950 reconsidered. *Women's Studies International Forum, 1*, 29–39.

Rich, A. (1976). *Of women born*. New York: Norton.

Rossi, A. (1981). On the reproduction of mothering, a methodological debate. *Signs, 6*, 482–514.

Segal, L. (1983). *What is to be done about the family?* Harmondsworth: Penguin.

Smit, J. (1967). *Het onbehagen van de vrouw*. Amsterdam: de Gids.

Wilson, E. (1977). *Women and the welfare state*. London, Tavistock.

Contemporary American Motherhood

Paralleling contemporary American society, in which new family forms are becoming more prominent, Part III highlights the experiences of diverse groups of mothers. These groups are increasing in prominence in the general population but the faces of the members of such groups are often misperceived and sometimes barely visible.

Kathleen McCartney and Deborah Phillips (Chapter 7) discuss the experiences of the majority of American mothers whose children are in day-care; Valora Washington (Chapter 8) discusses the experience of black motherhood in contrast to the myth of the black matriarchy; Martha Straus (Chapter 9) examines the economic, social, and psychological realities that face divorced mothers; Barbara Holland Baskin and Elizabeth Riggs (Chapter 10) highlight an often-forgotten group of mothers, those who are themselves disabled; and Joan Kuchner and Jane Porcino (Chapter 11) describe the experiences of women who have become mothers relatively late in life.

Before taking up each of these topics, however, it is useful to consider some of the facts concerning contemporary American motherhood. Motherhood as an American experience reflects both historical influences and contemporary change (see Table 1).

MOTHERHOOD AND CHILD CARE

In discussing motherhood and child care, McCartney and Phillips address an issue faced by the majority of American mothers. In 1970, only 30% of all mothers were employed but by 1985 this figure rose to 58% (Hofferth & Phillips, 1987). The greatest change, however, is in the number of mothers of infants who are now in the paid labor force. In 1975, this figure was 31%; by 1987, it rose to over 50% (Phillips, 1987).

A major federal and state policy question has become how to provide the best care for infants when mothers work. McCartney and Phillips trace the social history and contemporary manifestations of American ambivalence about maternal employment and child care. Noting that the earliest provision of day care

TABLE 1.

Facts about Mothers in the Late-Twentieth-Century United States[a]

1. 1985—20 million or 62% women with children under 18 in labor force.
2. 1984—proportion of poor families maintained by women was 48%.
3. 1984—women maintained 73% of poor black families.
4. 1985—17% of all families maintained by a woman.
5. Current estimated divorce rate—50% of all marriages.
6. 21% of families are comprised of a husband as earner, a mother at home, and children under age 18.
7. Most women work because of economic need. Nearly 2/3 are single, divorced, widowed, separated, or had husbands earning less than $15,000.
8. 1985—79% of women with 4-plus years of college in labor force. For women with less than 4 years of high school the figure is 44%.
9. 1984—Median income of married couples with wife in the paid labor force was $34,668; for married couples with the wife not working, $23,582.

[a]U.S. Department of Labor, Women's Bureau, 1986, *20 Facts on Women Workers*. Miller, G., *Child Care Opportunities for Families Act of 1985: A Fact Sheet*.

began in the mid-nineteenth century and was predicated on the belief that poor immigrant mothers were "inadequate," child care was established to rescue the children. By the 1930s Depression and World War II, the economic requirements of American society led to government-funded centers: working women, including middle-class women, were now considered "patriotic." After the war, most centers closed. By the 1960s, child care again became targeted for the poor, and mothers who used day care were labeled "disadvantaged." By the 1970s, things changed again. The authors call contemporary working mothers the "conflicted mothers." The need and the scarcity of adequate child care for the nation's several million children of working mothers is carefully documented.

McCartney and Phillips (Chapter 7) comment on the current debate concerning child care and the mother–child relationship. They indicate that shared child care does not negatively influence the child's emotional development and discuss shared childrearing in other cultures. McCartney and Phillips see the guilt some mothers feel as the major effect of the authorities who claim that day care is harmful to children. They document the need for social supports and social ideology that deal with today's realities for American women and children.

BLACK MOTHERS

Black mothers may be the most written about and most inaccurately portrayed women in America. Washington (Chapter 8) describes how psychologists, sociologists, and policy analysts have projected a pejorative image of the black matriarch, whereas black writers have typically idealized the image of mother. Washington demonstrates the fallacy of the myth of the black matriarch and describes the strengths of black women who rear their children in a racist society. Above all, she culls from the vast and frequently misleading studies some of the realities of the lives of black mothers. Washington documents the economic hardships faced by black mothers that are predicated on discrimination in education, employment, and housing and lead to problems in the health and well-being of their children.

But most of the research and policy analysis concerning black mothers is criticized in her article. By defining new research goals and a priority list of needed social policy for the black community, Washington's contribution stands among the chapters that will generate debate about how best to provide women, many of them poor, with viable options.

DIVORCED MOTHERS

Martha Straus (Chapter 9) demonstrates that divorced mothers share certain attributes with the other groups of mothers described in this book. They are a heterogeneous group, little understood, rarely studied, and surrounded by myths. However, divorced mothers also have unique characteristics. Their lives are marked by an event that heralds a change in status. This makes them and their children an important group for study. Furthermore, the social policies governing their lives have changed dramatically in the last two decades.

Straus pinpoints the fallacies that arise when social scientists focus solely on "psychological" issues. She notes that, from the psychological and sociological perspective, "single mothers" have been considered deviant. They have been described as unstable and incapable of adequate parenting. Without denying the fact that divorced mothers are frequently distressed by the dissolution of their marriages, Straus reviews the evidence suggesting that it is the sudden, instant poverty rather than psychological absence of the children's father that is the greatest problem for divorced mothers. She notes that, after the initial period of crisis and "diminished parenting," some women find their lives enhanced by divorce, particularly if the marriage that ended had been extremely conflicted. Straus's chapter documents the importance of asking the right question of the right people and the need for the study of the ecology of divorced mothers that goes beyond the characterization of their lives as deviant.

DISABLED MOTHERS

Baskin and Riggs (Chapter 10) make clear that, among the many faces of motherhood in the late twentieth century, the face most obscured is that of the disabled mother. The disabled are even more heterogeneous as a group than the other mothers discussed in this section. Whereas all black women have in common the experience of racial discrimination, and all divorced women share a sudden change in status, women with different disabilities are least likely to form a support group or even encounter other women with similar problems. The struggle for survival as mothers and the limited possibility of getting to know others who share their problems add to the isolation of handicapped mothers. Disabled mothers have not organized politically, and their particular needs have been ignored by both policymakers, concerned with the handicapped, and activists, concerned with women's issues.

Baskin and Riggs could not draw upon formal studies as their data base. Rather, they explored the lives of women with disabilities either as described to them in personal interviews or in the few autobiographies that exist. They have also drawn on data concerning education and employment, insofar as those are critical issues for disabled mothers. Similar to other mothers, the disabled are least handicapped when they are well educated and financially independent. Similar to all parents, they function best when they have the support of friends, families, and professionals. However, most professionals are ill-informed, if not misinformed, about the ability of handicapped women to successfully bear and rear their children.

More than any other group of mothers discussed in this section, disabled women have been explicitly discouraged from choosing motherhood. Baskin and Riggs's chapter is ground breaking in documenting how parents, schools, and the helping professions systematically discourage disabled women from having children and sometimes are active in separating them from their children.

Delayed Motherhood

The study of women who postpone childrearing is less than a decade old. Whereas in the 1950s most women (70%) who were to become mothers did so by the age of 25, in the 1980s this percentage dropped to 53% (Kuchner & Porcino, Chapter 11). Women who postpone childrearing are most likely to be well-educated and employed. For these women several questions are posed and answered before they become mothers. Some questions are: Should I have children? When is the right time? How will children affect my career? Should I have children if not married?

Kuchner and Porcino discuss the medical and psychological factors specific to this group of women. They also summarize the small (but interesting) number of studies of these women when they do become mothers. Whereas there is an increase in medical risks for older first-time mothers, there are also many benefits. Older mothers are usually financially secure, well-educated, and resourceful. Their enhanced self-esteem is also a benefit. As this phenomenon is relatively new, we still know very little about how these mothers will fare when at an age when most women are grandmothers they will be the parents of teenagers.

Chapter 7

Motherhood and Child Care

Kathleen McCartney and Deborah Phillips

A Changing Conception of Motherhood

Although the women's movement could not produce the symbolic equal rights amendment, it did produce the beginnings of needed social change for women. The effects of this social change are evident today in evolving professional and family roles of men and women. For many women, perhaps the greatest change concerns the conception of motherhood. Motherhood is now discussed in the context of child care, that is, shared childrearing between the family and child-care providers. In fact, the psychological study of mothering has always focused almost exclusively on the effects of various childrearing strategies on the developing abilities of children (Gerson, Alpert, & Richardson, 1984).

The role of child care in our society subsumes the issues of raising children, being parents, and defining social responsibilities. Child care is surrounded by controversy precisely because it touches upon basic values. It is for this reason that a chapter on child care earns its place in a volume on motherhood. Both public and private conceptions of the mothering role are intimately linked with the social and scientific histories of child care. Moreover, it is an easy prediction to make that the future conception of motherhood will be profoundly affected by the adequacy and quality of the child-care system that evolves during these changing times for women.

Our society's profound ambivalence about child care reflects concerns that child care poses a threat to motherhood and the sanctity of the family. Until recently, in western industrial society, any role for women other than motherhood has been portrayed as deviant (Hoffman & Hoffman, 1973). Although the employed mother is normative demographically (Piotrkowski & Repetti, 1984), concern about the effect of child care continues. On a political level, debates about child care revolve around fears that public support for child care

Kathleen McCartney • Department of Psychology, University of New Hampshire, Durham, New Hampshire 03824. Deborah Phillips • Department of Psychology, University of Virginia, Charlottesville, Virginia 22904.

will weaken the family's role and lend undesired credibility to nonfamilial forms of childrearing. Consequently, child-care providers become cast as competitors to parents, rather than as partners. Child-care services are rarely portrayed as supportive and complementary to the family, unless accompanied by paternalistic motives to rectify the effects of deprivation.

The effects of this adversarial relation between child care and parenting are great. As families' reliance on child care continues to rise for economic and social reasons, legislators, educators, and scientists continue to question the wisdom of sharing the mothering role. The result of this well-motivated questioning is a lack of support for child care, despite historical, cross-cultural, and developmental evidence that child care neither harms children nor erodes the mother–child bond. Although mothers are not aware of such evidence, they are aware of ever-present cultural perceptions, and so they, too, question.

Sylvia Ann Hewlett's (1986) recent personal view in *A Lesser Life* is poignantly illustrative:

> As a conscientious new mother I read the child-rearing manuals and found, to my dismay, that much of the experts' advice was incompatible with a professional existence . . . I failed to find any child-rearing book that expended more than two pages on the problems of the working mother; most experts were more or less hostile. Benjamin Spock told me that unless a mother absolutely must work, it makes no sense for her to "pay other people to do a poorer job of bringing up [her] children," while Berry Brazelton argued that "two mothers are not as good as one" and urged mothers to delay their return to work. (p. 20)

In nearly all societies, parental expectations of fathers continue to be different. Despite evidence that babies become attached to fathers (Lamb, 1980), and despite an increasing interest, at least among some fathers, in childrearing (Lamb, Frodi, Hwang, & Frodi, 1982), child care is never discussed in the context of paternal deprivation. From an egalitarian perspective, child care should be discussed in the context of parenting. From the contemporary societal perspective, it is, in fact, discussed in the context of mothering. This bias is reflected in the fact that, comparatively, the father is only a recent object of study (Lamb, 1976; Parke, 1979).

This chapter examines the sources, manifestations, and consequences of the uneasy relation between motherhood and shared childrearing. The evidence supports the view that the uneasiness, or conflict, is a cultural byproduct that reflects and in turn promotes current American values. We begin with analyses of the social and scientific legacies concerning mothering and child care. The effects of these legacies on motherhood are then examined through the lives of six women and through a questionnaire study. The chapter concludes with suggestions for social action to ameliorate the unnecessary guilt employed mothers in our culture share about child care.

MOTHERHOOD AND CHILD CARE: THE SOCIAL LEGACY

Today's concerns that child care poses a threat to a mother's natural and exclusive responsibility for childrearing is the direct inheritance of a social history that was carved around the need to avoid, at all costs, the legitimization of nonmaternal childrearing (Blum, 1983; Joffe, 1977; Long, Peters, & Garduque, 1985; Steinfels, 1973). This section will trace the various ways in which prevailing values about motherhood have affected the social history of child care and, in turn, have been affected by the functions of child care in our society.

Child care first emerged as a social institution at a time when the sanctity of motherhood had become firmly entrenched. The nineteenth century was a time of transition in social conceptions of the family. Two developments are primarily responsible. First, lower infant mortality rates led to a greater emotional investment in children. Second, the industrial revolution led men away from home to the workplace, which increasingly segregated women at home to manage household responsibilities and childrearing. What followed was the progressive separation of a man's public, ambitious world from a woman's private, nurturing world (Lasch, 1977).

It is important to emphasize the newness of the cultural ideas that evolved as a consequence of these two developments. Aries' (1962) treatise on the history of childhood first led scholars to recognize that past generations did not hold the kind of sentimental ideas about childhood that are with us today. As Kessen (1979) noted, the child is a cultural invention; indeed, the mother is a cultural invention as well (Dally, 1982).

Attitudes changed in accordance with increasingly narrow sex roles. Women were romanticized as loving, cultured, and in need of protection. Thus, the working-class woman who once toiled beside her husband in the field was now viewed, for the most part as incapable of "serious," that is, paid work. The childrearing function of women exacerbated this stereotype in light of the natural vulnerability of children. The isolation and close association of mother and child, which was an economic byproduct, became viewed as necessary for the healthy development of the child. Any effort to share childrearing responsibilities was portrayed as intrusive and detrimental; hence, the very great potential for a mother's conflict about child care.

From the outset, then, child care posed a challenge to prevailing views about what is best for children, suitable for women, and convenient for an industrial society. However, in the long evolution of the human species, women have engaged in productive labor concurrent with childbearing and childrearing (Rossi, 1977). It is only since the industrial revolution that a society's economy has afforded *some* women with what amounts to the luxury of motherhood as a profession. Women have always engaged in productive labor and women have always relied on shared childrearing to accomplish this. It is only because memories are short that child care, our society's form of shared childrearing, has seemed somehow new.

Social ideals about motherhood have provided a pivotal point around which justifications for child care revolve. Although previous analyses of the functions of child care have focused on its social roles (Fein & Clarke-Stewart, 1973), its policy functions (Belsky, 1985; Phillips & Zigler, 1987), and its effects on children (Clarke-Stewart & Fein, 1983), this analysis focuses on how these various justifications have been shaped by social conceptions of the mothering role. Specifically, four different prototypes of mothers are evident from the different functions served by child care: the inadequate mother, the patriotic mother, the disadvantaged mother, and the conflicted mother.

The Inadequate Mother

Until recently, mothers who used child care were stigmatized as somehow unable to provide an adequate childrearing environment. The origins of this stigma lie in the purposes and populations served by our nation's earliest child-care programs: the day nurseries.

Day nurseries first emerged in response to the unprecedented influx of immigrants during the mid- to late 19th century (Joffe, 1977; Rothman, 1973; Steinfels, 1973). Initially, the motive behind the day nurseries was largely benevolent, albeit disparaging of immigrants and poor mothers. The nurseries were specifically designed to create a family-like alternative to the orphanage and other permanent, institutional responses to "unacceptable" home conditions for children. Unacceptability was determined by a blend of concerns about children's whereabouts while their mothers worked and about the effects of "unfit" home conditions on children. In fact, there was a real fear that, in the absence of the morals and hygiene exemplified by the day nurseries, children from poor populations would fail to be socialized into American culture or worse would become delinquents or relief cases.

Although they had been prompted by a humanitarian zeal, the day nurseries, in practice, supported a nontraditional and problematic family form; moreover, they supported class division. Accordingly, the day nurseries came to be characterized as a temporary relief service for mothers who were not fulfilling their maternal responsibilities, mothers who were thus viewed as inadequate.

This portrayal of the day nurseries as a service for inadequate mothers became firmly entrenched during the 1920s and the 1930s, when responsibility for these services shifted from the charitable sector to professional social workers and teachers (Fein & Clarke-Stewart, 1973; Ruderman, 1968; Steinfels, 1973). Social welfare was viewed as an essential and beneficial service that was targeted on families who by definition failed to exemplify the American ideals of self-sufficiency, privacy, and domesticity.

As a consequence, child care became increasingly associated with welfare casework and pathological families, rather than with families who simply were poor. A statement by Grace Caldwell before the 1919 National Conference of Social Work is illustrative: "That we spend the greater part of our funds for the care of children does not alter the fact that the reason we do so is because of some maladjustment in the families of which they are members . . ." (Steinfels, 1973, p. 61).

The Patriotic Mother

The link between use of child care and maternal inadequacy established in the early 1900s held firm until the economic depression of the 1940s and World

War II, both of which necessitated that women, and not just poor women, enter the labor force. For the first time, the use of child care could not be justified with the traditional child welfare arguments.

The alternative involved linking child care to patriotism. Mothers who relied on child care were rescuing the country, first from economic failure and then from war. These middle-class mothers' use of child care was also characterized as a temporary expedient. When the crises passed, mothers would return home to their children. Many working-class mothers remained in the labor force, a situation that was made more difficult by the fact that all federal funds for the support of child-care programs were withdrawn immediately after the national crises passed (Fein & Clarke-Stewart, 1973; Steinfels, 1973).

Thus, under extraordinary circumstances, the mothering role can be supplanted by other national needs. The justifications for maternal employment and the concomitant use of child care emphasized the national interest and economic necessity, rather than family inadequacy. Perhaps most important for the preservation of motherhood was the portrayal of child care as a necessary, not beneficial, expedient, which constituted a very short-term deviation from rightful roles. Great steps were taken to assure that child care would not become an acceptable part of family life.

The Disadvantaged Mother

By the mid-1960s, public disparagement of the poor was tempered somewhat by the ideology of cultural deprivation. There was a growing appreciation of how conditions in society, not just personal inadequacies, contributed to poverty. With respect to mothers, their ability to provide a nurturing home environment became viewed as a function, in part, of social conditions such as discrimination, inequality of educational opportunities, and job shortages.

Two kinds of child care emerged from this new mentality. One emphasized children's need for an educational environment during their early years; the other linked child care to welfare reform. The Head Start Project exemplifies the first kind, because it arose from theories that stressed the significance of children's early experiences for their later achievements (e.g., Bloom, 1964; Hunt, 1961). The variety of federal child-care programs that have been tagged onto welfare reform proposals exemplify the second kind (Phillips & Zigler, 1987). Both kinds of child care were viewed as more constructive than the day nurseries, because of their emphasis on intervention. Head Start and welfare-linked child-care programs were framed within a problem-solving approach—one to launch children on a path of school and career success and the other to promote the economic independence of families.

Nevertheless, these approaches to child care failed to escape all associations with inadequate mothering. Indeed, when the Head Start model of early childhood education was extended to nonpoor families in the Comprehensive Child Development Act of 1971, it was greeted with a veto message by President Nixon that criticized the legislation for its "family weakening" implications and for advocating "communal approaches to childrearing over the family-centered approach" (*Congressional Record*, December 1971, p. S1129–30).

In a society that values both independence and middle-class style mothering, families that need to rely on public subsidies to achieve these goals are automatically suspect (Grubb & Lazerson, 1982), hence, the label "deprived mothers." The deprived mother's use of child care derives from the fact that she does not satisfy our society's image of the teacher-mother in an economically independent family. Her inadequacy, however, is defined in terms of external factors and so does not carry the same degree of blame associated with child-welfare-based child care.

The Conflicted Mother

The women's movement for equality, an increase in divorce rates, and economic need all have contributed to the unprecedented growth in women's participation in the labor force. Since 1947, the labor force participation rate of women has increased in all but 4 years (Smith, 1979). Among mothers, the rate of labor force participation has tripled during this time span (U.S. Department of Labor, 1983). Thus, rather than serving as a temporary expedient, child care did in fact become an integral part of American family life.

In a society that defines the home as the sole institution for childrearing, mothers who work outside the home are problematic. At the same time, there is a growing recognition that, like it or not, mothers are no longer staying home. The younger the child, the more rapid the rate of increase in labor force participation among mothers (Hofferth & Phillips, 1987).

This situation poses the greatest challenge to the ideal of the stay-at-home mother, who not only does not need child care, but also may view it as threatening to her identity. The issue becomes one of endorsing child care as part of normative family life and supporting its use or one of tolerating the growing use of child care as a necessary evil for mothers who must or choose to work outside the home.

The label for these mothers, "conflicted," portrays two aspects of how the "myth of motherhood" (Scarr, 1984) has been maintained despite the unprecedented growth in reliance on child care. First, mothers who use child care are among those who share public perceptions that the use of child care is a necessity, rather than one of many suitable options. A survey conducted by Yankelovich (1983) revealed that 43% of working mothers believed that work-oriented women should not be mothers and 42% believed that mothers, especially those with children under 6 years, should not work. Rather than redefine the childrearing role that has been reserved for mothers, the ideal of the stay-at-home mother continues to provide the norm against which personal decisions are judged, even by those who make the decisions.

In addition, it is important to remember that parents who use child care are largely on their own. No public effort has been made to accommodate their need to combine parental and work responsibilities. Only 2,500 companies from a possible 400,000 large businesses and 6 million companies nationwide provide any form of child-care support (Friedman, 1985). Although the dependent care tax credit maintains strong support, it largely benefits the middle-class and it reimburses these families for at most 30% of their child-care expenses.

To summarize, mothers who use child care have been characterized as inadequate, patriotic, deprived, and now, conflicted. These portrayals have carefully protected our deeply held belief that children fare best when they are reared exclusively by their mothers. The question remains, what is the scientific evidence concerning motherhood and child care?

MOTHERHOOD AND CHILD CARE: THE SCIENTIFIC LEGACY

Attachment Theory

The purpose of the preceding brief social history of shared childrearing is to demonstrate that social ideology guides our ideas about the family, which in turn guides our ideas about policy. Not surprisingly, social ideology similarly guides our ideas about research (Scarr, 1985). The romanticized mother and child of this century are most clearly reflected in the scientific literature in mother–child attachment theory.

Children become attached to primary caretakers, typically mothers, early in infancy. The beginnings of attachment can be observed in the fourth month of life, when infants begin to discriminate familiar from unfamiliar people. Clear attachment can be observed in the sixth month of life, when infants begin to show preferences for caretakers. Preference is indicated primarily via proximity-seeking behavior. Bowlby (1951, 1958, 1969) established that infants accomplish this feat through the behaviors most commonly observed during infancy: crying, cooing, babbling, smiling, clinging, sucking, and following. Bowlby's main contribution was to suggest that attachment behavior is "biologically biased," that is, innate, for its survival value. An infant who maintains proximity with mother is more likely to be cared for.

The influence of ethology on Bowlby's theory of attachment is evident in references to the evolutionary significance of attachment behavior. The influence of psychoanalytic theory is evident in references to the importance of the primary relationship with mother. Following Freud, Bowlby believed that early attachment with mother is of special significance, because this relationship serves as the prototype of future relationships. The term "monotropism" was introduced by Bowlby to refer to "the tendency for instinctual responses to be directed toward a particular individual or group of individuals and not promiscuously toward many." (Bowlby, 1958, p. 370). In his report to the World Health Organization, Bowlby (1951) asserted that the emotional development of the child depended in large part upon a relationship with "one person who steadily 'mothers' him." Other attachment theorists, notably Ainsworth (Ainsworth & Wittig, 1969), similarly stress the importance of the primary attachment with mother.

As a consequence of attachment theory, the psychological study of childrearing has focused almost exclusively on the mother–child relationship. Shared childrearing is discussed within the context of maladjustment, for example, whether day care leads to attachment insecurity. This bias in psychological study merely reflects relatively new Western cultural attitudes about both childhood and motherhood.

Following evolutionary theory, polymatric infant-care systems, in which mother shares childrearing responsibilities with interested others, would appear to be more adaptive than monotropism in most cases. For the infant, close relationships with a few familiar adults would seem to have increased survival benefits over a close relationship with a single caregiver. Multiple caregivers in a child's life increase the likelihood that a child will be cared for and protected from danger. For females, close relationships with related offspring should maximize inclusive fitness, that is, the continuation of one's genes in future generations.

The central tenet of evolutionary theory is that the primary function of an organism is to reproduce genes (see Dawkins, 1976). Evolutionary biologists argue that inclusive fitness is the motivating force behind maternal nurturance. Mothers are willing to invest valuable resources in their offspring to ensure the replication of shared genes. The survival of a child benefits all relatives who will share a percentage of genes with the child. Thus, it is not surprising from an evolutionary perspective that relatives of a child such as an aunt, sibling, or grandmother have been willing to undertake childrearing responsibilities.

Allomothering, caregiving by a nonrelative, is even explainable within an evolutionary context. Reciprocal allomothering by two women would increase the inclusive fitness of both. These two women would form an implicit altruistic social contract (Trivers, 1971)—for example, if I care for or protect your baby now, then you will care for or protect my baby tomorrow. Thus, shared caregiving is a comprehensible strategy from both the child's perspective and the mother's perspective. Although evolutionary theory hardly supports monotropism, as Bowlby suggests, it does support the adaptive function of attachment with some moderate number of interested caretakers.

Cross-Cultural Studies of Shared Childrearing

Cross-cultural data support the view that the American emphasis on mother–infant attachment reflects a cultural theory of development rather than a scientific theory of development. Weisner and Gallimore (1977) surveyed 186 nonindustrial societies and found that exclusive childrearing of infants was rare. Rather, shared childrearing with others, with, for example, younger or older relatives, is more the norm. Additional caretakers were present in 40% of societies during infancy and 80% of societies during early childhood.

Anthropologists have long recognized that childrearing arrangements are largely based on economic considerations. In foraging groups, mother and child stay in close proximity for the protection of the child in a potentially dangerous environment. For example, among the Bushmen, a hunting and gathering tribe, the mother is typically the exclusive caregiver for the first 3 years of the child's life (Konner, 1972). In agricultural groups, a mother will rely on childrearing assistance, because she is needed for work away from home. For example, among the Taira of Okinawa the young mother shares childrearing responsibilities with the grandmother, who is a less valued worker (Maretzi & Maretzi, 1963). Among the Kikuyu of Nairobi the young mother shares childrearing responsibilities with a young girl, often a relative, who again is a less skilled worker. By the time Kikuyu infants are about 6 months of age they are cared for by child nurses for about half the day (Leiderman & Leiderman, 1973). It is known that in hunter-gatherer societies women produce half or more of the food through their productive labor (Rossi, 1977). As such, shared childrearing has been both a necessity and a way of life.

Smith (1980) concludes that the fact that shared childrearing with one or a few subsidiary caregivers is frequent and perhaps even predominant through most of human history, including modern times, suggests that such practices are in no sense harmful for the child. In other words, there is no reason to believe that shared childrearing interferes with the development of the child's attachment with the mother. Attachment behaviors may be highly canalized, because of their survival importance (Scarr-Salapatek, 1976). In addition, shared childrearing would not seem to interfere with the mother's bonding with the child. Hinde (1983) has noted that the styles of mothering that are biologically advantageous will vary with circumstance and that an argument that any one mothering style is best, for example, monotropism, is on dangerous grounds. Humans are no doubt adapted to adapt.

Yet, research queries are based on social ideology and not historical analysis and evolutionary theory. Thus, there is a substantial literature on child care and attachment. Two questions have been asked: (a) Does substitute child care, specifically center-based day care, disrupt the formation of attachment and lead to felt insecurity and (b) Do children develop stronger attachment relationships with caregivers than with mothers?

Child Care and the Child's Attachment to Mother: A Meta-Analysis

Research on attachment has burgeoned since the late 1960s with the development of a measurement tool, Ainsworth's Strange Situation (Ainsworth & Wittig, 1969; Ainsworth, Blehar, Waters, & Wall, 1978). As we have seen earlier, Ainsworth and her colleagues designed a procedure to measure attachment that consists of seven 3-minute episodes involving the primary attachment figure, typically the mother, the baby, and a female stranger: mother and baby are alone (Episode 1), a stranger joins mother and baby (Episode 2), mother leaves so that stranger and baby are alone (Episode 3), mother returns and stranger departs (Episode 4), mother departs and baby is left alone (Episode 5), stranger returns (Episode 6), stranger departs and mother returns (Episode 7).

Attachment is operationalized primarily in three child behaviors: ability to use the attachment figure as a secure base, reaction to a stranger, and reaction to separation and reunion with the attachment figure. Observers rate how well the stressed baby is able to organize his or her behavior around the mother while under stress. Particular attention is paid to both departure and reunion behavior. The set of behaviors most often rated in early attachment research include exploratory manipulation, exploratory locomotion, crying, proximity to mother, avoidance of mother, resists mother, proximity to stranger, avoidance of stranger, and resists stranger. In more recent studies, babies are then classified as either avoidant (A), secure (B), or ambivalent (C) (Sroufe & Waters, 1977).

Although the Strange Situation is a stable and reliable measure (Sroufe, 1985), critics have focused on its validity. The primary criticisms concern the ecological validity of the Strange Situation. First, parents are directed to behave in an atypical manner (Hinde, 1983), and second, individual differences in temperament are confounded with performance in the Strange Situation (Campos, Barrett, Lamb, Goldsmith, & Sternberg, 1983). Furthermore, the predictive validity of the Strange Situation has been questioned by Lamb and colleagues in light of the failure to find evidence that variations in parental behavior within the normal range are related to performance in this task (Lamb, Thompson, Gardner, Charnov, & Estes, 1984). Most important here, it would be surprising if the Strange Situation was equally valid for all children. For example, separation and reunion must be perceived as different events for children in child care, who experience both during every workday, than for children at home with mother (Clarke-Stewart & Fein, 1983).

These criticisms are important in the present context, because social policy and public opinion have been affected by research using the Strange Situation. There are 25 studies concerning whether there are differences in attachment behavior between children attending day care and children cared for at home by mothers. Studies were identified from two sources: (a) *Child Development Abstracts and Bibliography* and (b) an excellent handbook chapter on "Early Childhood Programs" by Clarke-Stewart and Fein (1983). Clarke-Stewart and Fein (1983) focus on the two most commonly assessed variables, proximity seeking and proximity avoidance. They conclude on the basis of a consistent pattern from a subset of studies that children in day care tend to spend less time close to or in physical contact with mother and to ignore or avoid mother after a brief separation. They suggest that a meta-analysis might reveal a significant difference overall. We decided to conduct such a meta-analysis.

Fourteen of the twenty-five studies employed the strange-situation methodology, or a variation of it, and assessed one or more of the four most commonly investigated variables that operationalize attachment: exploratory behavior, crying, proximity to mother, and avoidance of mother. The studies that were excluded either used a different methodology (e.g., Caldwell, Wright, Honig, & Tannenbaum, 1970), used a different operationalization of attachment (e.g., Vaughn, Gove, & Egeland, 1980), or did not directly compare children in child care with children in home care (Cochran, 1977).

A meta-analysis is quite simply an analysis of analyses. An effect-size estimate, typically r, is computed for each study and an aggregate effect size is then computed. The effect of moderators on effect size can be computed using contrast weights (meta-analytic procedures are described in detail in Rosenthal, 1984). Four separate meta-analyses were conducted for each of the four attachment variables. Six moderators involving methodological considerations were also investigated: (a) whether the examiner was blind to group status, (b) the sex of the examiner, (c) the mean age of the children, (d) the age range of the children, (e) whether the Strange Situation paradigm was modified in any way, and (f) the length of time in months children had spent in day care. The moderators concerning the ages of subjects are particularly important, because the strange situation was designed for infants from 12 to 18 months. The moderator concerning amount of time in day care is important, because of the possibility that children first entering day care may show a transitory reaction to their change in environments (Belsky & Steinberg, 1978; Clarke-Stewart & Fein, 1983).

The 14 studies are listed in Table 1 with corresponding effect-size estimates for the four dependent variables and codes for the six-moderators. The combined effect-size estimates are .105 for explore, $-.008$ for cry, .011 for proximity to mother, and .156 for avoid mother. These four affect-size estimates are quite low. Cohen's (1969) rule of thumb is that .30 is low, .50 is moderate, and .80 is high. All four effect-size estimates are considerably below what is generally considered to be low, which suggests that children attending day care are no different than children reared at home on mother attachment as assessed through the Strange Situation.

Potential critics may argue that the effects of studies with better controls are being diluted by studies with poorer controls. For this reason, the effect of six methodological moderators was examined (see Table 2). Whether the examiner was blind to group status was significantly related to effect size for avoidance, such that studies in which the examiner was not blind were more likely to report that day-care children were more avoidant. There was a complementary trend for proximity, such that studies in which the examiner was not blind were more likely to report that day-care children were less likely to seek proximity with mother. Thus, researchers who are not blind are biased toward judging that children in day care differ from children in home care.

Sex of examiner was unrelated to effect size for the four variables. The mean age of the children was also unrelated to effect size, while age range was related to avoidance, such that studies with larger ranges were more likely to report that day-care children were more avoidant. Neither modification of the Strange Situation nor mean time in day care was related to effect size. The latter finding suggests that there is no transitory reaction to day care. In terms of attachment, children appear to adapt easily; in fact, this finding is demonstrated empirically in the longitudinal study reported by Roopnarine and Lamb (1979).

There were few care by sex interactions reported. Of the four studies that examined this interaction for avoidance and the two that examined it for crying, none were significant. Only one of the care by sex interactions for explore was significant: Moskowitz, Schwarz, & Corsini (1977) report that day-care boys explore more than girls, who explore more than home-reared boys. Four of the six studies report an insignificant care by sex interaction for proximity. Of the remaining two studies, one reports that home-reared boys are lowest (Cornelius

TABLE 1.

Meta-analysis of Strange Situation Studies Comparing Children in Day-Care with Children in Home Care

Author	Effect size (r)				E Blind (1=yes)	Sex E (1=male)	Mean age Ss (months)	Age span (months)	Modified strange situation (1=yes)	Mean time in day-care (months)
	Explore	Cry	Proximity mother	Avoid mother						
Blehar, 1974	0	.354	0	.582	0	0	34.8	9.4	0	4.6
Brookhart & Hock, 1976	—	—	0	0	0	0	11.3	—	1	2.0
Cornelius & Denney, 1975	0	0	0	—	0	1	60.1	23.0	1	15.2
Doyle, 1975	—	0	0	0	0	0	18.5	25.0	1	7.0
Kagan et al., 1978	—	0	0	—	1	1	20.0	0	1	16.0
Moskowitz et al., 1977	0	0	0	0	1	0	42.4	—	1	5.6
Portnoy & Simmons, 1978	0	0	0	0	1	0	45.0	—	0	24.2
Ragozin, 1980	.561	—	-.442	.760	0	0	29.5	21.0	1	3.0
Ricciutti, 1974a	0	—	0	—	0	1	16.0	—	1	10.0
	—	0	—	—	0	1	12.5	—	1	8.5
Roopnarine & Lamb, 1979b	—	0	.526	0	1	1	37.2	0	0	0
	—	-.413	0	0	1	1	40.8	0	0	3.0
Schwartz, 1983	—	—	.074	.158	0	0	18.0	0	0	10.0
Hock, 1980	—	—	-.018	-.094	0	0	12.0	0	0	9.0
Cummings, 1980	—	—	0	—	1	1	21.1	16.0	1	10.8
Hock & Clinger, 1980	—	0	0	0	0	0	12.0	—	0	6.3
Combined r	.105	-.008	.011	.156						

[a]This paper contains two studies with separate samples.
[b]This paper describes a two-wave longitudinal study.
NOTE: A positive r indicates that the day-care group exceeds the home-care group.

TABLE 2.
Z-scores of Contrasts for Moderating Variables

Moderators	Explore	Cry	Proximity mother	Avoid mother
E blind	.538	1.461	−1.624	1.980[a]
Sex of E	−1.273	1.544	− .098	1.135
Mean age Ss	−1.347	− .463	.990	.900
Age range	0	.815	−1.043	2.550[a]
Modified strange situation	− .670	− .108	1.535	−1.196
Mean time in day-care	.884	.240	−1.314	−1.361

[a]$p<.05$

& Denney, 1975) and one reports that home-reared boys are highest (Moskowitz *et al.*, 1977). Thus, the sexes are not differentially affected by day-care experience on attachment.

Admittedly, this is a limited set of studies. A set of 14 studies is a small one. Failure to find significant moderators may reflect lack of power. More important, the median age of children was 21 months. Thus, these studies do not speak directly to the question of infant day care (Gamble & Zigler, 1986). Nevertheless, an overall picture emerges of a child in day care who is capable of developing a secure attachment with his or her mother.

This meta-analysis may also be criticized for its focus on attachment behaviors. In recent research, attachment quality (avoidant, secure, resistant) and not attachment behaviors are scored from strange-situation protocols, because of increased concurrent and predictive validity (see Ainsworth, Blehar, Waters, & Wall, 1978). Only one research group has compared children in child care with children at home with mother on attachment quality. Vaughn, Gove, and Egeland (1980) compared three groups of mother–child dyads on the Strange Situation: mothers who returned to work early (prior to 12 months), mothers who returned to work later (12 to 18 months), and mothers who did not return to work. There was a significant increase in anxious-avoidant attachment relationships at 12 and 18 months for infants whose mothers returned to work during the first year of life. At 2 years, the three groups no longer differed (Farber & Egeland, 1982). Vaughn, Deane, and Waters' (1985) reanalysis of Farber and Egeland's data is interpreted to show an interaction between attachment history and child-care experience, but only when a liberal alpha is used.

Although researchers and policymakers alike need to continue to consider the effects of infant day care, too much has been made of these isolated findings (see Belsky, 1986, and reply by Phillips, McCartney, Scarr, & Howes, 1987). In addition, they need to be considered in light of the subject sample. Mothers in the study were "economically disadvantaged" and using "unstable" care arrangements (Vaughn *et al.*, 1980). Mothers' return to work was associated with being single and with higher life stress. Thus, truly significant effects are probably not generalizable to middle-class populations (Gamble & Zigler, 1986). However, the finding that unstable care arrangements have negative consequences for children remains important to document with a proper comparison group.

The Child's Attachment to Caregivers

A mother typically has mixed feelings about how her child's relationship with substitute caregivers will affect her own relationship with her child. On the one hand, child–caregiver attachment is something to be desired rather than feared, given the amount of time children spend with their caregivers. On the other hand, fears of being replaced or supplanted are also prevalent and natural (Ainslie & Anderson, 1984). There are a handful of studies that compare children's attachment relationships with mothers versus caregivers. The existing research consistently documents that children are more attached to their mothers than to their caregivers. Farran and Ramey (1977) observed 23 black infants attending an early childhood intervention child-care program in a room with mother, day-care provider, and a stranger. Children showed a strong preference to be near and to interact with their mothers. Similar findings are reported by Ainslie and Anderson (1984) and by Kagan, Kearsley, and Zelazo (1978).

In a more naturalistic study, Ragozin (1980) observed children's actual behavior in child-care settings during mother's morning departure, immediately following the departure, 1-hour postdeparture, and during mother's afternoon arrival. The children showed extremely low rates of crying, search, and calling for mother upon her departure. Yet, children's preference for mother was evident in the fact that children were more likely to seek proximity, touch, and move with mother than caregiver. Thus, children seem to adapt well to transitions that accompany the child-care experience. Moreover, they seem to recognize and treat their mothers as primary attachment figures.

In at least one study, it is suggested that infants never develop true attachment relationships with child-care teachers (Farran, Burchinal, Hutaff, & Ramey, 1984). In an observational study, Farran and her colleagues demonstrated that teachers and infants are continally sorting themselves into preferred patterns of interacting. The researchers attribute "shifting allegiances" to the continually changing day-care environment.

Two cross-cultural studies provide a more stringent test of the effect of shared childrearing on attachment preference than do the day-care studies, because in both cultures shared childrearing is part of the cultural norm and therefore an accepted practice. The first study examines the modern Israeli kibbutz and the second examines a preindustrial tribe near Nairobi.

Approximately 2% of Israelis live on kibbutzim. Fox (1977) compared kibbutz infants' attachment relationship with their mothers and with their metapelets, who are professional caregivers. In some sense, the metapelet is the primary caregiver. Shared childrearing begins on the fourth day of the infant's life when the baby is placed in an infant house under the care of the metapelet. The child lives in this house with the metapelet and other children, while mothers are encouraged to nurse and visit their babies. Children visit their parents between 4:00 and 7:00 every day; this is a special time, which is reserved for family interaction. Fox studied 122 children from three age groups: 8- to 10-month-olds, 12- to 15-month-olds, and 21- to 24-month-olds.

A 13-episode experimental procedure modeled on the strange situation was developed so that subjects would witness the arrival, presence, and departure of the mother, the metapelet, and a stranger in a neutral environment. Attachment behaviors coded across the 13 episodes included proximity seeking, touching, crying, and playing. There were no differences in children's reactions to the departure of the mother versus the metapelet. Thus, Fox concludes that these children are able to form an attachment relationship with both mother and metapelet. There were differences in children's reactions to the reunion with mother versus metapelet. Younger and older children played less and cried more during the reunion with the metapelet than with the mother. Younger and middle-aged children spent more time near the mother than near the metapelet. Fox interprets the reunion findings as evidence of children's greater attachment to their mothers than to their metapelet.

In a conceptually similar study, Leiderman and Leiderman (1973) assessed the effect of predominantly single (or monomatric) childrearing and shared (or polymatric) childrearing on attachment among the Kikuyu, an East African tribe near Nairobi. Monomatric and polymatric childrearing arrangements exist throughout the community and are not related to socioeconomic indicators. All mothers share childrearing with a young girl, aged 7 to 12 years, who is often a relative. This helper accompanies the mother on trips to the fields and has responsibility for the infant during these trips. The helper will also be left at home to care for the infant, during which time she will have sole responsibility for the child's care. The amount of help determines whether a childrearing arrangement is considered to be monomatric or polymatric. For the purposes of the study, a monomatric arrangement was defined as one in which the mother was the principal caregiver in over 75% of observations.

Sixty-seven mothers and their infants participated in the study. Attachment was assessed in a seminaturalistic session, which took place in front of the family's home. While the mother held the child, a stranger approached the child with friendly overtures. Later the stranger offered to hold the infant, the mother presented the infant to the stranger, and the mother departed for a short period. The same procedure was used with a caregiver helper and a stranger. Infant behavior was assessed using a 5-point scale for positiveness of response to both the stranger approach and the mother/caregiver helper departure. Infants were tested twice, at 7 to 9 months and at 10 to 12 months. There was no difference in the infants' responses to mothers and caregiver helpers in the approach situation. Based on this finding, Leiderman and Leiderman conclude, as Fox (1977) does, that infants can and do form attachments to more than one individual. Surely, research on fathers (e.g., Lamb, 1980) demonstrates this also.

The prevailing evidence, therefore, demonstrates that there is very little reason to suspect that a child would develop a stronger relationship with a caregiver than with a mother. In light of this, the prevalence of questions about the attachment relationships between children and their parents versus caregivers is indicative of our cultural bias. Of course, mothers in the labor force, like all mothers and like fathers, love their children in a special way and fulfill their children's basic needs—no doubt very young children are able to identify parents, regardless of work status, as primary caregivers. In fact, we know that mothers and caregivers interact differently with children, such that mothers provide more positive affect, social play, and so on (Rubenstein, Pedersen, & Yarrow, 1977); it would appear that children are sensitive to these differences. Interestingly, working status does not appear to affect a mother's playing time with her children. Rather, education of the mother exerts a stronger effect (Hill & Stafford, 1978).

THE EFFECT OF THE SOCIAL AND SCIENTIFIC LEGACIES ON MOTHERHOOD: CASE STUDIES AND STATISTICS

Most mothers are not familiar with the scientific evidence just presented. Rather they are familiar with advice from friends, family, and "experts" (Ehrenreich & English, 1978), all of which reflects beliefs of the larger culture and most of which promotes conflict between working outside the home and motherhood.

Concern from experts about the effects of infant day care, in particular, is rising (Belsky, 1986; Brazelton, 1986; Gamble & Zigler, 1986). For example, Brazelton warns that mothers who work outside the home are likely to develop defenses, such as denial of a problem, projection of important caregiving responsibilities onto substitute caregivers, and detachment. Most mothers do not realize that such claims are based on clinical judgment and not experimental findings. In addition, most mothers do not realize that developmentalists are not unanimous in this clinical judgment. In contrast, Scarr (1984) argues that employed mothers are for the most part happier and therefore better mothers.

Ironically, in contemporary American society, women feel pressure both to stay at home and raise their children *and* to enter the labor force. This double pressure leads to role conflict, which for employed mothers results in guilt, regardless of their attitude toward work. It is no wonder that employed women reveal more guilt feelings and more doubts about their childrearing competencies than do homemakers (Birnbaum, 1971).

This guilt is no doubt manifest in a number of ways. Hock (1985) has recently demonstrated that many employed mothers experience maternal separation anxiety, which is an unpleasant emotional state that reflects a mother's apprehension about leaving her child with a substitute caregiver. There are vast differences in maternal separation anxiety that are mediated by various personality attributes of a mother, a mother's perception of her child's ability to adapt, a mother's set of beliefs regarding women's role in society, and perhaps most important, the degree to which a mother believes that she is uniquely capable of caring for her child.

The guilt theme was the clearest one to emerge in exploratory interviews we conducted with six women of various occupations with various childrearing arrangements. Their guilt reflects three beliefs: first, that working outside the home will disrupt their role as primary caregiver; second, that working outside the home will prevent them from observing important developmental accomplishments; and third, that working outside the home will adversely affect others' attitudes about a woman's mothering abilities. One can only speculate about the origins of these fears. Our main thesis here is that they are the byproduct of rapid social change. Nevertheless, there is something peculiarly American about women's guilt over career and family, as Hewlitt (1986) demonstrates in her comparison of American and European women. This is demonstrated here, as well, in a comparison of case studies.

These women were simply asked "What have been your experiences as an employed mother and how do you feel about sharing childrearing responsibilities with a caregiver?" All six women spontaneously mentioned experiencing guilt in the context of these three themes. Consider the following excerpts.

Linda is a 36-year-old business manager and the mother of 2-year-old Alex. Alex is in family day care 3 days a week and center day care 2 days a week. The conflict Linda feels is evident in her discussion of the family day care provider. "I like the fact that she (the caregiver) provides a strong mother influence. She provides a real family environment and I like that. . . . Alex gets love, attention, and play time, but her approach to life is different . . . I just feel that a bond with parents affects peace of mind. I don't spend as much time with him in everyday play situations and you need to commit time for a child's growth, especially from 2 to 5. . . . One day I hope I won't feel regret for having worked this time. I'd feel terrible the rest of my life thinking that if something went wrong it would be my fault—but I know it probably wouldn't be."

For most women there is a fear of the unknown consequences. Even though women know of no evidence that their children will be adversely affected by child care, they worry. Doreen is a 30-year old speech and language pathologist, who admits that her concern drove her to read everything she could get her hands on about child care and its effects. Her son, Patrick, just celebrated his first birthday. Doreen started working a couple of days a week when he was 2 months old and yet recalls, "When people would inquire whether I was working or not I would reply, 'No, I stay home with my baby.' I wonder why I said that when in fact I was working. I realize now that I was a new mom and felt I should be home with the baby. . . . There's this feeling that it is going to make a difference someday, not now maybe, but someday. Now he is in family day care situation four days a week. I still keep wondering about when he is 16—if there is some sort of incidence that will emerge during a more stressful time in our relationship. Intellectually, I say probably not. On the other hand, I really sort of do believe that deep down it might." Doreen is able to justify her working status in light of these feelings with the following philosophy: "In order to be the best mother I can be to this baby I've got to be a happy person. If I were home 24 hours a day, I'd go crazy."

Many women alleviate concerns about the effects of child care by enlisting the help of family. However, this can bring a set of problems all its own. Teresa is a 26-year-old assistant buyer for a large department store chain and mother of 2-year-old Jennifer. Teresa's husband, Jim, is an academic with a flexible schedule. Because Jennifer was born in the spring, Jim was able to care for her over the summer following Teresa's maternity leave. Having Jim as the primary caregiver was difficult for Teresa. "Because of Jim's great involvement, Jennifer was more attached to him. At first this was very difficult. He would correct me on how to satisfy her needs and lots of times he would be right. I found myself making a special effort to spend all my spare time with Jennifer to make up for what I missed. Now that Jennifer is in day care it is a lot easier. Jen goes to me for some things and to Jim for other things." It is ironic that an involved father can actually add to a employed mother's feelings of guilt and inadequacy.

It is more common for grandmothers to help with child care. Mary, a 23-year-old project control coordinator for a mid-size engineering firm and mother of 1-year-old Laura, had no reservations about child care because her mother provided it. Her reservations, like Teresa's, involved relinquishing the role of primary caregiver. "I started back at work when Laura was 10 weeks old. After only 2 or 3 weeks I knew I wanted to go back. I missed Laura so much. And I started to see that Laura depended on my mother and wanted my mother, not me. I had given birth, but I didn't feel like a mother. . . . Then I realized how much I was going to miss—her first step, her first tooth. These feelings built up inside me. Kevin and I decided to cut back on the extras so that I could stay home. And I am very happy right now."

Can you win by staying home? The experiences of Phyllis, a 31-year-old former office manager and mother of two daughters, Devon and Jillian, suggest that you pay a price. Phyllis decided to stay home during the preschool years, because, like Mary, she wanted to enjoy the experiences of young motherhood. She feels that for these experiences she has had to sacrifice the respect of some peers. "If I am at a party and I offer a political opinion some people make me feel that I don't have a right to that opinion because I 'only stay home.' People can be very patronizing. They assume that if you stay home with your children then your brain must be made of pudding." Role conflict *for* women has led to interpersonal conflict *among* women, because once you are a mother you have to choose sides on the child-care issue. Teresa remarked that, "I feel like I can't ask a co-worker or a friend whether she is going back to work. Women feel bad about either decision. My sister-in-law is pregnant now and is going to stay home with the baby. I think she anticipated that I wouldn't be able to tear myself away from Jen and I think she hoped I would throw the towel in and stay home." The division between women over employment status has only recently been seriously considered (Berg, 1986).

Then how do you win? Women who work part-time appear to experience the least role conflict and the least guilt. They have the best of both worlds. Mary Kay is a dental assistant and mother of preschoolers Patrick and Courtney. She works about 20 hours per week, during which time her children are with either their father or a family day-care provider. Mary Kay believes she has "the best of both worlds." And yet for many women part-time work is unacceptable, either for economic reasons or career demands.

A change in cultural perceptions is the only sure way to win. Ann is a 31-year-old neuroscientist and mother of 2-year-old Patrick. Ann is American, but gave birth to Patrick while working in France, where attitudes about child care are very different. Patrick started day care when he was 4 months old. "Day care is not an issue over there. No one would say, 'What are you going to do after the baby is born? What are your feelings about going back to work?' About 80% of mothers of infants in France work. The Office for Children organizes what is called "la creche," which is essentially family day-care . . . his day-care mother was very maternal, but the response I got at the end of the day when I would pick him up was so clear—he knew who his mother was. And so I never worried really."

The cultural bias argument is particularly compelling to Kathleen Mc-Cartney because, despite her knowledge about child development and despite having cowritten this chapter, she has not been able to escape the working mother's guilt trip altogether. She expresses her concern this way:

> It is not clear to me the degree to which my concerns reflect my own beliefs or the beliefs of others. People let you know in subtle and not so subtle ways that you will never be mother of the year. A friend is surprised that your baby is attached to you. A relative asks how you can leave to go to an important conference. A colleague tells you that his wife is staying home, because they think it's important for their child. It does not feel good to know that others do not think you are a good mother.

Employed mothers are faced with the task of reconciling two selves. One self believes that a happy mother who works outside the home is better than a resentful mother who stays home. A second self believes or at least fears that one's work somehow hurts one's child. Suleiman (1985) conducted a literary analysis of working woman's guilt in comtemporary feminist fiction. She cites Gerda, a writer in Rosellen Brown's novel *The Autobiography of the Mother*, who speaks of her failed relationship with her daughter: "I had not known we were to share but one life between us, so that the fuller mine is, the more empty hers." Our clinical interviews with women revealed similar sentiments, presumably because we reached this second self.

Questionnaire studies, however, are more likely to document maternal satisfaction, because through this methodology the researcher reaches the self who has come to terms with child-care decisions. The beliefs of both selves are valid. Consider the following data on maternal attitudes toward substitute child care collected as part of the Bermuda Day Care Study (McCartney, Scarr, Phillips, Grajek, & Schwarz, 1982; McCartney, Scarr, Phillips, & Grajek, 1985; McCartney 1984). Attitudes toward substitute child care, particularly day care, may be more progressive in Bermuda than in the United States—about twice as many 2-year-olds, 84%, are in some form of substitute care. Most of the mothers of these young children work outside the home. We interviewed 166 mothers of children attending one of the nine day-care programs on the island that provide services for children from infancy through the preschool years about the child-care arrangments they had made for their children.

Because we did not wish to bias these mothers, we asked open-ended questions and then coded their responses. When we asked them "How has enrolling your child in day care affected you personally?" only 29% reported any effect. As Table 3 shows less than 3% of the sample spontaneously reported that enrolling a child in substitute care led to any guilt feelings. In fact, mothers were more likely to mention positive consequences of enrolling their children in day care, for example, having more time and improving the mother–child relationship. Mothers were better able to describe how day-care had affected their children. As Table 4 shows, 71% reported some effect; 52.8% of this sample reported positive changes in social skills, 17.4% reported positive educational changes, and 16.0% reported an increase in independence.

When we asked mothers directly what aspects of the day care center they were satisfied and dissatisfied with, an interesting pattern emerged (see Table 5). Nearly all, 95%, were able to report some satisfaction, while far fewer, 39%, were able to report some dissatisfaction. Among the dissatisfactions, concerns about caregivers ranked first; among the satisfactions, praise for caregivers ranked second. Mothers also discussed satisfactions with educational, social, and health and safety aspects of the center. However, mothers realize, quite rightly, that caregivers *are* the center and for this reason when they discuss their feelings about the center, they discuss caregivers. They also realize that caregivers are viewed by society at large as replacements or mother substitutes and that this fact underlies much of their inner conflict as well as their conflict with caregivers. Yet, on the whole, these findings suggest that mothers report being satisfied with center care arrangments they have made. It is important to remember that all of the mothers participating in this study had a child 3 years and older; no doubt satisfactions and dissatisfactions of mothers vary as a function of the child's age.

THE NEED FOR SOCIAL ACTION

To summarize, psychological studies document that child care does not disrupt the mother–child relationship, anthropological studies demonstrate that

TABLE 3.
*How Has Substitute Care Affected
You Personally?*

Code	Percentage[a]
More time	7.6
Enable mother to work	.7
Improve mother–child relation	7.6
Guilt	2.8
Question role as parent	1.4
General negative	9.0

[a]Because only 29% reported some effect, because mothers were permitted to report multiple effects, and because some mothers could not offer specific effects, column does not sum to 100.

TABLE 4.
*How Has Substitute Care Affected
Your Child?*

Code	Percentage[a]
Educational	17.4
Social	52.8
Obedient	4.9
Independent	16.0
Initial adjustment problem	1.4
General negative	5.1

[a]Because only 71% reported some effect, because mothers were permitted to report multiple effects, and because some mothers could not offer specific effects, column does not sum to 100.

shared childrearing is the norm in nonindustrialized societies, and evolutionary theory explains why shared childrearing might even be adaptive. It is worth repeating Hinde's (1983) point that any argument that one mothering style is best is on dangerous grounds. Rather, mothering styles reflect differing economic and social considerations. Why, then, do we *not* live in a society that is "pro-choice" about alternative mothering styles?

The answer, quite simply, is that current American trends and traditional American values are at odds. The 1980s, like the preceeding decade, continue to serve as a time of change for women, especially mothers. Although our economic system allows for and in many cases necessitates employed mothers, our social ideology does not. The result for employed women with children is tre-

TABLE 5.
*Percentage of Satisfactions and
Dissatisfactions of Mothers in the Bermuda
Day-Care Study*

Code	Satisfied[a]	Dissatisfied[a]
Educational	41.5	2.1
Social	17.0	0
Health and safety	17.0	4.8
Caregivers	28.6	13.1
Peers	4.8	6.2
Convenience	8.8	3.4
Atmosphere	15.0	6.9

[a]Because only 95% reported as some satisfaction and 39% reported as dissatisfaction, because mothers were permitted to report multiple satisfactions and dissatisfactions, and because some mothers could not offer specific satisfactions and dissatisfactions, columns do not sum to 100.

mendous conflict about the use of child care. As more mothers of young children enter the labor force, concerns about child care and shared childrearing would be expected to diminish. Social action will follow support from fathers, caregivers, and friends.

Support from fathers has been slow in coming. Employed women of all social classes have retained primary responsibility for "family work" (Pleck, 1979). In their effort to fulfill multiple-role expectations employed mothers may be hesitant to ask their spouses for help, especially with child care. For example, in one study fathers in dual-earner families were observed to interact less with their infants than fathers in male-breadwinner families, presumably because employed mothers were making up for lost time during evenings and weekends (Pederson, Cain, Zaslow, & Anderson, 1982). Clearly, employed mothers feel a need to compensate for lost time in a way that employed fathers do not. The importance of equal participation in family work is critical for social action, in that it provides an important model for children and in that role strain is shared. In fact, there is a growing body of evidence that multiple roles for women and men may serve a protective function (Gove & Geeken, 1977).

Second, caregivers, who are often young, single women, need to be aware of and sensitive to the kinds of conflicts employed mothers experience. Early childhood staff were shown in one study to rate the childrearing abilities of the parent clientele as significantly below their own standards of "good" parenting (Kontos, Raikes, & Woods, 1983). It is not clear to what extent these attitudes reflect cultural bias about shared childrearing or to what extent these attitudes are transmitted to mothers either explicitly through constructive criticism or implicitly through suggestion.

Yet, caregivers have been shown to perform an important support service to their parent clientele (Hughes & Durio, 1983). For example, Joffe (1977) writes of her discovery of an "underlife" in the Berkeley child-care program she investigated. Caregivers in this program provided a range of counseling services for a receptive parent clientele on both child-related topics, for example, discipline strategies, and broader-ranging topics, for example, career goals. Because caregivers and parents typically meet on caregiver turf and because not all parents know that caregivers are willing to discuss parent-initiated topics (Powell, 1980), it would seem to be the responsibility of caregivers to place parents at ease.

No matter how open the lines of communication are, it is unlikely that a mother will voice a concern she has concerning the strength of her child's attachment to a caregiver, yet this is likely to be a problem for a mother who is beginning to share childrearing responsibilities for the first time. It is important for teachers, especially teachers of young children, to realize the different roles of mother and teacher. Surely the roles overlap in function. Mothers and teachers both promote optimal child development through nurturance and education. The younger the child, the less distinguished these two roles are. The difference becomes one of degree. Katz (1980) describes the difference in terms of scope of function: A mother's function is diffuse and limitless, while a teacher's function is specific and limited.

Third, friends need to learn to be accepting of different attitudes and different choices, so that the question "Do you plan to return to work after the baby is born?" is neither asked nor responded to judgmentally. Women themselves need to unite on the issue of shared childrearing and realize that there is no evidence to suggest that one's decision about it should reflect anything more than a matter of choice.

CONCLUSION

The findings from historical, anthropological, and psychological studies on motherhood and shared childrearing converge: Shared childrearing in a variety of forms has existed throughout human history and it does not interfere with a child's socioemotional development. Nevertheless, we live in the age of the conflicted mother, especially in the United States, where rapid social change has left mothers and the larger society with the task of redefining motherhood to include the option of child care. The conflicted mother is the result of a short historical perspective. The recently romanticized social construction of motherhood is largely taken to be equivalent to the natural image of motherhood. Eventually, societal attitudes will parallel societal behavior. We hope that social action will be expedited through an awareness of the social and scientific legacies presented here.

ACKNOWLEDGMENTS

We would like to acknowledge the help of Monica Harris and Kathryn Dobroth, who provided invaluable consultation on the meta-analysis; Beverly Birns, Dale Hay, and Michael Lamb, who provided constructive criticism on an earlier draft of this paper; and Sandra Scarr and J. Conrad Schwarz, who collaborated with us on the Bermuda Day-Care Study. We would especially like to thank the six mothers who shared their experiences with us.

REFERENCES

Ainslie, R. C., & Anderson, C. W. (1984). Day care children's relationships to their mothers and caregivers: An inquiry into the conditions for the development of attachment. In R. C. Ainslie (Ed.), *The child and the day care setting*. New York: Praeger.

Ainsworth, M. D. S., Blehar, M. C., Waters, E., & Wall, S. (1978). *Patterns of attachment*. Hillsdale, NJ: Lawrence Erlbaum.

Ainsworth, M. D. S., & Wittig, B. A. (1969). *Attachment and exploratory behavior of one year olds in a strange situation*. In B. M. Foss (Ed.), *Determinants of infant behavior* (Vol. 4). London: Methuen.

Aries, P. (1962). *Centuries of childhood: A social history of family life*. (R. Baldick, Trans.). New York: Knopf.

Belsky, J. (1985). The science and politics of day care. In K. L. Shotland & M. Maks (Eds.), *Social science and social policy*. Beverly Hills, CA: Sage.

Belsky, J. (1986). Infant day care: A cause for concern? *Zero to Three: Bulletin of the National Center for Clinical Infant Programs*. Washington, DC.

Belsky, J., & Steinberg, L. D. (1978). The effects of day care: A critical review. *Child Development, 49,* 929–949.

Berg, B. J. (1986). *The crisis of the working mother.* New York: Simon & Schuster.

Birnbaum, J. (1971). *Life patterns, personality types and self-esteem in gifted family oriented and career committed women.* Unpublished doctoral dissertation, University of Michigan.

Blehar, M. C. (1974). Anxious attachment and defensive reactions associated with day care. *Child Development, 45,* 683–692.

Bloom, B. (1964). *Stability and change in human characteristics.* New York: Wiley.

Blum, M. (1983). *The day care dilemma: Women and children first.* Lexington, MA: Heath.

Bowlby, J. (1951). *Maternal care and mental health.* Geneva: World Health Organization.

Bowlby, J. (1958). The nature of the child's tie to his mother. *International Journal of Psychoanalysis, 39,* 350–373.

Bowlby, J. (1969). *Attachment and loss: Vol. 1. Attachment.* New York: Basic.

Brazelton, T. B. (1986). Issues for working parents. *American Journal of Orthopsychiatry, 56,* 14–25.

Brookhart, J., & Hock, E. (1976). The effects of experimental context and experiential background on infants' behavior toward their mothers and a stranger. *Child Development, 47,* 333–340.

Caldwell, B., Wright, B., Honig, A., & Tannenbaum, G. (1970). Infant day care and attachment. *American Journal of Orthopsychiatry, 40,* 397–412.

Campos, J., Barrett, K., Lamb, M., Goldsmith, H., & Sternberg, C. (1983). Socioemotional development. In M. Haith & J. Campos (Eds.), *Handbook of child psychology: Vol. 2. Infancy and developmental psychobiology.* New York: Wiley.

Clarke-Stewart, K. A., & Fein, G. G. (1983). Early Childhood Programs. In M. Haith & J. Campos (Eds.), *Handbook of child psychology: Vol. 2. Infancy and developmental psychobiology.* New York: Wiley.

Cochran, M. M. (1977). A comparison of group day and family child-rearing patterns in Sweden. *Child Development, 48,* 702–707.

Cohen, J. (1969). *Power analysis for the behavioral sciences.* New York: Wiley.

Congressional Record (1971, December 9). Veto of Economic Opportunity Amendments of 1971. Washington, DC: U.S. Government Printing Office.

Cornelius, S. W., & Denney, N. W. (1975). Dependency in day care and home care children. *Developmental Psychology, 11,* 575–582.

Cummings, E. M. (1980). Caregiver stability in day care. *Developmental Psychology, 16,* 31–34.

Dally, A. (1982). *Inventing motherhood.* London: Burnett.

Dawkins, R. (1976). *The selfish gene.* New York: Oxford University Press.

Doyle, A. (1975). Infant development in day care. *Developmental Psychology, 11,* 655–656.

Ehrenreich, B., & English, D. (1978). *For her own good: 150 years of the experts' advice to women.* New York: Doubleday/Anchor.

Farber, E. A., & Egeland, B. (1982). Developmental consequences of out-of-home care for infants in a low-income population. In E. F. Zigler & E. W. Gordon (Eds.), *Day care: Scientific and social policy issues.* Boston: Auburn.

Farran, D., Burchinal, M., Hutaff, S. E., & Ramey, C. T. (1984). Allegiances or attachments: Relationships among infants and their day care teachers. In R. C. Ainslie (Ed.), *The child and the day care setting.* New York: Praeger.

Farran, D., & Ramey, C. (1977). Infant day care and attachment behaviors toward mothers and teachers. *Child Development, 48,* 1112–1116.

Fein, G. G., & Clarke-Stewart, A. (1973). *Day care in context.* New York: Wiley.

Fox, N. (1977). Attachment of kibbutz infants to mothers and metapelet. *Child Development, 48,* 1228–1239.

Friedman, D. E. (1985). Corporate financial assistance for child care. *The Conference Research Bulletin* (No. 177). New York: The Conference Board.

Gamble, T., & Zigler, E. (1986). Effects of infant day care: Another look at the evidence. *American Journal of Orthopsychiatry, 56,* 26–42.

Gerson, M., Alpert, J. L., & Richardson, M. (1984). Mothering: The view from psychological research. *Signs, 9,* 434–453.

Gove, W., & Geekin, M. (1977). The effect of children and employment on the mental health of married men and women. *Social Forces, 56*, 66–76.

Grubb, W. N., & Lazerson, M. (1982). *Broken promises: How Americans fail their children*. New York: Basic.

Hewlett, S. A. (1986). *A lesser life*. New York: Morrow.

Hill, C. R., & Stafford, F. P. (1978). Parental care of children: Time diary estimates of quantity predictability and variety. *Institute for Social Research Working Paper Series*. Ann Arbor, MI: University of Michigan.

Hinde, R. A. (1983). Ethology and child development. In M. M. Haith & J. J. Campos (Eds.), *Handbook of child psychology: Vol. 2. Infancy and psychobiology*. New York: Wiley.

Hock, E. (1980). Working and non-working mothers and their infants: A comparative study of maternal caregiving characteristics and infant social behavior. *Merrill-Palmer Quarterly, 26*, 79–102.

Hock, E. (1985). The transition to day care: Effects of maternal separation anxiety on infant adjustment. In R. C. Ainslie (Ed.), *The child and the day care setting*. New York: Praeger.

Hock, E., & Clinger, J. B. (1980). Behavior toward mother and stranger of infants who have experienced group day care, individual care, or exclusive maternal care. *Journal of Genetic Psychology, 137*, 49–61.

Hofferth, S., & Phillips, D. (1987). Children in the United States, 1970 to 1995. *Journal of Marriage and the Family, 49*, 559–571.

Hoffman, L., & Hoffman, M. (1973). The value of children to parents. In J. Fawcett (Ed.), *Psychological perspectives of population*. New York: Basic.

Hughes, R., & Durio, H. F. (1983). Patterns of childcare information seeking by families. *Journal of Applied Family and Child Studies, 32*, 203–212.

Hunt, J. McV. (1961). *Intelligence and experience*. New York: Ronald.

Joffe, C. E. (1977). *Friendly intruders: Childcare professionals and family life*. Berkeley: University of California Press.

Kagan, J., Kearsley, R. B., & Zelazo, P. R. (1978). *Infancy: Its place in human development*. Cambridge: Harvard University Press.

Katz, L. (1980). Mothering and teaching: Some significant distinctions. ERIC Clearinghouse on Elementary and Early Childhood Education (ED 190 204).

Kessen, W. (1979). The American child and other cultural inventions. *American Psychologist, 34*, 815–820.

Konner, M. (1972). Aspects of the developmental ethology of a foraging people. In N. Blurton-Jones (Ed.), *Ethological studies of child behavior*. Cambridge: Cambridge University Press.

Kontos, S., Raikes, H., & Woods, A. (1983). Early childhood staff attitudes toward their parent clientele. *Child Care Quarterly, 12*, 45–58.

Lamb, M. E. (1976). *The role of the father in child development*. New York: Wiley.

Lamb, M. E. (1980). The development of parent–infant attachments in the first two years of life. In F. Pederson (Ed.), *The father–infant relationship: Observational studies in the family setting*. New York: Praeger.

Lamb, M. E., Frodi, A. M., Hwang, C., & Frodi, M. (1982). Varying degrees of paternal involvement in infant care: Attitudinal and behavioral correlates. In M. E. Lamb (Ed.), *Nontraditional families: Parenting and child development*. Hillsdale, NJ: Lawrence Erlbaum.

Lamb, M. E., Thompson, R. A., Gardner, P., Charnov, E. L., & Estes, D. (1984). Security of infantile attachment as assessed in the "strange situation": Its study and biological interpretation. *The Behavioral and Brain Sciences, 7*, 127–171.

Lasch, C. (1977). *Haven in a hearless world: The family besieged*. New York: Basic.

Leiderman, P., & Leiderman, G. (1973). Polymatric infant care in the East African highlands. In A. D. Pick (Ed.), *Minnesota Symposium on Child Development*. Minneapolis, MN: University of Minnesota Press.

Long, F., Peters, D. L., & Garduque, L. (1985). Continuity between home and day care: A model for defining relevant dimensions of child care. In I. Sigel (Ed.), *Advances in applied developmental psychology*. Norwood, NJ: Ablex.

Maretzi, T. W., & Maretzi, H. (1963). Taira: An Okinawa village. In B. Whiting (Ed.), *Six cultures*. New York: Wiley.

McCartney, K. (1984). The effect of quality of day care environment upon children's language development. *Developmental Psychology, 20*, 244–260.

McCartney, K., Scarr, S., Phillips, D., & Grajek, S. (1985). Day care as intervention: Comparisons of varying quality programs. *Journal of Applied Developmental Psychology, 6*, 247–260.

McCartney, K., Scarr, S., Phillips, D., Grajek, S., & Schwarz, J. C. (1982). Environmental differences among day care centers and their effects on children's levels of intellectual, language, and social development. In E. F. Zigler & E. W. Gordon (Eds.), *Day care: Scientific and social policy issues*. Boston: Auburn.

Moskowitz, D. S., Schwarz, J. C., & Corsini, D. A. (1977). Initiating day care at three years of age: Effects on attachment. *Child Development, 48*, 1271–1276.

Parke, R. D. (1979). Perspectives on father–infant interaction. In J. D. Osofsky (Ed.), *Handbook of infant development*. New York: Wiley.

Pedersen, F. A., Cain, R. L., Zaslow, M. J., & Anderson, B. J. (1982). Variation in infant experience associated with alternative family roles. In L. Laosa & I. Sigel (Eds.), *Families as learning environments for children*. New York: Plenum Press.

Phillips, D., McCartney, K., Scarr, S., & Howes, C. (1987). Selective review of infant day care research: A cause for concern! *Zero to three: Bulletin of the National Center for Clinical Infant Programs*. Washington, DC.

Phillips, D., & Zigler, E. F. (1987). The checkered history of federal child care regulation. In E. Rothkepf (Ed.), *Review of research in education, Vol. 14*. Washington, DC: American Education Research Association.

Piotrkowski, C. S., & Repetti, R. L. (1984). Dual-earner families. *Marriage and Family Review, 7*, 99–124.

Pleck, J. H. (1979). Men's family work: Three perspectives and some new data. *The Family Coordinator, 28*, 481–488.

Portnoy, F. C., & Simmons, C. H. (1978). Day care and attachment. *Child Development, 49*, 239–242.

Powell, D. R. (1980). Toward a sociological perspective of relations between parents and child care programs. In S. Kilmer (Ed.), *Advances in early education and day care, Vol. 1*. Greenwich, CT: JAI.

Ragozin, A. (1980). Attachment behavior of day care children: Naturalistic and laboratory observations. *Child Development, 51*, 409–415.

Ricciuti, H. (1974). Fear and development of social attachments in the first year of life. In M. Lewis & L. A. Rosenblum (Eds.), *The origins of human behavior*. New York: Wiley.

Roopnarine, J. L., & Lamb, M. E. (1979). Effects of day care on attachment and exploratory behavior in a Strange Situation. *Merrill-Palmer Quarterly, 24*, 85–89.

Rosenthal, R. (1984). *Meta-analytic procedures for social research*. Beverly Hills, CA: Sage.

Rossi, A. (1977). Biosocial perspectives on parenting. *Daedalus, 106*, 1–31.

Rothman, S. (1973). Other people's children: The day care experience in America. *The Public Interest, 30*, 11–27.

Rubenstein, J., Pederson, F., & Yarrow, L. (1977). What happens when mother is away: A comparison of mothers and substitute caregivers. *Developmental Psychology, 13*, 529–530.

Ruderman, R. (1968). *Child care and working mothers*. New York: Child Welfare League of America.

Scarr, S. (1984). *Mother care/other care*. New York: Basic.

Scarr, S. (1985). Constructing psychology: Making facts and fables for our times. *American Psychologist, 40*, 499–512.

Scarr-Salapatek, S. (1976). An evolutionav perspective on infant intelligence. In M. Lewis (Ed.), *Origins of intelligence: Infancy and early childhood*. New York: Plenum Press.

Schwartz, P. (1983). Length of day care attendance and attachment in eighteen month old infants. *Child Development, 54*, 1073–1078.

Smith, P. K. (1980). Shared care of young children: Alternative models to monotropism. *Merrill-Palmer Quarterly, 26*, 371–389.

Smith, R. E. (1979). The movement of women into the labor force. In R. E. Smith (Ed.), *The subtle revolution: Women at work*. Washington, DC: The Urban Institute.

Sroufe, L. A. (1985). Attachment classification from the perspective of infant-caregiver relationships and infant temperament. *Child Development, 56,* 1–14.

Sroufe, L. A., & Waters, E. (1977). Attachment as an organizational construct. *Child Development, 48,* 1184–1199.

Steinfels, M. O. (1973). *Who's minding the children: The history and politics of day care in America.* New York: Simon & Schuster.

Suleiman, S. (1985). Writing and motherhood. In S. N. Garner, C. Kahane, & M. Sprengnether (Eds.), *The (m)other tongue.* Ithaca: Cornell University Press.

Trivers, R. L. (1971). The evolution of reciprocal altruism. *Quarterly Review of Biology, 46,* 35–37.

U.S. Department of Labor (1983). *Time of change: 1983 handbook on women workers.* Bulletin 298. Washington, DC: U.S. Department of Labor.

Vaughn, B. E., Deane, K. E., & Waters, E. (1985). The impact of out-of-home care on child–mother attachment quality: Another look at some enduring questions. In I. Brethton & E. Waters (Eds.), *Growing points of attachment theory and research. Monographs of the Society for Research on Child Development, 50* (Serial No. 209).

Vaughn, B. E., Gove, F. L., & Egeland, B. (1980). The relationship between out-of-home care and the quality of infant–mother attachment in an economically disadvantaged population. *Child Development, 51,* 1203–1214.

Weisner, T. S., & Gallimore, R. (1977). My brother's keeper: Child and sibling caretaking. *Current Anthropology, 18,* 169–190.

Yankelovich, D. (1983). *Work and human values: An international report on jobs in the 1980s and 1990s.* New York: Public Agenda Foundation.

CHAPTER 8

The Black Mother in the United States
History, Theory, Research, and Issues

VALORA WASHINGTON

Well, son, I'll tell you:
Life for me ain't been no crystal stair.
It's had tacks in it,
And splinters,
And boards torn up,
And places with no carpet on the floor—
Bare.
But all the time
I'se been a-climbin' on,
And reachin' landin's,
And turnin' corners,
And sometimes goin' in the dark
Where there ain't been no light.
So boy, don't you turn back.
Don't you set down on the steps
'Cause you finds it's kinder hard.
Don't you fall now—
For I'se still goin', honey,
I'se still climbin',
And life for me ain't been no crystal stair.

—Langston Hughes
"Mother to Son"

INTRODUCTION

"Life for me ain't been no crystal stair." The message in Langston Hughes's classic poem "Mother to Son" continues to bear a perennial truth for black

---

VALORA WASHINGTON • Dean of Faculty, Antioch College, Yellow Springs, Ohio 45387.

mothers. As long-time survivors of the triple jeopardies of sexism, racism, and relative poverty, black mothers are objects of curiosity observed and judged by a myriad of others. Memories of black childhoods and poets have tended to idolize them as standard bearers, as those who have sowed the seeds of faith and love in the midst of their own suffering. In contrast, the microscopic images of empirical studies, clinical observations, and educational analysis accuse them of fostering social defects, deviance, and deficiencies.

Whether revered or despised, the circumstances of their history have required exceptional valor among the most common of women. Yet, their courage and resourcefulness have been obscured by the familiar demographic profiles of good-time girls with too many children and not enough to eat.

The strengths of black mothers may seem remote to scientists and public opinion makers for other reasons. These "well-informed" Americans are often physically segregated and psychologically distant from the demographers' "typical" black mothers. These women are aliens to be read about or discussed. Yet, through all the volumes of analyses of black mothers, the women's own voices are faint or omitted altogether.

There is a scandalous paucity of scientific work about black mothers by the women themselves. Compounding this tragedy is the fact that black mothers, economically and politically depressed as a group, have been unable to shape or influence widespread myths and assertions about them.

Black motherhood is a topic about which many Americans have ready beliefs, but actually studying black mothers is a formidable and challenging task. Much of the literature about black mothers is intricately intertwined with other related topics such as analyses of black women in general or of their impact on their children. Further, the study of black mothers is necessarily interdisciplinary, drawing upon child development, psychology, sociology, literature, economics, and many other fields. Understanding black mothers is also complicated by the fact that, perhaps more than any other group of American mothers, these women have given birth and reared children under conditions of social instability, societal discontinuity, and rapid social change.

This chapter synthesizes the historical, theoretical, empirical, and popular views of black motherhood. These perspectives form the context through which new investigative questions can be identified, myths refuted, and the continuing relevance of cherished beliefs about, and expectations for, black mothers challenged. In an effort to understand these women, we realize that black mothers are not a monolithic group. Yet there is considerable empirical evidence for common personality patterns and world views based on history, culture, and social circumstances. Through this composite discussion of black mothers, we seek to move analysis toward an ecological and liberating perspective on black motherhood.

This chapter is organized into eight subsections, beginning with a brief history of black motherhood in the United States. We then examine the black matriarchy theory, which still forms the core of discussion about these women. Images of black mothers in literature are outlined. The status of black mothers is presented, including data on fertility rate, economic preparation for parenthood, maternal and infant mortality, and educational outcomes. The family support systems available to black mothers are explored and five characteristics of the black mothering process are identified. Finally, current issues for black mothers are raised with conclusions relevant to preparing these women and their families for the 21st century.

HISTORICAL BACKGROUND

Understanding black mothers in the United States must begin in the context of their cultural and political history because the strength, form, and function of mothering is deeply rooted in the framework in which it occurs.

Black Mothers in Africa

Nobles (1974a,b) explains that the special bond between the black American mother and child is deeply rooted in an African heritage and philosophical orientation that places a special value on children because they represent the continuity of life. The mother–child relationship was important in all of West Africa from which American slaves were drawn (Frazier, 1932, 1939). There are also reports that West African women were viewed like gods because they bear children and therefore the future. In African mythology, the universe was conceived and delivered by a woman; only women have the ability to give birth, to ensure the ever-increasing number of ancestors, to link the past with the present (see Rodgers-Rose, 1980).

Black Mothers in Bondage

The experience of slavery served to reduce black mothers from a revered place in society to that of a breeder and worker. As slaves, women were deprived of legal marriage, male protection, and maternal rights. Woloch (1984) writes that slave mothers customarily were released from field work a month before and after delivery and were usually allowed to leave a field a few times a day to nurse infants who might be left in the care of another child or an aged slave. These mothers prolonged nursing as long as possible, even for several years. Nevertheless, after childbirth, as they labored in the fields with the pain of full breasts, slave mothers were often beaten raw by the overseer when they did not keep up with the men (Davis, 1971; Owens, 1976).

In slavery, the black male was used systematically as a stud and the black female used primarily for purposes of breeding or for the gratification of the white male. The sons of white planters were often encouraged to rape black women. It was also common for planters to command slave women and girls to have children.

The offspring of slave women and white males derived their condition from that of their mother. Although this was not unique to American slavery, there could be little doubt about how such a question would be resolved: Had status been defined on a paternal basis, there would instantly have arisen the question of parental obligation for the numerous mulatto children.

Thus, the father among slaves was legally "unknown." When planters spoke of slave families, they often referred to husbandless mothers and their children (Owens, 1976). Consequently, the only source of family continuity was through the female, the dependence of the child on the mother. In this pattern we see that the matrilineal system among blacks, a basis for the so-called black matriarchy, was a creation of a racist system, not of indigenous values held by the enslaved.

Slave women were active resisters to the brutality they experienced (Davis, 1971; Cole, 1978). Some slave mothers rejected their children because of the traumatic nature of childbearing and the extra work it entailed (Frazier, 1939). Abortions and infanticide were performed by some black mothers rather than produce a family for use by slave masters (Steady, 1981).

Yet, numerous slave accounts and narratives support the fact that there was also a special value placed on children. Although many slave children were born not out of love but under adverse circumstances, slave mothers were found to be "fiercely maternal." Lantz's (1980) analysis of slavery-related narratives indicates that blacks resisted efforts to disperse the family. These narratives reveal the strong attachment mothers held for their children and provide dramatic accounts of forced separation. Among plantation slaves, the assertion that a woman could not have children constituted a slur.

The masters' economic interest in the survival of children caused them to recognize the dependence of the young children upon their mothers. Whether out of humanity or self-interest, the masters were compelled to respect the mother's strong attachments to their children (Owens, 1976). Maternal indifference, where it existed, can be explained by the forced pregnancies and harsh experiences attending motherhood. Most of the evidence indicates that slave mothers were devoted to their children and made tremendous sacrifices for their welfare. Under such circumstances, a maternal family group took form and the tradition of the black mother's responsibility for her family took root (Frazier, 1949).

The black mother's role in the slave family contrasted sharply with that of white women in their families, beginning a host of differences between the two groups (see Woloch, 1984). Anger about illicit interracial sex was usually directed at women slaves instead of unfaithful husbands. When southern white women denounced slavery, they usually did so on a pragmatic basis rather than a moral one, as they focused on the evils of slaves rather than the curse of slavery. Further, although black women were active in the abolitionist movement, one female antislavery society ws almost disbanded as a result of controversy about black female members. Clearly, slave women had more in common with enslaved men than with free white women.

Postslavery Experiences

Black family units were revitalized after the Civil War (Lantz, 1980). Legal marriage and a stable household characterized by female domesticity were commonly viewed as the major privileges of freedom (Woloch, 1984). This ideal proved increasingly fragile.

Historians report that throughout the chaotic situation of the Civil War and Emancipation, black mothers held their families together and supported their children (Frazier, 1949). Moreover, because black men continued to suffer overt discrimination in jobs and opportunities for upward mobility, black mothers continued to play important roles in contributing to the overall support of the black family.

There have been many postslavery investigations of black women's view of their role as mothers. Many researchers asserted that "bitterness, despair and futility" were often associated with motherhood (Jeffers, 1967). Bernard (1966) claimed that because motherhood does not fulfill the black woman, her "poor performance in the role" (p. 103) is inevitable.

Other researchers (Bell, 1965; Jeffers, 1967) found that black mothers had a strong commitment to the mother role. Being a mother was an important source of identity and meaning, and experience that, like none other in their lives, provides immediate and frequent rewards. For many poor black mothers, motherhood is the only honorable status that they can reasonably expect to have.

Indeed, many researchers have stated that motherhood is more highly valued than wifehood (Bernard, 1966; Bell, 1965, 1971). Rodgers-Rose (1980) asserts that the West African practice of polygamy had historically made the wife role less demanding. In America, the restricted opportunities for black men to fill the family breadwinner role has been alleged to make marriage udesirable for some lower class black women. Joseph (Joseph & Lewis, 1981) states that there appears to be an unconscious and conscious bias toward the maternal because the emotional primacy, the social constancy, and solidarity of mother–child ties eclipse marital bonds, which tend to be brittle.

Black women have continued to regard children as a value in themselves, and, by extension, have heavily invested in a family/community "caring" role, which has been reinforced by postslavery experiences. Moreover, Rodgers-Rose (1980) notes that cultural and historical forces combined to place black women in a role in which the family structure expected them to show responsibility for a wide range of "others." Their caring role extended from their own children and families to their communities and even to white children and families. Being mothers, being caretakers, formed the core of these women's existence and their economic survival.

THE BLACK MATRIARCHY: A PERSISTENT MYTHOLOGY

Black mothers have been labeled as matriarchs by those who ignore the cultural and historical context of black motherhood. Although there have been numerous critiques of the matriarchal model of black family analysis, the image of structurally dysfunctional, woman-dominated households has remained a strong theme of discussion about black mothers.

Although the matriarchy concept was advanced by both black (eg., Frazier, 1939) and white researchers, it was popularized by a white sociologist, Daniel P. Moynihan, in the 1960s (1965a,b). Moynihan's views received wide attention because he was not just a sociologist; he served as an Assistant Secretary of Labor and an advisor to several presidents. In these roles, he advanced a policy platform that would compel the federal government to "intervene" in black family life.

In "The Negro Family: A Case For National Action," Moynihan reported that black families were crumbling in a "tangle of pathology." To advance this thesis, he minimized the fact that a large majority of black families of all economic levels then had both parents present. Instead, Moynihan envisioned an emerging black matriarchy rooted in the disproportionately high number of out-of-wedlock births, female-headed households, and employed black women. "Deviant" family structure and organization, coupled with high unemployment among black men, led to Moynihan's focus on imminent disaster.

The family roles of black mothers were unusual among middle-class white women—and perhaps even more unimaginable to the white males who studied them. In a possible projection of the ego damage these white males would feel under similar circumstances, it was readily presumed and scientifically concluded that the status of black males was being undermined by black women.

Indeed, Moynihan asserted that "a fundamental fact of Negro American family life is the often reversed roles of husband and wife." The matriarchy perspective heightened sensitivity to the fact that black women have been, for a long time, important in family decision-making processes, an antithesis of the traditionally accepting female role in white middle-class America.

A critical error in the matriarchy concept is the failure to recognize that acceptable male and female roles reflect cultural values rather than inherent appropriateness. Few research studies have investigated black marriages or families on their own merits with attempts at illustrating the positives or testing the accusations made by critics (Rodgers-Rose, 1980). There has also been little recognition of the fact that slavery compelled an unbalanced husband–wife relationship.

Further, research has not recognized the cultural continuity between West African and black American people in family definition, character, form, and function. An important example of this historical continuity is seen in the flexible family roles in which men and women more easily interchange the domestic and economic roles that are sex-specific in Euro-American traditions (Nobles, 1974a,b). Whereas matriarchal perspectives interpret this sharing as "female dominance" or confused sexual identity, other scholars (Staples, 1973; Cazenave, 1983; Scanzoni, 1971; Mack, 1974) see lower- and middle-class black families as more equalitarian than white families at the same status levels.

Both classic and contemporary research refute assertions of wife dominance (Schultz, 1968) and family disorganization (LaBarre, 1968) among blacks. Allen (1985) recently found that, although black mothers have comparably more central roles in their family lives, their centrality is not purchased at the father's expense. Black women realize that a sense of personal independence, in contrast to perceived powerlessness, can be maintained in intimate interpersonal relationships (Joseph & Lewis, 1981).

In addition to cultural variables, historical factors also account for the structural and functional differences in black and white families. These differences may be an unintended consequence of long-standing economic, educational, and occupational discrimination against black men (Scanzoni, 1971; Steady, 1981; Allen, 1979). They also reflect the result of large social forces impinging differently upon white and black family systems (Scanzoni, 1977). Further, studies (e.g., Parker & Kleiner, 1969; St. Pierre, 1982) have found the relationship between socioeconomic discrimination and family instability to be direct; problems of instability in the black family often appear to be created and maintained not by a deviant subculture but by the social and psychological consequences of unemployment and discrimination.

Robert Staples (1970) calls the black matriarchy theory a myth and "a cruel hoax" since black women are economically exploited because they are both Black and female and because of the shortage of black males. The cultural stereotype of the domineering black woman is an ironic contrast to the masses of black women who constitute a defenseless group against white racism in its most virulent sexual and economic manifestations.

However, like most myths, it contains some elements of truth. Black women have not been passive objects who were satisfied with watching their menfolk make history. The highly functional role that the black female has historically played makes it more appropriate to describe the black woman as strong rather than domineering (see Rodgers-Rose, 1980).

Instead of being criticized, the survival of black mothers and their offspring against multiple attacks to their endurance should be applauded. The greater tenacity of black women and their ability to adapt to nontraditional roles should have led to social scientists' recognition and study of positive survival strategies rather than to negative labeling. Ironically, these long-established cultural patterns and historical factors have created models of womanhood and of family functioning in the black community toward which middle-class whites now are moving.

IMAGES OF BLACK MOTHERS IN LITERATURE

Myths about black mothers have predominated in a scientific tradition in which these women have not been permitted to speak for themselves. Their experiences have been interpreted and analyzed rather than presented on their own merits.

It appears that since the 1970s and the civil rights movement, some studies, historical works, and novels are better representing voices from the black experience. Some white scholars have also recognized the racism inherent in the previous literature. Consequently, there have been numerous challenges to the concepts of cultural deviance and deprivation and a greater acceptance of cultural relativism.

Recognizing diversity is an important and necessary step to enhance the validity of the investigative process in cross-cultural settings. Yet, there still lacks the proper respect for alternative research designs, methods, tools, and approaches that add substance to the acknowledgment of certain inherent weaknesses in the scientific process.

One critical missing element is the absence of black mothers who are also social scientists. The number of black women engaged in the scientific process has remained small; blacks are seriously underrepresented among graduate and professional school students (The College Board, 1985).

Consequently, to get balanced perspectives and a more accurate representation of the reality of the experience of black motherhood, we must turn to those sources produced by black women themselves. One readily available source is black literature, including biography and fiction. Mary Helen Washington (1975) observes that since *Iola Leroy*, the first novel written by a black woman, was published in 1862, one of the primary preoccupations of the black woman writer has been the black woman herself.

The portrait of black women presented by black women writers contrasts sharply with that offered by social scientists. In Mary Washington's anthology of classic stories by and about black women, black women writers did not present black women as the legendary and romanticized superwoman or as a perversion such as the super sex object or the domineering matriarch. Rather, Washington was impressed with the frequency of the image of a woman of towering strength who was fiercely protective of her children, often sacrificing herself to prepare them to live in a violent and racist world. However, black writers also depict the black mother as a woman faced with harsh responsibilities, which she accepts and carries out to the fullest of her powers. These women are not composites of statistics, but are people living their daily lives to the best of their abilities.

In an analysis of the works of Maya Angelou, Alice Walker, and Ethel Waters, Burgher (1979) concluded that the literature views black motherhood as a nonindividualistic, cultural force that is *not* based solely on procreation, but on being individually creative in whatever task one undertakes. It is not uncommon for the black mother to be the strongest member of the community spiritually. She also assumes the responsibility of communicating values and ideals that encourage and support the black community as a viable entity separate from the larger society that almost suffocates the black race. The black mother sees herself not as a breeder or as a matriarch but as a builder and nurturer of a race, a progeny, a nation.

According to Andrea Rushing, the most prevalent image of black women in

Afro-American poetry is the image of the mother. Almost all the images of mother revolve around her strength under stress. In Afro-American tradition, mother is not a cushion from troubled and chaotic conditions but the impetus and example for perseverance in a hostile world. Langston Hughes' "Mother to Son" is the best-known example of this. Black attitudes toward mother are extremely complex, but in almost all the mother poems, mother is above criticism, the almost perfect symbol of black struggle, suffering, and endurance. The strong black "mammy" does exist in the literature, but she is humanized by being scaled down. Rushing asserts that images of black women are not as varied in Afro-American poetry because women often symbolize aspects of black life that are valued by the race (see Steady, 1981).

Comparing black literature with sociological studies is one method of assessing the validity of each. Wade-Gayles (1980) studied the interrelations between art and science in the analysis of the role of the black mother as she is presented in selected novels and sociological studies published between 1940 and 1970. Wade-Gayles found that the studies by sociologists emphasize the black mother's fatalistic attitude toward life, while fiction emphasizes the frustration and struggle, but not fatalism. She further maintains that sociologists' perceptions of the black mother do not reflect the reality of the women's lives but the narrowness of sociologists' understanding of that reality. Whereas sociological studies present data on "effects" without discussion of "cuases," the two are inseparable in fiction. Moreover, the sociological studies considered two factors in interpreting childrearing postures (family structure and class) but fiction suggested that other factors also affect the way a black mother treats her children.

In a comparison of selected works from sociology with contemporary black music, Stewart (1980) found that the art form paralleled the sociological data, supplemented empirical evidence, and suggested further research questions. Stewart concluded that some important aspects of black culture are lost through scientific analysis; data obtained from folk culture provide a unique cross-check on the validity of sociological data.

THE STATUS OF BLACK MOTHERS

In the face of multiple sources of evidence against the black matriarchy hypothesis, one must wonder what accounts for the perennial strength of this idea. Would not scientists, if not the public, refute the notion and continue more productive efforts to understand black mothers and their families?

The power of the black matriarchy thesis may be rooted in the history of racism and the continuing public refusal to accept any direct responsibility for the plight of black mothers and their children. Thus, looking for internal causes to the poverty they face, the matriarchy theory serves as an "explanation" that is all-encompassing, has historical continuity, and is easily "proved" by descriptive statistics on family structure. Rather than confront institutional racism or structural barriers to black advancement, "cultural explanations" for "deficiencies" evolved. It may be more comfortable to argue that mother-dominance smothers the spirits of unemployed black boys or that the mother's laziness fails to provide a model of self-sufficiency, thus leading her children to lives of welfare dependency, crime, delinquency, drug addiction, and premature death.

Howard and Scott explain the logic behind the deficit approach to black families as "poverty causes family disorganization, which in turn causes socialization failures, which cause character defects, which perpetuate poverty" (Munroe, Munroe, & Whiting, 1981, p. 123). Such premises appeal to those scientists sympathetic to social problems because they place the blame on poverty and imply that a redistribution of resources would alter the behavior patterns of the affected groups. This approach, however, reduces the importance of culture and elevates the idea that group differences are primarily reactions to external contingencies.

Nevertheless, black mothers in the United States *do* face challenges related to changes in family life unprecedented in the history of black people. They are more likely than the majority of their countrywomen to be employed yet economically unprepared for motherhood. Yet, they bear more children and have them at earlier ages than nonblack mothers. The pre- and postnatal risks to black mothers and their offspring remain comparably high. Throughout the cycle of mothering, they are more likely to raise their children alone, to be poor, and to witness their children succumb to a variety of horrors ranging from inadequate health and nutrition to unemployment. Black mothers are also faced with the awesome task of preparing their children to confront racism and discrimination and ensuring that this preparation is simultaneously realistic but does not immobilize youngsters.

Fertility Rate

A primary public concern about black mothers is the sheer number of children they bear. Woloch (1984) found that the childbearing rate of seventeenth-century immigrant slave women was extremely low because of factors such as high adult mortality, poor health, the relative old age of the women, and the desperate condition of new women slaves, their inability to adjust to slavery, and their alienation, depression, and morbid state of mind. According to Moynihan (1965a), at the time of the founding of the nation, one American in five was black. The proportion declined steadily until it was only one in ten by 1920, where it held until the 1950s when it began to rise. One American in nine was nonwhite in 1965.

Today the black population is approximately 12% of the U.S. total, a proportion that is likely to increase. There were 400,000 fewer white children under 5 in 1984 than in 1970, which had the highest number in a decade, but there were 280,000 more black children under 5. The Census Bureau's 12% growth projection from 1985 to 2000 reflects increases of 23% among blacks and 9% for whites (Feistritzer, 1985).

As increases and declines in black fertility have tended to parallel those within white society, the major reason for racial differences in fertility seems to be the control of fertility rather than the number of children desired. For many blacks, particularly nonusers of birth control and males (Farrell, Dawkins, & Oliver, 1983), family planning continues to evoke fears of race genocide.

Racial divergences in family planning may be due to the fact that blacks (males especially) have been systematically denied equal access to educational and occupational opportunity structures in which individualistic aspirations are most generally carried out (Scanzoni, 1975). Thus, for decades higher-income, better-educated blacks have had fewer children than lower-class blacks have. Moynihan (1965a) called this phenomenon "the Frazier effect," after the distinguished author of *Black Bourgeoisie* (1962) and several books on the black family between 1930 and 1940.

Today, middle-class blacks have the greatest proportion of unmarried and childless women during their most fertile years. High-income blacks have even fewer children than their counterparts in the general population. Two-parent families among blacks are concentrated among middle-class blacks, but it is precisely among these families that the greatest reductions in childbearing are occurring (Darity & Myers, 1984).

Economic Preparation for Motherhood

Although black mothers have more children than their white counterparts, they face enormous challenges in providing adequately for their care. Ironically, although the matriarchy theory implies female leverage, black women are more disadvantaged overall than either blacks, females, or white males in terms of employment, income, education, and health (Gary, 1981; CDF, 1985).

This situation is likely to continue since during the 1970s and early 1980s, there was a worsening of living standards for blacks, particularly in terms of unemployment and income (Willhelm, 1983). This is particularly bad news for black mothers; annual statistical data since 1930 reveal a black underclass characterized by mother-headed families with low income and mobility levels. The children in these families are the poorest in the nation; they are three times more likely to be poor than white children in such families (CDF, 1985).

The comparably weak economic status of black mothers holds true regardless of whether they are in two-parent or female-headed households. Black children in two-parent families are twice as likely as white children in two-parent families to live below the poverty level. Further, the median income for all black families is less than 60% of that of white families, an increasing gap between 1970 and 1983 (CDF, 1985).

Black middle-class mothers also face economic challenges. Research has cast doubt on the use of established measures of middle-class status with blacks (Smith, 1979). The black middle-class remains fragile and segregated in institutions dependent on federal government subsidy and concentrated in functions created to serve the black consumer and community (Collins, 1983).

Maternal and Infant Mortality

The Children's Defense Fund (1985) reports that, compared with white mothers and children, twice as many black mothers die in childbirth and twice as many black infants die. One in eight black babies is born underweight compared with one in 18 white babies.

The black American infant mortality rate has been reported as higher than that of Cuba, Jamaica, Puerto Rico, and four Eastern block countries (Bulgaria, Czechoslovakia, East Germany, and Poland) (CDF, 1985). Billingsley and Giovannoni (1972) argue that there is a "racist dimension of infant mortality" (p. 13) because, regardless of the economic status of the parents, white children have a better chance of living beyond their first birthday.

Inadequate prenatal care is implicated in many of these tragic deaths. Whereas 80% of white women receive first trimester care, only 60% of all black women do. Nearly 10% of all black women and 20% of black mothers under age 15 receive last-trimester or no prenatal care.

Education, Earnings, and Employment

While education generally facilitates health care, employment, and income, black women do not reap the full measure of their academic achievements and potential contributions. The reasons for these low attainments have been subject to both research and debate (see Rodgers-Rose, 1980), but the racial gap in income is linked more to different reward structures than to worker characteristics (Hanushek, 1982).

Although black women work more years of their lives than do their white counterparts, they have the lowest median level of occupation and earnings and their unemployment rate is greater (Rodgers-Rose, 1980). Black females also have higher unemployment rates at both the high school and college levels (CDF, 1985).

Although blacks earn less than whites with comparable education and training (Hanushek, 1982), black students, particularly black female students, are more likely than whites to end their high school careers in vocational rather than academic programs. Moreover, more black women than white drop out of school because of home responsibilities, particularly pregnancy (CDF, 1985).

Clearly, the presumed "power" of the "matriarchal" black mother does not reflect economic security. Indeed, their relative status in the family is not due to their greater earning power, but to the lack of opportunities for black males. Although black mothers are vital to the well-being of their children, they command little respect from the culture at large. In a twist of fate, black mothers are at once powerful and without any power at all.

FAMILY SUPPORT SYSTEMS

The fragile living standards of many black mothers have required a high degree of sharing and cooperation within a network of black mothers. Thus, black mothers have survived by means of their high participation in the work force, their participation in helping networks of kin and non-kin, public assistance, and assistance from the fathers of their children. It is important to recognize that a *combination* of support systems continues to be necessary to sustain a modest or stable living standard. For example, the low wages earned by black women often makes it difficult for them to purchase child care; therefore they must rely on relatives and friends. The level of child support that many black fathers can afford makes it necessary to receive public assistance. A picture emerges wherein typical black mothers of all social classes are involved in complex family support systems integral to their survival. Nevertheless, despite multiple sources of support, nearly half of all black children continue to live in poverty.

Labor Force Participation

Primary among the black mothers' means of support is their own employment. The weight of evidence suggests that labor force participation is an enculturated aspect of black women's sex-role identity and of black community life. From emancipation onward, black women have been employed in disproportionate numbers to white women (Woloch, 1984; Moynihan, 1965a). Whereas the labor force participation rates of white women have catapulated during the past quarter century, black women's rates have been fairly constant (Engram, 1980). Consequently, female employment has become much more institutionalized and normative among black families.

The perennial pattern of a higher proportion of working black wives than any other group of married women can be accounted for by economic need and a desire to sacrifice for their children (Pleck, 1970; Woloch, 1984). Also, black women are more likely than white women to work whether or not it is necessary (Beckett, 1976). Thus, history has had a strong bearing on intergenerational labor force activity, thereby strengthening cultural imperatives that transcend major social and economic trends in American society.

The high rates of labor force participation among black women have also been less sensitive to the effects of assuming maternal roles (Rodgers-Rose, 1980). Compared with white mothers, black mothers enter or return to the labor force when their children are younger and they are more likely to work full-time. As a result, four out of five black mothers with preschool children work compared with three out of five white mothers; young black children in two-parent families are more likely than white children to have working mothers (CDF, 1985).

Family income also is related to maternal employment. Among children in families with income under $17,000 a year, maternal employment rates are about the same for blacks and whites, but the gap widens as incomes increase. Among children in families earning over $25,000, 80% of black mothers work compared to 60% of white mothers. In the top income bracket, 94% of all young black children and 57% of young white children have mothers who work (CDF, 1985). The high employment rates among black mothers, especially those in the upper-income brackets, demonstrate their importance as wage earners.

On the other hand, many black women may actually desire homemaking roles but have been denied the freedom to choose between work or family. To the contrary, the matriarchy hypothesis precluded the notion that work may be associated with role conflict. Black women are reared with the expectation that whether or not they marry, whether or not they have children, they will work most of their adult lives. Rather than being a liberating goal, work is another fact of life. Now, many white women are coming to define work as their right and not as an option—a perspective characteristic of black women for decades (see Rodgers-Rose, 1980).

Extended Family Relationships

The employment pattern of black mothers indicates their greater need for inexpensive and full-time child care. Black preschoolers are enrolled in full-time day-care programs at two to three times the rate of white preschoolers. Black working mothers are more likely to use child-care centers or relatives for their preschool children (CDF, 1985).

In child care as well as other areas of life, both fictive and blood "relatives" are integral to the survival of black mothers. Many scholars have documented the stabilizing influence of the extended family among poor, single mothers. It is likely that the extremely poor black family has not developed along the nuclear pattern because there is a need to provide an alternative system of savings and insurance (see Gary, 1981; Rodgers-Rose, 1980).

However, as Harriette McAdoo's research (1978) points out, it is incorrect to view the extended family support network as a "coping mechanism" needed only as a defense against poverty. McAdoo found that both single and married middle-class black mothers also were involved extensively in the kin-help exchange network including child care, financial assistance, and emotional support (see Rodgers-Rose, 1980).

Family stability is also maintained by the role of grandparents in children's lives. Allen (1985) observed the profound influence of the black grandmother on the mother's childrearing practices and thus the next generation's socialization. Moreover, grandparenting remains a significant, highly respected role.

In sum, research indicates that black family forms reflect deeply rooted value commitments and are not merely abnormal reactions to situational pressures. The hapless charge of family instability in the face of evidence on family structure ignores the extended family adaptation based on kinship bonds.

Paternal Support

Another implication of the matriarchy theory is the weakness of black fathers, with many research reports that the lower-class black man considered his marital and parental roles of little importance (Bell, 1971). Yet, recent studies have found that black husbands are more accepting of maternal employment and are active in child care and socialization (see Beckett, 1976; Gary, 1981).

Part of the "matriarchy" stereotype may be related to the difficulty with which some black mothers acquire income support from the fathers of their children. However, this observation must be closely followed by the realization that this problem is hardly unique to black families. Research has found that the provider role is salient to the identities of middle-class black men (Cazenave, 1979).

As divorce and separation have increased in nonblack communities, society now is more vigorously assisting custodial parents in enforcing child-support obligations. Still, custodial white mothers are twice as likely as custodial black mothers to be awarded, and to actually receive, child support (CDF, 1985).

Some scholars (e.g., Stack & Semmel, 1975) point out that black mothers often receive support from the paternal relatives and that society's punitive attempts to collect from fathers increases family stress without increasing funds to children, particularly for those children receiving public assistance. Further, Wilson and Neckerman (1985) point out that without jobs, black men cannot support families; whereas the labor force participation patterns of white men have changed little since the late 1940s, the labor force participation of black men declined substantially from 84% in 1940 to 67% in 1980. The increasing rate of joblessness among black men merits serious consideration as a major underlying factor in the rise of black single mothers.

Public Assistance

When the mother's sources of income are inadequate, the state and federal governments *supplement* family support. (Public assistance should clearly be considered as partial support, given the fact that official documents indicate the levels of aid are below the standard of need) (Washington, 1984).

The proportion of black mothers and children on "welfare" rolls have been fairly stable. In 1961, not quite half of all children receiving aid were black (Moynihan, 1965a); the figure was about 44% in 1985 (CDF, 1985).

Not surprisingly, four out of five AFDC (Aid to Families with Dependent Children) families are headed by single mothers. For some black lower-class women, marriage appears to have limited possibilities for acquiring a husband to fill the breadwinner role. A poor woman who decides to marry may be gambling her control over a stable low income against an income that may be even lower and less stable.

Yet, despite assertions to the contrary, Darity and Myers (1984) argue that research fails to demonstrate a statistical link between variations in AFDC payments relative to typical black male income and variations in the proportion of black families headed by women. Further, they concluded that the evidence so far suggests that welfare benefits do not provide an incentive to teenagers to bear children. Research is similarly unable to establish a direct link between welfare and the incidence of out-of-wedlock births. Nevertheless, social transfer programs may have contributed to an environment less conducive to the financial necessity of and support for the traditional two-parent family.

CHARACTERISTICS OF THE BLACK MOTHERING PROCESS

As early as 1870, John Van Ervie's book *White Supremacy and Negro Subordination* asserted that "the Negro isolated by himself, seems utterly incapable of transmitting anything whatsoever to the succeeding generation" (cited by R. Jones, 1973, p. 121). Yet, much of the traditional literature is so lacking in ecological perspectives and is so methodologically flawed as to offer few useful or authentic insights about the lives of black mothers.

Gloria Wade-Gayles (1980) reports numerous examples of methodological inadequacies in the scientific literature, such as merely theorizing about black family life without presentation of data and small sample sizes. Another problem is the level of analysis used by investigators; explanations and inferences based on either a macro- or micro-unit of analysis may be extremely limited. Validity of the observations is also a concern; Wade-Gayles states that, as outsiders with preconceived, negative notions of the black experience, researchers have been as crippled as the people they studied were victimized. Another difficult problem is the sheer complexity of family life and the need for multiple measures, multiple observations, an ecological perspective, and a representative sample. Yet, social scientists have generally studied the structure of the most economically deficient, socially vulnerable, problematic black families and inferred negative interaction patterns from the structural viewpoint based on comparisons with economically stable white middle-income families (Allen, 1985).

Despite the predominance of flawed research on black mothers, even in the early literature (e.g., Jeffers, 1967), there are illustrations of the creativity, coping skills, love, and positive nurturing patterns shown by many black mothers. Indeed, five characteristics can be highlighted as typical of the black mothering process:

1. Adaptation to cultural and economic imperatives
2. High aspirations for children
3. Emphasis on people rather than objects
4. Focus on physical care and development and early training
5. Clear expectations for discipline and obedience.

Adaptation to Cultural and Economic Imperatives

Most black women realize that their mothering, and their parenting goals, are influenced by cultural and economic imperatives. Indeed, the childrearing goals of blacks across social classes have been found to be similar (Kamii & Radin, 1967). Generally, successful black childrearing must resolve a basic conflict that exists between the Euroamerican world views of competition, individualism, and independence and the African-American world views of cooperation, interdependence, and collective responsibility (Nobles, 1974a,b).

Janice Hale (1982) states that black mothers have had to ignore white childrearing norms that are irrelevant to the existential situation of their children. Indeed, exposure to informational sources in the realm of childrearing may be more widespread among white than among black mothers regardless of class position or educational level. Yet, a recent study of black teen, black adult, and white adult mothers suggests that knowledge of "normative" development may not be essential to parent effectiveness (Stevens, 1984).

Nowhere is the issue of cultural adaptation more important to recognize than in discussion of the impact of father absence on black children. Model studies in the 1950s and 1960s asserted that delinquency and hypermasculinity as a consequence of the sex-role identity problems resulted from the father's absence in black males. Moynihan (1967) offered a solution:

> Given the strains of the disorganized and matrifocal family life in which so many Negro youth come of age, the Armed Forces are a dramatic and desperately needed change: a world away from women, a world run by strong men of unquestioned authority. (p. 42)

In contrast, research has found that black sons generally develop a close nurturing relationship with their mothers (Gary, 1981). Since strong mothers are normative in black families, black boys are more likely to grow up successfully in a relatively matrifocal family pattern rather than in a pattern that is deviant for the culture. It is the *meaning* of father absence in the culture rather than the fact itself that influences adult behavior (Munroe, Munroe, & Whiting, 1981).

High Aspirations for Children

Another characteristic of black mothering is high aspirations for children, a characteristic with historical continuity. Both slave and emancipated blacks held a strong desire for literacy and a willingness to endure the hardships necessary to attain it (Bullock, 1970; Owens, 1976). Strong maternal and cultural approval was an important factor in the success of black students; studies found that black mothers wanted their children to acquire an education even if it resulted in estrangement from the family (Ramirez & Price-Williams, 1976; Kriesberg, 1967; Powell, 1963).

Early research frequently dismissed or ignored these maternal expectations for achievement as "unrealistically high" (Bernard, 1966, p. 105) or as reflecting "an element of wishful thinking" (Kandel, 1967). Rosen (1959), for example, concluded that since slavery taught blacks to believe in their helplessness, the black mother could not teach her child to strive for success. Bell (1965) argued that the black mother simply "does not believe in success" (1965, p. 449). Erikson (1965) stated that, in sharp contrast to Jewish mothers, the black mother attempts to "keep her children, and especially the gifted and questioning ones, away from futile and dangerous competition, imposing on them 'a surrendered identity'" (Erikson, 1965, p. 200). Recently, Howard and Hammond (1985) explained that black youth avoid intellectual competition because of "rumors" about their inferiority; these rumors are a hidden obstacle to black success.

Many indicators of educational attainment reveal clear racial differences. From kindergarten through 12th grade, black children's scores on reading and mathematics tests lag behind the scores of white children. Black youth are also more likely to be enrolled in special education or vocational programs and to drop out of school; they are less likely to be enrolled in gifted and talented or academic programs or to graduate from college (The College Board, 1985).

Yet tremendous progress has been made. Between 1971 and 1980, elementary school black children made larger gains in reading and mathematics than did nonblack students. Black high school graduation rates have improved dramatically over the past two decades. Like whites and Hispanics, greater percentages of each succeeding generation of blacks have completed high school.

Although all ethnic Americans desire a better life for their children, this vision has required extraordinary faith and perseverance in the face of formidable odds against black achievement. Instead of implicating family structure and process in the poor academic performance of black children, it is more relevant to highlight the impacts of discrimination (Bullock, 1970), the instructional process (Hale, 1982; Washington, 1983), and federal educational policy (The College Board, 1985) for the academic failure of black children.

A "People" Orientation

Part of the inspiration for high achievement comes from the group or people orientation of black Americans, which stems from the African ethos "I am because we are, and because we are, therefore I am" (Mbiti, 1970). Indeed, because blacks have historically been denied material possessions, a strong cultural imperative is the disdain for bragging about "things" (Kochman, 1981).

Thus, black home environments have a "people" rather than the "object" orientation of white homes. Although the variety and stimulation provided by the home environment of blacks and whites are similar, in black homes babies see more people and have fewer toys (Hale, 1982). Although compensatory programs have sought to "remediate" these practices, Morgan (1976) indicts these efforts:

> Little thought was given to the fact that the tinker-toy concept dictates that children are expected to sit in the crib or thereabouts and play quietly with their toys until their

favorite TV program comes on. Without these toys, of course, mother and child touch, exchange various forms of communications and learn from one another. (p. 133)

Physical Care, Development, and Training

Although there is evidence to the contrary, it is commonly asserted that American black infants show a precocity for early motor development similar to that found in African groups (see Munroe, Munroe, & Whiting, 1981). This may be attributed to fewer restrictions on the infant's behavior and permissive parental attitudes.

Consistent with the people orientation of black homes, many researchers suggest that black mothers tend to emphasize children's physical development and care including "early" toilet training and walking in contrast to the educational emphasis. However, black mothers do not focus on physical development at the expense of cognitive skill (Rosser & Randolph, 1985).

Black preschool children are believed to possess a greater movement repertoire than both lower- and middle-class white children (Guttentag, 1972). It has also been shown that black children learn faster or more easily with techniques that utilize movement than when they are taught by a more traditional format (Hale, 1982).

As black children are not taught according to their cultural styles, it is not surprising that studies have found that children who can inhibit movement have higher IQ scores (see Hale, 1982). Morgan (1976) believes that black mothers often ignore their children's motoric precocity and do not seek to extend it because development in that area might interfere with the child's ability to be integrated into the school system of white low-motor expectations. This situation, he maintains, is detrimental to the natural learning styles of black children.

Clear Expectations for Discipline and Obedience

Both the classic and contemporary literature cite examples of relatively strict child disciplinary patterns in black families, although the underlying interpretations of this behavior have varied. A recent report found that white mothers envied the way the black mothers commanded respect and obedience from their own children and from white children, exceeding that of the white mothers (see Rodgers-Rose, 1980). Similarly, Hale (1982) found a tendency for the punishments of the black grandmothers to be more severe, with black grandmothers preferring to use a switch, an African-derived instrument. Black grandmothers were significantly more concerned about disobedience, disrespect to elders, and talking back to adults. Whereas white grandmothers stated that they would punish children for fighting back when assaulted, black grandmothers were very emphatic that children should defend themselves and that they would punish any child reluctant to do so.

Reconciling the seeming contradiction between black parental ratings of ambition and obedience as their top childrearing goals, Allen (1985) points out that these parental goals reflect the reality that black children confront. Black parents recognize that future success and survival depends on the child's ability to be alternately and selectively assertive and acquiescent. Quite simply, black people (and particularly black men) at all levels of this society periodically encounter "attempts to keep them in their place." Again, the cultural context of mothering must be considered; similar disciplinary strategies have been found to have different impacts on children across ethnic groups (Baumrind, 1972).

CURRENT ISSUES FOR BLACK MOTHERS

Despite the many positive aspects of black mothering that can be synthesized from both research and literature, much of the current public and scholarly focus remains fixed on the problematic aspects. Although the term "matriarch" has come into disfavor, its underlying notions are evident in current "concern" about adolescent mothers and/or the rise in female-headed households. Indeed, the specters of illegitimacy or welfare dependency that were invoked by the pejorative term "matriarchy" are now raised by disarmingly innocuous descriptive labels (e.g., "single-parent household").

Clearly, the rise in single-parent households, the high rates of adolescent parenting, and the consequent overrepresentation of children among the poor are serious causes for concern. These issues have led to the open discussion of black family life among black leaders, a sensitive, volatile issue arrested significantly by fallout from "The Moynihan Report." Now some blacks concede that "Moynihan was right" since he predicted accurately the increasing deterioration of black family structure. Others regret that Moynihan's recommendations for strengthening the family were overlooked as a result of reaction to his thesis.

An observer of social trends, Daniel P. Moynihan, a senator from New York since 1977, has again turned his attention to the status of American family life (Moynihan, 1986). In his 1985 Godkin lectures at Harvard University, Moynihan examined the relationship between the growing erosion of "traditional" family structure and child poverty. His 1965 treatise compared "the Negro family" with the white family, which he felt had "achieved a high degree of stability and is maintaining that stability" (p. 5). Moving from the extreme implication that race and culture was a significant correlate of family dysfunction, Moynihan now asserts that the problem of family disorganization is no longer racial.

Although we appreciate Moynihan's universal approach, a realistic attack on family crises and poverty must appreciate the fact that there are commonalities and differences in the family experiences of black and white families. A universal approach to the problem fails to consider that blacks have a peculiar history and presence in the United States that provides insight into the causes, consequences, and cures of their family concerns (see Washington, 1985). For example, where out-of-marriage birth may represent radical choice or pathology in the Euroamerican situation, for black mothers this phenomenon may too often be a practical or bitter adaptation to ecological constraints.

However, we are in agreement with Moynihan that the problem can no longer be ignored. The profound anguish that blacks have experienced as a result of attacks on their family life must be overcome in an objective effort to confront painful realities.

Adolescent Mothers

The personal, social, and economic consequences of being a teenage parent are usually tragic. The birth of children to a teenaged woman entails a substantial risk for the well-being of both mother and child. Social isolation for the mothers and social and physical maladaptations of children threaten optimal development (Kellam, Adams, Brown, & Ensminger, 1982; Washington & Glimps, 1983).

Concern about black adolescent parenting is not new. It was significant to Moynihan (1965a) that the gap between the "generation rate" between whites and nonwhites was particularly wide and concentrated among the poor. Today, about 30% of all births to teenagers are to black females; teenagers account for about 25% of all black births and about 12% of all white births. Further, almost 6 out of 10 births to teens under age 15 were to blacks. Consequently, black children are twice as likely to be born to a teenage or single-parent family (CDF, 1985).

The proportion of black women who were mothers by the time they are age 20 has increased slightly since 1940, from 40% to 44%. However, birth rates for black teens, married and unmarried, have been declining while the birth rate among white unmarried teens has been increasing in recent years (CDF, 1985).

Out-of-Marriage Childbearing

What has changed dramatically is the marriage pattern for black teens. In 1950, only about 18% of all black infants born to teenagers were out of wedlock; today that figure is almost 90%, about two and one-half times the white rate.

Further, in 1982, about 57% of *all* births to black women were out of wedlock. Black children are 12 times more likely than white children to live with a parent who never married. One black child in 4 lives with a parent who has never married, compared to one white child in 48.

What is significant is that the driving fact in this trend has not been an increase in the number of black infants born to teenage mothers. Rather it has been a decline in the marriage rate among black women generally (CDF, 1985). According to the Children's Defense Fund, these high levels of out-of-marriage childbearing essentially guarantee the poverty of black children for the foreseeable future.

Female-Headed Households

The twin trends in adolescent parenting and out-of-wedlock births for all black women has led to a rise in the incidence of female heads of households.

Black mothers are far more likely to raise their children alone. Whereas 80% of white children live in two-parent families, only 40% of black children do. Today, half of the black children (15% of white children) live in female-headed households compared with one-fourth in 1960 (CDF, 1985).

Several decades ago, some researchers thought that as blacks migrated to Northern urban areas, family characteristics such as the female-headed family and the unwed birthrate (eight times the white rate in 1940) would decrease (MacIntyre, 1964). Not only did this prediction fail to occur, as Darity and Myers (1984) point out, for blacks the female-headed family has rapidly moved toward becoming the norm as the rate grew from 21% in 1960, to 28% in 1970, to 46% in 1981.

Contrary to some assertions, the female-headed household is not a legacy of slavery. Rather, between 70 and 90% of postbellum black families had two parents (Woloch, 1984).

Darity and Myers (1984) show that the cause of female-headed households has changed from the death of the husband at the turn of the century through the early 1960s; after 1963, desertion and divorce become the primary immediate source of marital disruption; by 1970, more black families were being formed by women who never married (see Woloch, 1984). The marked fall in fertility among husband—wife black families in the 1970s, bears statistical responsibility for the growing proportion of black children born out of wedlock (Darity & Myers, 1984).

Many authors have asserted that the female-headed household is a self-perpetuating institution. St. Pierre (1982) found that black single-parent females in both the middle and lower classes had themselves come from single-parent families and had close relationships with their mothers. Becoming an "adult" in this manner is reinforced by the shortage of young black men who would make suitable marriage partners as a consequence of the black males' shorter life expectancy and higher rates of infant mortality, drug addiction, accidents and homicides, incarceration, and military participation (Darity & Myers, 1984; Gary, 1981).

Thus, many young black men and women come to expect adult life without spouses, even if they desire a traditional family. After a relatively long period of greater incidence of female headship coupled with poverty, cultural elements may emerge that treat the female-headed family as the normal or accepted form (Darity & Myers, 1984).

The Feminization of Poverty

These contemporary concerns about black mothers have serious economic considerations: these families are very likely to be impoverished. Four out of every five families receiving AFDC are female-headed.

Young mothers under age 25 heading families are very likely to be poor whether they are black (85%) or white (72%). However, black female-headed families are much more likely to stay poor. In female-headed families with older mothers ages 25 to 44, there is a 25-percentage-point gap between black and white poverty rates (CDF, 1985).

The feminization of poverty is cause for alarm. Hill (1979) states that if he were forced to choose what group to target to reduce poverty, he would focus on female-headed families, which in his view are the main cause of the underclass. There appears to be at least two distinct minority communities—one consisting mainly of female-headed households who slip more deeply into poverty and the other of two-parent families who move toward the middle class (Auletta, 1982).

TOWARD AN ECOLOGICAL MODEL OF BLACK MOTHERHOOD

> The woman of a race should be its pride;
> We glory in the strength our mothers had,
> We glory that this strength was not denied
> To labor bravely, nobly and be glad.
>
> —Paul Lawrence Dunbar

This review of the history, status, perspectives, and current issues related to black motherhood reveals the complexity of these women's lives. Accurate interpretation of these findings about black mothers requires an avid appreciation of the context in which their nurturing occurs. Several conclusions and observations can be made about black mothers:

First, we must withdraw the notion that mothers are totally responsible for the outcomes of their mothering. We must lose the sense of the isolation of the mother–child dyad in the face of other social experiences and forces. Social change affects the mothering process as well as the scientific analysis of black mothers.

Second, there is a need for research that focuses on black mothers in a balanced and nonbiased perspective. I concur with Rodgers-Rose's (1980) call for research that neither denigrates black women because of the very functional roles they have had to play nor idealizes them in the process of black family survival and stability almost to the exclusion of black men. Black mothers must be recognized as a distinct segment of society that cannot effectively be studied as "blacks" or as "women." Researchers should respect the integrity of all black families, recognizing the cultural variations in the concept of motherhood.

Third, in a sense, black mothers have been in the vanguard of family trends in the general American society. Movements toward maternal employment, equalitarion sex roles, and female-headed households were all preceded by the black mothers as a model of possibilities for other women. Ironically, as whites move toward black models in their relationships, the pejorative labels appear to soften (Rodgers-Rose, 1980).

Fourth, policymakers must realize that attempts to eradicate poverty require explicit attention to the black mother, particularly those in female-headed households. It is important to bear in mind that family structure does not *cause* poverty or developmental dysfunction. Also, the degree to which society supports black mothers through the community and family determines the extent to which they will function adequately. Instead of offering such mothers tears and damnation, training and development should be provided. In this way, poor single mothers can be prepared to move themselves and their families from public dependency to self-sufficient heads of households. The ultimate solution to black mothers' general poverty is racial and gender equality including access to educational and employment opportunities for black women and black men.

Fifth, although the strong work orientation of black mothers has been a strength, it is timely to reexamine what work means to them. There is increasing evidence that black mothers are enslaved by the lack of choices, not because of the previously assumed lack of proper work attitudes and skills. The black mothers' participation in the labor force may have also been oversold as a model of black womanhood. While it has been important to dispel the myth that black mothers are "living off of the fat of the land," one must be careful not to romanticize the plight of those working women.

Sixth, a comprehensive picture of black mothers necessitates understanding of the black father. Unfortunately, the view of the black woman as a matriarch and the focus on family structure have led researchers to ignore the role of the black man in family survival (Gary, 1981). Few studies have addressed the black father and child. Yet, as McCray (1980) points out, it is difficult to believe that black families could have survived if it were not for some strengths attributable to the black male, the black female, and to that combination (Rodgers-Rose, 1980).

Finally, black family survival for the twenty-first century mandates change in the images and expectations of the black mother that are held by the community, the family—and above all, by the mothers themselves. Indeed, after less than a decade, white women are questioning the "superwoman" role—a role that black American mothers have been required to endure for centuries.

The larger-than-life worker, homemaker, lover, mother, churchwoman, and friend, though born of cultural necessity, is more difficult to negotiate and justify in modern life. Traditional cushions of support for black mothers are weakening under social strain. Many grandmothers, for example, are young, working parents themselves who are both unable and unwilling to assume the traditional role of caretaker for their grandchildren. Although child support enforcement has increased, the high unemployment rate of black men makes it unlikely that some black families will reap substantial benefit from this effort. Moreover, public policy, grounded in the false assumption that black mothers must be forced to work, thrusts some poor mothers into unskilled, minimum-wage labor that makes it arithmetically impossible to raise the family above the poverty level.

We understand that motherhood is an institution with customs, traditions, and expectations. Yet these notions are based largely on expectations rooted in the lives of black mothers of yesterday. Black mothers have changed—they are working, they are poorer, using more organized, substitute care. What has not changed are our expectations of mothers. We expect them to be responsible for all the same functions as yesterday without appropriate changes in fathering, business practices, and social support.

CONCLUSION

Historically, the broad experiences of black mothers were similar. They have been the symbolic guardians of faith and ethnic identity. Typically, black mothers were also wives and employees who saw their potential reduced by the unyielding walls of segregation and discrimination. With their husbands, black mothers prepared their children to endure the limited present and to be ready for unlimited possibilities. For black mothers—whether educated or uneducated, middle-class or poor—their foremost goal was to attain the rights of citizenship set forth in the Constitution of the United States. Their problem was the failure of their government to safeguard their freedom.

The controversial Moynihan Report (1965b) was issued as challenges to lawful segregation were intensifying. The report's conclusions about black family deviance and pathology were attacked as a racist attempt to undermine the civil rights movement that was then in its heyday.

Since the 1960s, many civil rights victories have been won. These rights resulted in employment and educational opportunities that boosted many black families into the middle class. At the same time, changes in the American economy have reduced the need for unskilled or semiskilled black workers, particularly males. As evident in this chapter, the consequences for family life have been devastating.

As we approach the twenty-first century, the experiences for black mothers will be widely divergent. Those women who are highly skilled or married to men who have sophisticated training will see their incomes increase and their children prosper. On the other hand, poor, single, or adolescent mothers are likely to become increasingly alienated and distant from mainstream American life.

Whereas the black underclass becomes more firmly rooted in poverty, the black working class, formerly the backbone of the black community, faces an increasing challenge to maintain economic self-sufficiency. Moreover, the children of the working class, impatient with the pace of racial progress, often have little desire or motivation for the blue-collar work of their parents. Too often, these children are among the rolls of the undereducated and unemployed.

Further compounding these difficulties, as Darity and Myers (1984) point out, given the differential birthrates between the black middle and lower classes, it is the poorest black women who carry the heaviest responsibility for having and raising black children. The black women of the underclass appear to be the only segment of the black population that remains strongly committed to the traditional childrearing function of family life. Yet these women have the least resources and they are obliged to nurture the new generations in the most nontraditional settings for family life. Moreover, their motives for childrearing are most frequently impugned in discussions among policymakers about the consequences of the existing structure of social transfer payments.

The psychological and material resources now existing in black communities will become even more strained by this dilemma. Accustomed to the appearance of racial unity, it will be more difficult to ignore the important constellation of family income and experiential factors that separate the black middle-class from the black poor.

Yet, the social classes of black mothers are not neatly divided into totally segregated worlds. Most middle-class black mothers probably have poor sisters, cousins, aunts, other relatives, and girlfriends with whom they are in frequent contact. These natural alliances, buoyed by community support, provide distinct possibilities for both *preventing* public dependence (for example, through youthful mothering) and for ameliorating the impact of changing social conditions. These relationships offer a solid vehicle for consciousness-raising as black mothers shape their self-definitions, roles, and responsibilities for the twenty-first century.

Many white feminists have envied the role, value, and economic importance of black mothers to their families. Yet, aside from theoretical plaudits to the concept of gender equality, few women of any race envy the *lives* of black mothers. Their so-called "liberation" is rooted in hardship, suffering, circumstance, and freedom *from* choice.

This review of the status of black mothers reminds us that not all black mothers are able to handle the multiple, insidious pressures of economic deprivation with work and family demands. Yes, black mothers and their families have survived—indeed some have prospered. Yet, this survival has been with a great cost unworthy of either favorable or disparaging mythology.

The romantic notion of the black mother as martyr is an obstacle to changing the realities that black families face today. It may be a long time before the negative images and connotations of black mothers are dispelled from scientific and popular discourse. However, the survival, development, and ultimate liberation of black communities necessitates immediate attention to, and adjustments in, the weight carried by black mothers in America.

In addressing these issues, much of today's debate is whether blacks should continue to emphasize the need for government action or to target their energies on self-help. Although a combination of government and community initiative is essential, blacks are now focusing on what can be done using their own resources. For example, because almost half of black females in America become mothers while they are teenagers, the predominant, radical cries that birth control is genocide have given way to a declaration of war against adolescent pregnancy by many black organizations. Amid the correct demands that society fulfill the promises of the Constitution, there is a persistent call for self-reliance. By promoting and extending values and traditions, it is certain that the dilemmas facing black mothers and their families will be resolved.

REFERENCES

Allen, W. R. (1979). Class, culture and family organization: The effects of class and race on family structure in urban America. *Journal of Comparative Family Studies, 10*(3), 301–313.

Allen, W. R. (1985). Race, income and family dynamics: A study of adolescent male socialization processes and outcomes. In M. B. Spencer, G. K. Brookins, & W. R. Allen (Eds.), *Beginnings: The social and affective development of Black children* (pp. 273–292). Hillsdale, NJ: Lawrence Erlbaum.

Auletta, K. (1982). *The underclass*. New York: Random House.

Baumrind, D. (1972). An exploratory study of socialization effects on Black children: Some Black-White comparisons. *Child Development, 74,* 261–267.

Beckett, J. (1976, November). Working wives: A racial comparison. *Social Work,* 463–471.

Bell, R. (1965). Lower class Negro mothers' aspirations for their children. *Social Forces, 43,* 130–138.

Bell, R. (1971). The relative importance of mother and wife roles among Negro lower-class women. In R. Staples (Ed.), *The Black family: Essays and studies* (pp. 248–255). Belmont, CA: Wadsworth Press.

Bernard, J. (1966). *Marriage and family among Negros*. Englewood Cliffs, NJ: Prentice-Hall.

Billingsley, A., & Giovannoni, J. M. (1972). *Children of the Storm: Black children and American child welfare*. New York: Harcourt Brace Jovanovich.

Bullock, H. A. (1970). *A history of Negro education in the South*. New York: Praeger.

Burgher, M. (1979). Images of self and race in the autobiographies of Black women. In R. P. Bell, B. J. Parker, & B. Guy-Sheftall (Eds.), *Sturdy Black bridges: Visions of Black women in literature* (pp. 107–122). Garden City, NY: Anchor/Doubleday.

Cazenave, N. A. (1979). Middle-income Black fathers: An analysis of the provider role. *The Family Coordinator, 28*(4), 583–593.

Cazenave, N. A. (1983). A woman's place: The attitudes of middle class Black men. *Phylon, 44*(1), 12–32.

Children's Defense Fund. (1985). *Black and white children in America: Key facts*. Washington, DC: Children's Defense Fund.

Cole, J. (1978). Militant Black women in early U. S. history. *The Black Scholar, 9*(7), 38–44.

The College Board. (1985). *Equality and excellence: The educational status of Black Americans*. New York: College Board Publications.

Collins, S. (1983). The making of the Black middle class. *Social Problems, 30,* 369–381.

Darity, W. A., & Myers, S. L. (1984, Summer/Fall). Public policy and the condition of Black family life. *The Review of Black Political Economy,* 164–187.

Davis, A. (1971). Reflections on the Black woman's role in the community of slaves. *Black Scholar, 3,* 2–15.

Engram, E. (1980). Role transition in early adulthood: Orientations of young black women. In L. Rodgers-Rose (Ed.), *The Black woman*. Beverly Hills: Sage.

Erickson, E. (1965). The concept of identity in race relations: Notes and queries. *Daedalus, 95,* 200–215.

Farrell, W. C., Jr., Dawkins, M. P., & Oliver, J. (1983). Genocide fears in a rural Black community: An empirical examination. *Journal of Black Studies, 14*(1), 49–67.

Feistritzer, C. E. (1985, July 16). A new baby boomlet hits the schools. *The Washington Post,* p. Cl.

Frazier, E. F. (1932). *The free Negro family: A study of family origins before the Civil War*. Nashville: Fisk University Press.

Frazier, E. F. (1939). *The Negro family in the United States*. Chicago: University of Chicago Press.

Frazier, E. F. (1949). The Negro family in America. In R. N. Anshen (Ed.), *The family: Its function and destiny* (pp. 65–79, 82–84). New York: Harper & Row.

Frazier, E. F. (1962). *Black bourgeoisie*. New York: Collier.

Gary, L. D. (Ed.). (1981). *Black men*. Beverly Hills, CA: Sage.

Guttentag, M. (1972). Negro-White differences in children's movement. *Perceptual and Motor Skills, 35,* 435–436.

Hale, J. E. (1982). *Black children: Their roots, culture and learning styles*. Provo, UT: Brigham Young University Press.

Hanushek, E. A. (1982). Sources of black-white earning differences. *Social Science Research, 11*(2), 103–126.

Hill, R. (1979). *The widening economic gap*. Washington, DC: National Urban League Research Department.

Howard, J., & Hammond, R. (1985, September 9). Rumors of inferiority. *The New Republic,* 17–21.

Jeffers, C. (1967). *Living poor.* Ann Arbor: Ann Arbor Publishers.

Jones, R. (1973). Proving blacks inferior. The sociology of knowledge. In J. A. Ladner (Ed.), *The death of White sociology* (pp. 114–135). New York: Random House.

Joseph, G. I., & Lewis, J. (1981). *Common differences: Conflicts in Black and White feminist perspectives.* New York: Anchor/Doubleday.

Kamii, C. K., & Radin, N. J. (1967, May). Class differences in the socialization practices of Negro mothers. *Journal of Marriage and the Family, 29,* 302–310.

Kandel, D. (1967). Race, maternal authority and adolescent aspiration. *American Journal of Sociology, 76,* 999–1004.

Kellam, S. C., Adams, R. G., Brown, C. H., & Ensminger, M. E. (1982). The long-term evolution of the family structure of teenage and older mothers. *Journal of Marriage and the Family, 44,* 343–359.

Kochman, T. (1981). *Black and White styles in conflict.* Chicago: University of Chicago Press.

Kreisberg, L. (1967). Rearing children in fatherless families. *Journal of Marriage and the Family, 39,* 229–234.

LaBarre, M. (1968). The strengths of the self-supporting poor. *Social Casework, 49*(8), 459–466.

Lantz, H. R. (1980). Family and kin as revealed in the narratives of ex-slaves. *Social Science Quarterly, 60*(4), 667–675.

MacIntyre, D. M. (1964, December). *Public assistance: Too much or too little:* New York: New York State School of Industrial Relations, Cornell University, Bulletin 53-1, pp. 73–74.

Mack, D. (1974). The power relationship in Black families and White families. *Journal of Personality and Social Psychology, 30,* 409–413.

Mbiti, J. S. (1970). *African religions and philosophies.* Garden City, NY: Doubleday (Anchor Books).

McAdoo, H. (1978). The impact of upward mobility of kin-help patterns and the reciprocal obligations in black families. *Journal of Marriage and the Family, 40,* 761–776.

McCray, C. A. (1980). The Black woman and family roles. In L. Rodgers-Rose (Ed.), *The Black woman.* Beverly Hills: Sage.

Morgan, H. (1976). Neonatal precocity and the Black experience. *Negro Education Review, 27,* 129–134.

Moynihan, D. P. (1965a, Fall). Employment, income and the ordeal of the Negro family. *Daedalus, 94*(4), 745–770.

Moynihan, D. P. (1965b). *The Negro family: The case for national action.* Washington, DC: U. S. Government Printing Office.

Moynihan, D. P. (1967). The Negro family: The case for national action. In L. Rainwater & W. Yancy (Eds.), *The Moynihan Report and the politics of controversy.* Cambridge: MIT Press.

Moynihan, D. P. (1986). *Family and nation. The Godkin Lectures, Harvard University.* San Diego: Harcourt Brace Jovanovich.

Munroe, R. H., Munroe, R. L., & B. B. Whiting (Eds.). (1981). *Handbook of cross cultural human development* (pp. 73–90). New York: Garland STPM Press.

Nobles, W. W. (1974a). African root and American fruit: The Black family. *Journal of Social and Behavioral Sciences,* 52–78.

Nobles, W. W. (1974b). Africanity: Its role in Black families. *Black Scholar, 5,* 10–17.

Owens, L. H. (1976). *This species of property: Slave life and culture in the old South.* New York: Oxford University Press.

Parker, S., & Kleiner, R. (1969). Social and psychological dimensions of the family role performance of the Negro male. *Journal of Marriage and Family, 31*(3), 500–506.

Pleck, E. (1970). A mother's wages: Income earning among married Italian and Black women. 1896–1911: In M. Gordon (Ed.), *The American family socio-historical perspective* (pp. 490–510). New York: St. Martin's.

Powell, C. N. (1963). *Factors affecting the educational and vocational plans of high ability Negro students in the high schools of Alabama.* Doctoral dissertation, Pennsylvania State University. University Microfilms No. 64-5382.

Ramirez, M., & Price-Williams, D. R. (1976). Achievement motivation in children of three ethnic groups in the United States. *Journal of Cross Cultural Psychology, 7,* 49–60.

Rodgers-Rose, L. F. (Ed.). (1980). *The Black woman.* Beverly Hills, CA: Sage.

Rosen (1959). Race, ethnicity and the achievement syndrome. *American Sociological Review, 24,* 47–60.

Rosser, P. L., & Randolph, S. (1985). *Maternal perceptions, CNS organization and cognitive development.* Report of the National Technical Information Service, U. S. Dept. of Commerce. 22161.

Scanzoni, J. (1971). *The Black family in modern society.* Boston: Allyn & Bacon.

Scanzoni, J. (1977). *Sex roles, life styles and child bearing.* New York: The Free Press.

Schultz, D. (1969). *Coming up black.* Englewood Cliffs, NJ: Prentice-Hall.

Smith, E. J. (1979). Reference group perspectives of middle-class Black workers and college bound Black youth. *The Journal of Negro Education, 48*(4), 479–487.

Stack, C. B., & Semmel, H. (1975). Social insecurity: Welfare policy and the structure of poor families. In B. R. Mandell (Ed.), *Welfare in America.* Englewood Cliffs: Prentice-Hall.

Staples, R. (1970). The myth of the Black matriarchy. *The Black Scholar, 1,* 8–16.

Staples, R. (1973). Public policy and the changing status of Black families. *The Family Coordinator, 22,* 345–351.

Steady, F. C. (1981). *The Black woman cross-culturally.* Cambridge: Schenkman.

Stevens, J. H. (1984). Child development knowledge and parenting skills. *Family Relations, 33,* 237–244.

Stewart, J. B. (1980). Perspectives on Black families from contemporary soul music: The case of Millie Jackson. *Phylon, 41,* 57–71.

St. Pierre, M. (1982). Black female single parent family life: A preliminary sociological perspective. *The Black Sociologist, 9*(1), 28–47.

Wade-Gayles, G. (1980). She who is Black and mother in sociology and fiction, 1940–1970. In L. F. Rodgers-Rose (Ed.), *The Black woman* (pp. 89–106). Beverly Hills, CA: Sage.

Washington, M. H. (Ed.). (1975). *Black-eyed Susans: Classic stories by and about Black woman.* Garden City, NY: Doubleday (Anchor Books).

Washington, V. (1983). Observations of teacher behavior in desegregated reading groups. *The Urban Review, 15,* 53–68.

Washington, V. (1984, Winter). Continuity of care in American support for dependent children. The AFDC example. *International Journal of Mental Health, 12*(4), 59–77.

Washington, V. (1985). Social policy, cultural diversity and the obscurity of Black children. *Journal of Educational Equity and Leadership, 5*(4), 320–335.

Washington, V., & Glimps, B. (1983). Developmental issues for adolescent parents and their children. *Educational Horizons, 61*(4), 195–199.

Willhelm, S. M. (1983). Black/white equality: The socioeconomic conditions of blacks in America, Part II. *Journal of Black Studies, 14*(2), 151–184.

Wilson, W. J., & Neckerman, K. M. (1985, Fall). Without jobs, black men cannot support families. *Point of View, 2*(3), 1, 3–5.

Woloch, N. (1984). *Women and the American experience.* New York: Knopf.

CHAPTER 9

Divorced Mothers

MARTHA B. STRAUS

DIVORCE REFORM AND FEMINISM

Divorce reform and the women's movement have a curious shared history. The search for the meaning of equality between the sexes has been particularly complicated in the divorce arena. Feminist thinking on alimony, child support, and the division of property has undergone radical change since the early 1970s as the stark economic realities of postdivorce independence have been acknowledged. The social and emotional consequences of divorce for women and mothers have also been scrutinized anew as we have seen our friends and sisters struggle to rebuild their personal lives following divorce. Though still the "chance of a new lifetime" as feminists of a decade ago proclaimed (Brown, Feldberg, Fox, & Kohen, 1976), divorce for mothers can also thrust numerous legal, economic, social, psychological, and parenting hurdles in the way. Because divorce has become so common, these hurdles are well understood now.

Divorce statistics are cited widely by the media, and there is now an extraordinary amount of speculation about what it all means—for individuals and for society. Although "women's liberation" has, incorrectly, borne the brunt of blame for the increase in divorce (Emery, 1982), few technological changes or social trends have been spared from analysis, and recently, even men have been implicated (Ehrenreich, 1983). It is well known that some demographers predict that, by 1990, 49.2% of all marriages will end in divorce (Davis, 1983) and that more than a third of those who remarry will divorce again (Cherlin, 1981). The average marriage now lasts just 6.8 years (McKay, Rogers, Blades, & Gosse, 1984), and every year more than 2 million people file for divorce (Saunders, 1983).

The divorce statistics involving parents and children are also described frequently since more than 60% of divorcing couples have children (Bane, 1979). Back in 1970 there were 2.3 million children living with a divorced mother. However, by 1982, that figure had risen by 122%, to 5.1 million (SCCYF, 1983).

MARTHA B. STRAUS • University Associates in Psychology, 222 West Street, Keene, New Hampshire 03431.

Mother-headed families continue to be the predominant result of divorce involving children, even in states like California that have an explicitly sex-neutral
custody law (Weitzman, 1981). The national nine-to-one ratio (Emery, Hetherington, & Dilalla, 1984) favoring maternal custody may reflect judicial bias and
may also reflect the fact that fewer fathers seek custody.

Statistics like these have been used for scholarly research projects and for
policy decisions. Both purposes have taken long to get past the assumption,
both tacit and stated, that the female, single-parent household is deviant and
pathological (Brandwein, Brown, & Fox, 1974; Glasser & Navarre, 1966). Father
absence rather than mother presence is the focus of most early and even much
recent divorce work. Here a twofold deviance is often implied: the family type is
deviant and the mother assumes a deviant role by becoming a father substitute.

These researchers and policymakers have focused primarily on how growing up with mothers after divorce affects children's cognitive development,
achievement, and social and emotional adjustment. In the area of social and
emotional effects of divorce, researchers have emphasized sex typing, moral
development, and locus of control. Such emphases are the legacy of conceptualizing divorce and one-parent families in terms of father absence and "broken
homes."

The thinking of feminists involved with the legal system clearly has evolved
in the past 15 years. Their original position has also turned out to be based on
many false assumptions. Divorce reforms, including no-fault divorce, joint custody, and divorce mediation, have each turned out to be less beneficial, both
economically and psychologically, than they were initially anticipated to be. The
recent press for mediation and joint custody, for example, even in situations
where they may be untenable, suggests the ways in which policy and legislation
have used the value-laden assumptions of research and early feminist strivings
for equality.

LEGAL CONSEQUENCES OF DIVORCE

> Of course I thought joint custody would be best for Michael—he should have two
> parents raising him. But then I found out we couldn't agree on anything and we've
> been in court three times just this year alone over ridiculous stuff like whether Michael
> could play hockey or take ski lessons. Also, his father uses it to pay me just $25.00 a
> week child support even though he only has Michael every other weekend—it's totally
> unfair. If I had to do it again, I never would be so reasonable. (Carol, mother of a 6-
> year-old boy, 5 years after the divorce)

No-Fault Divorce

Since divorcing parents have been cluttering court dockets, laws guiding
court decisions have also been developed to clean up the mess. It seems apparent that California's 1970 no-fault divorce law set into motion a kind of legal
revolution. Since then, all of the states have adopted some form of this law.

Before no-fault divorce, one member of the couple had to be judged guilty of marital fault such as adultery or cruelty before a divorce could be granted. The new laws permitted either party to divorce when "irreconcilable differences" caused the breakdown of their marriage (Freed & Foster, 1984). No-fault divorce laws have shifted the legal process from moral questions of blame and responsibility to economic issues of ability to pay and financial need (Weitzman, 1985).

Feminists initially were quite enthusiastic about these divorce reforms as they quickly spread over the country. The law's aim of equality between men and women in divorce promised to eliminate the anachronistic legal assumptions about women's subordinate role and to recognize wives as full equals in the marital partnership. However, as divorced mothers soon learned better than anyone, when the legal system treats men and women "equally" at divorce, it ignores the very real economic inequalities that marriage creates. It also ignores the economic inequalities between men and women in the larger society. Betty Friedan (1976) describes part of the reversal in feminist thinking:

> The women's movement had just begun when the so-called divorce reform law was passed. At that time, we were so concerned with principle—that equality of right and opportunity had to mean equality of responsibility, and therefore alimony was out—that we did not realize the trap we were falling into . . . We fell into a trap when we said, "no alimony!" becuase housewives who divorced were in terrible straits. We fell into another trap by accepting no-fault divorce without provision for mandatory economic settlements. (p. 325)

In California, the no-fault divorce law acknowledges the special needs of young mothers, older housewives, and women in transition and, in principle, provides for their continued support. In all three cases, however, the data reveal these women are also often denied the support that they were promised (Weitzman, 1985).

Even before no-fault divorce, women were experiencing the legal system as unable to advocate for them in divorce. For example, in one study conducted in Pennsylvania before divorce reform, 84% of women asked expressed great dissatisfaction with their legal experience and thought the laws should be changed (Spanier & Anderson, 1979). Perhaps the hopes offered by the legal reforms made the actual consequences seem worse in contrast. Whether or not they were designed that way, the current rules for property, alimony, and child support create severe financial hardships for most divorced women and their children. Gender-neutral rules designed to treat men and women "equally" have in effect served to deprive divorced women of the legal and financial protections that the old law provided.

Child Custody

No-fault divorce also opened the door to custody reforms. Joint legal custody was believed to be a Solomon-like compromise that would, at very the least, decrease conflict and inequality in this one hot arena. Experts originally predicted that fathers would request and receive both physical and legal custody of their children in increasing numbers as states adopted a sex-neutral "best interests of the child" doctrine. Contrary to expectations, there has been little change in custody arrangements in the last 15 years. Overwhelmingly, it is mothers who continue to be the children's primary caretaker before and after divorce. Except in the rare cases where parents are friendly and cooperative through the divorce, the move toward joint custody has, on the balance, been a disappointment, revealing initial hopes to be unfounded.

However, as with no-fault divorce, joint legal custody on first reading looks like it has some clear advantages for divorced mothers. First, it is widely asserted that children benefit from such an arrangement because the continued postdivorce involvement of both parents is a practical and psychological necessity. Needless to say, this presupposes that the joint-custody plan is at least agreed upon by both parents. Second, it might increase the chances that child support will be paid. Since most women retain primary physical custody of their children, this is a clear advantage. Third, joint custody could eventually reduce conflict between the spouses. Tension might be decreased if mothers were to have respite from the sole responsibility of caring for children and fathers were given legal rights they would not otherwise have. Finally, the assumptions of equality here—that both parents are equally capable of raising children, and should do so—are straight from a feminist utopia.

However, for divorced mothers, each of these four initial advantages requires greater scrutiny. First, most children of divorce will have little contact with their fathers, regardless of the custody plans. In one national study, it was reported that only 16% of the children actually saw their fathers at least once a week. Another 16% of the children reported that they saw their fathers at least once a month, and 15% reported at least annual visits with their fathers. Remarkably, the remaining 52% of the children had had no contact with their fathers whatsoever in the preceding year (Furstenberg, Nord, Peterson, & Zill, 1983). The father's estrangement often begins soon after the marriage ends and continues to increase over the years. (These data are affected by race, educational level, remarriage, and propinquity). Fathers interested in obtaining sole legal or joint custody tend to be better educated and in white-collar jobs. Despite a general increase in numbers of fathers staying involved with their children, the actual percentage remains small.

The second compelling reason for joint custody—to ensure child-support payments—also does not appear to be based in reality. More than half of the women who are due court-ordered child support never receive it (Weitzman, 1985), and a significant percentage who get some money end up with less than the amount agreed upon. It is widely held also that even the court-ordered sum is generally inadequate (Weitzman, 1985). Whether or not a father has joint legal custody does not seem to affect his compliance with child-support orders: support payments, at least in preliminary studies, appear to be comparable across the custody groups (Pearson & Thoennes, 1984). Some researchers have even gone so far as to observe that joint custody may be used as a device to lower child-support awards to begin with. As Lenore Weitzman (1985) has pointed out:

Fathers who spend more time with their children, even if they have them two days a week, argue that they should not have to pay any child support because they are "sharing" the actual costs of the child. (p. 255)

The third common explanation given for joint custody—that interpersonal conflict will be reduced—has also been questioned in recent years. Several research studies suggest that the incidence of postdivorce conflict is substantial (Pearson & Thoennes, 1984) and that a greater percentage of parents awarded joint legal custody return to court to resolve child-related matters than parents awarded sole maternal custody (Phear, Beck, & Hauser, 1986). Notably, when interviewed, mothers who initially agree upon joint custody later say they were talked into it and had really wanted sole custody because of the sustained acrimony with their ex-spouse (Weitzman, 1985). There is little to suggest that the arrangement decreases conflict—rather it intensifies it. The above discussion refers to voluntary joint-custody arrangements. Court-ordered joint-custody results are likely to be more divisive. Parents who opt for joint custody are probably less acrimonious than those who contest the custody plan. Thus those litigated cases in which a judge is forced to make a difficult custody decision may be exactly the ones for whom joint custody will not work. Neither voluntary nor mandatory joint custody appears to decrease postdivorce conflict.

Finally, it should be quite obvious now, that the ideal of equality has not been attained through changes in custody laws. Divorced mothers who initially believed that such an arrangement was proper for all concerned often find out too late how naive they were. Although joint-custody laws hold the promise of men assuming equal responsibility for postdivorce parenting, in practice these laws have given men equal authority but not equal responsibility (Weitzman, 1985). As most children continue to live with their mother while fathers are not even required to visit, laws that force custodial mothers to consult with and gain the father's approval on all major decisions about their children serve primarily to give fathers more power and control over their former wives and their lifestyles. The vision of feminists that had fathers and mothers sharing in the care of their children after divorce appears to bear little resemblance to the actual lives of divorced mothers.

Divorce Mediation

No-fault divorces and joint-custody decisions were expected to reduce the acrimonious nature of divorce. Yet the adversarial process by which these standards are now applied inherently breeds acrimony. Divorce mediation has become a widely touted alternative to the adversarial model. Like these other reforms, for divorced mothers, mediation has also fallen short of its promise.

In divorce mediation, the divorcing couple employs a consultant who works with both parties to facilitate agreement on disputed custody and/or property issues. The key benefits of mediation have been called the "four C's" (Emery, 1982): reduced conflict, increased cooperation, maintenance of parental control, and lower cost. California, which has set the pace for divorce reform in this country, has had a mandatory mediation law since 1981. All divorcing couples who have disputes must first attempt to resolve their differences through mediation prior to appearing before a judge. Many other states have mediators who, either attached or unattached to the court, adopt as their goal the voluntary resolution of divorce disputes (although mediators in courthouses may have a closer connection to judges than truly voluntary mediation might dictate).

On the surface, preliminary research examining whether mediation works better than the adversarial method appears to be encouraging at least in terms of reaching agreement. Various mediation programs that have been instituted in the United States, Canada, and Australia have been successful in getting from 22% to 67% of divorcing couples to reach voluntary out-of-court settlements (Irving, Bohm, MacDonald, & Benjamin, 1979). In one study where couples who applied for a court hearing were randomly assigned to mediation or to the usual litigation, 22% of the mediation cases as opposed to 8% of the litigation cases were settled out of court (Bahr, 1981). Furthermore, one research group found that couples who failed to reach an agreement in mediation were still more likely than those in the traditional adversarial system to settle out of court subsequently, with the aid of attorneys, rather than proceed with litigation (Pearson & Thoennes, 1982). It must be emphasized that success in these studies is measured solely by whether agreement was obtained.

In addition to mediation aiding the resolution of disputes, it also appears to cost less to the state and to individuals; one estimate has projected an annual private savings exceeding $88 million (Bahr, 1981). Further, there may be fewer repeat costs. Studies of both randomly assigned and nonrandomly assigned subjects conclude that significantly fewer couples who use mediation return to court because of allegations of noncompliance in comparison with couples who use litigation (Bahr, 1981; Doyle & Caron, 1979; Milne, 1978).

While there are not much data supporting either the positive emotional effects of mediation on divorcing parties or on their children, the little evidence there is also seems promising. One investigator found that 25% of those randomly assigned to mediation reported that "things had gotten much better" six weeks after the divorce in comparison with 9% of those who went through litigation (Irving et al., 1979). Others have noted that couples involved in mediation are more pleased with their agreement and more likely to cooperate with it than couples who went to court (Pearson & Thoennes, 1982). Even without hard statistics, it might follow that parents who are more satisfied with the plan they arrived at together have a better prognosis for caring cooperatively for their children.

In light of the generally favorable review of the divorce mediation literature, it is noteworthy that advocates for divorced mothers have begun to raise serious doubts about it. Despite the advantages of the "four C's," it appears that the mediation process potentially is quite perilous for divorced mothers for several reasons.

First, mediation is designed for disputes between parties of equal bargaining power. The divorcing couple must be able to communicate freely and to negotiate with each other as equals. However, women are likely to be disadvantaged on many fronts. They are likely to have less experience in bargaining and negotiating; be less informed about financial issues, including family finances; be economically dependent (whether they work or not); have a stronger tendency than men to give in to demands in order to make peace and to withhold demands of their own; and/or be the victims of physical, verbal, or emotional abuse. In any and all of these instances, there is inequality indicating that mediation may be contraindicated.

Second, agreement, the goal of custody mediation, may not be in the "best interests" of the involved children or their mothers. Mothers who did not feel their ex-husbands would be fit parents would lose in mediation if they compromised or refused to compromise. Even more important, perhaps, custody disputes have potentially dire legal and economic consequences from which women may not be protected adequately in mediation. Sally Goldfarb (1985), Staff Attorney for the NOW Legal Defense and Education Fund, offers these examples:

> A crucial distinction between adversarial legal proceedings and mediation is that there are no legal mechanisms to compel financial disclosure by a party in mediation. Without full disclosure of the financial situation of the economically more secure partner— usually the man—any child support agreement is likely to be based on erroneous facts, and therefore, to be unjust. . . . The custody decision may also affect who receives the marital home, the amount of the maintenance award, and so on. In the absence of full information about her legal rights, a parent may give up custody because she thinks she cannot afford it. . . . Even the question of whether to choose joint physical custody, which has often been viewed as a purely psychological matter, raises potential legal problems: Who will take the tax deduction for the child? Will a parent's eligibility for AFDC be endangered? (p. 7)

Given the hazards of voluntary mediation, it is clear how mandatory court-ordered mediation would be rife with additional problems. The NOW Legal Defense and Education Fund lobbied against a mandatory mediation bill in New York State. Foremost in their objections is the difficulty with forming standards for cases that might not be suitable for mediation. No one yet knows which cases are more appropriate than others or which types of mediation are suitable for whom. It is clear that many women are unable to bargain as equals and that couples who are in intense conflict will have trouble compromising.

Finally, many women will benefit from having an attorney represent their interests in child-custody disputes. As Goldfarb (1985) describes:

> A parent involved in child custody litigation deserves access to the full range of protections of the legal system, including representation by counsel. There is no justification for furnishing unfettered access to legal process for litigants in every other type of case, but denying it to parents involved in disputes about the lives of themselves and their children. (p. 8)

Participants in mediation forego much of the legal protection guaranteed them in the adversarial system.

Mediation that is ordered or even just "recommended" by judges can have deleterious consequences for a divorcing mother if she is not more or less a psychological, economic, and intellectual equal to her husband, with a full grasp of her rights and the meaning of different choices she might make during the mediation. Even voluntary mediation, which at first review of the literature looks superior to litigation, appears to be risky in many instances.

ECONOMIC CONSEQUENCES OF DIVORCE

All three recent divorce reforms—no-fault divorce, joint custody, and divorce mediation—are reforms that were initially hailed as progress for women, but in each case they have fallen short of their promise. At the root of the discrepancy between expectation and reality is economics. Divorce reforms such as these have only served to *increase* the economic inequality between men and women in this country. Without the potential for at least sustaining a predivorce financial situation, no-fault divorce, joint custody, and mediation all become weapons in the hands of a sexist society:

> Lizzie wanted some of those sneakers like all of the kids have but they cost $50 or something so I had to say "no"—and ask your father. But he told her I would have the money if I didn't spend all his child support on myself. That's such a laugh—I haven't seen a penny from the jerk since December. (Mary, mother of 12-year-old girl, divorced 2 years)

Much of the fallout from divorce can be described as family problems, but the economic consequences of divorce are women's issues. As Weitzman (1985) has described at great length: When income is compared with needs, divorced men experience an average 42% rise in their standard of living in the first year after the divorce, whereas divorced mothers (and their children) experience a *73% decline*. The social and economic results of this outrageous discrepancy are not difficult to imagine: residential moves, inferior housing, drastically diminished or nonexistent funds for recreation and leisure, and relentless psychological pressure. Many divorced mothers "live on the edge," eating macaroni and cheese five nights a week, going on public assistance, or moving back to their own parents' home (Weitzman, 1985).

The rise in divorce has been the major cause of the increase in female-headed families and that increase has been the major cause of the feminization of poverty (Pearce, 1978). The National Advisory Council on Economic Opportunity estimates that if current trends continue, the poverty population of the United States will be composed solely of women and children by the year 2000 (National Advisory Council on Economic Opportunity, 1980). The Council declares that "the feminization of poverty has become one of the most compelling social facts of the decade". While it has been well documented that mother-headed families are the fastest-growing segment of the American poor, the link among divorce, the economic consequences of divorce, and the rise in female poverty has, until recently, been unexplored (Weitzman, 1985). Contrary to popular perception, only 18% of the nearly 10 million female-headed families in the United States are headed by an unwed mother; over 50% are headed by divorced mothers and the remaining 31% by separated mothers (Weitzman, 1985). The high divorce rate had vastly multiplied the numbers of women who are left alone to support themselves and their minor children.

The divorced mother confronted with such economic hardship has essentially four options: immediate employment, seeking public or private assistance, job retraining, or remarriage, none of which consistently compensate for the postdivorce economic losses.

Employment of Divorced Mothers

First, when the courts deny divorced women the support they require, they are assuming that the woman can get a job and support herself. As is now well known, however, with a mother's current disadvantages in the labor market, getting a job is not necessarily the answer. The structure of the job market is such that only half of all full-time female workers are able to support two children without supplemental income from either the children's fathers or the government (Pearce & McAdoo, 1981). A third of all working mothers cannot earn enough to enable them and their children to live above the poverty level (Weitzman, 1985). Getting a full-time job simply does not guarantee a mother a way out of poverty in the United States. Moreover, finding a job can be particularly difficult for women who have been out of the workforce for any period of time and who have no particular job skills. Although younger divorced mothers may be in a better position to begin or continue in a career, they often have other problems, including child care and smaller property, alimony, and child-support settlements. There are many advantages to employment—among them increase in income, social security and health benefits, and the chance to get out of the house and be with other adults. However, for many divorced mothers, these advantages still may not outweigh the economic hardships they face.

Alternative Sources of Support

Second, in addition to or instead of employment, divorced mothers can also seek out private and public support. Many divorced mothers are able to obtain financial help from relatives (Weiss, 1975a), but it is likely to be temporary and it may be problematic in other ways. As many as 34% of divorced mothers are also forced, at some point, to resort to welfare or Aid to Families with Dependent Children (AFDC) to support their families (Bradbury, Dansinger, Smolensky, E., & Smolensky, P., 1979)—an alternative that certainly can create emotional and social stress. Not only are welfare benefits insufficient to raise a family's income above the poverty level, but the process of obtaining welfare can also be both demeaning and arduous (Weiss, 1975a).

Job Retraining

A third alternative for financially troubled mothers with few job skills is retraining: returning to school or entering a job training program. Ultimately, mothers who are well trained can then obtain higher paying, more satisfying jobs. However, job training can be quite expensive because it requires that time be spent learning with little or no income generated during that time. Paradoxically, divorced mothers who need it most cannot afford to get through this costly process (Emery *et al.*, 1984). Also, for many mothers, no amount of job training will suffice to make up for earning potential sacrificed through years of homemaking.

Remarriage

A final economic alternative available to divorced mothers is remarriage. At least for women under 30, about 75% remarry and 10% of these remarriages involve at least one child from a previous marriage (Baker, Druckman, & Flagle, 1980). At the present time, it is estimated that over 35 million adults are step-parents, and that one child in six is a stepchild. However, before viewing remarriage as a viable economic solution, it is important to note that as many as 40% of second marriages end in divorce within 5 years, with the presence of children from the previous marriage predisposing in favor of the divorce (Becker, Landes, & Michael, 1977). Much research concludes that remarriage families have *more* stress and are less cohesive than nuclear families (Cherlin, 1978; Fast & Cain, 1966; Visher & Visher, 1982). Even if the presence of children were not a deterrent to remarriage or to the duration of the remarriage, economic incentives are still unlikely to be a sound basis for a second marriage.

Social and Legal Reforms

In recent years, there have been many suggestions for combating the feminization of poverty. Most of these have focused on remediating discrimination in the labor market and on expanding social welfare programs to compensate above the poverty line. Redesigning alimony to include financial aid for job training has also been suggested (Emery *et al.*, 1984). In her thorough study of the economic consequences of divorce, Weitzman (1985) added to this list:

> . . . change the way that courts allocate property and income at divorce. If for example, custodial mothers and their children were allowed to remain in the family home, and if the financial responsibility for children were apportioned according to the means of the two parents and if court orders for support were enforced, a significant segment of the population of divorced women and their children would not be impoverished by divorce. (p. 351)

Without change in many spheres, the present system will, in all likelihood, lead to a permanent underclass of women and children. It is vital that the economic independence of the divorced mother be assured. Property, alimony, and child-support awards must reflect need. Moreover, continued efforts to eliminate sex discrimination in the workplace will benefit all women, but divorced mothers in particular. Women still earn just 60% of what their male counterparts earn. They also have available to them predominantly more clerical and service type jobs, which tend to pay poorly and have less room for advancement than other types of jobs. Further, low-cost child care continues to be a scarce necessity for many divorced mothers. Finally, public assistance can be augmented by economic support services that train mothers to enter the workforce. Higher initial public expenditures that subsidize, for example, career counseling and retraining programs may lead to lower long-term costs, and improved family functioning (Emery *et al.*, 1984). The current economic structures, reflected in and exacerbated by divorce, make it extremely difficult for divorced mothers to improve their economic situation by hard work or any of the other traditional routes to economic mobility. Without changes in these structures, divorced mothers will continue to face severe hardships as they try to provide for their families.

SOCIAL SUPPORTS FOR DIVORCED MOTHERS

> Who is helping me get through this? My mother, my best friend, Dennis (new boyfriend) . . . mostly the kids. (Rachel, mother of a 5-year-old boy and an 8-year-old girl, divorced less than a year)

When a mother divorces, she redefines herself in a relation to other people. Particularly during the first months after divorce, newly single mothers need extra support from others with whom they previously exchanged care more equally.

Family of Origin

Members of the family of origin are generally most supportive of the divorced mother. They may provide financial assistance, housing, child care, and other services. In general, mothers experience an increase in contact, with more kinship support than when they were married (Gibson, 1972; Hetherington, 1978; Spicer & Hampe, 1975). Although some women may perceive that their standing in their families of origin drops with the failure of their marriage (Weiss, 1975a), most studies investigating family interaction and support indicate that these factors are positively associated with divorce adjustment particularly when children are involved (Anspach, 1976; Colletta, 1979a; Spicer & Hampe, 1975).

However, many mothers feel they pay a price for the return to dependency upon their families following divorce. Although a divorced mother's kin are a potential source of support, their help is not always beneficial and can sometimes become another source of stress. Especially if the divorced mother must return to her parents' home, she is likely to feel infantilized and to have reciprocal demands placed upon her. Most divorced mothers, when asked, say they prefer to live alone and to be independent from their families of origin—if adequate resources are available (Hetherington, 1978).

The Former Spouse

Perhaps surprisingly, the former spouse is also a source of support for some divorced mothers. Divorce does not end a relationship although it changes it (Weiss, 1975), and, even in the face of conflict, attachment to the former spouse can persist for some time after the divorce. For example, in one study, many mothers reported that, in the months following divorce, in case of emergency, the ex-spouse would be the first person they would call (Hetherington, Cox, & Cox, 1976), and several of the couples continued to be sexually involved as well. Such involvement generally decreases over time. It is widely reported that, after a couple of years, most divorced mothers no longer rely upon their former spouses for emotional support (Hetherington *et al.*, 1976; Spanier & Casto, 1979; Weiss, 1975). Similarly, the conflict between the ex-spouses also decreases over time, although women are reported to sustain anger and resentment longer than men (Hetherington *et al.*, 1976). Whereas there is a wide range of relationships between ex-spouses, for some mothers, some of the time, former husbands are a source of potential emotional support.

In-Laws

Attendant to divorce, many mothers seek out the support of their in-laws, although many others lose that support. If the children have had ongoing relationships with their paternal grandparents, most divorced mothers say they want to try to maintain contact—though it generally decreases sharply (Anspach, 1976). In-laws may also provide financial assistance for these women. For example, in one study 38% of the females interviewed were receiving some type of economic aid from their former in-laws (although only 1.6% of the males were receiving similar support) (Spicer & Hampe, 1975). Therefore, for some mothers who divorce, a relationship with the family of their former spouse remains very much an important part of their support system.

Friends

For most divorced mothers, friends and acquaintances are the most vital sources of support during the divorce process. Social participation has been found to have many benefits, including lowering stress and improving coping skills (Hetherington, Cox, & Cox, 1982). Ultimately, however, mothers are often excluded from former social networks and are likely to become more isolated after divorce. Robert Weiss (1975) described a three-phase process of postdivorce friendships. The first state is a period of "rallying round." Friends typically move to support the divorcing mothers in their stress immediately after divorce. As time passes, each friend moves into a stage of "idiosyncratic reaction." Certain friends might respond with reactions of envy, condemnation, fright, intrigue, or support. The last stage is one of "mutual withdrawal." Both the divorced mother and her friends slowly allow the friendships to fade.

Weiss describes the final stage as a mutual decision. Other researchers have also noted that many divorced mothers isolate themselves from family and friends, feeling that they no longer "fit in" with the group (Spanier & Casto, 1979). Moreover, maintaining social relationships is difficult for these women. For example, the women in one study complained that American culture designs social activities for couples rather than single adults. Some mothers, particularly those not employed, felt like prisoners trapped in a child's world, with little time for themselves (Hetherington, 1978). Working divorced mothers are further limited in the resources they have to devote to their own lives, with little time, energy, or money to spend on socializing (Goetting, 1981).

It is clear that, despite an increased need for the social support of friends, divorced mothers are, in fact, more isolated than other single people. Interaction with married friends tends to decline at a faster rate for divorced mothers than divorced fathers (Hetherington et al., 1976), and so they seek out other divorcees rather than coupled people for companionship. Many mothers report that they "grow away" from their close friends after divorce, particularly if the connection had been made through their former husband. Further, as one study concluded, some mothers are simply unable to replace lost friendships and for them adjustment is very difficult (Spanier & Casto, 1979). Although finding new friends to replace the old is a primary chore following divorce, this task is particularly arduous for women with children. As Longfellow (1979) stated, divorce "intensifies the single mother's need for an external support system, while at the same time it throws up obstacles aginst her ability to build or maintain such a network" (p. 297). Despite the numerous obstacles in the way of keeping friendships alive, most divorced mothers report one or two friends upon whom they can rely.

Dating

Finally, divorced mothers are also likely to seek out support through dating and sexual relationships and, possibly, remarriage. In most studies, divorced mothers cite meeting new single people as one of their most difficult problems (Hetherington et al., 1976; Kohen, Brown, & Feldberg, 1979; Spanier & Casto, 1979; Weiss, 1975). Despite this many women date in the years immediately following divorce. Although divorced mothers tend to date less than their exhusbands, most of them eventually do begin to have other relationships (Hetherington et al., 1976; Spanier & Casto, 1979). It has also been found that financially secure mothers have more opportunities to meet men, have more dates, and have more steady relationships than those who are less economically secure (Ambert, 1983). They are also more likely to break up relationships that do not suit them, they are less likely to tolerate abusive male behavior toward them, and less likely to flatter a man's ego. Economic well-being, as in many spheres, appears to have a beneficial effect on dating for divorced mothers.

Another aspect of dating—sexual relationships—is also an important concern for divorced mothers. In one study, of 30 such women who had been divorced between one and five years, many reported that they enjoyed the greater control over their sexuality; 19 of them said their sex lives had improved since they divorced. Eleven of the 30, however, were less satisfied; they reported having less sex than they wanted, feeling ambivalent about unmarried sex lives, and desiring more stable relationships with fewer partners (Kohen et al., 1979). Despite the stated desire for monogamy, dating a variety of people has been shown, repeatedly, to be just as helpful in aiding adjustment to divorce (Spanier & Casto, 1979).

Although after 1 year, few mothers are actively considering remarriage (Brown et al., 1976), this form of support is not uncommon (Weitzman, 1981). However, the likelihood of a mother's remarriage is largely a function of her age at the time of divorce. As suggested earlier, if she is under 30, she has a 75% chance of remarrying. But her chances diminish significantly as she grows older; between 30 and 40, the proportion is closer to 50%, and if she is 40 or older, she has only a 28% chance of remarriage (Rheinstein, 1972). Moreover, it has been found that, although more fathers of higher socioeconomic status (SES) who are divorced remarry and do so more rapidly than their lower SES peers, the reverse relationship may exist among mothers (Carter & Glick, 1976). This observation has led some researchers to conclude that remarriage attracts more mothers who are less able to take care of themselves (Edwards, 1967; Renne, 1971). It follows, then, that although remarriage might be considered a source of support by older mothers, this is frequently not a visible option. Moreover, younger, poorer mothers are most likely to remarry (although younger, wealthier mothers have the option to do so). Both age and economics play a role in determining the degree to which remarriage can be a source of social support for divorced mothers. There is little doubt, however, that remarriage involving children is generally quite stressful and often results in a second divorce (Visher & Visher, 1982).

At the root of much social change for mothers is their increased isolation after divorce, compounded by a diminished social and economic status. Although the need for support from family is most often fulfilled, this carries with it a return to dependency that many mothers would prefer not to have. Ex-spouses and their families are sometimes supportive in limited ways, but these contacts decrease dramatically and, in some cases, produce additional stress anyway. Well documented as well is the difficulty that divorced mothers have maintaining old friends and making new friends. Fortunately, most appear to have one or two friends upon whom they can rely following divorce, even though their networks do become smaller. Finally, many mothers eventually find support in dating relationships, with younger and less financially secure mothers more likely to remarry sooner, and to divorce again. Despite all of the possible places a divorced mother might turn for support, many such mothers do not have adequate social resources to penetrate their isolation and offer them meaningful adult contacts.

PSYCHOLOGICAL EFFECTS

> I can't stop crying. I force myself to do stuff with the kids but all I want to do is be
> in my room crying. I don't think I'm going to be able to make it alone and I'm so scared.
> (Susan, mother of three children under 5 years, divorced 1 month)

The emotional consequences of divorce have been described at length in recent years; some turmoil appears to be a near-universal hurdle for divorcing individuals. On life-stress indices, divorce is second only to death of a spouse in its potential impact (Dohrenwend, 1973), and clear epidemiological data indicate that in terms of psychiatric hospitalizations, death due to automobile and other accidents, suicide and death from homicide, as well as overall mortality, the rates for the divorced (of both sexes) are higher than for others (Bloom, Asher & White, 1978). The psychological distress engendered by divorce is further revealed by the fact that divorced men and women exhibit more symptoms (e.g., anxiety, depression, "nervous breakdowns" and "inertia") and in more serious degree than others (Landbrook, 1976).

Although signs of emotional distress are indicated by both sexes following divorce, it is clear that mothers experience significantly greater stress than fathers, with more severe consequences. The relationship between low SES and mental and physical illness has been well documented, and, for divorced mothers, there are data to suggest that these stresses are compounded (Berkman, 1969). Many studies have concluded that most divorced mothers experience moderate to high levels of emotional distress at some point during the divorce process (e.g., Campbell, Converse, & Rogers, 1976; Chiriboga, Roberts, & Stein, 1978; Goode, 1956; Hetherington, 1978; Mitchell, 1983). In national samples, divorced mothers appear to be consistently more distressed than any other group. They are more likely to have fears of an impending nervous breakdown, more likely to have sought psychotherapy or to have felt they could have benefited from it, and more likely to have the lowest sense of well-being and feel least satisfied with their lives (e.g., Campbell *et al.*, 1976; Goode, 1956; Gunn, Veroff, & Feld, 1960).

Although the association with economics is strong, many other theories have been developed to explain why mothers are so often distressed by divorce and to determine some of the variables that mediate adjustment. Despite the devastation experienced by some women, others are affected less intensely and/or for a shorter duration. Moreover, a small but significant number of women perceive divorce to be a long-awaited opportunity (Brown *et al.*, 1976). Whereas adjustment difficulties have been well documented, the consequences of divorce must be reexamined in the context of the full range of emotional impact that it can have.

Divorce Adjustment Theories

Theories of divorce adjustment abound in the literature. These include stage theories that parallel Kubler-Ross's stages of response to death—denial, mourning, anger, readjustment (Kressel, 1980). Other stage theories describe stages of completion of the different aspects of divorce—the emotional divorce, the legal divorce, the community divorce, etc. (Bohannan, 1971). Some other theories draw from Bowlby's infant attachment work (Weiss, 1976) and Freud's explanations of ego development. For example, Rice (1977) describes the "narcissistic injury" in divorce in which the damage inflicted by the loss of the spouse is caused by the deflated primitive fantasies of infantile greatness. Many theorists have also noted the loss of self-esteem and the perception of many women that they are unlovable following divorce (Kressel, 1980; Weiss, 1975b). Studies have reinforced these intrapsychic explanations by demonstrating the relatively poor self-concept held by many women 2 years and more after the divorce (Goode, 1956; Hetherington, 1978). Such theory and research are the continuing legacy of deviancy models of divorce.

There is a growing body of literature, taken directly from the life experiences of divorced mothers, that appears to look beyond the inevitable adjustment period and probe more deeply into their overall functioning. It is perhaps a curious result of the fact that most divorced mothers begin their postdivorce lives with a long list of negatives—less money, inadequate vocational skills, low self-esteem, heightened anxiety and stress, and great fear about the future—that they are likely to find their lives following divorce better and more satisfying than they anticipated. These findings have been repeated in several studies now. For example, Weitzman (1985) found that most of the women in her study reported a rise in competence and self-esteem at some time during the first year after divorce. A total of 83% reported that they were functioning better than during the marriage. They also felt better about themselves (88%), considered themselves more competent in their work (68%), more physically attractive (50%), and that they possessed better parenting skills (62%). Similarly, women in other studies have reported feeling better off psychologically despite financial problems because they had more control over their lives (Brown et al., 1976); and, after 3½ years, divorced mothers do not differ on indicators of maladjustment from continuously married mothers (Saul & Scherman, 1984). Further, compared with the husbands, the mothers interviewed in another study (Kressel, 1980) could identify more concrete postidvorce accomplishments— purchase of a house, establishment of their own credit, completion of a degree or obtainment of full-time employment. These achievements, as visible demonstrations of their coping ability, reportedly imbued them with a sense of pride and self-confidence.

Thus, in spite of the pervasive economic difficulties that divorce brings, a portrait of resilience and resourcefulness also emerges from these accounts. Perhaps these reactions also expose the extent to which the self-confidence and self-esteem of so many mothers are stifled during marriage, leaving them with the most minimal expectations for themselves and their lives after divorce. As Weitzman (1985) hypothesized, for women who have defined themselves in terms of their husbands and children, this may be the first time in their lives that they have felt free to focus on themselves and to develop their own interests.

The Range of Reactions

Naturally, there is a wide range of reaction to divorce. One review of the factors reported to be associated with more positive postdivorce adjustment included the following: nontraditional sex role, being prepared for the divorce decision, agreeing with the divorce decision, high marital conflict, a decreased degree of attachment to the ex-spouse, maintenance of interests and hobbies separate from those of the ex-spouse, engaging in social and dating activities, being involved in a new intimate relationship, having adequate finances, and receiving social support (Kurdeck & Blisk, 1983). Factors negatively related to adjustment included age, length of marriage, continuing emotional relationship with ex-husband, high family orientation and low self-orientation (Bloom & Clement, 1984), and the prospect of continuing low income. Anticipated income for the coming year is related to both physical and mental health following divorce: the lower the anticipated income, the less favorable the mother's physical and psychological well-being (Weitzman, 1985).

It is clear that many factors are associated with differences in adjustment for mothers following divorce. While the postdivorce period is obviously one of many contrasts, and while there is a great deal of variation in reactions to divorce among different individuals (and, of course, within the same individual at different times), a surprisingly large percentage of divorced mothers ultimately report that they are functioning better and are more competent than they were during marriage. Here it is significant that mothers often exceed fathers in their own reports of postdivorce coping. Divorced mothers appear to take tremendous pride in surviving the economic hardships they face and in finding their greatest fears about the future to be unrealized. Given the stressful circumstances of most divorces involving children, the resiliency of these mothers is perhaps more striking than the adjustment difficulties they initially have.

Mental health professionals have responded to the increase in divorce by developing a wide array of programs aimed at aiding adjustment. These include groups to address employment problems, legal and financial issues, parenting concerns, housing and homemaking arrangements, and social and emotional well-being; individual and family therapy; and general self-help groups (Bloom et al., 1982; Camara, 1982 [cited in Emery et al., 1984]; Kurdek & Blisk, 1983; Wallerstein & Kelly, 1980). Whereas controlled evaluations of such efforts are rare, it appears that any form of treatment can be effective and improves adjustment better than no organized help at all (Bloom et al., 1982). A major benefit of therapy for divorced mothers may well be the social support it provides, although this can be artificial. Wahler's (1980) suggestion that therapists build naturally occurring social supports into treatment is important to consider. It is possible that self-help groups, in which parents supply their own support networks within a structured, problem-solving format, is a more practical approach to postdivorce adjustment (e.g., Camara, 1982; [cited in Emery et al., 1984]; Kessler, 1978). Most programs run by professionals treat divorce as a crisis rather than as a long-term, gradual process. Although crisis intervention can be beneficial, the long-term emotional consequences of divorce are also important to consider, particularly as they affect the evolving relationship between a mother and her child(ren).

THE MOTHER–CHILD RELATIONSHIP

> At first I thought there would be all of this change to get used to, and, for a while it was weird not having Bill around to be mad at. But I always did everything for Josh anyway, you know, and so it was like everything was really the same. No, its better, because on the weekends, it's Joshy and me and we have fun. (Debbie, mother of a 4-year-old boy, divorced 2 years)

Much has been written about how children respond to changes in their care and how they perceive relationships with their caretakers (usually mothers) following divorce. Relatively less is known about the stresses and supports that divorced mothers may encounter during this same period and ways in which this relationship changes for them.

The Stresses

It has been concluded widely that custodial mothers experience more difficulty in their parental role than do nondivorced mothers (e.g., Furstenberg et al., 1983; Hetherington et al., 1982). Past research has frequently sought out and discovered the deficits in postdivorce mother–child relationships. As the divorced mother attempts to manage household, economic, and social responsibilities on top of childrearing, the mother–child relationship is quite commonly found to be disrupted. Some research further demonstrates that custodial mothers with three or more children, very young children, or male children show more signs of depression and role difficulty than mothers with fewer, older, or female children (Colletta, 1979a) and that with young children they tend to use more negative and restrictive sanctions, be more inconsistent with their discipline, and demonstrate less affection toward their children (Burgess, 1978; Hetherington et al., 1982). This disruption in childrearing following divorce is so common that it has been called a "period of diminished parenting" (Wallerstein & Kelly, 1980). Much of this research is intuitively right; it lends empirical confirmation to some of the stress we might expect. It also makes postdivorce difficulty appear to be normal. Women who might be seen as deviant or inadequate can instead be viewed as undergoing rather predictable changes. It should be expected that immediately following divorce, mothers will experience a decrease in their ability to parent effectively. What is remarkable is that some mothers have little or no difficulty with their children in this major transition and that most mothers get over the hurdle within a moderate amount of time.

There is some longitudinal research that provides evidence for a perpetuation of diminished parenting, particularly when the involved children act out or become resistant to maternal authority (Hetherington et al., 1982). Custodial mothers display increased anxiety and depression, and decreased feelings of internal control when their children become troubled after divorce, particularly mothers with sons—it appears that mothers with daughters have an easier time (Weiss, 1975b). There is, of course, also a body of literature describing the multiple problems of inpoverished mothers, which in turn exacerbate difficulties in mother–child relationships (e.g., Colletta, 1979b).

Although the picture painted by a deviancy model is rather gloomy, there are a few additional points that should be added. First, when divorced parents are able to keep their own conflict at a minimum, mothers experience less tension with their children as well. Second, when other variables like socioeconomic status are held constant, differences in married and divorced parenting skill disappear (Kurdek & Blisk, 1983). In other words, much of the diminished parenting appears to be part of a diminished pocketbook. Finally, patterns of difficulty in discordant two-parent homes and high-conflict divorces are the same (Emery, 1982). Women who are fighting with their spouses have the same amount of trouble with their children as those struggling with "father absence" and all it implies.

The Benefits

A tiny but growing field of inquiry includes asking women about their experience. Findings in this literature reveal some of the tacit biases of traditional research. Most women say that as bad as times get in their single-parent role, the conflict-ridden marriage was worse (Brown et al., 1976). Further, it is also common for mothers to feel closer to their children following divorce. Given the fact that, in general, women had been doing most of the caretaking before the divorce, they do not experience a major role change. Instead, they note the peace and lack of conflict. Contrary to the attitudes of the society around them, most women, when asked, say they feel they are doing well with their children. Similarly, there are studies that indicate that mothers experience an improvement of mood and communication with their children upon resolution of an acrimonious divorce (Brandwein et al., 1974; Hetherington et al., 1979).

In sum, current perspectives on mother–child relationships following divorce have evolved from two sets of assumptions. The first, traditional view is based in theory describing how the family type is deviant, so assumes there are bound to be problems stemming from the deviancy. The second, more inclusive view tries to explain ways in which the new family structure also can have some assets it didn't have before. Research questions in the first mode center on examination of deficits and weaknesses. Research questions in the second mode center on examination of improvements and strengths. The study of father absence, mode two suggests, can be replaced by the study of conflict absence. In neither case is this the whole picture (most divorces conclude with both fathers and conflict still present at least some of the time) but the bigger picture suggests that there are positive outcomes that have been largely overlooked.

Divorced mothers attempting to raise their children independently face a variety of barriers that are, in large part, due to our public policies—policies based squarely on old research from the traditional perspective. The women's movement has much to offer divorced mothers in this arena. Quality day-care, adequate low-cost housing, equal credit rights, equal access to job training and employment, equal pay for equal and comparable work, and so on—the very goals of the women's movement—have clear and tangible consequences for the mother–child relationship. A mother who is able to provide confidently and consistently for the well-being of her children can readily overcome the inevitably difficult postdivorce period with them.

THE FUTURE

We now know a great deal about the experiences of divorced mothers—through daily contact with them as well as research. We can identify, with some accuracy, the range of stresses and supports they are likely to encounter. More study is not necessary to begin to shape policies that will protect these women from many of the inequities of the present system.

Money

It is clear that at the foundation of the struggle for most divorced mothers is money, plain and simple. The harsh financial consequences lurk in every unexamined corner and bear on all aspects of their lives. Although economics are not the only hurdle to overcome, it is apparent that other hurdles shrink when a women leaps off from financial security. Women who receive equitable divorces, who have access to adequate, low-cost child care, and who have assurance of sufficient income through employment or other means have resources. These resources can be used to penetrate social isolation, to offer hope about the future, and to provide extra resilience in the face of inevitable troubles and setbacks.

Our current public policies offer a number of costs and barriers to divorced mothers. With great overlap, these women are affected by their status as poor, as women, and as parents, and policies that help any of these groups in general will also help divorced mothers specifically. It is possible that some momentum for needed changes has gathered in the past several years. Women have made significant advances in their efforts to seek legal recognition of their work and their rights in the family. These advances have occurred on both the state and federal level, in both the courts and the legislatures. Particularly significant is the federal government's recent shift in position from one of noninvolvement in family law issues to one of involvement. There is, obviously, much still to be done, but relevant work (e.g., child-support enforcement, stronger marital property laws, prosecution of batterers, etc.) has begun.

Families in the Courts

Large-scale changes are not likely to come about in the near future. First, as Woods (1985) has noted, it is no coincidence that there is also a growing trend in the United States to exclude family law issues from the courts and to undermine many of the gains women have made over the years. Second, the costs of public policies at present are placed squarely upon divorced mothers. Solving the economic and social inequities caused by divorce would distribute these costs onto governmental policymakers and onto men—an unlikely current event. Finally, despite its prevalence, divorce is still not accorded a major place in policy decisions, and divorced mothers are still viewed by many as deviant from the traditional community, thus not meriting advocacy.

Advocacy

However, if mobilized, divorced mothers might offer a persuasive advocacy of their own. Women's centers, which now exist in many communities, might expand their outreach more specifically to divorcing mothers. These centers can provide, for example, legal counsel and assistance, vocational and educational counseling, information about custody and child support, assistance in obtaining welfare benefits, and aid in finding day care, housing, and therapeutic services. Women's centers can do more than create a necessary base for political activism—though that is a vital function. They can provide the resources that ease costs to divorced mothers and provide the conditions through which she can remain a part of the larger community, breaking the social isolation that debilitates.

Legal reforms, including enforced payment of child support and alimony and more equitable distribution of marital property coupled with such community activism, may help protect future divorced mothers from the economic devastations of divorce. The road to more equitable divorces is paved by policy initiatives. Divorced mothers and those who choose to advocate for them now have the information needed to prescribe enduring remedies to the economic and personal costs of divorce.

REFERENCES

Ambert, A. (1983). Separated women and remarriage behavior: A comparison of financially secure women and financially insecure women. *Journal of Divorce, 6*(3), 43–54.

Anspach, D. F. (1976). Kinship and divorce. *Journal of Marriage and the Family, 38,* 323–330.

Bahr, S. J. (1981). An evaluation of court mediation for divorce cases with children. *Journal of Family Issues, 2,* 39–60.

Baker, O. V., Druckman, J. M., & Flagle, J. E. (1980). *Helping youth and families of separation, divorce and remarriage.* Palo Alto, CA: American Institutes for Research.

Bane, M. J. (1979). Marital disruption and the lives of children. In G. Levinger & O. C. Moles (Eds.), *Divorce and separation: Context, causes and consequences.* New York: Basic.

Becker, S., Landes, E. M., & Michael, R. T. (1977). An economic analysis of marital instability. *Journal of Political Economy, 85,* 1141–1187.

Berkman, P. (1969). Spouseless motherhood, psychological stress, and physical morbidity. *Journal of Health and Social Behavior, 10,* 330.

Bloom, B. L., Asher, S. J., & White, S. W. (1978). Marital disruption as a stressor: A review and analysis. *Psychological Bulletin, 85,* 867–894.

Bloom, B. L., & Clement, C. (1984). Marital sex role orientation and adjustment to separation and divorce. *Journal of Divorce, 7*(3), 87–98.

Bloom, B. L., Hodges, W. F., & Caldwell, R. A. (1982). A preventive intervention program for the newly separated: Initial evaluation. *American Journal of Community Psychology, 10,* 251–264.

Bohannan, P. (1971). *Divorce and after: An analysis of the emotional and social problems of divorce.* New York: Anchor/Doubleday.

Bradbury, K., Dansinger, S., Smolensky, E., & Smolensky, P. (1979). Public assistance, female leadership, and economic well-being. *Journal of Marriage and the Family, 41,* 519–535.

Brandwein, R. A., Brown, C. A., & Fox, E. M. (1974). Women and children last: The social situation of divorced mothers and their families. *Journal of Marriage and the Family, 36*(3), 498–514.

Brown, C. A., Feldberg, R., Fox, E. M., & Kohen, J. (1976). Divorce: Chance of a new lifetime. *Journal of Social Issues, 32*(1), 119–133.

Burgess, R. (1978). *Project Interact: A study of patterns of interaction in abusive, neglectful and control families* (Final Report). Washington, DC: NCCAN.

Campbell, A., Converse, P. E., & Rogers, W. (1976). *The quality of American life: Perceptions, evaluations and satisfactions.* New York: Sage.

Carter, H., & Glick, P. C. (1976). *Marriage and divorce: A social and economic study.* Cambridge: Harvard University Press.

Cherlin, A. J. (1978). Marriage as an incomplete institution. *American Journal of Sociology, 84,* 634–650.

Cherlin, A. J. (1981). *Marriage, divorce, remarriage.* Cambridge: Harvard University Press.

Chiriboga, D. A., Roberts, J., & Stein, J. A. (1978). Psychological well-being during marital separation. *Journal of Divorce, 2,* 21–36.

Colletta, N. D. (1979a). Support systems after divorce: Incidence and impact. *Journal of Marriage and the Family, 41,* 837–846.

Colletta, N. D. (1979b). The impact of divorce: Father absence or poverty? *Journal of Divorce, 3,* 27–36.

Davis, K. (1983). The future of marriage. *Bulletin of the American Academy of Arts and Sciences, 36*(8), 33.

Dohrenwend, B. (1973). Social status and stressful life events. *Journal of Personality and Social Psychology, 28,* 213–218.

Doyle, P. M., & Caron, W. A. (1979). Contested custody intervention: An empirical assessment. In D. H. Olson, M. Cleveland, P. M. Doyle, & M. F. Rockcastle, (Eds.), *Child custody: Literature review and alternative approaches.* St. Paul, MN: Hennepin County Domestic Relations Division.

Edwards, J. N. (1967). The future of the family revisited. *Journal of Marriage and the Family, 29,* 505–511.

Ehrenreich, B. (1983). *The Hearts of Men.* Garden City, New York: Anchor/Doubleday.

Emery, R. E. (1982). Interparental conflict and the children of divorce and discord. *Psychological Bulletin, 92,* 310–330.

Emery, R. D., Hetherington, E. M., & Dilalla, L. F. (1984). Divorce, children and social policy. In H. W. Stevenson & A. F. Siegel (Eds.), *Child development research and social policy.* Chicago: University of Chicago Press.

Fast, I., & Cain, A. C. (1966). The step-parent role: Potential for disturbances in family functioning. *American Journal of Orthopsychiatry, 36,* 485–491.

Freed, D. J., & Foster, H. H. (1984). Family law in the fifty states: An overview. *Family Law Quarterly, 17,* 365–447.

Friedan, B. (1976). *It changed my life.* New York: Random House.

Furstenberg, F., Nord, C., Peterson, J., & Zill, N. (1983). The life course of children of divorce: Marital disruption and parental contact. *American Sociological Review, 48,* 656–668.

Gibson, G. (1972). Kin family network. *Journal of Marriage and the Family, 34,* 13–23.

Glasser, P., & Navarre, E. (1966). Structural problems of the one-parent family. *Journal of Social Issues, 21,* 98–109.

Goetting, A. (1981). Divorce outcome research: Issues and perspectives, *Journal of Family Issues, 2*(3), 350–378.

Goldfarb, S. (1985). Statement of NOW Legal Defense Education Fund of Mediation of Child Custody Disputes. Unpublished.

Goode, W. J. (1956). *Women in Divorce.* New York: Free Press.

Gunn, G., Veroff, J., & Feld, S. (1960). *Americans view their mental health.* New York: Basic.

Hetherington, E. M. (1978). Stress and coping in divorce: A focus on women. In J. H. Gullahorn (Ed.), *Psychology and transition*. New York: Winston.

Hetherington, E. M., Cox, M., & Cox, R. (1978). The aftermath of divorce. In J. H. Steven & M. Matthews, (Eds.), *Mother–child, father–child relations*. Washington, DC: National Association for the Education of Young Children.

Hetherington, E. M., Cox, M., & Cox, R. (1976). Divorced fathers. *The Family Coordinator*, 25, 417–428.

Hetherington, E. M., Cox, M., & Cox, R. (1979). The development of children in mother headed families. In D. Keiss & H. Hoffman (Eds.), *The American family: Dying or developing*. New York: Plenum Press.

Hetherington, E. M., Cox, M., & Cox, R. (1982). Effects of divorce on parents and children. In M. Lamb, (Ed.), *Nontraditional families*. Hillsdale: Erlbaum.

Irving, H., Bohm, P., MacDonald, G., & Benjamin, M. (1979). *A comparative analysis of two family court services: An exploratory study of conciliation counseling*. Toronto: Department of Mental Health and Welfare.

Kessler, S. (1978). Building skills in divorce adjustment groups. *Journal of Divorce*, 2, 209–216.

Kohen, J. A., Brown, C. A., & Feldberg, R. (1979). Divorced mothers: The costs and benefits of female family control. In G. Levinger & O. C. Moles (Eds.), *Divorce and separation*. New York: Basic.

Kressel, K. (1980). Patterns of coping in divorce and some implications for clinical practice. *Family Relations*, 29(2), 234–240.

Kurdek, L. A., & Blisk, D. (1983). Dimensions and correlates of mothers' divorce experiences. *Journal of Divorce*, 6(4), 1–24.

Landbrook, D. (1976). The wealth and survival of the divorced. *Conciliation Courts Review*, 14, 21–33.

Longfellow, C. (1979). Divorce in context: Its impact on children. In G. Levinger & O. C. Moles (Eds.), *Divorce and separation*. New York: Basic.

McKay, M., Rogers, P., Blades, J., & Gosse, R. (1984). *The divorce book*. Oakland, CA: New Harbinger.

Milne, A. (1978). Custody of children in a divorce process: A family self-determination model. *Conciliation Courts Review*, 16, 1–10.

Mitchell, K. (1983). The price tag of responsibility: A comparison of divorced and remarried mothers. *Journal of Divorce*, 6(3), 33–42.

National Advisory Council on Economic Opportunity. (1980). *Critical choices for the 80's*. Washington, DC: Author.

Pearce, D. (1978, February). The feminization of poverty: Women, work and welfare. *Urban and Social Change Review*.

Pearce, D., & McAdoo, H. (1981, September). Women and children: Alone and in poverty. Washington, DC: National Advisory Council on Economic Opportunity.

Pearson, J., & Thoennes, N. (1982). The mediation and adjudication of divorce disputes: The benefits outweigh the costs. *Family Advocate*, 4, 26–32.

Pearson, J., & Thoennes, N. (1984). *Child custody, child support arrangements and child support payment patterns*. Unpublished paper.

Phear, P. W., Beck, J. C., & Hauser, B. (1986). An empirical study of custody agreements: Joint vs. sole legal custody. *Journal of Law and Psychiatry*, 14.

Renne, K. S. (1971). Health and marital experience in an urban population. *Journal of Marriage and the Family*, 33, 338–350.

Rheinstein, M. (1972). *Marriage Stability, Divorce and the Law*. Chicago: University of Chicago Press.

Rice, D. G. (1977). Psychotherapeutic treatment of narcissistic injury in marital separation and divorce. *Journal of Divorce*, 1, 119–128.

Saul, S. C., & Scherman, A. (1984). Divorce grief, and personal adjustment in divorced persons who remarry or remain single. *Journal of Divorce*, 7(3), 75–85.

Saunders, B. E. (1983). The social consequences of divorce: Implications for family policy. *Journal of Divorce*, 6(3), 1–17.

SCCYF (Select Committee on Children, Youth and Families) (1983). *U.S. children and their families: Current conditions and recent trends*. Washington, DC: U.S. Government Printing Office.

Spanier, G. B., & Anderson, E. A. (1979). The impact of the legal system on adjustment to marital separation. *Journal of Marriage and the Family, 41*(3), 605–625.

Spanier, G. B., & Casto, R. (1979). Adjustment to separation and divorce. *Journal of Divorce, 2,* 241–253.

Spicer, J. W., & Hampe, G. D. (1975). Kinship interaction after divorce. *Journal of Marriage and the Family, 37,* 113–119.

Visher, E. B., & Visher, J. S. (1982). Stepfamilies and stepparenting. In F. Walsh, (Ed.), *Normal family process.* New York: Guilford.

Wahler, R. G. (1980). The insular mother: Her problems in parent–child treatment. *Journal of Applied Behavior Analysis, 13,* 207–219.

Wallerstein, R. S., & Kelly, J. B. (1980). *Surviving the breakup.* New York: Basic.

Weiss, R. S. (1975a). *Marital separation.* New York: Basic.

Weiss, R. S. (1975b). Growing up a little faster: The experience of growing up in a single-parent household. *Journal of Social Issues, 35,* 97–111.

Weitzman, L. J. (1981). *The divorce revolution.* New York: The Free Press.

Weitzman, L. J. (1985). *The marriage contract.* New York: The Free Press.

Woods, L. (1985). Medication: A backlash to women's progress on family law issues. [Special summer issue]. *Clearinghouse Review.*

CHAPTER 10

Mothers Who Are Disabled

BARBARA HOLLAND BASKIN AND ELIZABETH P. RIGGS

INTRODUCTION

> The difficulty is neither in being [disabled] nor in being a mother. It is in the attitudes of others, the invisible barriers which can separate me from other mothers and my children from their children. (Kendrick, 1983, p. 18)

It is common wisdom that disabled women cannot be capable mothers. This misconception is not surprising since the public tends to equate disability with general incompetence, lack of intelligence, and passivity on the part of the mother. Dailey (1979) asserts that the stereotypes for women and for the disabled are identical and reinforcing:

> Both are encouraged to be helpless, nonassertive . . . nonathletic, dependent, passive, grateful, and apologetic for a less than perfect body.

Linda Pedro, a disabled Hispanic single parent states that "disabled women are the last minority" (Neel, 1981, p. 13).

Events heralding "The Year of the Disabled" or "The Decade of the Disabled" have recently become part of the domestic as well as the international political scene, promising, at minimum, visiblity, if not political gain, for citizens with impairments. The last 10 years have seen revolutionary changes in schools and other public settings which have made life considerably easier for the disabled.

Similarly, feminists have fought for and won significant changes for women in the traditional social order. Disabled women hoped that, as a group whose needs overlapped both advocacy movements, their voices would be heard. Unfortunately, few feminists or disability activists perceived the unique concerns of disabled women as worthy of their attentions. Women with impairments remain disadvantaged by their "double handicap," and disabled women who are also

BARBARA HOLLAND BASKIN • Interdisciplinary Program in Social Sciences, State University of New York, Stony Brook, New York 11794.   ELIZABETH P. RIGGS • (retired) Department of French, State University of New York, Stony Brook, New York 11794.

mothers share their unfavorable status. Further, they shoulder the burden of society's perception of them as incompetents who have irresponsibly become mothers who will, along with their offspring, unquestionably become a burden on society.

The intent of this chapter is to consider some aspects of this group, particularly how their childhood, adolescence, family, and personal lives affected their goals and thoughts about motherhood. Special attention is given to the adaptations required by these mothers and the benefits derived from the status of motherhood. The individuals who influenced them, such as family, spouse, teachers, friends, counselors, physicians and the mothers' limited social support system, are also examined.

Data on Disability

By and large, this information is derived from testimonial material by disabled women, supported by studies and reports based on a small number of subjects. An examination of the bibliography will reveal the currency of most references. It is quite clear that until now, demographers, physicians, sociologists, psychologists, and others neither counted, described, nor reported such information in meaningful quantity. Holcomb (1984) stated that "a frequent assumption in the studies was that what applies to men with disabilities also applies to disabled women" (p. 18). As a result of this widespread neglect, we have only a rough estimate of the number of disabled women and therefore an even less reliable notion of the number of disabled mothers.

Focus

In this chapter, we focus on mothers who have sensory, physical, neurological, orthopedic, or debilitating health impairments who are living "in society."

In order to explore how the disabled mother responds to the challenges of daily living, this chapter examines issues that at first glance may seem peripheral, for example, education and work experience. Yet these matters bear heavily on her available resources. As disabled women may be heads of households in addition to being mothers, they are often the chief economic providers as well.

THE EDUCATION OF DISABLED WOMEN

The disabled woman is heavily disadvantaged in educational experience. One in every six disabled women had less than 8 years of formal education compared with one out of every 28 nondisabled woman, according to the U.S. Department of Labor (1985). When they did attend school, Holcomb (1984) reported that progress was often irregular because of interruptions and complications due to illness.

Gillespie and Fink (1974) found that disabled girls in public schools were directed toward occupational training that focused on such gender-related programs as laundry work and housekeeping, in contrast with disabled boys who were informed about and guided to higher paying career options. Rosenstein and Lerman (1963) reported gender-distinctive educational tracks in residential facilities as well.

Reports of inadequate educational experiences, particularly at the secondary level, are corroborated in the testimonies of disabled women and in the recent reports of researchers on educational inequity. Thus, many emerged from high school with a diploma but ill-prepared for the social, marital, and employment world of their able-bodied peers (Corbett & Weeks, 1981).

THE EARLY LIVES OF DISABLED GIRLS

Their early years contribute markedly to disabled women's perception of themselves as wives and mothers. Childhood accounts show wide variations from loving acceptance to painful rejection (Campling, 1979).

Disabled adults frequently report family disorganization as a result of their disability. They also suffered from limitations in their own adolescent socialization and sexual experiences. Many have noticed negative attitudes in the school and neighborhood and most reflect concern about such personal issues as independence and self-worth.

Two Contrasting Life Stories

In the following excerpts from two interviews, the impact of two vastly different parental attitudes is contrasted (Riggs & Baskin, unpublished).

Emily's photo, taken at 2½ just before polio, reflects a doll-like perfection. Apparently, neither of her parents, traumatized by what had happened, could accept the end of this flawlessness. Emily, now in her 60s, says most of her life she felt guilty for her "failure" to remain the perfect doll.

Her parents responded to the calamity by keeping their "damaged" daughter within the privacy of their house to "spare her feelings." She was tutored at home and lived as a recluse during her childhood and adolescence.

When a favorite uncle bought her a beautiful doll, her mother allowed Emily only about an hour a week to hold the doll; then it was put away. Even at 7, Emily understood that her mother wanted to keep *that* doll undamaged.

One of her tutors recognized Emily's capabilities and arranged a scholarship at Columbia but her parents would not permit her to go. Because of her inexperience, she was grateful to the man who offered the only way out of limbo that was acceptable to her parents: marriage. The residence he chose was accessible only by two long flights of stairs, an impossibility for her polio-wasted legs. She became a prisoner. From a totally isolated childhood, she went directly into an adulthood that was eerily similar. In 33 years, she never once went out in the company of her husband.

She had five babies who never ceased to delight her, especially because doctors had told her she could never have children. The marriage was a disaster and after 15 years, she planned her exit. Lacking the means to be independent, she had to postpone her escape until the last child left.

When her moment of freedom arrived, she "walked out." She became Nora in Ibsen's *A Doll's House,* bravely slamming the door on security. Her divorce horrified her Catholic parents, but led to her marriage to another man, whose own impairment made him understanding of hers. He was as tender and supportive as her first husband had been cold and uncaring.

Her parents' disapproval did not lessen when she found a job as a receptionist, where her disability was visible to everyone. At the age of 50, Emily had come out of the closet.

Her newfound independence has led to self-confidence and a kind of blooming. She now takes college courses through supervised home study, she paints, and writes searing poetry about her parents and her childhood.

Recently, her husband bought her a beautiful doll to replace the one she could not really play with when she was a child. Somehow she felt this gift was symbolic of the control that she now has—at last—over her own life.

Millie represents the opposite side of the coin from Emily. You would first notice her intelligence, her energy, and her fierce independence. Legally blind, she functions with an enviable efficiency and decisiveness. You will feel sorry for this woman at your peril; she makes no excuses for herself and asks none from you.

Her income, at $24,000, is well above the average for women in general. She is self-employed, a social worker with a graduate degree.

Millie, a widow, lives with her two daughters in a middle-class nieghborhood. She is lucid about the problems faced by the children of severely disabled mothers—first, their self-consciousness about having a "different" parent, and second, their extra responsibilities:

> It is O.K. to ask children for help so long as it is appropriate to their [stage of] development . . . but it is damaging to children to overburden them. They must feel that they can depend on us more than we do on them.

Her most serious problem in day-to-day functioning is her inability to drive; she depends on friends for help.

She characterized her marriage as "fairly happy." Her husband was totally blind, but very involved in child care. He was loving and—as a teacher of rehabilitation—taught his wife skills she didn't yet have.

Millie has been fortunate in her relationships. Not only were both her parents and her husband supportive, even her ophthalmologist encouraged her to "live a normal life." Millie advises visually handicapped mothers who are considering the pros and cons of having children:

> Blind mothers . . . must have close friends and relatives (who are sighted) and must allow these people to provide the child with certain experiences that [such mothers] cannot. . . . Teaching about colors, answering questions about things the child sees,

these are necessary educational tools . . . Where eyesight is absolutely necessary, you
borrow or purchase it.

Parental Attitudes and Overprotection

Corbett and Weeks (1981) report a fairly constant element in the lives of
young disabled women—overprotection. The traditional family behavior of
minimizing or eliminating what is perceived of as risky is usually closely followed by parents of disabled girls. Adults find it particularly difficult to identify
realistic dangers, and many women complain of the oppressiveness of their
childhood. Girls like Emily passively accept this well-meant but infantilizing
behavior and become fragile "objects" throughout their lives.

As the disabled girl develops into adolescence, she is "protected from" or
denied the sexual education of her able-bodied counterparts. Her physical status
may hinder social contacts with young adults her age for whom discussions of
dating and sex are normal and instructive. Further, many parents may find it
hard to believe that their daughter is interested in sex education (Robinault,
1978). Sex and sexuality are extremely difficult issues for parents of disabled
women and such taboos quite naturally affect young women's sense of femininity, desirability, and understanding of themselves as sensual and sexual beings
(Connors, 1985).

Perceptions of Adulthood

Berta, a mobility-impaired woman, reported that as a teenager, she expected to be "an old maid" but was "passionately determined to experience
life . . . at any cost." She married a man who, though spurning housework and
child care, nevertheless gave her great emotional support, assuring her that she
was "beautiful" and "sexy," words disabled women rarely expect to have applied to them (Riggs & Baskin, unpublished).

Moreover, disabled girls see so few adult role models that they have no idea
what to expect for themselves when they grow up (Corbett & Froschl, 1983).
Corbett and Weeks (1981) found that 60% of their respondents had no memory
from their childhood of contact with a disabled woman. Phillips (1984) also
argued that the development of femininity and sexuality is further sabotaged by
restrictive social models that equate beauty with desirability and, by definition,
exclude those with "imperfections." The disabled woman may associate her
impairment with a conviction of her own unworthiness, resulting in repression
of her emergent sexuality or in feelings of uncertainty with potential sexual
partners. Achieving independence will increase the likelihood of her seeking
adult satisfaction in a mate.

Attitudes about Disability

Two women give accounts that reveal how attitudes about disability influenced their future:

> My family always assumed that I would one day get married and have children.
> Disability was no excuse. And that is exactly what I did—married and gave birth (no
> miracle) like any "normal" woman does and parented those children through sickness,
> etc. My personal life has changed recently from a married wife and mother to a di-
> vorced, single working parent. Sometimes when I think about it, I have to gasp. (Maine
> Association of Handicapped Persons, 1984, p. 7)

An artist whose shoulders, arms, and hands were affected by rheumatoid
arthritis, recollected:

> When I was about eighteen, I decided . . . that I would have an absolutely normal
> life . . . a marriage, a family, a career in the arts, and that's what I've had. I've been
> lucky. Pain is a constant in my life, always has been. But in the interest of living, the
> pain became tolerable. And I've always thought that was the prize—living. (Carrillo,
> Corbett, & Lewis, 1982, p. 88)

Despite a host of such examples, Robinault (1978) claims that society assumes that females are automatically rendered physically inadequate or sexually
incompetent as a result of impairment. Many disabled women state they were
encouraged to attend college since their families felt they were unlikely to marry
and, as a result, they report being the first in their family to go to a university.

THE WORK EXPERIENCE OF DISABLED WOMEN

Paid labor force participation is important for the disabled mother. It provides knowledge about the world and financial independence. Like other employed women, she can enter marriage as a partner, feeling confident that she
could reenter the economic world if necessary. Such a background provides
essential economic and psychological comfort.

However, some of the conditions that hampered the disabled woman's
education also hinder success in work settings. Bird (1979) asserts that sexism
plays a powerful role:

> Disabled women are not meaningfully present in the work place. The leaders of the
> disabled rights movement are, more often than not, male; the rehabilitation establish-
> ment is dominated by men. When women with disabilities are trained for jobs, they are
> frequently trained for less skilled jobs because they are female. (p. 104)

According to the U.S. Department of Labor (1985), in 1980, only one in three
young disabled women (16 to 34) had jobs at all.

Special Problems in the Workplace

All women workers are affected by sex discrimination but disabled women
often have a secondary problem. Their disorder may decrease their perceived
physical attractiveness. Because some women are hired to "glamorize" the office, restaurant, or other enterprise, and disabled women are often perceived as
unsightly or asexual, their opportunities are further limited (Brown, 1981). As
data reveal that attractiveness is positively related to success for all workers, the
disabled woman, even after she is hired, may be disadvantaged in the job

market (Vash, 1982). Matthews (1983) recalled an employer saying to her "I don't want someone in a wheelchair messing up the look of my office" (p. 158).

Disability and Benefits

Even when women have worked and are eligible for benefits, they are the victims of discrimination. Thurer (1982) asserts that disabled women are unfairly disadvantaged by policies originally designed for disabled males:

> Today, women receive not only fewer but also less generous benefits from . . . disability insurance, supplemental security income, workers' compensation, and vocational rehabilitation. Since eligibility for benefits includes participation in the labor force for a prescribed period of time, and since disability insurance benefits correlate with earnings, women, in this sense, are punished for having been unpaid homemakers prior to the onset of disability. Conversely, women are overrepresented under supplemental security income, which is a public assistance program that supports disabled individuals *below* [italics added] the poverty level. (p. 195)

Squeezed between their low income level and high cost of living, disabled women face an impossible situation. Despite problems of mobility, deteriorating vision, and isolation, Bonnie, a single parent with multiple sclerosis, states with some optimism:

> I believe I can overcome my disability if my financial situation will let me. There have been times when Medicaid would not cover a certain medication I needed. I had only enough money to buy it or food for my children. As a mother, what would you do? (Riggs & Baskin, unpublished)

Effects of Premarital Factors

Why, in a discussion on motherhood, should any attention be given to such factors as education, work history, and income? These factors shape the disabled woman's situation as she comes to marriage, define her as dependent or independent, limit or expand her knowledge of the world, affect her relationship with her husband, and influence her choices should she want to terminate the marriage. Moreover, like most parents, she wants to be able to go places with her children, buy them clothes, books, and magazines, and the "necessities" of a comfortable life. Without the education, training opportunities, and sense of competence and freedom that employment can bring, she faces a grim and disproportionate reduction in the options available to her as a disabled wife and mother. If the marriage dissolves, she will have to support her children through her own efforts, supplemented by inadequate income support programs.

FAMILY PLANNING AND PREGNANCY

For obvious reasons, the couple must begin to think early in their relationship about family planning.

> The medical diagnosis has less to do with the question of whether or not to have
> children than the balance between a couple's capabilities and inabilities, mentally,
> physically, emotionally, and socially. (Robinault, 1978, p. 133)

Even today, some disabled women who wish to conceive find it difficult to
locate a responsive physician. One woman reported:

> The first doctors I contacted were very negative. One told me to get into analysis and
> report back to him after 6 months of intensive therapy.

Other women experienced psychological stress stemming from their own
disorder. A legally blind woman reflected on her worries during her pregnancy:

> I'm not sure my concerns were all that different from those that anyone would
> have. . . . My husband [also blind] was in rehabilitation, he was very competent, [he
> was] a good cook. I learned a lot of skills from him. I felt that if I didn't know how to do
> something, he would know or he would find out and he would show me.

In 1979, Hale claimed that information on the extent of childbearing among
physically disabled mothers was not readily available. However, "experts agree
that more chronically or seriously ill women are choosing to have babies these
days" (Gross, 1986, p. C1).

From testimonial sources, it does not appear that disabled women have
exceptional pregnancies. Clearly, this varies by disability and the mother's general health. Interviews with doctors of chronically ill women revealed that they
"are largely motivated by a desire to be normal, to test the body that has so often
failed them, to be like everyone else" (Gross, 1986, p. C10).

It is imperative for women to seek out obstetricians who understand the
effects of motherhood on the disability but who also empathize with the woman's wishes to become pregnant and deliver a child (Campling, 1981).

The obstetrician will often recommend special supervision for the pregnant
woman and suggest that she not give up active recreational activity (Turk, Turk,
& Assejev, 1983). Exercises specifically designed for disabled expectant mothers
are now available.

Careful obstetricians advise their patients to check with them with regard to
prescriptions written by other doctors or when planning to take over-the-coun-
ter drugs. A very cautious stance is suggested, that is, certain medications
should be avoided during pregnancy. Instructions in how the woman may assist
in delivery are provided even when such problems as partial paralysis are
present.

In their small sample, Shaul, Bogle, and Norman (1977) reported conventional experiences with labor and delivery. Carrick and Bibb (1982) state that:

> The major problems relating to pregnancy and/or delivery were the attitudes of the
> physician or hospital staff in accepting the fact that women with disabilities often desire
> to have children, are happy to be pregnant, and sincerely desire motherhood. (p. 31)

HOMEMAKING BY DISABLED WIVES AND MOTHERS

What are the circumstances in which the disabled woman brings up her
children? How does the disability influence other family members? What effect
does the disability have on her role as mother?

Although obtaining housing is a necessity for every family, finding accommodations that are both accessible and affordable often presents problems (Carrillo *et al.*, 1982; Matthews, 1983). A Social Security Administration survey analyzed by Franklin (1977) described the typical disabled married woman as living within a nuclear family structure, having relatives who lived both within and outside the house and at least one relative who lived an hour or less from them. Most, however, reported no household help from relatives.

Disability and Divorce

As with other American marriages, those with an impaired partner tend to be precarious, particularly when it is the woman who is disabled (Fink, Skipper, & Hallenbeck, 1968; Kutza, 1981). Women frequently reported that their marriage ties dissolved after they became disabled (Neel, 1981). Nagi and Clark (1964) noted that separation and divorce typically take place within 5 years from the onset of the disability. This disruption frequently occurs during an early period in the partners' lives: 37% of the divorced individuals were less than 25 years old.

Whereas some of the unions dissolve for reasons similar to those of their able-bodied sisters, unique pressures exist when the woman is the disabled partner (Rezen & Housman, 1985). Many disabled wives question their own self-worth and that of their husband. They report suspicions about the quality of a man who would choose them and are often pressured by in-laws, friends, and even strangers about their partners. One woman disabled by an accident reported this incident in the hospital. A staff member commented: "You're married, aren't you? Well, that won't last."

Spousal Assistance

Cogswell (1976) suggests that sex-role reversal is extremely stressful, particularly when rigid sex-role boundaries existed prior to the onset of the disorder. Although assuming "male" tasks does not appear stigmatizing to a woman, some males have great difficulty in assuming traditional "female" tasks such as household management and child care.

One woman, still married, reported on the trials she and her husband underwent. Severely disabled by polio, and needing to use a respirator to breathe, she was sent to a rehabilitation center for 2½ years. She recalls: "My husband . . . told me that the hardest thing in the world for him was to accept the fact that I was like I was." But he cared for the three children while she was away, fixed her portable respirator so it could run off the car battery, and made rubber armrests and double seat belts for her comfort when they went on rides (Orlansky & Heward, 1981, pp. 67–70).

When disabled women have partners who make similar adaptations, their lives are considerably easier. However, Merchant (1969) found that the major helpers of physically impaired homemakers were their children and not their spouse.

Information for the Homemaker

Particularly for the blind or orthopedically impaired mother, adaptations are usually necessary, and are available from disability-associated agencies, county consultants, rehabilitation centers, or mobile rehabilitation libraries (Bopp, 1981). They are given instruction in meal preparation and service and in laundry and cleaning tasks. Those with orthopedic problems learn about specialized clothing and its availability.

Women also receive information on home remodeling, safety considerations, and conservation of energy since fatigue is often a problem. Many women have learned to improvise, modifying their working environment to circumvent the restrictions resulting from their impairments. The deaf mother may install electronic devices at her door to inform her if someone is there and one at the crib to tell her if the baby is crying. In *No More Stares*, disabled mothers can observe, through the photographs, how some of their disabled peers do parenting (Carrillo *et al.*, 1982).

Transportation and the Disabled Mother

As so many disabled mothers are heads of households, they often have to do the shopping themselves. Homemakers with mobility, visual, or auditory impairments are often obliged to make heavy use of catalogs, personal shoppers, or local stores that will take phone orders and deliver.

Shopping is not the only reason extensive transportation is needed. Disabled women need access to medical and dental care for themselves and their children, access to schools, camp, day care, and the other components of modern life. Some independent disabled women use an adapted van or have modified car controls, either of which is costly. The absence of affordable, adapted transportation necessitates heavy taxi costs or the awesome prospect of going long distances by wheelchair or on crutches.

As an example of how complex the transportation problem can be, a blind woman reported on her efforts after deciding to surprise her husband at the airport. With her 4-year-old and 2-year-old on tethers, a diaper bag over one shoulder and purse over the other, and her white cane in hand, she walked to one bus, changed to another, and next sought out a limousine, then located, at some distance, the gate where he would deplane (Kendrick, 1983, p. 19). Even if women are able to transport children in their own cars, they may find that access to some shops, libraries, museums, and so on, may be beyond their capability, if ramps or elevators (in working order) are not provided or if designated parking spaces have been appropriated by others.

Day-Care

What is particularly galling to the disabled mother is lack of access to child-care centers (Glass, 1982). The disabled mother may need respite for personal reasons, and she may require child care if she works at home or obtains external employment. If there are limitations to the enriching experiences she can provide for her children, the social and psychological benefits of day-care become especially important.

A blind woman reported:

> We moved to the suburbs from Brooklyn when she [the baby] was about 10 months old and, until she began nursery school at 2, . . . I was trapped in this house with no adult companionship except my husband. When she enrolled in a cooperative nursery school . . . , I began to meet people and my whole life changed. [It] was a way of breaking down the isolation of living in a suburban area with a little kid when you couldn't drive. (Riggs & Baskin, unpublished)

Support Networks

Many women have learned to rely on support networks to help them in the activities of daily life (Brown, 1984; Green, 1984). These women share advice about how to deal with recalcitrant agencies, how to solve problems of child care, where to find resources, and they give one another general emotional support (Daley, Kaplan, & Hochberg, 1983; Ellis & Sewell, 1984; Women and Disability Awareness Project, 1984).

MOTHERHOOD AND THE DISABLED WOMAN

The trials of disabled mothers are daunting and dispiriting. Their survival, and even successes, are a testament to their incredible determination to prevail. Many face abandonment by their husbands, humiliation at home. One woman told her daughter-in-law (after hearing about her miscarriage), "Blind people aren't meant to have children" (Asrael, 1982, p. 214). Expectant mothers hear doctors say their children will hate them when they grow up (Matthews, 1983). They are confronted with physical as well as psychological barriers in their daily lives.

What is even more astonishing is that the prejudice of researchers about the parenting abilities of the disabled has been allowed to stand unchallenged. A thorough examination was made of the literature relating to parental disability and child adjustment and the results were reported in the *Annual Review of Rehabilitation*. Criticizing those previous studies because of serious methodological inadequacies, as well as their limited scope, Buck and Hohmann (1983) conclude that:

> The widespread belief among professionals that disability severely limits parenting ability and often leads to maladjustment in children . . . has not been supported by

well-designed studies. We believe [that there] is a negative bias in . . . the consensus
of opinion and uniformity of the hypothesized ill effects of parental disability on
children, despite the absence of empirical evidence to support them. (p. 204)

In fact, they assert that:

Methodologically acceptable data available to date demonstrate that disabled parents
can successfully raise children and that their children as adults are normal, well-
adjusted individuals. (p. 237)

One parent remarked:

I can't see any place where the disability was harmful to my family. Sure, I had to be
inventive about holding, lifting and handling my children. As my sons became older,
they began to carry things for me, help out. I think it was good for them, helped them
mature. (Carrillo *et al.*, 1982, p. 98)

Indeed, it would not be very difficult to hypothesize that women who
assumed the maternal role were essentially those who had reached adulthood
by overcoming innumerable roadblocks in their own lives and, by so doing, had
learned how to bypass obstacles. Many reported that, as they planned their own
pathways pragmatically and efficiently, so they learned to cope with their children's crises. Blind mothers, for instance, color code their children's clothing as
they do their own. They braille baby food labels, medications, poisons, and so
on, for their own and their children's protection. They read to their young
children by using twin vision books (facing pages are braille and print), scratch
and sniff books, or use audio tapes (Baskin & Harris, 1984). They correctly give
allowance money since they know the shapes of coins and fold bills differently
by denomination. Owen (1983) learned skills during rehabilitation that she later
applied to her domestic demands. She learned how to use a braille watch and
thermometer, how to read temperatures and settings on electrical equipment,
how to sew by hand or by machine, even how to use a lathe, which she subsequently used to make furniture.

Other disabled women raise both psychological issues and practical ones for
the visually impaired parent. A blind woman commented:

I learned that you have to have ways of circumventing difficulties. Your whole life is
involved with doing that, and we were highly motivated to be successful parents.
(Riggs & Baskin, unpublished)

Another mother added:

Travel and mobility for blind parents is a problem because a child wants to be cared for
and secure. It's very frightening for a kid to be with an adult, traveling in a strange
situation when that adult isn't in control and needs help. When you are blind . . . , you
must ask for information from sighted people and this makes the child feel you are not
in control. (Riggs & Baskin, unpublished)

Blindness involves small frustrations as well as the obvious ones—trying to
locate a lost toy for a crying child, ascertaining whether homework is indeed
done, noticing when a child is pale or apathetic, etc. At those moments, blind
mothers figure out an alternative solution, ask for assistance from another child
or family member. Frequently, someone in their support network can suggest

ways to handle the problem (Arsnow, Dichiera, Mould, Sauerburger, & Peaco, 1985).

Effects of Children on Mothers

Many women report that having to deal with the ongoing demands of children strengthened their resolve to go on with their lives, despite pain, loneliness, or despair. BM (personal communication, September 4, 1985) recalled that with an iron lung outside her room, she kept her spirits up while acutely ill with polio by gazing at her child's picture. She intensified her will to recover by thinking about her commitment to her 2 year old. During her speech therapy period, only her daughter seemed to be able to understand her garbled speech.

D. spoke of the pleasure she got from breast feeding her son and the sense of being, for once, the giver not the receiver of care. The blind woman explained: "Tactile sensation has been emphasized for a handicapped baby, but it's just as important for a handicapped parent." She added, "It was the one thing I could do that nobody else could" (Orlansky & Heward, 1981, p. 131).

Davies (1981) considers the tasks associated with raising children as "occupational therapy." She reported that, with the assistance of a loving husband and friends, she raised four children:

> They never [catered] to me and . . . they expected school uniforms, sports gear, and jeans to be washed, ironed, and mended whenever necessary. This attitude was invaluable because . . . keeping four children fed and clothed ensured against me giving up the battle (against severe rheumatoid arthritis], and encouraged me to fight on when it would have been only too easy to throw in the towel. (p. 2ABPN)

Her children ignored her awkwardness and responded with humor to various predicaments. Once when she returned home from the hospital with her wrists fused and pinned, one remarked, "Poor mum is working her fingers to the metal!"

Children's Responses to Maternal Disability

Cogswell (1976), in *The Sociology of Disability*, concluded from her examination of such families that assuming responsibility contributed to the positive self-image of youngsters and that there was apparently little resentment about peforming additional tasks. Concerns about mortality prompted one couple to promote independence in their children (Shaul, Dowling, & Laden, 1985). Peterson (1974), a deaf mother, believed that, although her children were often exasperated at having to repeat conversations, it ultimately helped them express their own thoughts better. Further, she insisted that the children interpret when they all were with hearing people. The youngsters also interpreted television news programs, corrected their parents' pronunciation, and made business calls for them.

Kendrick's inability to see required certain behaviors from her children. They were always to keep pathways clear, avoid leaving any objects on a stairway, and come to her immediately when called (1983).

In her excellent book of interviews with disabled Canadian women, Matthews (1983) provides harrowing accounts of how determined these women were about caring for their children. One woman confessed to being terrified she would drop her child:

> To leave my hands free to push my wheelchair, I used to wrap her in a receiving blanket and carry her around in my teeth. Her body rested in my lap. . . . I even shopped with her that way, until she was old enough to sit in the cart.

Hale (1979) believes that most of the practical problems of being a disabled parent are limited to the child's early years. She comments:

> Rather than depending on threats of punishment, which a disability can make difficult to implement, it's far better to develop your own powers of persuasion and to rely . . . on the cooperative behavior of the child. (p. 163)

The age of children, asserts Green (1984, p. 10), also plays a decisive role in their reactions to impairment. Her youngest played crawling games with her but her oldest viewed her mother's multiple sclerosis with distaste because it brought additional responsibility as well as embarrassment. In a therapeutic workshop, the girl wrote the following: "Work, Work, Work. I have to do my mother's work. That's what MS means to me."

Sometimes, seemingly minor issues disturb children. Nettie said, "my daughter has had great difficulty accepting my [blindness]—she doesn't want to admit it. One of the things she resented is that it's hard for me to light the candles on her birthday cake." (Riggs & Baskin, unpublished). In the same study, Molly, a mobility-impaired mother, reinforced that concern:

> Reflecting back when my children were young and inquisitive, I regret not being more open and relaxed about my disability. My advice to a young disabled mother would be to discuss her disability with her children and provide the environment for them to feel comfortable [enough] to share their concerns, fears, and feelings.

Adolescent years are difficult, but for adults with disabilities, unique problems arise. A social worker polled blind parents to identify those concerns. He discovered: (a) Sighted parents can obtain and verify information at a glance, blind parents have to rely more on trust; (b) sighted parents can ascertain whether the child's appearance is appropriate (blind parents cannot tell if the child is dirty, has too much makeup); (c) blind parents tend to ask sighted children to drive them places, creating a sense of dependency; (d) there is reliance on children to read to parents, even including certain papers parents would like to keep private (Arsnow et al., 1985).

Two personal accounts from No More Stares highlight stories of role reversal between parent and child. Overwhelmed by a sense of self-defeat and despair, a young woman responded negatively to her son's inquiry about when she was going to walk. He declared, "I'm going to make you get up and put your braces on." Even more dramatic was the account of a woman who became quadriplegic after being shot. She refused advice about relinquishing responsibility for her

2½-year-old triplets, who subsequently cooperated in cleanups and would help her if she fell. She claimed that without such assistance, she "wouldn't have made it" (Carrillo et al., 1982, p. 99).

On the other hand, some women perceived themselves as failures in their maternal role. A woman with multiple sclerosis expressed her feelings of inadequacy and her poor relationship with three teenage sons. Her sense of depression was exacerbated when her husband exchanged his good job for a less lucrative one so he could care for her at night, and subsequently was fired (Matthews, 1983). But on the whole there are more successes than failures reported in the literature. The self-reports may be biased toward favorable accounts of the mother–child dyad, but these personal statements are supported by studies that tend to reaffirm essentially constructive relationships.

Two parents comment on some of the particular features of these relationships. A mother who is blind asserts:

> My children have learned to see the strengths in a human being, and not to concentrate on what a person lacks. Already the payoffs are apparent. Both my children have chosen playmates from different racial groups, and they are also attracted to a cross-section of adults—including some with disabilities. (Kendrick, 1983, p. 18)

LeMaistre (1985) movingly sums up the impact a mother's disability has on her children:

> I've come to realize that we may give our children something which is uniquely the result of our . . . disabilities. If we are self-accepting, our children will learn not to be afraid of disabled people, will admire and wish to emulate the strength in our daily struggle, and will accept for an entire lifetime the simple but too often hidden fact that there are no perfect people, no perfect lives, and that physical distress is very much a part of living. To our children, we can give a zest for human contact and the examples of myriad ways in which it is possible to get going productively when the going gets very rough indeed. To have a hand in producing emotional resilience, compassion, and the willingness to set reasonable goals for oneself is a very fine expression of parental love. (p. 291)

E. C., a woman with a degenerative nerve disease, believes her children are better people in that they've observed her problems and her ability to cope. She adds, "They are proud of the things I've done [and] they're fighters too" (Riggs & Baskin, unpublished). A woman who became a paraplegic after a ski accident reports that although her teenage sons are sometimes embarrassed by her condition and frequently irritated by the demands she must make on them, they are also occasionally "lovingly helpful," and she believes they are now more mature, sensitive, responsible, and aware of others as a result of learning to cope with the problems presented by their mother (Riggs & Baskin, unpublished).

In sum, Vash (1981) concludes that:

> The children of reasonably well-adjusted [disabled] parents differ from children of nondisabled parents mainly in that they are more affectionate and appreciative toward their parents and more responsible or mature than the typical child of the same age. (p. 68)

RECOMMENDATIONS FOR FUTURE RESEARCH

We need cross-disciplinary, longitudinal, and comprehensive studies to develop a multidimensional portrait of this group.

First, basic demographic data on disabled mothers must be obtained: prevalence, age, race, marital status, educational achievement, number of children, particular disability and age at onset, etc., and the interrelationships among these variables. Much more information is needed on family characteristics: sex experiences; courting; marriage, birth control, pregnancy, and childbearing; roles and decision making; contributions of teachers, counselors, social workers, and therapists; family stresses, including deteriorating physical conditions, illness, unemployment, child care, and availability of aides; the role and the influence of friends, church, networks, government assistance; employment data; etc.

This chapter summarizes much of what is available. What emerges is a mosaic of small-scale reports, modest and limited, rather than in-depth, carefully monitored investigations. Both microscopic and macroscopic studies must be undertaken. What is needed is a large-scale, long-term examination of the lives of disabled women.

Disabled Mothers' Responses to Maternity

In a collateral unpublished study, the authors interviewed numerous disabled mothers. The second author, herself a disabled mother of two, synthesized the responses she received to the question: What does it mean to be a handicapped mother?

For every woman, giving birth represents a watershed: she will never be quite the same again. For the woman with disabilities, there are added dimensions to the experience. Giving birth represents a kind of validation: this child proves that her imperfect body can function as it was meant to. This child is a connecting link to all women, indeed to the human race in all its variations and imperfections.

Her pregnancy may have been more difficult than the norm. She may have had to battle her own doubts as well as those of her doctor and family. Can you hear your baby cry? Can you see the baby's rash? Can you carry an infant safely when you can barely get around yourself? These are valid concerns and in the still of the night these questions gnaw at her, for she knows she has no easy answers.

Birth itself challenges the musculature as never before. By successfully bringing forth a child, the disabled woman may feel ineffable elation and, perhaps for the first time, a pride in her body.

Although all parents take pleasure in their newborns, the experience of the disabled mother is particularly emotional. The woman may have placed her own life in jeopardy by the pregnancy, she may have wondered about the impact of the disorder on her child, she may have questioned the potential burden the newcomer would place on her marriage.

As the baby grows, new problems arise. Disabled mothers are ingenious at finding ways to cope with the physical problems of their disorder, but they may not anticipate the social implications for their school-age child. Children are notoriously conventional; they feel anguish at being "different" in any way, and this includes having a mother who is "different." They may feel embarrassment at being seen with her and at the same time feel shame for being disloyal to a dearly loved parent. Mothers need to be aware of these natural but painful feelings.

Another danger is that the mother in her need may lean too much on the child, may unwittingly take advantage of the child's love and willingness to help. There is a fine line between every child's need to feel truly useful, a fully functioning member of the family, and the need to feel that parents are strong enough to direct and control their lives without any help from the child. If this delicate balance is maintained, disabled mothers often find that their children actually benefit from the experience of being needed.

It is most important to note that among disabled mothers the similarities are more striking than the differences. Disabled or not, a mother is first and foremost: a mother.

REFERENCES

Arsnow, G. A., Dichiera, J., Mould, L., Sauerburger, D., & Peaco, F. (1985). Blind parents rearing sighted children. *Journal of Visual Impairment and Blindness, 79*, 193–198.

Asrael, W. (1982). An approach to motherhood for disabled women. *Rehabilitation Literature, 43*, 214–218.

Baskin, B. H., & Harris, K. H. (Eds.). (1984). *The mainstreamed library: Issues, ideas, innovations.* Chicago: American Library Association.

Bingham, B. (1985). *Cooking with fragile hands: Kitchen help for arthritics.* Naples, FL: Creative Cuisine Press.

Bird, C. (1979). What women want. New York: Simon & Schuster.

Bopp, R. E. (1981). Consumer publications for disabled persons. *Ilinois Libraries, 63*, 540–546.

Brown, D. (1981). Jobs are disabled women: Double discrimination and little help from the women's movement. *Disabled USA, 4*, 20–21.

Brown, D. (1984). Self-help groups for learning disabled people and the rehabilitation process. *Journal of Rehabilitation, 50*(9), 92–93.

Buck, F. M., & Hohmann, T. W. (1983). Parental disability and children's adjustment. In E. Pan, T. Backer, & C. Vash, (Eds.), *Annual Review of Rehabilitation, 3*, 203–241.

Campling, J. (1979). *Better lives for disabled women.* London: Virago.

Campling, J. (Ed.). (1981). *Images of ourselves: Women with disabilities talking.* Henley-on-Thames: Routledge & Kegan Paul.

Carrick, M., & Bibb, T. (1982). Women and rehabilitation of disabled persons: Disabled women and access to benefits and services. Report of the Mary E. Switzer Memorial Seminar, *6*, 28–35.

Carrillo, A. C., Corbett, K., & Lewis, V. (1982). *No more stares.* Berkeley: Disability Rights Education and Defense Fund.

Cogswell, B. E. (1976). Conceptual model of family as a group: Family responses to disability. In G. L. Albrecht (Ed.), *The sociology of physical disability* (pp. 139–168). Pittsburgh: University of Pittsburgh Press.

Connors, D. (1985). Disability, sexism, and the social order. In S. E. Browne, D. Connors, & N. Stern (Eds.), *With the power of each breath* (pp. 92–107). Pittsburgh: Cleis.

Corbett, K., & Forschl, M. (1983). Access to the future: Serving disabled young women. In S. Davidson (Ed.), *The second mile: Contemporary approaches in counseling young women* (pp. 161–181). Tucson: New Directions for Young Women.

Corbett, K. J., & Weeks, C. (1981). Invisible women. *Off Our Backs, 11,* 6–7.

Dailey, A. L. T. (1979). Physically handicapped women. *Counseling Psychologist, 8,* 41–43.

Daley, E., Kaplan, C. (Producers), & Hochberg, V. (Director). (1983). *Tell them I'm a mermaid* [Film]. Hollywood, CA: KTTV & Mark Taper Forum.

Davies, H. A. (1981). A disabled mother. *Nursing Times, 77,* 2 ABPN.

Ellis, R. J., & Sewell, J. C. (1984). Sensible products. *Disabled USA, 2,* 32–35.

Fink, S. L., Skipper, J. K., Jr., & Hallenbeck, P. N. (1968). Physical disability and problems in marriage. *Journal of Marriage and the Family, 30,* 64–73.

Franklin, P. A. (1977). Impact of disability on the family structure. *Social Security Bulletin, 40,* 3–18. *Disabled USA, 2,* 16–18.

Gillespie, P. H., & Fink, A. H. (1974). The influence of sexism on the education of handicapped children. *Exceptional Children, 41,* 155–161.

Glass, R. (1982). Meeting the program needs of women: Mainstream child care. *Rehabilitation Literature, 7–8,* 220–221.

Green, C. (1984). An exchange of feelings. *Disabled USA, 2,* 8–9.

Gross, J. (1986, February 12). Having children despite illness. *New York Times,* pp. C1, C10.

Hale, G. (Ed.). (1979). *The source book for the disabled.* New York: Paddington.

Holcomb, L. P. (1984). Disabled women: A new issue in education. *Journal of Rehabilitation, 50,* 18–22.

Kendrick, D. (1983). Invisible barriers: How you can make barriers easier. *Disabled USA, 1,* 17–19.

Kutza, E. A. (1981). Benefits for the disabled: How beneficial for women? *Journal of Sociology and Social Welfare, 8,* 194–215.

Le Maistre, J. (1985). Parenting. In S. E. Browne, D. Connors, & N. Stern (Eds.), *With the power of each breath* (pp. 284–291). Pittsburgh: Cleis.

Maine Association of Handicapped Persons (1984, May). Handicapped people and sex: Disabled people speak about experiences. *Coping, 4,* pp. 6–7, 11.

Matthews, G. F. (Ed.). (1983). *Voices from the shadows: Women with disabilities speak out.* Toronto: Women's Press.

Merchant, M. (1969). Homemaking time use of homemakers confined to wheelchairs. Unpublished master's thesis. University of Nebraska.

Nagi, S. Z., & Clark, D. L. (1964). Factors in marital adjustment after disability. *Journal of Marriage and the Family, 26,* 215–216.

Neel, C. E. (1981). Surviving our society with its limitations. *Off Our Backs, 11,* 12–13.

Orlansky, M. D., & Heward, W. L. (Eds.). (1981). *Voices: Interviews with handicapped people.* Columbus, OH: Merrill.

Owen, M. J. (1983). Doors are for opening. *Disabled USA, 1,* 1–5.

Peterson, R. (1974). The deaf woman as wife and mother: Two views. *Rehabilitation Journal, 5,* 21–22.

Phillips, M. J. (1984, December). *Straight talk from "crooked women."* Paper presented at the Barnard College Meeting, Women and Disability.

Rezen, S. V., & Housman, C. (1985). *Coping with hearing loss: A guide for adults and their families.* New York: Dember.

Robinault, I. P. (1978). *Sex, society and the disabled: A developmental inquiry into role, reactions, and responsibilities.* Hagerstown, MD: Harper & Row.

Rosenstein, J., & Lerman, A. (1963). *Vocational status and adjustment of deaf women.* New York: Lexington School for the Deaf.

Shaul, S., Bogle, J., & Norman, A. D. (1977). *Toward intimacy: Family planning and sexuality concerns of physically disabled women.* Everett, WA: Planned Parenthood.

Shaul, S., Dowling, P. J., & Laden, B. F. (1985). Like other women: Perspectives of mothers with physical disabilities. In M. J. Deegan & N. A. Brooks (Eds.), *Women and disability: The double handicap* (pp. 133–142). New Brunswick, NJ: Transaction.

Thurer, S. L. (1982). Women and rehabilitation. *Rehabilitation Literature, 43*, 194–197.

Turk, R., Turk, M., & Assejev, V. (1983). The female paraplegic and mother–child relations. *Paraplegia, 21*, 186–191.

U.S. Department of Labor, Women's Bureau. (1985, July). *Working age disabled women*, Fact Sheet #85-3.

Vash, C. L. (1981). *The psychology of disability*. New York: Springer.

Vash, C. L. (1982). Employment issues for women with disabilities. *Rehabilitation Literature, 43*, 198–207.

Women and Disability Awareness Project. (1984). *Building community: A manual exploring issues of women and disability*. New York: Educational Equity Concepts.

CHAPTER 11

Delayed Motherhood

JOAN F. KUCHNER AND JANE PORCINO

The trend in the 1950s was to have large families (Ford, 1981). It was considered the "American thing to do." As politicians and the mass media waved the banner of home and hearth and sang the idealized virtues of motherhood (Margolis, 1984), women felt this as a personal call. World War II had disrupted their lives, and they had a strong need to be surrounded by the security of family (Daniels & Weingarten, 1982). Although many women who had entered the labor force during the war years returned to full-time homemaking in response to the cultural and inner directives (Margolis, 1984), others remained in the workforce. For the most part, those women employed outside of their homes became part of the economy's expanding service sector, taking on roles compatible with the image of women as caretakers and nurturers (Margolis, 1984). The conditional approval of women's work outside the home was based on the idea that the woman's income helped the family by providing for extra discretionary indulgences (Margolis, 1984). Today, these items are viewed as necessities.

In the 1950s, the ideal for women was to marry early and have children. Women as homemakers had babies and juggled jobs but generally did not define this choice as "having a career" (Daniels & Weingarten, 1982). Between the 1950s and the 1960s, the ideal age for starting a family began to shift, particularly for college-bound women who planned a pause between marriage and children (Daniels & Weingarten, 1982). The "baby boom" of the 1950s ended 10 years later, as women across all sectors of the population acted on their desire to limit their family size (Belsky, Lerner, & Spanier, 1984), encouraged by the ease and availability of improved methods of birth control, as well as the option of a legal therapeutic abortion (Wilkie, 1981). A rising economy plummeted more and more married women into the workforce in order to provide the housing, clothing, and education associated with the secure middle-class life that was envisioned for these planned children.

By the late 1970s, the two-income family was becoming the norm (Margolis,

JOAN F. KUCHNER • Social Science Interdisciplinary Program, State University of New York, Stony Brook, New York 11794.   JANE PORCINO • Continuing Education Department, State University of New York, Stony Brook, New York 11794.

1984), and the clinical literature was beginning to echo the strains on these dual-career families (Moulton, 1979). As women postponed childbirth in order to pursue a career and/or education, the overall fertility rate in the United States dropped (Wilkie, 1981). Two decades ago, approximately 76% of women ages 31 to 35 had given birth to their first child by age 25 (U.S. Bureau of the Census, 1978). However, in 1985, only 39% of ever-married women had become mothers before reaching 25 years of age (U.S. Bureau of the Census, 1987). Women of today are caught in a historically unique conundrum, deciding whether or not to commit themselves to motherhood (Potts, 1980). The attempt to understand the motivations to parent has by itself generated a significant body of research (Rapoport, Rapoport, & Strelitz, 1980).

The stress of this struggle for mid-life couples is documented in the personal revelations gathered by Leah Potts (1980) in the context of group discussion. The basic ambivalence expressed by 40 self-selected primarily middle-class professionals between 28 and 34 years old is a testimony to the conflicts that surface in this decision process.

The recurring need to weigh the potentially disruptive elements of parenting against the problematic pleasures of raising a child was similarly voiced by the 24 white, childless, married middle-class career women, 27 to 35 years old, studied by Carole Wilk (1986). In addition to individual interviews, she used two projective instruments in order to expose hidden or camouflaged feelings about spouse, parents, and self that might not have been revealed in the interview process.

However, research examining the effect of delaying motherhood until mid-life is itself in its infancy. A computer literature search covering the past 10 years revealed fewer than 10 references to the psychological or sociological aspects of postponed parenting.

The ground-breaking study of Pamela Daniels and Kathy Weingarten (1982) was the first to explore the impact of the timing of parenthood on adults' perceptions of the experience. These researchers interviewed three groups of couples: (a) early-timing parents, who had their first child in their late teens and early 20s; (b) late-timing parents, who first became parents in their late 20s and early 30s; and (c) mid-life parents, who began parenting in their late 30s and early 40s. The personal accounts, memories, and feelings of 86 white parents from a cross-section of occupations, incomes, and age cohorts is the only available baseline data on this range of family groups.

Steven Frankel and Myra Wise's (1982) more narrowly focused account is based on selected professional women and their husbands. They interviewed 15 older mothers, who were on the average 36 years old before the birth of their first child, and 10 "on-time" mothers between the ages of 23 and 29 at the birth of their first child. The women as well as their husbands were asked to reflect on the experiences surrounding their changed role as parents.

The most recent study is an in-depth look at the current generation of mothers conducted by Carolyn Walters (1986). Early-timing mothers (women 19 to 25 years of age at the birth of their first child) and late-timing mothers (30 to 41 years of age when they first became mothers) probed their own attitudes, feelings, and beliefs through the medium of semistructured small group discussions complemented by an individual questionnaire and an adjective checklist. A core group of 53 self-selected women participated in Walters' (1986) age-limited discussion groups. Along with the core group, an additional 27 mothers from similar urban and suburban communities completed the questionnaire and the adjective checklist.

This initial research has studied a remarkably homogeneous population of predominantly white, married, and middle- to upper-middle-class women. Drawing on the limited research that focuses on first-time mothering as a mid-life option, this chapter explores the issues surrounding postponed childbearing and the concerns of women who delay motherhood until their mid 30s and beyond.

MOTHERHOOD AS A DECISION

Postponing Motherhood

Motherhood was rarely viewed as a decision among early-timing and "on-time" mothers (Daniels & Weingarten, 1982; Frankel & Wise, 1982; Walters, 1986). In this sense, younger mothers appeared to be less aware of a conscious choice (Frankel & Wise, 1982). Motherhood was experienced as a natural progression following marriage (Daniels & Weingarten, 1982).

The decision to delay childbearing until mid-life is often the result of a two-tiered process. A decision to postpone conception is followed by a frequently more difficult decision to have a child. For some "late-blooming" mothers, the postponement of childbearing into their fourth decade is the outcome of a well-articulated conscious choice (Daniels & Weingarten, 1982; Frankel & Wise, 1982; Wilk, 1986). Many of these women appear to respond to the idea of becoming a young mother by conjuring the image of their mothers' generation learned firsthand or filtered through the media (Potts, 1980; Wilk, 1986). They acknowledge women locked into intolerable marriages for the sake of children hastily conceived (Wilk, 1986). They recall women with no time or resources to care for themselves (Potts, 1980; Wilk, 1986). They describe divorced or widowed women without marketable skills or women who are ill equipped to fill their time once children leave home (Wilk, 1986). Reacting against a perceived void in their own mothers' lives, these women seek to establish an autonomous life for themselves before beginning the task of parenting (Daniels & Weingarten, 1982; Frankel & Wise, 1982; Potts, 1980; Wilk, 1986). An increasing expectation that a woman will be employed outside the home during a substantial portion of her life may also influence these young women to consider the option of solidifying career objectives before raising children (Wilkie, 1981).

Delaying the Decision

Even when couples discuss the potential options of parenting prior to marriage, the decision of whether or not to have children may be postponed

(Daniels & Weingarten, 1982; Potts, 1980; Wilk, 1986). At times, this deferral itself becomes the issue. Women contemplating motherhood question whether their own health or their child's will be jeopardized by a later-life pregnancy (Daniels & Weingarten, 1982; Fabe & Wikler, 1979; Potts, 1980). They are concerned with the social consequences of continued delay, how their children might feel about having older parents, or how friends may respond to this change in status (Fabe & Wikler, 1979). The problem of placing an age deadline on when to decide may be compounded by the concern for the "irrevocable nature" of this decision (Potts, 1980). Wilk (1986) found that women in their late 20s placed the decision deadline at 30 years old; whereas women in their 30s felt that they could continue to postpone making a definitive decision about childbearing until their late 30s, easing that limit up to 40 years old with increasing age. The first-birth rate of women age 35 to 39 years old has increased by 8% since 1972 (Resnick, 1986). For the 40- to 44-year-old age group, this rate has increased by 33% within the same time period (Resnick, 1986).

Choosing the Right Time

Among career women contemplating motherhood in their 30s, there is very little agreement about the right time to have a baby (Wilk, 1986). The decision to become pregnant while maintaining continued involvement in the world of work is fraught with uncertainty. Thus, this *decision* may prove to be more difficult than the initial desire to postpone parenting.

The concern that maternity is a threat to career momentum may still be well founded in today's climate (Wilkie, 1981). Women contemplating pregnancy express awareness that their appearance alone may have an adverse effect on their acceptability in the workplace (Wilk, 1986). The physical reminder of their impending change in status may promote others to consider them less serious about their profession (Wilk, 1986).

Both women and the men in their lives were apprehensive that a child would have a negative impact on their life-style and intrude on their relationship with each other (Potts, 1980; Wilk, 1986). Women expressed doubt that they had the emotional resources to expend on a child (Potts, 1980; Wilk, 1986). Wilk (1986) found that the women she interviewed expressed these same doubts in financial terms. The need for two incomes to meet financial commitments, particularly home mortgages, was voiced by many women (Potts, 1980; Wilk, 1986; Wilkie, 1981).

For many career women, the establishment of nontraditional roles involved an extensive struggle. They believe that pregnancy and motherhood will tip a delicate domestic balance, throwing them back into the traditional role of housekeeper (Fabe & Wikler, 1979). Women expressed discomfort with the specter of financial dependence should they opt to stay at home (Rubin, 1980). At the same time, they are concerned about the high cost as well as the scarcity of quality child care, which they perceive as necessary to ensure continued involvement with their career (Wilk, 1986). The stress for mothers that surrounds maintaining quality child-care arrangements is well documented (Bronfenbrenner & Crouter,

1982; Clarke-Stewart, 1982). However, for many of these women the concern for loss of personal privacy and private time for the couple appears to stand out even when economic pressures are not paramount and child-care issues are put aside.

Finding Role Models

The complexity of a woman's conflict may be accentuated by her perception of her own mother. Women seriously considering remaining childless expressed a fear of replicating the undesirable qualities of their own mother (Kaltreider & Margolis, 1977; Moulton, 1979; Potts, 1980), while those beginning to decide to bear children felt guilty about the possibility of being better than their own mother in the area of parenting (Potts, 1980). Wilk (1986) found that images of lost youth and inevitable death were also associated with the decision process. Adding to the delicacy of the decision is the possibility that the would-be father's desire to reproduce will be interpreted as an insensitivity to the intrapsychic needs of the woman.

Wilk (1986) found that the availability of a familial role model who successfully combined childrearing and a commitment to work, whether defined as a career or a job, facilitated a woman's decision to parent. Women in Wilk's (1986) study who reported a high level of satisfaction with their career did not feel that an addition of a baby would dramatically change their professional development. But they did anticipate that their career course might evolve in a different direction as they combined childrearing and work commitments.

Answering the Question "Why Have Children?"

Given the apparent benefits to childlessness the question remains, why bear and raise children? The traditional definition of a family as adults with children is a powerful normative influence, despite the increasing prevalence of alternative life choices (Fabe & Wikler, 1979; Rapoport et al., 1980). The decision to have a child, at any age, is formed around a variety of individual conscious and unconscious motivating forces (Rapoport et al., 1980). These may include the desire to maintain family continuity, an attempt to resolve issues of one's identity in relationship to parents, a need to have someone to love who will love in return, the search for a purpose for work or for life, and the insurance of someone to provide care in later life. Most of the women in both Wilk's (1986) and Potts' (1980) studies recognized a nonrational element in their decision process. Issues of sexual identity may be one unconscious component (Moulton, 1979; Wilk, 1986). In some cases, women perceive a child as a public proclamation of sexual maturity (Moulton, 1979). For other women, pregnancy is symbolically associated with a loss of sexuality (Wilk, 1986). In this regard, Wilk (1986) found that career women who had made a clear-cut decision to have children were comfortable with both the nurturant and sexual components of their identity as women.

Disillusionment with the world of work may precipitate a childbearing decision (McCauley, 1976). Alternatively, the decision to have a child later in life may represent a reassessment of values. As part of a mid-life review of priorities, women who previously had focused on career achievement may begin to look for an opportunity to connect to the rest of the world, to add a new dimension to their lives (Walters, 1986), to try to experience everything that is open to them as women, "to have it all." As one woman said:

> I was married when I was 38, and had my first baby at 40. I'd been working for 23 years, and the only thing I thought I was missing was a child. Otherwise I was very happy, and might never have married.

Or as another mid-life mother described her decision, "My marriage was good and my career secure. And yet I had an overwhelming feeling that I wanted more: I needed to have a baby."

Delayed motherhood is not always voluntary. Daniels and Weingarten (1982) found that for 77% of the mid-life women in their sample, motherhood was postponed for lack of a suitable partner or for infertility. As one woman recently interviewed put it, "I simply didn't find anyone I wanted to marry until I was 35."

Whereas the specter of a biological clock winding down may cast a shadow on individual decision making, it is usually interpreted as a foreboding of risk for infant or mother (Wilk, 1986) and not in terms of decreased fertility. Yet, in spite of the medical profession's increasing ability to stretch the limits of a woman's reproductive years, it is statistically more difficult for a woman in her mid 30s to conceive a child than it is for a younger woman (Davajan & Mishell, 1986). For the woman who has planned her life and has finally decided that she is ready for motherhood, the loss of personal control symbolized by the difficulties encountered in becoming pregnant may prove an additional burden to combat in the quest for motherhood.

MEDICAL PROBLEMS OF DELAYED MOTHERHOOD

Infertility

One of the major problems of postponing childbearing is the risk of decreased fertility. Approximately 10% of American couples are infertile (those who have failed to conceive after a year or more of trying) (Davajan & Mishell, 1986; Reeder, Mastroianni, & Martin, 1983). Although fertility in women exhibits a substantial decline after 35 years of age (Davajan & Mishell, 1986), it is the intersection of age, health, and fertility that is the most critical. Aging increases the likelihood that accidents and/or a wide range of illness will occur that will ultimately affect fertility (Dewhurst, 1981). From 30 to 50% of infertility problems have been attributed to endometriosis (in which the tissue that normally grows in the uterine wall has been displaced to other locations), fibroid tumors, and infections (Davajan & Mishell, 1986). Although a man may continue to produce sperm well into his later years (Nieschlag & Michel, 1986), a drop in hormone levels, exposure to toxic environmental chemicals, infections, chronic disease, and stress affect male fertility in mid and later life (Davajan & Mishell, 1986). Female fertility rates are thus combined with potentially lower rates for the older male partner.

Treatment is available for some forms of male and female infertility. Surgical procedures will often correct structural problems. Naturally occurring and synthetically produced hormones may be effective in stimulating ovulation even in mid-life women (Davajan & Mishell, 1986). A 23% spontaneous cure rate for infertility has also been reported (Davajan & Mishell, 1986). Increased medical knowledge and technology, such as *in vitro* fertilization, have raised the hopes of women who in earlier decades would have certainly faced a childless future. However, this hope cannot always be realized. Incidences of miscarriage increase dramatically in women over 35, with the neonatal mortality rate reaching 30% of live births in women over 45 years old (Danforth & Scott, 1986; McCarthy, 1987).

Risks to the Child

A decision to postpone childbearing to the years after age 30 includes accepting not only increased risks of neonatal death, but also increased probability of chromosomal and congenital abnormalities. The occurrence of Down's syndrome, which is associated with mental retardation, heart disease, hypothyroidism, and immunological disorders, is the most frequent chromosomal anomaly. Incidence of Down's syndrome begins to rise dramatically after the mother reaches 30, increasing from 1 in 2400 conceptions for mothers 15 to 19 years old to 1 in 109 for mothers age 40, and 1 in 32 conceptions among mothers 45 years old (NIH, 1979). Recent techniques that permit the identification of the source of the extra chromosome also point to a correlation between Down's syndrome and advanced paternal age (Hook, 1986; Iffy & Kaminetzky, 1981). Other chromosomal abnormalities also occur with increased frequency in mothers over 40 (Fraser, 1984).

Although the exact nature of the intervening variables is not clear, studies of children born to women over 35 suggest that these children continue to be at risk for problems beyond infancy, including increased frequency of fine motor problems, visual–perceptual dysfunction, attentional problems, and incidence of Type I diabetes mellitus in childhood (Resnik, 1986).

Major advances in human genetic diagnosis, particularly amniocentesis and chorionic villus sampling, permit chromosomal analysis of the fetus in the early stages of pregnancy but cannot detect the presence of many congenital abnormalities. In amniocentesis, a needle is inserted through the mother's abdominal wall, guided by concurrent ultrasound imaging of the fetus, and amniotic fluid containing fetal cells is withdrawn (Reeder et al., 1983). This technique enables professionals to detect the presence of trisomy 21 (the cause of Down's syndrome), as well as 40 other potentially life-threatening genetically controlled abnormalities, with diagnostic accuracy of close to 100% (Latt, 1984). Although the procedure of amniocentesis can safely be performed between the 15th to

19th week of pregnancy, the results are not known until 4 weeks later. In addition, the procedure itself does involve some risks (NIH, 1979), including the possibility of triggering a spontaneous abortion, rupturing the amniotic sac, and inflicting injuries due to needle puncture or placental separation (Elias & Simpson, 1986). Sensitization following amniocentesis of Rh negative mothers who are carrying an Rh positive fetus has been documented, and vaginal bleeding and leakage of amniotic fluid, as well as uterine contractions immediately following amniocentesis, are common occurrences (Elias & Simpson, 1986).

A more recently developed diagnostic procedure, chorionic villus sampling, can be performed during the first 8 weeks of pregnancy. It involves the aspiration of the hairlike projections (villi) of the preplacental structure that surround the developing embryo during the stage of implantation (Blakemore & Mahoney, 1986). This biopsy is generally performed either transabdominally or transcervically under ultrasound guidance (Blakemore & Mahoney, 1986). It can detect the same range of disorders discernible through amniocentesis, with the exception of spina bifida and neural tube defects. However, chorionic villus sampling is not risk free. Several independent studies place the estimated risk of a spontaneous abortion between 2 and 5%, with increased risk associated with increasing maternal age (Blakemore & Mahoney, 1986). The possibility of intrauterine infection poses a serious threat to both "mother-to-be" and the fetus, as does the potential risk of Rh sensitization in Rh negative women (Blakemore & Mahoney, 1986).

Whereas chorionic villus sampling and amniocentesis offer the promise of medical technological answers to counter some of the reproductive risks of midlife childbearing, these procedures may also create additional profoundly personal, emotional, and moral burdens for mothers-to-be should fetal defect(s) be diagnosed. The results of amniocentesis may not be available until the middle of the second trimester. Although the technique of chorionic villus sampling provides tissue suitable for analysis within the first trimester of pregnancy, offering the option of a safer first trimester abortion, it is less widely available and it may involve a greater risk for mother and infant (Blakemore & Mahoney, 1986). For later life mothers, the conflicts involved in the decision of whether or not to carry to term a fetus with identified deficits may be accentuated by an awareness that their own age presents an additional impediment to the long-term care of such a child (Daniels & Weingarten, 1982). Nevertheless, the potential of these prenatal diagnostic procedures, in and of itself, can become part of a persuasive argument for some women over 35 years old who might otherwise not consider or attempt pregnancy (Daniels & Weingarten, 1982; Wilk, 1986).

Risks to the Mother

The risks to mothers who delay first-time pregnancy until their mid-30s are complicated by preexisting conditions. In addition to potential individual medical histories, a woman bearing her first child in her late 30s has increased risk of developing toxemia and hypertensive disorders of pregnancy (conditions characterized by high blood pressure, sudden weight gain from fluid retention in tissues, and the presence of protein in the woman's urine) and placental previa (a condition in which the fertilized egg implants itself low in the uterus covering part or all of the cervix). Both conditions correlate with advancing age and each presents a risk to both mother and child (Iffy & Kaminetzky, 1981).

Among women 35 years old and older, the leading causes of maternal death are obstetric hemorrhage, embolism from a blocked artery, and high blood pressure (Resnik, 1986). Complications from abortion and Cesarean delivery are also more serious with advancing years (Resnik, 1986). Women over 35 years old are more likely to die from pregnancy-related causes than women in their 20s (McCarthy, 1987). Additional risk factors are generated by somewhat slower cervical dilation and the possibility of lessened muscle tone and weaker contractions, which may lead to longer labors (Iffy & Kaminetzky, 1981; Resnik, 1986).

DIAGNOSTIC TESTING AND THE PSYCHOLOGICAL TIMETABLE OF PREGNANCY

Motherhood in Suspense

The decision to have diagnostic testing appears to alter the psychological reality of pregnancy (Daniels & Weingarten, 1982). Instead of the first trimester being a time devoted to accepting the pregnancy, this psychological task is postponed until the health of the fetus is confirmed. Fears of miscarriage are combined with anxiety over the possible need to confront elective abortion if abnormality is evident, placing women in a state of suspension that may stretch into the second trimester. Prior to the availability of modern medical technology, the second trimester was characterized as a period in which the mother-to-be was imbued with a sense of well-being and relative calm (Galinsky, 1981). "Quickening" or the mother's first sensation of fetal movement is generally experienced during this trimester, spurring the mother to acknowledge the growing separateness of the fetus. Thereafter, the presence of fetal movement may be singled out by the mother as an indication that the fetus is healthy.

For many mid life mothers, the timing of amniocentesis divides the experience of pregnancy in half (Daniels & Weingarten, 1982). The most trying period for these mothers occurs between the time they see a sonogram of the fetus and hear its heartbeat as part of the procedure surrounding amniocentesis and the time when the amniotic fluid is cultured and the fetal cells are analyzed. This visual and auditory connection to the unborn may then make the decision to terminate pregnancy even more difficult than it might have been without these concrete amplifiers of attachment. At the same time, the sonogram may provide sufficient criteria to identify the sex of the fetus. Mothers who opt to have access to this information gain a gender label around which may crystallize a culturally powerful array of stereotypes (Daniels & Weingarten, 1982). Daniels and

Weingarten (1982) point out that it may be too soon to gage the full impact of unleashing these images prior to birth, at a time traditionally allowed for a moratorium on gender labels. Without gender information, mothers experiment with alternative, frequently androgynous interpretations of temperament and ability.

The Experience of Childbirth

Contrary to public concern over the misuse of amniocentesis and abortion for preselecting an infant by its sex, Daniels and Weingarten (1982) found that among those couples conceiving first babies in mid life, the knowledge of fetal gender did not lead to abortion. Rather, this knowledge provided additional time for both parents to deal with any disappointment they might have had concerning the sex of the conceived child. Maternal realization that this may be their only child, combined with the reassurance that this child is in apparent good health, may alleviate disappointment in the sex of the child. All of the 13 mid-life mothers studied by Daniels and Weingarten (1982) described the moment they learned of the results of their amniocentesis as a pivotal event in their journey to parenthood. Only two mothers out of this group singled out the moment of birth as carrying such psychological importance. The shift in emphasis may be partially explained by the prevalence of Cesarean births among mid-life mothers (Resnik, 1986). Recognizing the potential for increased difficulties in conceiving and carrying a healthy infant to term, obstetricians may intercede more actively at any sign of possible complicating factors during labor and delivery with older mothers (Price, 1977). Nevertheless, in Daniels and Weingarten's (1982) study, only one-half of their group of midlife mothers had babies delivered by Cesarean section. Irrespective of delivery method, childbirth was viewed by midlife mothers as part of a series of critical events leading up to their new role, rather than as a culminating experience. This phenomenon is even more striking when compared with the emotionally charged detail with which childbirth, as an event, was described by the mothers whose first child was born when they were in their 20s or early 30s (Daniels & Weingarten, 1982).

TRANSITION TO PARENTHOOD

The Expectations and Demands of Motherhood

The transition to motherhood begins during pregnancy, as mothers rethink their relationship to their own parents, create an image of the infant-to-be, and rehearse possible childcaring scenarios. From the moment the infant is born, mothers begin the task of discovering their infant and attempting to integrate the reality of their infant's needs and behaviors with the fantasized infant and the imagined motherhood of pregnancy. After childbirth, a precipitous drop in estrogen and progesterone levels may trigger a period of crying and diffuse sense of unhappiness and anxiety (Livingston, 1987). These "baby blues" are short lived, but problems associated with fatigue coupled with the unrealistic expectations of resuming all of one's previous responsibilities within weeks of childbirth may persist (Reeder *et al.*, 1983). In the words of one mid life mother, "It's amazing the amount of patience and thought you need to put into being a mother. That's the biggest surprise to me. I'm also surprised at what a perfectionist I've become."

Mothers of all ages confront an array of social expectations associated with the role of mother filtered through a web of interpersonal emotional and financial commitments. Many mothers wooed by the media anticipate their spontaneous ability to function as "supermom" (Griffin, 1987). Even medical texts perpetuate the assumption that women will return to their prepregnancy shape, physically and psychologically, within weeks of delivery (Griffin, 1987). Although the first few months immediately following the birth of a child have been referred to as the "baby honeymoon" (Hobbs, 1968), the first weeks through the first year may be increasingly stressful for mothers. Miller and Sollie (1986) found that middle-class mothers reported not only more personal stress after the infant's birth than during pregnancy, but also increased personal and marital stress 8 months after their infant was born. Fathers' marital stress scores remained approximately the same throughout this postpartum period (Miller & Sollie, 1986).

New mothers are often unprepared for the around-the-clock reality of motherhood and for the accompanying rearrangement of professional, familial, and social activities. In Daniels and Weingarten's (1982) sample of 14 couples who became first time parents over 40, three mothers reported having difficulty absorbing and accepting the demands of motherhood. These new mothers were not only disappointed when the reality of their infants' and their husbands' behavior collided with their own expectations, but they were also distressed by their own inability to function at the level of competence, expertise, and control they had come to demand of themselves. In discussion groups, late-timing mothers (women who ranged in age from 31 to 40) revealed that the first 3 months of parenthood were the most difficult (Walters, 1986). They were uncomfortable with someone being so dependent upon them. They missed the positive feedback built into their job structure. They reported difficulty both in defining parenting goals and accomplishing projects they set for themselves during this period. The accretion of small daily discrepancies between their lives before baby and the nature of the demands placed upon them caring for their new infant led to a lowered sense of self-esteem as compared with their antepartum state.

Several of the women in Walters' (1986) discussion groups of late-timing mothers described difficulty in playing with their babies. Basically, they were dissatisfied with preverbal interactions. They were looking for companionship instead. In contrast, the early-timing mothers found the opportunity for physical closeness with their babies and the immersion in the feelings and tempo of their babies the most pleasurable aspects of mothering. They took pride in their ability to interpret nonverbal messages and they drew satisfaction from being needed by their infants. Late-timing mothers interpreted their own dissatisfaction as related to their later life parenting (Walters, 1986). In general, late-timing mothers studied by Walters (1986) agreed that the most difficult aspect of motherhood was not having enough time for oneself, whereas early-timing mothers saw their babies as "extensions of themselves" (Walters, 1986).

A New Chapter

The majority of mid life and late-timing mothers felt that they were ready for parenthood without feeling that they had missed out on life experiences (Daniels & Weingarten, 1982; Frankel & Wise, 1982; Walters, 1986). As one 41-year-old mother said, "Having my children later in life, circumscribes my world much less than it would have when I was young. I've traveled enough for awhile, seen enough plays, and gone to enough parties." A contemporary of hers at 44 years of age adds, "I've had a fabulous time in my life. I've worked and played all over the world—so settling down now feels okay."

Half of the mid life women interviewed by Daniels and Weingarten (1982) perceived their infant as fitting into an ongoing lifestyle and saw mothering as a further ramification of a pre-existing self. All of these women continued to work, arranging for alternative infant care. This same perspective was reported by the majority of older mothers interviewed by Frankel and Wise (1982).

For other midlife women, motherhood marked a "new chapter" in their lives. As one such mother expressed:

> My baby has given me a chance to start over in life. I worked for a long time, and although I enjoyed it, I was tired of the routine. This is a new beginning, at age 40, for both my husband and me.

BENEFITS OF DELAYED MOTHERING

A Sense of Identity

Women who first experienced motherhood in their 30s and 40s bring to this experience a firmer sense of their own abilities, interests, and emotional needs than do women who enter motherhood early (Daniels & Weingarten, 1982; Frankel & Wise, 1982; Walters, 1986). The younger mothers were more apt to use this role to define themselves, separate from their parents, and assert their adult status (Daniels & Weingarten, 1982), while deriving a main source of their own identity from their husbands (Walters, 1986). In the words of a first-time mother, at age 37:

> I'm such a different person now than when I was 20. Then I had undeveloped ideas about what I wanted to be—but I knew who I was; I knew I wanted to marry, and I did. We had enough money to have a big house, a summer place, and a good social life. When you are 20, you don't have those things. We'd done quite a bit of living; traveled

independently and together—and we didn't feel deprived of anything, except perhaps children. I think there are definite advantages to having children when you are older.

Thus, for many women who undertake motherhood in the fourth and fifth decade of life, the experience becomes just one of many pieces to a complex sense of personhood. Late-timing mothers in Frankel and Wise's (1982) study emphasized their feelings of competence. Walters (1986) found that late-timing mothers frequently introduced themselves to the research discussion group in terms of their own accomplishments in the world of work and community or through enduring interests and commitments. On an adjective checklist, the late-timing mothers described themselves as more achievement-oriented, autonomous, self-reliant, and individualistic than did the early-timing mothers. The late-timing mothers were less apt to question their childbearing decisions in the context of group discussion than the early-timing mothers. Similarly, the late-timing mothers were less prone to call upon their own parents for support or advice (Daniels & Weingarten, 1982; Frankel & Wise, 1982; Walters, 1986). Yet many late-timing mothers felt that the experience of motherhood enabled them to see their own mothers more as individuals. This new recognition of their mothers' personal needs and parenting history enhanced the current relationship between mother and daughter (Walters, 1986).

Financial Security

Late-timing mothers are accustomed to taking control of their own lives. These women were producers and providers before they were parents, and many of the professional women studied were used to both personal freedom and material comforts. In Walters' (1986) sample, late-timing mothers had worked an average of 9 years before the first of their children were born, three times the number of years the early-timers worked prior to motherhood. A total of 97% of the late-timing mothers in her sample had graduated from college, and 62% had graduate degrees. Their work choices reflected this opportunity for advanced study, although approximately equal numbers of late-timing and early-timing mothers were working outside of the home during the course of the study.

One of the outstanding differences in the situations of late-timing and midlife mothers as compared with women who became mothers in their early 20s is increased financial security (Daniels & Weingarten, 1982; Frankel & Wise, 1982; Walters, 1986; Wilkie, 1981). Population statistics from the U.S. Census Bureau from 1982 confirm that a woman 30 years or older when compared with a woman 18 to 24 years old at the birth of her first child is more likely to have completed at least one year of college, to be employed in a professional occupation, and to live in a family with a relatively high income (U.S. Bureau of the Census, 1987).

Reciprocity as an Ideal

The experience late-timing mothers gained in exerting their own influence within the workplace was also felt within the family (Daniels & Weingarten, 1982). The extended years prior to parenthood not only contribute to financial security, but also give women time to practice negotiating shared household responsibility. The more typical experience for early-timing mothers was to care for the baby while nurturing her husband as well (Daniels & Weingarten, 1982; Walters, 1986). The recognized goal for late-timing and mid-life parents was reciprocity in meeting emotional needs and accomplishing household and child-care tasks (Daniels & Weingarten, 1982; Frankel & Wise, 1982; Walters, 1986). In this regard, it is interesting to note that none of the late-timing mothers mentioned the need to obtain approval from her husband before taking part in an activity, whereas early-timing mothers reported seeking the approval of their husband for their own "leisure" activities (Walters, 1986).

A changed intrafamily dynamic may be one of the benefits of delayed mothering. The time spent developing the relationship within a marriage is one source of interpersonal strength (Daniels & Weingarten, 1982). In addition, late-timing fathers have been found to be more involved with the parenting role (Daniels & Weingarten, 1982; Frankel & Wise, 1982).

JUGGLING WORK AND CHILDREN

Setting Priorities

Over 50% of women with children under 3 years old in the United States are gainfully employed outside the home (Szanton, 1986), while over 60% of women with children 5 years old and under are in the labor force or looking for work (Hayghe, 1986). Although the majority of employed mothers work full time, the orchestration and supervision of the myriad details of daily household maintenance, from food purchase and preparation, room care and cleanliness, to appropriateness and availability of apparel is ultimately the woman's responsibility (Bronfenbrenner & Crouter, 1982; Clarke-Stewart, 1982; Daniels & Weingarten, 1982). In all three generations of early- and late-timing mothers studied by Daniels and Weingarten (1982), women who worked beyond their family conceived of their efforts and responsibilities at home as "a job." Overall, they had to combine the roles of two occupations on a day-to-day basis, in contrast to fathers, who may have provided assistance but rarely acknowledged household chores as a primary role (Bronfenbrenner & Crouter, 1982; Daniels & Weingarten, 1982; Johnson & Johnson, 1977).

Daniels and Weingarten (1982) found that women from all the generations initially decreased their involvement with outside work upon becoming mothers. This technique for "managing" the demands of two simultaneous primary occupations in dual-career families has been repeatedly documented (Frankel & Wise, 1982; Johnson & Johnson, 1977; Skinner, 1986). Integrating these two roles involves placing limits on time and continually tapping emotional reserves. The integration of both identities and roles is a psychological task that women predominantly face alone (Skinner, 1986). Daniels and Weingarten (1982) found that the women's experience and hidden work histories at home and in the paid labor force were more like each other's than the men's throughout the generations interviewed.

The difference was that women planning pregnancy in mid-life anticipated that having a baby might require some readjustment. Their expectation was that when work and motherhood were juxtaposed, careers would be preferred. However, they were unprepared for their feelings that work was interfering with their own desires to be available for their babies (Daniels & Weingarten, 1982; Walters, 1986). Late-timing mothers appear to have a more clearly differentiated sense of themselves as workers and mothers, which strengthens their ability to cope with the sometimes conflicting demands of each role (Frankel & Wise, 1982; Walters, 1986). However, less than half of the late-timing mothers in Walters' (1986) study were working and only 24% were working full time. As one midlife mother put it, "Motherhood is my profession now." Late-timing mothers were often surprised at the satisfaction that they derived from motherhood. Walters (1986) found that a greater percentage of late-timing mothers than early-timing mothers ranked their children as their number one source of satisfaction.

Nevertheless, several homebound late-timing mothers were frustrated by the loss of a "work identity" and disenchanted with the assumption that they could perform at the same level of competence in all areas while combining motherhood with full-time work. They used their expertise and seniority to create part-time or flexible work schedules (Daniels & Weingarten, 1982; Walters, 1986). In some cases, this represented a reprioritizing of career aspirations and a redefinition of personal success.

Social Support

Frankel and Wise (1982) found that the late-timing mothers more often selected home or family day-care arrangements as a child-care option, while younger mothers predominantly used group child-care centers or a patchwork arrangement with friends and neighbors. The reliance on family for child care was notably absent in both on-time and late-timing mothers studied by Frankel and Wise (1982). Daniels and Weingarten (1982) found that early-timing mothers were likely to turn to their families, fathers, mothers, grandparents, sisters, and brothers for understanding and child-care assistance.

Social isolation is one of the stresses of mothering in the first few years of life, which both on-time mothers (Frankel & Wise, 1982) and late-timing mothers (Walters, 1986) experience. Women who have been employed outside of the home may never have established contact with neighborhood social networks.

Opting for longer periods at home after the birth of a child may entail a subtle distancing from colleagues at work. New mothers may find themselves seeking more family-oriented social situations. The nurturing aspect of motherhood brought out a renewed awareness of the value of friendships for many late-timing mothers (Frankel & Wise, 1982; Walters, 1986). This group of mothers in Walters' (1986) study took advantage of the discussion groups to reach out for social contacts.

TIME AND MOTHERHOOD

Time for Self

Late-timing and mid-life mothers called upon their organizational skills to cope with the demands of motherhood (Daniels & Weingarten, 1982; Walters, 1986). Walters (1986) reports that a larger percentage of late-timing mothers than early-timing mothers indicated that their own needs were the main factor influencing daily decisions. Early-timing mothers ranked their child's needs as being given greater priority. Late-timing mothers approached mothering as a "planned project." This enabled them to maintain career direction and set aside time for themselves. Nevertheless, their need to function in structured situations under their own control may also be their "Achilles' heel."

Time for the Child

Late-timing and mid-life mothers expressed difficulties in circumstances that required spontaneity and flexibility in order to meet children's needs, feeling more at ease in the context of well-established routines. Although some late-timing mothers in Walters' (1986) study commented that breast feeding was a high point of mothering, the majority appeared to be most comfortable with evidence of maturing verbal and motor abilities. This emphasis on achievement and milestones reflects their own successfully reached goals. The child's growing independence complements the mothers' need for time for themselves.

Walters (1986) asked both early- and late-timing mothers to rank various aspects of their lives according to the degree of satisfaction they derived from them during the preceding month. Statistical analysis revealed that late-timing mothers more frequently ranked relationship with child/children as the most satisfying. However, they maintained more of a sense of personal distance within their relationship and actually spent only half as much time with their children as the early-timing mothers.

Sense of Time and Mortality

An increased awareness of time appears to be incorporated into the experience of mid-life parenting, both as a greater appreciation of the time spent with children and as an increased pressure to fill that time spent with meaningful experiences (Daniels & Weingarten, 1982; Walters, 1986). The mid-life mothers in Walters' (1986) study were more ready to recognize the changing nature of development. This recognition of the inevitability of change helped to balance momentary frustrations. However, late-timing mothers were simultaneously shadowed by a sense of their own mortality. The voiced concerns of late-timing mothers that they might have less physical energy than younger mothers (Daniels & Weingarten, 1982; Frankel & Wise, 1982; Walters, 1986) may offer one safety valve for their expression of more general worries over diminished capacities associated with aging.

Older mothers perceived a need to teach their child everything in a short period of time (Walters, 1986). In the words of one mid-life adoptive mother:

> For 10 weeks now, I've been living a new lifestyle. I'm a first-time mother at age 45. This state drastically alters my perception of time, and aging as well. Each day is really a new beginning. I don't magically become a young mother. My concerns and delights have to do with a full nest, as opposed to the proverbial empty nest of mid-life. My worries about starting so late have to do with having to deal with an adolescent at age 58, when I should be taking things easy. But I'm putting those concerns "underground" for the time being.

The importance of time in the life choices of these mothers is evidenced in the question of whether or not to have another child (Daniels & Weingarten, 1982). The question "Is there time for another child?" speaks to both the organization of daily lives and the biological ceiling.

ADOPTION

An Antidote for Infertility

Adoption as a strategy to ensure motherhood has become an increasingly acceptable alternative to childlessness (Tizard, 1977). One such mother describing the decision to adopt said:

> After three or four years unsuccessfully attempting to have a child, we went to a fertility expert. He discovered that my husband had a low sperm count. Although that was a real trauma for both of us, we decided to pursue adoption. It was a long frustrating experience, but finally we flew to Columbia to pick up our three month old daughter. She was (and is) the highlight of our married life—a sheer delight.

Of all the roadblocks that pock the path to adoption, two of the most salient are the time and the cost. The wait for adoption may be as long as 5 or 6 years through agency channels (Kadushin, 1980). Although agencies recognize that adults 35 to 45 years old are good candidates as adoptive parents for an infant, the waiting time itself may place prospective adoptive parents beyond these agency-defined desirable age limits (Deutsch, 1983). "Gray market" adoptions based on individually negotiated contracts between biological parents, usually mothers, and potential adoptive mothers or parents account for approximately one-fifth of all adoptions (Kadushin, 1980). However, these brokered matches may carry a price tag ranging as high as $25,000 for a healthy infant (Zelizer, 1985). Minority children and older children are more difficult to place, partially because standards for family adequacy have included matching parents' religious and racial backgrounds (Deutsch, 1983). Criteria for parents also include evidence of a stable marital relationship, adjustment to infertility, financial stability, and an assessed capacity for parenthood (Deutsch, 1983; Kadushin, 1980).

An Option for the Nontraditional Mother

A redefinition of the goals of adoption from a compensation to infertile couples to a means of providing caring families for individual children has pried open doors of adoption agencies for the older and single mother, making possible a somewhat greater acceptance of these women as potential adoptive mothers, particularly in the case of older children (Kadushin, 1980; Tizard, 1977). Divorced as well as never-married mid-life women are increasingly considering and exercising this optional road to motherhood. One woman said that when she could afford to support a child and realized that marriage wasn't imminent, she decided to adopt. The issues for her were declared when she said, "I wanted to give love, to have a child, and to be a mother."

Lesbian women are among those for whom adoption may be a viable alternative to motherhood through impregnation, although methods such as artificial insemination from either an anonymous or a known donor or becoming pregnant through a male friend are also possibilities. Lesbian couples may delay the decision to raise a child until they feel that both their relationship and their finances are secure, reasons that are similar to those of their heterosexual counterparts.

The Adjustment to Motherhood

For older mothers who successfully run the adoption gamut, the first year of mothering may be fraught with the same range of stresses as those experienced by first-time biological mothers. In a comparison of biological and adoptive mothers with infants in the household for less than 12 months, McCaghren and Jackson (1987) found that both groups of mothers reported changes in their sleeping patterns accompanied by fatigue after the addition of the infant. Mothers from both groups reported occasional feelings of inadequacy and difficulties in concentrating (McCaghren & Jackson, 1987). However, they also experienced the same pleasures, including finding motherhood easier than anticipated (McCaghren & Jackson, 1987). One adoptive older mother simply said, "I am truly enjoying my adopted baby."

THE FUTURE

Research

The trend toward postponing the entrance into parenting to mid and later life is still a new phonemonon. Those mothers whose individual concerns, preferences, and decisions have become part of the public domain have just begun to experience motherhood and to taste the continuingly developing nature of that role and the multifaceted relationships that it encompasses. Research is needed to monitor the impact of the decision to delay mothering on both the children and parents. Daniels and Weingarten (1982) point out that the change in timing affects not only the years of parenting but also the years of nonactive parenting. One will need to consider in what way the age differences may affect interaction between late-timing mothers and their adolescent or young adult children. In what way might this relationship be different from the relationship that develops between mothers and their "last-chance babies" born after they already have teenage children.

The research literature suggests that mid-life first-time mothers view themselves as achievement-oriented and self-reliant. They prefer to function in structured situations with built-in mechanisms of rewards. As a group, they are least comfortable in caregiving circumstances that call for a realignment of their own needs to meet the pace and pattern of their young child's ability and interests. Instead, it appears that the tendency among late-timing mothers is to ask the child to participate in social settings defined according to adult capabilities and to provide evidence of accomplishing externally recognized concrete achievements.

The continued experience of mothering may be a force for growth for the mothers. The opportunity for personal development provided by motherhood may lead to a restructuring of intrapsychic and interpersonal priorities among midlife first-time mothers. The potential for this reorganization is hinted at by the first-time mothers who expressed surprise that they had begun to perceive of work as interfering with mothering, instead of the reverse as anticipated during pregnancy.

Current research has dealt exclusively with the self-reported perception of mothers and has yet to focus on observable behavioral differences. Future research needs to address the match between the feelings expressed by mothers and the specific behavior patterns of mothers, fathers, and children. The initial studies of mid-life mothers have not distinguished between mothers who postponed having children after marriage and those who married later in life. The interlude between marriage and children may provide a period crucial to the cohesiveness of the couple, affecting communication styles within the family as well as flexibility in response to the needs of children and of childrearing.

Studies focusing on postponed parenting households have primarily provided a window into the lives of intact middle-class, and professional, white families (Daniels & Weingarten, 1982; Frankel & Wise, 1982; Walters, 1986). The impact of postponed mothering on single women and within the diverse cultural communities that make up the American mosaic is largely uncharted.

Policy and Services

As increasing numbers of women postpone the decision to become parents, more children may be brought up in single-child households or with fewer siblings. The parents of these later-life children will also be at a different point in the course of their social and work lives (Bronfenbrenner & Crouter, 1982). The outcome of parenting and its potential to deflect life courses remains to be examined. However, one may begin to extrapolate some long- and short-term needs from current experiences of this emerging population of mothers and children.

The social isolation of new mothering for women of all ages may be accentuated for first-time mid-life mothers, who are less likely to turn to extended family members for practical assistance and emotional support and who may be removed from their workplace contemporaries. Sharing experiences with other mid-life mothers with infants and young children, whether first-born or "later-born babies," may alleviate some of this stress while providing guidance in adjusting to the nonverbal initiatives and cognitive configurations of infants, toddlers, and preschoolers.

Opportunities for flexible hours, professional level part-time employment, and quality child care can be seen as high on a social agenda that recognizes the needs of families. The question remains whether the trend toward postponed parenting among highly qualified workers will create additional pressure on business and government to facilitate the institution of these options, which could benefit individuals at all socioeconomic and educational levels.

The more advanced parental age may create long-range needs. Children of mid-life or later-life mothers may enter college at a time when their parents are contemplating retirement. These children may be faced with the predicament of providing financial and/or daily care to parents at a point when they themselves are trying to establish careers and nurture children of their own. These adult children may need guidance in taking on these responsibilities just as their own parents may want to seek out financial and legal advice to prepare for the juxtaposition of life events. Delaying motherhood into the fourth and fifth decade of life may have long-term societal and personal repercussions. The initial investigation of delayed motherhood has just begun to sketch the framework for further exploration.

REFERENCES

Belsky, J., Lerner, R., & Spanier, G. (1984). *The child in the family*. Reading, MA: Addison-Wesley.
Blakemore, K., & Mahoney, M. (1986). Chorionic villus sampling. In A. Milunsky (Ed.), *Genetic disorders and the fetus*. New York: Plenum Press.
Bronfenbrenner, A., & Crouter, A. (1982). Work and family through time and space. In S. Kammer-

man & C. Hayes (Eds.), *Families that work: Children in a changing world.* Washington, DC: Academic.

Clarke-Stewart, A. (1982). *Daycare.* Cambridge: Harvard University Press.

Danforth, D., & Scott, J. (Eds.). (1986). *Obstetrics and gynecology.* Philadelphia: J. B. Lippincott.

Daniels, P., & Weingarten, K. (1982). *Sooner or later: The timing of parenthood in adult lives.* New York: Norton.

Davajan, V., & Mishell, D. R., Jr. (1986). Evaluation of the infertile couple. In D. R. Mishell, Jr., & V. Davajan (Eds.), *Infertility, contraception and reproductive endocrinology.* Oradell, NJ: Medical Economics Books.

Deutsch, F. (1983). *Child services on behalf of children.* Monterey, CA: Brooks/Cole.

Dewhurst, J. (Ed.). (1981). *Integrated obstetrics and gynecology for postgraduates* (3rd ed.). Boston: Blackwell Scientific.

Elias, S., & Simpson, J. (1986). Amniocentesis. In A. Milunsky (Ed.), *Genetic disorders and the fetus.* New York: Plenum Press.

Fabe, M., & Wikler, N. (1979). *Up against the clock.* New York: Random House.

Ford, K. (1981). Socioeconomic differentials and trends in the timing of births. *Vital and health statistics.* National Center for Health Statistics, Series 23, No. 6.

Frankel, S., & Wise, M. (1982). A view of delayed parenting: Some implications of a new trend. *Psychiatry, 45,* 220–225.

Fraser, F. C. (1984). Gross chromosomal aberrations. In M. E. Avery & H. W. Taeusch, Jr. (Eds.), *Schaffer's diseases of the newborn.* Philadelphia: Saunders.

Galinsky, E. (1981). *Between generations: The six stages of parenthood.* New York: Times Books.

Griffin, J. (1987). Postpartum recovery; It takes longer than you think. *Genesis, 9*(2), 17–20.

Hayghe, H. (1986). Rise in mothers' labor force activity including those with infants. *Monthly Labor Review.* U.S. Department of Labor Statistics.

Hobbs, D. F., Jr. (1968). Parenthood as a crisis: A third study. *Journal of Marriage and the Family, 27,* 367–372.

Hook, E. S. (1986). Paternal age and effects on chromosomal and specific locus mutations on the genetic outcomes in offspring. In L. Mastroianni, Jr., & C. A. Paulson (Eds.), *Aging, reproduction and the climacteric.* New York: Plenum Press.

Iffy, L., & Kaminetzky, H. (Eds.). (1981). *Principles and practice of obstetrics and perinatology.* New York: Wiley.

Johnson, C., & Johnson, F. (1977). Attitudes toward parenting in dual career families. *American Journal of Psychiatry, 134,* 391–395.

Kadushin, A. (1980). *Child welfare services* (3rd ed.). New York: Macmillan.

Kaltreider, N., & Margolis, A. (1977). Childless by choice: A clinical study. *American Journal of Psychiatry, 134,* 179–182.

Latt, S. A. (1984). Prenatal genetic diagnosis. In M. E. Avery & H. W. Taeusch, Jr. (Eds.), *Schaffer's diseases of the newborn.* Philadelphia: Saunders.

Livingston, C. (1987). Postpartum women in crisis. *Genesis, 9*(2), 21–23.

Margolis, M. (1984). *Mothers and such.* Berkeley: University of California Press.

McCaghren, E., & Jackson, M. (1987). Maternal adaptation to parenthood: Responses of biological and adoptive mothers. *Genesis, 8*(6), 31–35.

McCarthy, M. (1987). Infant, fetal and maternal mortality in the U.S. *Vital and Health Statistics,* Series 20, No. 3.

McCauley, C. (1976). *Pregnancy after 35.* New York: E. P. Dutton.

Miller, B., & Sollie, D. (1986). Normal stresses during the transition to parenthood. In R. Moos (Ed.), *Coping with life crises: An integrated approach.* New York: Plenum Press.

Moulton, R. (1979). Ambivalence about motherhood in career women. *Journal of the American Academy of Psychoanalysis, 7*(2), 241–257.

National Institutes of Health. (1979). *Antenatal diagnosis: Report of a consensus development conference.* Bethesda, MD: (U.S. Department of Health, Education, & Welfare, Publication No. 79-1173).

Nieschlag, E., & Michel, E. (1986). Reproductive functions in grandfathers. In L. Mastroianni, Jr., & C. A. Paulson (Eds.), *Aging, reproduction and the climacteric.* New York: Plenum Press.

Potts, L. (1980). Considering parenthood: Group support for a critical life decision. *American Journal of Orthopsychiatry, 50*(4), 629–638.

Price, J. (1977). *You're not too old to have a baby.* New York: Farrar, Straus & Giroux.

Rapoport, R., Rapoport, R., & Strelitz, Z. (1980). *Fathers, mothers and society perspectives on parenting.* New York: Random House.

Reeder, S., Mastroianni, L., & Martin, L. (1983). *Maternity nursing.* Philadelphia: J. B. Lippincott.

Resnik, R. (1986). Age-related changes in gestation and pregnancy. In L. Mastroianni, Jr., & C. A. Paulson (Eds.), *Aging, reproduction and the climacteric.* New York: Plenum Press.

Rubin, S. (1980). *It's not too late for a baby: For women and men over 35.* Englewood Cliffs, NJ: Prentice-Hall.

Skinner, D. (1986). Dual-career family stress and coping. In R. Moos (Ed.), *Coping with life crises: An integrated approach.* New York: Plenum Press.

Szanton, E. (1986). *Infants can't wait: The numbers.* New York: National Center for Clinical Infant Programs.

Tizard, B. (1977). *Adoption: A second chance.* London: Open Books.

U.S. Bureau of the Census. (1978). Perspectives on American fertility. *Current Population Reports.* Series P-23, No. 338.

U.S. Bureau of the Census. (1987). *Statistical abstract of the United States.* Washington, DC: U.S. Government Printing Office.

Walters, C. (1986). *The timing of motherhood.* Lexington, MA: Lexington Books, D. C. Heath.

Wilk, C. (1986). *Career women and childbearing.* New York: Van Nostrand Reinhold.

Wilkie, J. (1981). The trend toward delayed parenthood. *Journal of marriage and the family,* 583–591.

Zelizer, V. (1985). *Pricing the priceless child.* New York: Basic.

Conclusion

BEVERLY BIRNS AND DALE F. HAY

The objectives we set at the outset were to examine mothers in their own right, in the context of their life experiences, of their own phenomenology, as well as their objective conditions, within their cultures. Authors were encouraged to explore the available empirical literature and to supplement their reading of existing research with interviews with mothers. What emerged from these efforts was a realization that we know relatively little about the subjective experience of motherhood. We know about the effects of certain experiences on children, about the psychology of women, but not very much at all about the lives of mothers.

This seemed particularly true with respect to the groups of contemporary American mothers discussed in the third section of the book. For example, in searching for information about disabled mothers, Baskin and Riggs (Chapter 10) found hundreds of references about the disabled, few that specifically focused on disabled women, and only biographical and autobiographical accounts of disabled mothers. Their interviews are the first empirical step in studying this important group of mothers.

In most other cases, empirical studies have focused on children, not their mothers. For example, the research on child care summarized by McCartney and Phillips (Chapter 7) indicates that care outside the home, by persons other than the mother, has positive effects on some children, little measurable effects on others, and negative effects for poor children in poor and discontinuous care. However, there is almost no information about the impact of shared caregiving on mothers and almost no analysis of how mothers' experiences of shared care arrangements may mediate the effects on children.

In still other cases, the available information about different groups of mothers is qualified by misleading assumptions about the pathological nature of motherhood. The assumption of pathology creates particularly clear problems

BEVERLY BIRNS • Child and Family Studies Program, State University of New York, Stony Brook, New York 11794.   DALE F. HAY • Institute of Psychiatry, De Crespigny Park, Denmark Hill, London SE5 8AF, England.

with respect to the literatures on divorced mothers and black mothers. Straus's review (Chapter 9) indicates that many of the psychological studies of divorce begun over a decade ago focused on the stresses experienced by divorced women and the negative effects of these stressors on their children. Studies tended to conclude that most women were psychologically devastated by divorce and had few successful coping strategies.

In contrast, current research focusing on the economic plight of divorced mothers (e.g., Weitzman, 1985) presents a more balanced picture. Nevertheless, in terms of the psychological experience of divorce, we know very little about the possible positive effects it has on mothers who leave abusive and destructive relationships. What resources and coping skills have they developed, and what is the outcome for their children? Only if we begin to see divorce as not inevitably pathological will we begin to understand the impact of what has become a part of life for many mothers and children.

Similarly, it is necessary to examine the lives of minority women in a manner free of assumptions about pathology. Washington (Chapter 8) demonstrates clearly that the notion of the "black matriarchy" has set back the course of sound research on the black experience of motherhood. This misguided assumption about black family structure has obscured the important issues that need to be studied. Rather than consider racial discrimination as the source of poverty among blacks, it has been easier for many social scientists and policymakers to fault black mothers. Rather than seeking the sources of strength and unique coping skills of black mothers, many have considered black youth unemployment or educational disadvantages to result from maternal dominance.

Given the many inadequacies of the existing literature on motherhood, what can we conclude from this effort to compile and synthesize existing findings? What do we need to know? And what do we already know we need to do?

WHAT WE NEED TO KNOW

The primary need in future research on motherhood is to examine mothers as whole human beings, with feelings, thoughts, actions, interests, relationships, histories, and futures. In previous research this has rarely been done. As we have seen, mothers have been viewed as ideals, as stereotypes, as public properties, as forces impinging on their children's development, but rarely as complex human beings in their own right. There is a need for a social psychology of motherhood. Furthermore, the beginning attempts made by the authors in this volume to address the phenomenology of motherhood needs to be systematized and continued. More formal interviews need to be designed and conducted.

The authors of chapters in this volume have examined a number of different samples of mothers in America and in other cultures; however, other samples also call out for investigation. For example, interviews should be conducted with teen mothers, with mothers whose children are cared for in group day care as opposed to those who are cared for in other arrangements, with various groups of working mothers who hold different positions in the job market and have different earning abilities. There is a need to interview stepmothers, foster mothers, and adoptive mothers and even grandmothers. In addition to interviewing "successful" mothers, one would wish to interview mothers of abused and neglected children.

There are a number of questions to be asked in such interview studies. For example, did the woman choose to become pregnant? When and under what conditions does a woman make the decision to become a mother? Why was the choice made when it was? What aspirations and expectations did she have at the time of conception and birth, and how did those change over time? what kinds of relationships and other forms of social support did she have as she entered the state of motherhood? From whom did she get advice, support, and criticism? What were her own criteria of success? When did she feel stressed? When did she think she had failed to meet her own expectations? How does her childrearing compare with that of her own mother? Is most maternal behavior learned from one's mother? What kind of advice would she herself give to a young woman contemplating motherhood? If she had to do it over again, would she still choose to become a mother?

Such interview studies would serve to define the subjective experience of motherhood. Once the subjective experience of motherhood is more fully known, dimensions of the experience can be examined both as dependent and independent variables. That is, one would want to ask: (a) what physical, social, and historical factors affect the mother's thoughts, feelings and actions, and (b) how do her thoughts, feelings, and actions affect the relationship she has with her children?

In addressing each of these questions, it will prove important to cast the net widely. Studies of the determinants of women's experiences of motherhood need to focus on the economics and sociology of motherhood as well as its biology and psychology. Thus, for example, cross-cultural analyses will prove very important, since the supports for mothers and the constraints on them differ from culture to culture. For example, even when examining motherhood in Western society, a limited perspective, one should still make careful comparisons between motherhood in countries with different policies and supports for childbirth and childrearing. What, for example, is the effect on mothers of the policy in the Netherlands for most births to take place at home? What are some differences between mothers of similar social class in Britain and the United States with respect to the routine use of community midwives and health visitors in the former country? One must also inquire very carefully about economic and political factors that shape mothers' lives in a variety of cultures.

In terms of the second set of issues, the impact of the mother's experience of motherhood on her relationship with her children and their subsequent development, again it becomes important to take a broad view of the questions. In the history of research on child development, some progress has been made from studying mothering purely in terms of retrospective accounts of grown-up children to actually observing mothers with their children. However, the latter set of studies are too often restricted to short-term analyses of mother–child dyads under particular experimental conditions. Experimental methods will continue to have a place in the study of motherhood, in terms of testing key hypotheses under controlled conditions, but such methods must be supplemented with other techniques. For instance, in the United States, the predominant mode of nonrelative day care for infants and toddlers is family day care. However, we know very little about how mothers or the children's caregivers feel about this shared childrearing (see McCartney and Phillips, Chapter 7). Mother–child dyads studied in isolation from either the mother's or the child's greater social worlds have limited value.

Furthermore, studies of the effects of mothers' experiences on children's lives must also take into account the effects of children's experiences on mothers' lives. It has been observed, for example, that intervention programs designed to facilitate children's development have a clear impact of mothers' lives as well. The mother–child relationship is not static; it should not be studied in terms of static maternal traits or simplistic child outcomes. Rather, motherhood itself deserves examination as a developmental process, one that meshes with but is not simply a function of the child's development.

WHAT WE ALREADY KNOW WE NEED TO DO

There is obviously much to learn about the experience of motherhood, and adequate theory is yet to be developed. Nevertheless, the information collected by the authors of chapters in this volume and by other writers (Weitzman, etc.), tells us much about the status of contemporary mothers in American society. These facts have direct implications for social policy. The following recommendations seem imperative:

1. Motherhood works best when it is freely chosen. Women should bear only those children they want to have, when they want them, and when they believe they can take care of them. Young men and women should learn about birth control; birth control should be both accessible and affordable. Women must continue to have the right to terminate unwanted pregnancies.

2. Efforts should be made to prevent teenage pregnancy. Adolescent parenting, dropping out of school, unemployment, and single parenthood are highly correlated with poverty. In 1983 in the United States, over 1 million teen pregnancies resulted in 500,000 births (Children's Defense Fund, 1986). Half of the young mothers do not receive adequate health care and therefore many have high-risk pregnancies and give birth to babies who are small and/or premature. These infants have higher than average mortality rates and are more likely to have serious health problems than babies born of mothers in their 20s. In one New York State county with lower than national average infant mortality rates, the mortality rates for black infants is three times as high as for white infants and is comparable to some of the poorest counties in the United States.

Most adolescent mothers are unable to complete high school and 43% of high school dropouts are attributable to pregnancy or marriage (Children's Defense Fund, 1986). Being economically disadvantaged should not be equated with inadequate mothering because many economically disadvantaged mothers have coping skills and strengths rarely discussed (see Washington, Chapter 8). However, mothers who are themselves youngsters are likely to be single and those who cannot provide their children with a safe environment, adequate food, excellent and regular health care, and good education are more often highly stressed than mothers who do not face these problems.

3. All pregnant women and all children must be guaranteed adequate health care and nutrition. Programs such as Medicaid should pay for the care of pregnant women as of the day that their pregnancy is confirmed. WIC (the supplemental food program for women, infants, and children) should be available to all needy pregnant women and all infants and children to guarantee nutritional adequacy. WIC provides pregnant women and children who are low income and nutritionally deficient with specified nourishing foods. Pregnant American women should be guaranteed free medication and dental care, services provided to all pregnant women in Britain. High-risk women, those with serious health problems that jeopardize infants, including alcoholism, substance abuse, and high blood pressure, should receive counseling and sufficient care to diminish the likelihood of giving birth to low-birth-weight or addicted babies.

Although the United States guarantees some health care to its aging population, there are still hospitals that refuse care to high-risk, uninsured pregnant women. Thousands of infants and young children receive no well-baby care and are only seen by physicians when they are seriously ill. It seems imperative that all health problems of children be treated, independent of the parents' ability to pay the cost. Children with problems of vision, hearing, or other development problems should receive early and continuous care.

During pregnancy, as part of health care, it should be determined that certain minimum standards of care and protection are in place for both mother and infant. No mother should be permitted to leave the hospital without a guaranteed safe, well-heated and well-ventilated home, a safe crib or crib equivalent for the baby, and access to a telephone for emergency use. There are cases of mothers leaving hospitals to dwell in their unheated automobiles, others who leave the hospital to bring their infants into broken cribs and unsafe and unsanitary environments.

4. Affordable, accessible day care of high quality must be available to all working mothers and others in need—that is, women with health or psychological problems or those with insufficient resources to provide adequate care. Insofar as the majority of American mothers are now employed, child care is not an indulgence but a necessity. Although the United States considers itself a "child-oriented society," the low pay for child-care workers and absence of federal regulation and sufficient support of child-care services make child care a major problem for 75% to 90% of working mothers. Current federal support for day care exists primarily as a tax benefit that offers greatest assistance to middle-class parents; support for low-income parents is critical.

Several steps must be taken to improve existing child-care facilities in the United States. There must be both federal and state support for day-care centers. There must be salary equity for day-care workers. Those who provide family day care in their homes should be given adequate training, pay equity, and benefits.

5. There must be systematic education for parenthood and family life. Al-

though some would argue that good parents, like good teachers, are born that way, and others would say that parents raise their children as they themselves were raised, whether lovingly or harshly, there is now sufficient evidence that certain kinds of parental treatment are more beneficial or less beneficial to children. There is also sufficient evidence that most human behavior is affected by experience and that learning is a lifelong process. Education for the most critical dimension of the human experience should be provided not only in the family but by the society as a whole, in the schools. Many high schools consider computer literacy a requisite skill, none require "parental" literacy.

6. Mothers must be aided in the attainment of economic self-sufficiency. Insofar as most mothers work for pay, and most do so out of economic necessity, the question becomes: Are their earnings sufficient to care for themselves and their children? As long as women earn less than two-thirds of what men do, and most women remain in low-paying fields, it seems clear that most mothers are not financially self-sufficient. Many single mothers—and, as we have seen, more and more mothers are single, some by choice but most as a result of divorce and separation—cannot adequately support their children. Therefore the issue of pay equity becomes a critical one for those concerned with the welfare ofmothers and children. Similarly, the issue of financial commitment by the noncustodial parent, who in most cases is the father, is of critical importance.

In general, then, as we conduct the research that is required to understand the complex psychological experience of motherhood, we know that many mothers in the United States are lacking very basic economic and social support. The chapters in this book have defined the study of motherhood as an important field of scientific inquiry; they have also identified an urgent need for a comprehensive social policy to ensure the well-being of mothers and children. In the next few years, we hope to see the design of informative, creative research and the formulation of humane, effective policy, which of course ought to go hand in hand.

REFERENCES

Birns, B., & Howell, J. (1987). *Suffolk County: A Profile*. Unpublished paper.
Children's Defense Fund. (1986). *Adolescent pregnancy: Whose problem is it?* Washington, DC: Children's Defense Fund.
Weitzman, L. (1985). *The divorce revolution: The unexpected social and economic consequences for women and children in America*. New York: Free Press.

Index